Close Calls

To Joe

With best wishes,

from

Elliott Abrams

ELLIOTT ABRAMS became president of the Ethics and Public Policy Center in July 1996. During the 1980s he held three Assistant Secretary posts at the U.S. Department of State: International Organization Affairs, in which he supervised U.S. participation in the United Nations system; Human Rights and Humanitarian Affairs; and Inter-American Affairs, in which he supervised U.S. policy in Latin America and the Caribbean. He is the author of *Undue Process* (1993), *Security and Sacrifice* (1995), and *Faith or Fear* (1997).

Close Calls

Intervention, Terrorism, Missile Defense, and 'Just War' Today

Edited by
Elliott Abrams

Essays by James Turner Johnson, Robert Kagan,
Oliver Revell, Eugene V. Rostow, Margaret Thatcher,
R. James Woolsey, *and Fourteen Others*

ETHICS AND PUBLIC POLICY CENTER
WASHINGTON, D.C.

The moral issues that shape foreign and domestic policy are central to the work of the Ethics and Public Policy Center. The Center is a non-profit institution established in 1976 to clarify and reinforce the role of the Judeo-Christian moral tradition in the American public policy debate. Its activities include research, writing, publications, and conferences. Current programs include Catholic Studies, Evangelical Studies, Jewish Studies, the Project on the Judiciary, the Program on Medical Science and Society, studies in religion and foreign policy, and the Marriage Law Project.

Library of Congress Cataloging-in-Publication Data:
Close calls: intervention, terrorism, missile defense, and 'just war'
    today / edited by Elliott Abrams; essays by James Turner Johnson
    . . . [et al.].
        p.   cm.
    Includes bibliographical references and index.
    ISBN 0-89633-187-3 (alk. paper)
    1. War—moral and ethical aspects.   2. Just war doctrine.
3. International relations.   I. Abrams, Elliott, 1948–   .
II. Johnson, James Turner.
U22.C537   1998   97-47718
172'.42—dc21   CIP

Ethics and Public Policy Center
1015 Fifteenth Street NW ✦ Washington, D.C. 20005
(202) 682-1200 ✦ *fax* (202) 408-0632 ✦ *website* www.eppc.org.

Contents

III. CAN DEMOCRACIES FIGHT TERRORISM?

IV. Is Missile Defense Moral?

Introduction

The frequency of U.S. intervention in other countries since the end of the Cold War has been a surprise to many Americans— and a source of alarm to some. From Somalia to Zaire, from Bosnia to Haiti to Kuwait, hundreds of thousands of American soldiers have taken part in actions designed to make or keep the peace or to relieve human suffering. These interventions have occurred within an international system still characterized by the threat and use of violence. States continue to maintain large armies, to seek and build weapons of mass destruction and the systems to deliver them, and to employ terrorism in the pursuit of foreign-policy goals. In the post–Cold War period, a war involving a million soldiers took place in the Persian Gulf; nuclear and missile proliferation continues at a rapid pace; and in locations as diverse as Israel and Argentina, spectacular and murderous acts of terror have taken place.

This is of course very far from the world widely anticipated after the collapse of the Soviet Union. Now as during the Cold War we are forced to prepare to use force, and today its proper use is even more difficult to determine. With the struggle against the evil combination of Communist ideology and Soviet power now over, when is the use of force defensible, indeed required? How shall we decide, employing what standards, what limits, what ideas about force? When is intervention justifiable, and when is it morally necessary? What is the nature of terrorism today, and how may we best defend against it? Is defense of the nation against missile attack possible? If so, is it sensible, warranted, even required?

In 1996 the Ethics and Public Policy Center undertook a project called "Just War After the Cold War," supported by a generous grant from the Smith Richardson Foundation. In a series of conferences, an outstanding array of experts reflected on the just war tradition itself and on its application to intervention and terrorism. (A fourth conference dealt with "Intangible Interests and U.S. Foreign Policy"; those papers are being published separately.) To the fourteen essays that emanated from these conferences we added, for this book, five on missile defense, along with a provocative speech by Margaret Thatcher that inspired them. Our goal in this project was to see what guidance the just war tradition provides for us today. After all, just war reasoning is an effort to discriminate between defensible and indefensible uses of military force. To the usual questions of statecraft it adds the dimension of human rights. It does not accept "state interest" as an unbeatable trump; it requires that moral distinctions be drawn.

Today's just war theorist responds to a novel situation. One state, the United States, has emerged as the preponderant world power. The dangers that provoke intervention are not only the fear of military attack but also such problems as terrorism, drug trafficking, migration flows, and humanitarian emergencies. And the risks we now face include not only conventional military attack but also the potential use of nuclear, biological, and chemical weapons of mass destruction whose impact on both military and civilian populations could be devastating.

But if the dangers have grown, so have the announced goals of many military actions. It is often argued that a particular action not only will be in the national interest but also will relieve human suffering, and may even help to establish a world order where peace and law prevail. Sometimes an action is defended despite its irrelevance to national interest in the traditional sense, and the argument is made that the United States has a strong interest in maintaining a reputation for benevolence and humanitarianism. The Roman Catholic Church itself, where the just war tradition was born and nurtured, seems torn. Church spokesmen nowadays usually hew to a narrow definition of just wars, limiting them to the purest cases of self-defense on the grounds that any other use of force now creates too much destruction and injustice to be defensible; yet the Church is naturally attracted by broad humanitarian goals such as the promotion of world peace and the relief of human suffering.

In this volume, three essays on the just war tradition itself (Part One) and seven on intervention (Part Two) provide a wealth of insights into when the use of force is justifiable and how just war reasoning helps us decide. **James Turner Johnson** surveys the history of just war thinking and explains why the requirement of just cause needs to be reassessed in our day. In revisiting the requirement of competent authority, **Eugene V. Rostow** reviews the relationship between just war doctrine and international law, and comments on how state conduct in the current international system is—and should be—affected by each. Then **Andrew Bacevich** asks how technological change has affected the conduct of war and our understanding of just war.

Intervention—humanitarian and otherwise—is the subject of Part Two. **Brad Roberts** examines the moral case for military actions aimed at preempting damaging actions by "rogue" states equipped with nuclear, biological, and chemical weapons. **John Langan** and **Andrew Natsios** take up the argument over humanitarian intervention—intervention occasioned not by the pursuit of narrow national interests but by broad humanitarian goals, such as the relief of famine. **John Bolton** and **Alberto R. Coll** provide perspectives, from the State Department and Defense Department, respectively, on the 1992 U.S. intervention in Somalia. **Drew Christiansen and Gerard Powers** apply just war reasoning to humanitarian intervention, finding that the fit between ends and means is "key to determining their moral validity." And **Robert Kagan** argues that the search for certainties in the conduct of world affairs can undercut both comprehension of the problems and our effectiveness in dealing with them.

Part Three, on terrorism, begins with **Anthony Arend**'s look at what just war doctrine has to teach about terrorism and our defense against it. Next, two practitioners of counterterrorism, one American and one Israeli, bring the theory into real-life experience. **Oliver "Buck" Revell** reflects on his long career at the FBI as domestic and foreign terrorism grew and our responses to it changed, while **Yigal Carmon**, a key counterterrorism adviser to two Israeli prime ministers, provides what is, unsurprisingly, a rather different perspective on how a democracy can defend itself. Finally, **Eric Breindel**, former editorial-page editor of the *New York Post*, discusses ongoing changes in how the American media have covered terrorism—from the TWA airliner hijacking by Shiites in 1985 to the trial of Lori Berenson for her activities on behalf of Shining Path in Peru in late 1995.

In the years ahead, the United States and its allies are likely to be menaced not by threats of traditional warfare, army against army on the battlefield, but by the new and horrific threats of the use of instruments of mass destruction—chemical, biological, and nuclear weapons delivered from afar by ballistic missiles. Can we defend ourselves, our friends, and our soldiers against such devices? If we can, should we? Must we? Part Four opens with Baroness **Margaret Thatcher**'s reflections on the new national-security threats we face in the post–Cold War world. **James Turner Johnson**, whose extraordinary essay on the just war tradition begins this book, here considers what that tradition has to say about our duty to defend ourselves against missile attack, especially when such defense might prevent far wider outbreaks of violence and far greater bloodshed. **Robert Kagan** considers the impact an effective missile defense system might have on U.S. foreign policy: would we feel safely walled off from threats and free to isolate ourselves from world politics, or able to engage more fully because we were no longer courting the danger of missile attack? **Jeffrey Salmon** asks why, given the need for missile defense and its apparent feasibility, those who opposed it during the Cold War continue to do so despite the radical change in the conditions that underlay their initial opposition. Former CIA director **James Woolsey** reviews the proliferation of nuclear weapons and ballistic missiles in the 1980s and 1990s. And, in the concluding essay of this volume, former SDI head **Henry F. Cooper** argues that missile defense is eminently feasible, and explains why.

Just war concepts first elucidated by Aquinas and Grotius proved to be extremely useful, as we had thought they would, in analyzing the foreign-policy and military challenges now facing U.S. leaders. As Drew Christiansen and Gerard Powers note in their essay, "The Duty to Intervene," the style of reasoning employed in just war thinking is indeed applicable today: "The kinds of issues raised, the tests to be met, and the moral distinctions to be drawn bear sufficient family resemblance to traditional just war analyses to be taken as a contemporary variation on a centuries-old theme." The Ethics and Public Policy Center is pleased to present this book, for we believe that these distinguished analysts and their wise arguments have made and will continue to make a signal contribution to the debate over the role of moral considerations in the nation's foreign and national-security policy.

— ELLIOTT ABRAMS

PART ONE

Can Modern Wars Be Just?

1

Just Cause Revisited

James Turner Johnson

Just war tradition addresses the morality of the use of force in two parts: when it is right to *resort* to armed force (the concern of *ius ad bellum*) and what it is right to do in *using* such force (the concern of *ius in bello*). While these two aspects are related, they are also distinct, and the former has priority: if a given resort to force has not been morally justified, then even the most strictly delimited uses are, according to just war tradition, unjust.

The moral requirements of *ius in bello* are that a use of armed force be discriminate and proportionate. For *ius ad bellum*, the requirements are that the resort to force (1) have a just cause, (2) be authorized by a competent authority, (3) be motivated by a right intention, and (4) pass four prudential tests: it must (a) be expected to produce a preponderance of good over evil, (b) have a reasonable hope of success, (c) be a last resort, and (d) have peace as its expected outcome. Some commentators include also the requirement that a war be formally declared, but I take this concern to be satisfied by the others. Either

James Turner Johnson is professor of religion at Rutgers University, where he also teaches in the graduate department of political science. Among the books he has written are *Can Modern War Be Just?* and *The Quest for Peace: Three Moral Traditions in Western Cultural History.*

way, formal declaration is required, and this serves two necessary purposes: to make public for all to judge the justification of the resort to force, and to serve fair notice to the enemy so he can make amends before being forced to do so.

In listing the *ius ad bellum* criteria I have distinguished the three requirements of just cause, competent authority, and right intention from the remaining four prudential concerns. This acknowledges the priority historically given those first three in the tradition as well as the internal logic of the tradition itself. Thomas Aquinas's treatment is typical as well as authoritative. "In order for a war to be just," he writes, "three things are necessary," and he lists sovereign authority, just cause, and right intention.[1]

The idea of just cause is thus one of the most fundamental elements in just war tradition. What are the implications of this idea for statecraft today? What sorts of contemporary situations would satisfy the requirement that for resort to armed force to be justified, a just cause must exist?

In what follows I will seek to answer this question by means of three steps. The first step is to identify the meaning given to just cause by the medieval and early modern thinkers who defined just war tradition in its classic form. My focus here will be on "benchmark" figures: the canonist Gratian and the theologian Thomas Aquinas from the Middle Ages, with reference to their use of earlier authorities, and the theologian Vitoria and the jurist Grotius in the reformulation of just war tradition for the modern age.

The second step is to see how the idea of just cause was affected by the experience of modern war, from the latter part of the nineteenth century through the twentieth. Here I will focus on two major carriers of just war tradition during the modern period: international law and Catholic teaching on war.

The third and last step is to assess just cause in its contemporary context. In defining this context I will look at two issues: (1) the difference between typical contemporary uses of military force and the image of "modern war" as a holocaust driven by the venality of states, and (2) the changing relationship between states and the international order exemplified by the United Nations. In assessing the concept of just cause in this modern context I will examine three questions: First, does the emphasis on defense found in both positive international law and recent Catholic teaching adequately render the classic requirement of just cause? Second, does the idea of just cause ever justify preemptive use of force? Third, may protection of ideals, and not simply of interests, constitute just cause for resort to force?

The Medieval and Early Modern Consensus

In his magisterial compilation of canon law from the middle of the twelfth century, the Italian legal scholar Gratian defined just war by citing two statements from authoritative Christian writers.[2] The first is from Isidore of Seville, writing around the year 600: "A war is just when, by a formal declaration, it is waged in order to regain what has been stolen or to repel the attack of enemies." The second definition is from Augustine, writing approximately a century earlier: "Those wars are customarily called just which have for their end the revenging of injuries, when it is necessary by war to constrain a city or a nation which has not wished to punish an evil action committed by its citizens, or to restore that which has been taken unjustly." Both these definitions have centrally to do with the idea of just cause, and together they set forth three purposes that justify resort to armed force: to regain something wrongly taken, to defend against attack, and to punish evildoing.

Over the next hundred years Gratian's canonist successors, the Decretists and the Decretalists, neither added to this conception nor subtracted from it; most of their attention went not to just cause but to a debate over how to define the authority necessary to declare a war just. Thomas Aquinas, writing during the last half of the thirteenth century, reflects the long established medieval consensus on the concept of just cause while revealing his dependence on Gratian and, through him, on Augustine. We recall from above that Thomas identified three conditions as necessary for a war to be just: sovereign authority, just cause, and right intention. On just cause he writes:

> Second, a just cause is required, namely that those who are attacked, should be attacked because they deserve it on account of some fault. Wherefore Augustine says (QQ. in *Heptateuchum*, qu. X, *Super Josue*): A just war is wont to be described as one that avenges wrongs, when a nation or state has to be punished for refusing to make amends for the wrongs inflicted by its subjects, or to restore what has been seized unjustly.[3]

The French commentator Alfred Vanderpol, writing in the immediate aftermath of the First World War, noted the centrality of punishment of evil in this passage and argued from it to a conception of Scholastic just war doctrine in which just cause is reduced to this alone.[4] I think this goes too far as an interpretation of Scholastic doctrine, and it certainly does not reflect the more balanced position of the canonists, who held to the formulation given by Gratian that there are three just causes for resort to armed force: not only punishment of evil but also defense against attack and recovery of something wrongly taken. This broader conception was reinforced by the acknowledgment that Roman law had recognized the same three just causes for a *iustum bellum*. At the same time, Vanderpol's formulation draws attention to the fact that the medieval world is not our world, and that the justification of resort to force for the cause of punishing evil, largely lost in the modern period, was emphasized there. Medieval writers on just war made widespread use of Romans 13:4 to define the role of the prince: "He is the minister of God to execute his wrath against the evildoer." The prince had the authority to employ the sword, not only defensively but proactively so as to punish evil persons and thereby right injustices.

Vanderpol's formulation also draws attention to the fact that Thomas's passage, as well as the citation from Augustine it includes, makes no specific reference to defense as just cause for resort to force. This is another reflection of the difference between medieval and modern sensibilities, a difference especially striking since, as we shall see, a hallmark of authoritative twentieth-century just war thought has been the effort to restrict just cause to defensive second resort to force in face of an attack. Now, as the canonical sources show clearly, the idea of defense against attack was in fact generally understood in the medieval period to constitute just cause for resort to force. But at the same time, that idea was somewhat problematical theologically in the context of a piety that required Christian participants in the use of force not to violate Jesus' command to turn the other cheek when struck on the one.

Ambrose's Paradigm

The pacifist wing of early Christianity had argued that this command of Jesus meant Christians could never participate in war, since doing so would violate this command of Jesus. The theological argument that made a Christian just war theory possible was developed by Augustine, building on the position of his mentor Ambrose of Milan. Praising the man who defended his country at personal risk,[5] Ambrose distinguished between using force to defend oneself (which was prohibited by Jesus' words and example) and using force to defend another person (which followed as a requirement of charity). Developing further the idea that charity sometimes requires resort to force against another person, Ambrose provided a paradigmatic example that was well known both by Augustine and by medieval writers on just war: A Christian is journeying alone in a remote area, carrying a weapon to use against animals he might encounter on the way. He instead encounters an armed bandit in the process of attacking another innocent wayfarer to rob him and perhaps wound or kill him. What is the Christian to do?

In his answer Ambrose did not challenge the accepted doctrine that if the itinerant Christian were himself the victim of the attack, he could not defend himself: the Christian "when he meets an armed robber . . . cannot return his blows, lest in defending his life he should stain his love for his neighbor."[6] But this is a different case: the attack is on a neighbor whom the Christian is commanded to love. For Ambrose, the Christian has a moral duty in charity to defend this innocent neighbor from the attack and may, to do so, use force if necessary, up to and including doing to the assailant what that assailant is capable of doing to the victim. Not providing such defense is itself morally wrong: "He who does not keep harm off a friend, if he can," Ambrose writes, "is as much in fault as he who causes it."[7] At the same time, the Christian should use no more force than necessary to subdue the attacker, for that person too is someone for whom Christ died. Charity thus justifies the resort to force in defense, not of self but of the other; yet at the same time it limits the force that can be used against the evildoer to what is necessary to end the evil. (Augustine's similar argument is found in *On the Freedom of the Will* I.5; cf. Paul Ramsey's development of this line of reasoning.[8])

Augustine argued from this to permission for Christians to take part in public warfare with the aim of defending their neighbors in the state, but not to use force as private persons.[9] For the medieval heirs of Augustine, this shifted the focus of the debate away from the question of just cause (the moral obligation to defend those wrongly attacked, which was consensually accepted) to the question of the authority necessary to authorize such resort to force. Thomas Aquinas exemplifies this way of casting the issue in his use of Augustine to refute an objection against Christians' resorting to armed force: "to have recourse to the sword (as a private person) by the authority of the sovereign or judge, or (as a public person) through zeal for justice, and by the authority, so to speak, of God, is not to *take the sword*."[10]

The Medieval Concept Summarized

In the medieval context, then, the theological argument for defense of the neighbor under attack by an aggressor complemented the conception drawn from Roman law through Gratian that defined three just causes for resort to armed force: defense, the retaking of something wrongly taken, and punishment of evil. At the same time, theological and canonical discussions of the obligation of defense focused more on the question of the legitimate authority to resort to armed force. The theologians, like Thomas, were motivated by a concern to deal with the Christian tradition that forbade Christians to "take the sword" in their own defense; the canonists added a second concern: to limit the overall level of violence in the society by emphasizing that only the highest officials had the right to authorize resort to the sword even for just cause.[11]

One of my purposes thus far has been to suggest that medieval concerns about justified warfare were focused quite differently from such concerns in the twentieth century. For much of the present century, as I will discuss in more detail below, there has been an effort to reduce just cause to the case of defense alone. For the medieval thinkers who helped to define the just war idea in its classic form, the emphasis was different. While they saw defense of the neighbor as being at the very basis of the Christian just war idea and as a just cause for resort to the sword, what they emphasized was the right and duty of sovereign rulers to authorize resort to force in order to correct violations of justice. Vanderpol summarized the actions of rulers in accord with the concept of just cause as acts of "vindicative justice"— uses of force to restore a balance that had been disturbed by the action of an evildoer. Evil acts that might be corrected by force did not have to involve force in themselves; they only had to be evil.

Taken in its totality, the medieval concept of just cause had centrally to do with establishing and enforcing a just political and social order, an order that was necessary for the presence of peace. Thus was the developing just war idea related to the three acknowledged goods of politics: order, justice, and peace.

The discussions in the churchly sources were complemented by reflections on Roman law and custom and, increasingly in the late Middle Ages, by a renewed interest in the concept of *ius gentium*, law of nations. Together these approaches defined a consensus: just cause for resort to armed force is provided when natural justice is disturbed by some act of evildoing. While such a resort to force must be authorized by sovereign authority and must be carried out with right intention, the justified cause itself may be either defending against unjust attack, punishing evil, or retaking something wrongly taken. This consensus constitutes the classic just war idea of just cause.

The Early Modern Thinkers

Two important changes adapted the idea of just cause to the modern period. First, the justifying causes for resort to force became located squarely within natural law and the law of nations (*ius gentium*), thereby ruling out appeals to religion (or, implicitly, other ideological causes) as justifying resort to war. Second, the recognition developed that in a given conflict both sides might appear to have just cause. Both these changes are marked in the important bridge figures Francisco de Vitoria, writing in the mid-sixteenth century, and Hugo Grotius, writing in the first half of the seventeenth.

The medieval theorists of just war mixed religious and natural-law concerns together in their concept of both *ius ad bellum* and *ius in bello*. This was understandable and appropriate within a culture that understood itself to be Christian and found it hard to define the line between the temporal and the spiritual. It meant in practical terms, however, that the developing consensus on just war applied only to wars among members of Christendom, not to wars with non-Christians.

The birth of the modern period was marked by two challenges that required rethinking the just war idea in terms accessible to all humankind, that is, in terms of the law of nature. The first of these challenges was the discovery of the New World, which raised, more acutely than the wars against Islamic enemies had done, the problems of the applicability of just war thinking to conflicts involving non-Christians. The second challenge was the division of Christendom into Catholic and Protestant, which brought home the problems of warfare justified by religious claims far more vividly than religious warfare on the fringes of Christendom had been able to do.

Vitoria: Just Cause and the Law of Nature

The context of Vitoria's thought on just war was the Spanish encounter with the New World, and his immediate opponents were those Spanish Catholic "developers" of the New World who sought to justify making war against the Indians by appealing to their religious difference and the need to convert them to Christianity. To this argument Vitoria replied flatly, "Difference of religion is not a cause of just war."[12] The only just causes—and this is a point to which he returns repeatedly, in different contexts—are those grounded in natural law and therefore knowable through the use of natural reason. Thus the idea of just war, as developed by Vitoria, is not uniquely Christian; it is in principle an idea common to all humankind. This meant for him both that European Christians should observe its requirements in making war against persons from other cultures and, reciprocally, that persons from other cultures could also be held accountable to fight according to just war principles.

What is just cause as provided for in the law of nature? Vitoria's general answer was that such cause exists whenever there is a fault knowable through natural reason: "[t]here is a single and only just cause for commencing a war, namely, wrong received."[13] In direct line with the tradition of just cause stretching through the medieval theorists back to the Romans, Vitoria recognized three such specific causes: defense, recovery of something wrongly taken, and punishment for wrongdoing.[14] Significantly, in contrast to the medieval tendency to emphasize the prince's responsibility to use force for the punishment of evil, Vitoria gave special emphasis to defense of the political community as just cause: "the end and aim of war is the defence and preservation of the state."[15] Indeed, in one place he defined the state as any political entity that has the power to use force to support its rights in the presence of any of the three recognized just causes.[16] Elsewhere, however, in a passage that both recalls the medieval concern that just resort to force be to combat evil and expresses his deeply modern interest in the proper conduct of just war, Vitoria specifically cited the right to use force to oppose pillage, rape, and killing.[17]

Vitoria worked within the framework of the established just war tradition, making especial use of Thomas Aquinas. Yet he was able to reshape the focus of the tradition in terms of the concerns of the modern era. His conception of just cause was based in natural law, not in a mix of natural law and Christian moral duty; its central paradigm was not the sovereign acting in God's stead to punish evil (as provided for by Romans 13:4, that favorite proof-text of medieval just war theorists) but rather the state acting to defend and preserve itself and its rights. In Grotius's just war thought, as we shall see, these same elements are at center stage.

Vitoria, and after him Grotius, also brought a new perspective to the question of where just cause lies in a conflict. Medieval just war theory required that just cause be determined and declared by competent authority, and by the end of the thirteenth century there was a consensus that this meant sovereign authority. But given a plurality of sovereigns, there arose the possibility of rival claims to just cause. Common in chivalric disputes, this problem was exemplified by the rival claims of the French and English monarchs in the Hundred Years War. By the time of Vitoria in the mid-sixteenth century, the concept I call "simultaneous ostensible justice" had eroded the self-confident assumption of the medieval just war theorists that the right and wrong sides in a dispute were simple matters to determine. The fundamental concept of just cause remained intact; the nagging problem was that sometimes both sides of a conflict could make plausible claims to just cause.

If, for example, one party used force against another to retake a piece of property judged to be wrongly taken, this party would by one measure have just cause; at the same time, if the attacked party believed it justly owned the property in question, it would have the right to defend itself and seek to punish the attacker. Vitoria wrote of such cases,

There is no inconsistency, indeed, in holding the war to be a just war on both sides, seeing that on the one side there is right and on the other side there is invincible ignorance. . . . [But] the rights of war which may be invoked against men who are really guilty and lawless differ from those which may be invoked against the innocent and ignorant.[18]

In other words, Vitoria argued that parties to a conflict must justify their resort to force by appeal to the established concept of just cause, but that they may not always be right in doing so; one (or both) may be invincibly ignorant, and no human judge may be able to find the truth between them. Such is "a just war on both sides," and Vitoria knew enough examples, historical and from his own time, to recognize it as a not uncommon problem. His response was to accept this possibility but to use it to raise a new argument for limits on the conduct of war; that is, he put forward a *ius in bello* response to an insoluble contradiction in the *ius ad bellum*.

Grotius: Permitting Preemption

Nearly a century later Grotius confronted the same problem and resolved it in essentially the same way. His resolution became normative for modern international law, which has constituted one of the major vehicles for development of just war tradition during the modern period. Grotius's treatment of simultaneous ostensible justice— wars in which there appears to be just cause on both sides—was brief but significant. So long as the requirements of justice set by natural law and *ius gentium* are met, when a war has been solemnly declared by both parties, it is clear that they are fighting by mutual consent to resolve a dispute, and in such a case what is most important is that they both observe the *ius in bello* limits.[19]

What, though, are these requirements of justice established in natural law and the law of nations? Following the inherited tradition, Grotius wrote, "Three justifiable causes for war are generally cited: defense, recovery of property, and punishment." He continued, however, by explicitly including preemption in his conception of defense: "The first just cause of war . . . is an injury, which *even though not actually committed*, threatens our persons or our property."[20] Medieval just war thought had defined the prince's role in using force to be proactive in response to evildoing; Grotius's shift of focus was to recognize that such evildoing extends to the preparations for armed attack, not simply the attack itself. "The danger [to be defended against] must be immediate, and as it were, at the point of happening," he said. "If my assailant seizes a weapon with an obvious intention of killing me, I admit too that I have a right to prevent the crime."[21]

In arguing explicitly for preemptive uses of force under certain clear conditions, Grotius was developing an implicit argument within just war theory, not introducing an innovation. James Brown Scott finds in Vitoria also an approval of preemptive defense against attack.[22] In both these early modern theorists, this position reflects the assumption that protection of justice centrally requires protection of the state, an assumption that led to an emphasis on the just cause of defense that is thoroughly modern. By contrast, we have seen that the idea of defense itself posed certain problems in the context of medieval piety. Medieval just war theorists were perfectly willing to justify many resorts to force that would, in a twentieth-century context, be rejected as cases of "first use" of force; yet they did so by appealing to the just causes of punishing evil and recovering things wrongly taken. Grotius built on this by allowing first use of force also in cases where the just cause is defense.

The most obvious feature in Grotius's argument for allowing the preemptive use of force in cases of just cause is that he undertook to discuss and justify preemption explicitly. Bringing it out into the open required him to confront two other issues: the sort of threat that in fact justifies preemption, and the kind of moral scrutiny that should be applied to it—and indeed, to all the accepted just causes for war. His discussion of preemption gave him the occasion to distinguish justified preemptive uses of force from unjustified offensive uses, thus demonstrating his conviction that the focus must be on the justice of a particular resort to force, not on the question of who first takes up arms.

Safeguards Against Abuse

No sooner did Grotius declare the preemptive resort to force to be allowable in *defense* than he began to erect safeguards against unwarranted *offensive* uses. "[P]ersons," he wrote, "who regard any sort of fears as a just ground for the precautionary killing of another person are themselves greatly deceived and deceiving to others."[23] Later he limited the resort to preemption still further:

> But quite inadmissible is the doctrine proposed by some, that by the law of nations it is right to take up arms in order to weaken a rising power, which, if it grew too strong, might do us harm. . . . [T]hat the bare possibility that violence may be some day turned on us gives us the right to inflict violence on others is a doctrine repugnant to every principle of justice.[24]

In short, to employ preemptive self-defense one must be absolutely certain that the enemy intends to attack. Even in such cases Grotius counseled caution and recommended other efforts to defuse the crisis, for undertaking war is a "horrible" thing.[25]

The final safeguard Grotius provided to prevent justified preemption from degenerating into unjustified attacks based on "any sort of fears" was the requirement that, when a war is begun, its causes be stated publicly so that "the whole human race, as it were, might weigh the justice of them."[26] Thus the right of sovereigns to judge whether they have a just cause to go to war is limited by their being implicitly held to account in a court of "the whole human race."

In summary, Grotius's treatment of the idea of just cause embodied the established tradition and further developed its implications. He adhered to the three long established ideas of defense, recovery of something wrongly taken, and punishment of evil as the just causes. Like Vitoria, he thought these derived entirely from the law of nature and could therefore be judged by all humankind. Of the three, he emphasized defense. His explicitly raising the possibility of a justified *preemptive* use of force served several ends. First, it drew attention to the importance of defense as a just cause. Second, it gave him a context within which to develop cautions and safeguards against unjustified resort to armed force. Third, it reinforced the principle that the just causes must be declared publicly for all to see and judge, thus imposing a moral restraint on the sovereign's claim to be the only judge—a concept inherited from the medieval definition of the just war criterion of right authority.

In all these respects, Grotius set the terms for the treatment of just cause (as well as of just war tradition generally) by the theorists of international law who followed him and, ultimately, for the development of the positive law of war.

One consequence of this was not entirely happy. In the modern state system ratified by the Peace of Westphalia, Vitoria's and Grotius's focus on defense of the state as just cause became increasingly more formalized into the concept that the sovereign of a state possesses, on its behalf, *compétence de guerre*, the right to decide when its interests require defending by resort to war. Grotius's stress on the need to declare publicly the causes of a resort to armed force was similarly formalized and emptied of moral content by later consensus. The result was that wars ostensibly just on both sides at once—just, that is, in that they were authorized by a sovereign possessing *compétence de guerre* for causes publicly declared—became increasingly the rule, not the exception as acknowledged by Vitoria and Grotius. Thus the idea of just cause, and indeed the *ius ad bellum* in general, was more and more rendered through legal formalities, rather than through reflection on its moral content. At the same time, another tendency set in motion by Vitoria was also apparent: an increased emphasis on limiting the conduct of war, the *ius in bello*.[27]

Modern War and Just Cause

In the thought of Vitoria and Grotius, just war tradition, including its idea of just cause, was established firmly on the ground of the law of nature. Other theorists, including Locke in England and the French *philosophes*, were shortly to argue for a conception of human rights also grounded in nature. These two theoretical developments came together in the two great revolutions of the end of the eighteenth century, the American and the French. The result, while it falls outside the development of just war tradition proper, did have an influence on this evolving tradition.

The difference these revolutions made to the developing concept of *ius ad bellum* was substantial in two areas. The first was the idea of the necessary authority to resort to armed force. Just war tradition had uniformly required the authority of a sovereign person or body. But by this, revolution was inherently unjust, since the requisite authority was lacking. The American and French revolutions challenged this conservatism in the name of the authority of the individual, who, possessing certain inalienable rights conferred by nature, could enter into a collective defense of those rights even against sovereign authority. More significant for our purposes here is the second development set in motion by these two revolutions: a kind of messianism whereby those who had established the right to govern themselves believed they possessed the right to expand this cause. In the aftermath of the French Revolution, the result was a new conception of just cause for war: exporting the Revolution. More broadly, the result was a new doctrine of national war, war justified by an appeal to the defining ideology of the nation and drawing on the resources of the nation's citizenry as a whole.[28] Thus was modern war begun.

Furthermore, in the post-Revolutionary French conception, offensive warfare, not merely defense, was justifiable by appeal to the ideology of the rights of man. The cautions set in place by Grotius to prevent resort to war because of private fears were swept aside by Napoleon's efforts to establish all around France nations brought under French control, in the name of the Revolution. This went far beyond the concept of preemptive defense against a real and imminent threat and did much to undermine the case for preemption within the framework of just cause.

From this new conception of just cause for war came two contradictory lines of development. One was the Marxist-Leninist "war of national liberation," which is beyond the scope of this essay. The other, which occurred variously within international law, church doctrine, and philosophical theory, took the form of efforts to set new, more restrictive limits on just cause, or even to deny outright the possibility that such cause might exist. In the following section I will explore two of the most important examples of this trend, positive international law and Catholic teaching on war.

International Law and Just Cause

During the nineteenth century, the trends set in motion by the French Revolution changed the face of war. Increasingly, war became a vehicle for nationalistic aspirations, while at the same time technology made it more destructive and the use of the resources of the whole nation exposed more and more people to its effects. The effort to hold these trends in check concentrated on restricting the incidence of war. It built on the emphasis given to defense of the state as just cause by Vitoria and Grotius at the dawn of the modern period, but drew out this emphasis so that defense became the *only* justification for resort to armed force. From the perspective of those who saw war itself as the evil to be avoided, the other classically recognized just causes—recovery of something wrongly taken and punishment of evil—were too easily made instruments of national self-interest. Appeal to these other causes also tended to produce wars in which both sides could claim to be fighting justly—a situation far easier to tolerate in the limited "sovereigns' wars" of the eighteenth century than in the rationalistically inspired, totalistic, and far more destructive warfare of the nineteenth. There were, of course, important efforts to limit the destructive impact of war: leading examples of this approach include the *Instructions for the Government of Armies of the United States in the Field* (General Orders No. 100 of 1863), the Geneva Conventions, the Oxford Manual of 1880, and the actions of the Hague Conferences of 1899 and 1907.[29] In the arena of limiting the resort to war, though, those who wanted to maintain the state system centered their efforts on restricting the resort to force to the case of defense. This effectively ignored the concern of earlier just war tradition—from Gratian through Grotius—that focused on violations of justice as the problem for just war. By the new measure, war itself was the problem.

The limitation of just cause for war to defense alone was attractive to two very different constituencies. From the point of view of those who wanted to limit the incidence of war, it took away the right to wage offensive war for the sake of self-defined national interest, while from the point of view of the states and their political leadership, it supported maintenance of the status quo against potential rivals. This odd confluence of positions masked an irony: by in effect ratifying the status quo of existing states, it served their most fundamental national interest, self-preservation.

In the law of nations, the first steps toward limiting resort to war to defense against attack took the form of major treaties in which groups of nations pledged to support one another defensively if they were attacked (e.g., the Three Emperors' Leagues of 1873 and 1881 and later the Triple Alliance and the Triple Entente).[30] When this approach broke down, however, as in the Crimean War and World War I, the results were the more destructive because the ensuing wars involved alliances of nations, not individual states.

Closing the Door to Preemption

The restriction of just cause for war to defense effectively closed the door on the openness to preemption found in Grotius. Preemption, despite Grotius's cautions and restraints, became identified with aggression. Indeed, aggression itself became identified with firing the first shot, a far less complex condition than what historical just war discussions had recognized as the nature of fault that could justify an armed response.

Article 51 of the United Nations Charter affirms "the inherent right of individual or collective self-defense if an armed attack occurs" against a U.N. member, until such time as the Security Council takes steps to deal with the breach of peace. Morton Kaplan and Nicholas Katzenbach comment about this, "[T]he restrictive term 'armed attack' was used deliberately and most commentators would read the Article to forbid self-defense except in case of armed attack."[31] French commentator Henri Meyrowitz has sharply criticized this language of the Charter, arguing that it has removed justice from the *ius ad bellum* by outlawing first use of force for whatever reason while permitting second, again regardless of circumstances.[32]

If defense is thus equated with second use of force in response to first use ("armed attack"), then the concept of defense does not include an armed response while an expected attack is still gathering but has not yet been launched. This is the possibility Grotius took into account in allowing preemption. If first use of force is prohibited, then even genuinely preemptive resorts to force are disallowed. Reading the Charter in the context of the Pact of Paris and the League of Nations Covenant suggests that this is what is intended; the goal is to prohibit states from initiating armed violence in a conflict with other states while preserving the right of victims of aggression to defend themselves.

Yet this is not the only possible meaning. Restricting just cause to defense against an armed attack already launched is a problematical doctrine that does not well suit the actual circumstances of many conflicts. Kaplan and Katzenbach note that the wording of the Charter "does not clearly forbid self-defense prior to armed attack but only sanctions self-defense as permissible in case of armed attack."[33] The judgments of states in actual cases have not shown a doctrinaire rejection of first use of force when it is judged genuinely to represent preemption of an attack about to be launched or under way but not yet landed. The United States, for example, accepted the Israeli preemptive strike at the beginning of the Six-Day War of 1967 as justified while disapproving the Indian military move into East Bengal during the war that led to the creation of Bangladesh. There have also been disagreements as to what constitutes "aggression" and what "defense." During the Cold War, the judgment normally depended on which side one was on. A "war of national liberation" was thus defensive in the Soviet view while aggressive from the perspective of the United States.

The effort to reduce just cause for resort to force solely to defense has had another unforeseen result: expansion of the concept of defense to include other categories as well. For example, nuclear deterrence has for decades routinely been characterized as "defense," though it actually rests on a threat of retaliation. Such retaliation would be, to be sure, a second use of force in response to a first strike; yet it is clearly something different from the root meaning of defense as an action or actions taken to prevent an attack from succeeding. A second example is provided by the war between Argentina and Britain over the Falkland Islands, which both sides characterized as "defensive," though both included in this concept the classic just war idea of recovering property wrongly taken. The Gulf War provides a third example. Here the West defined its action against Iraq legally as response to an "armed attack" that was under way, though the Iraqi takeover of Kuwait by force was quickly accomplished at the start of the crisis. Legally, the "armed attack" remained in process as long as Iraq continued its military occupation of Kuwait. Any theorist familiar with the concept of recovery of something wrongly taken would not, however, have had to stretch the concept of defense so far to find just cause for the coalition's armed action against Iraq.

Catholic Just War Thought and Just Cause

Like positive international law, twentieth-century Catholic doctrine has sought to limit resort to force by narrowing the concept of just cause to defense alone. The roots of this approach are in a perception of modern war as a *source* of injustice rather than a means of fighting injustice. Thus in 1870, five years after the end of the American Civil

War and in the same year as the Franco-Prussian War, a statement of several *postulata* was presented to the first Vatican Council in which the contemporary form of war as practiced by European nations was explicitly challenged as unjust. The document singled out large national standing armies as a special evil, arguing that they fostered a spirit of militarism, tended to foment wars in order to make them "pay for themselves" through conquest, and produced conflicts so destructive as to be "hideous massacres" the Church could not regard as just. So far as the *ius ad bellum* was concerned, this argument cut against the possibility of a justifiable first use of force, though it admitted the right of second resort to force in defense.[34]

Similarly, in 1931 the Conventus of Fribourg, a gathering of theologians, distinguished between war for "defense," which was "lawful," and war from national "necessity," which was not. In the context of the provisions for arbitration of disputes established by the League of Nations and the renunciation of first use of force established for the signatories to the Pact of Paris, the Conventus took the position that it is wrong to initiate resort to arms to settle a dispute without first recourse to arbitration.[35]

Since World War II, various official and non-official statements have gone a good deal further than this, calling into question whether, given the nature of modern war, even the just cause of defense can legitimize resort to armed force. In what follows I will concentrate on papal statements, which have undeniable authoritative force, though they represent only a fraction of the full range of recent Catholic thought on war.

Characterizing the position of Pius XII, John Courtney Murray wrote that this pope forbade "all wars of aggression, whether just or unjust" (*sic!*), while finding "morally admissible" "a defensive war to repress injustice."[36] Pius's language revealed his hesitation even about the defensive use of force. In his 1956 Christmas message, reflecting the context of the Hungarian revolution and its repression by Soviet armed force, he wrote:

There is no further room for doubt about the purposes and methods that lie behind tanks when they crash resoundingly across frontiers. . . . When all the possible stages of negotiation and mediation are by-passed, and when the threat is made to use atomic arms to obtain concrete demands, *whether these are justified or not*, it becomes clear that . . . there may come into existence in a nation a situation in which all hope of averting war becomes vain. In this situation a war of efficacious self-defense against unjust attacks, which is undertaken with hope of success, cannot be considered illicit.[37]

This is explicit just war language, but it has a very contemporary twist. Medieval and early modern just war theorists focused on the problems of injustice that a use of force by sovereign authority might set right; for Pius, as for the Fribourg theologians in 1931 and the 1870 *postulata* before that, it is the use of force itself, even to serve just ends, that is problematical and needs to be hedged about with safeguards. The threat to use atomic arms is a new element mentioned by Pius, but the basic shift in the focus within the *ius ad bellum* came earlier—as early, indeed, as the denunciation of large standing national armies in 1870 and the new emphasis on arbitration in 1931.

Giving his own weight to this new emphasis, in *Pacem in Terris* (1963) Pope John XXIII called for the banning of nuclear weapons, a general reduction of other arms, and the development of an international regime based on common consent that would be able to resolve disputes without resort to war. In a widely discussed passage he wrote, "[I]n this age which boasts of its atomic power, it no longer makes sense to maintain that war is a fit instrument with which to repair the violation of justice" (paragraph 127). Catholic modern-war pacifists argued that this statement not only condemned all war in the nuclear age but rejected just war theory as well.[38] By contrast, Paul Ramsey reasoned that John XXIII instead was working within the just war framework, ruling out only two of the three classical just causes, recovery of something wrongly taken and punishment of evil, while leaving defense as justified.[39] While I side with Ramsey's interpretation, I believe more attention has to be paid to what was given up here. To "repair the violation of justice," after all, was precisely what classic just war doctrine was about.

The "Presumption Against War"

By this point in the development of recent Catholic thought on just war it is clear that the focus has shifted to a concern that the resort to force, for whatever reason, itself holds great potential for injustice, and that this must be avoided. At the same time, defensive resort to arms remains a moral possibility, though an increasingly questioned one.

In Pope Paul VI's 1965 address to the United Nations General Assembly, this tortured line of reasoning reached for a new resolution. While issuing the ringing challenge "[n]ever again war, war never again!" Paul also admitted that so long as man remains "weak, change-able, and wicked," "defensive arms will, alas! be necessary."[40] But he stopped short of explicitly saying that it is morally allowable to use such arms; his point was rather to draw a distinction between the pos-session of offensive arms, which he regarded as morally evil, and the possession of defensive ones, which he permitted because of the cur-rent "weak, changeable, and wicked" state of humanity.

The concept that just war doctrine begins with a "presumption against war," which appears in the 1984 pastoral of the American Catholic bishops,[41] reflects the shift in focus illustrated by the exam-ples above. It is important to recognize that this is a change of major dimensions in just war theory. To put the matter plainly, this attitude toward armed force is not the problem that classic medieval and early modern Christian just war theory sought to deal with; that problem was injustice, and force (under the conditions established by the just war idea) provided the means to deal with it. The concept that force itself is a major problem originated only comparatively recently as a result of the encounter with modern war, judged as an enterprise whose great destructive potential will inevitably be realized once resort to arms has been allowed.

J. Brian Hehir traces the development of the "presumption against war" as also characteristic of the position of John Paul II. Citing a letter from this pope to President George Bush, Hehir remarks (in language reminiscent of John Courtney Murray's comment on Pius XII) that while John Paul's use of just war logic is "clearly evident," his conclusion is that "resort to force is not justified *even though* a just cause exists."[42]

The base line of post–World War II Catholic thought on just cause for war has, in general, formally paralleled the position defined in pos-itive international law by the United Nations Charter, that only defense against attack provides just cause for resort to force. Catholic thought, however, actually diverges from this formal similarity by imposing a further significant restriction: even when such just cause is present, the more moral course may nonetheless be not to resort to force. The weight of argument here has shifted away from the classic emphasis on the requirements of just cause, right authority, and right intention to the prudential considerations of overall proportionality, last resort, and reasonable hope of success. For recent official Catholic teaching, these have the power to overrule the presence of a recognized just cause.

Going still further than the papal statements we have reviewed, Brian Hehir regards as indicative of the trend of official Vatican doctrine an editorial severely critical of the Gulf War published in the influential Roman journal *Civiltà Cattolica* in 1991. According to this editorial, Hehir writes, modern war is inevitably unjust, with only one limited exception: "the single exception of a war of pure defense against an aggressor actually taking place."[43] There is a significant difference between the meaning of an aggression "actually taking place" in this passage and the meaning found in international law, as applied to Iraq's military occupation of Kuwait. While Catholic thought earlier in this century tended to reflect the state of positive international law, this editorial takes a considerably more restrictive position on the allowability of resort to force.

The underlying reason for this fundamental shift in the structure of the moral argument is a judgment about the nature of modern war as disproportionately destructive and itself the source of great injustice. This conception has repeatedly surfaced in the sources cited above representing official and near-official Catholic thought on war from the time of the first Vatican Council to the present. For the 1870 *postulata,* the threat to be avoided was that of large standing national armies and the militarism they inculcated, together with the destructiveness such armies entailed in wartime. For the 1931 Conventus of Fribourg, the same threat lurks in the background, magnified by the memory of the Great War, and arbitration is held up as an alternative to war for the future.

By the time of Pius XII the threat has taken the even more ominous shape of the destructive power of atomic weapons, and it is this theme to which subsequent popes return repeatedly in their own statements about the right to resort to war. While defense continues to be somewhat reluctantly permitted, even this is undercut by the position Murray and Hehir find in Pius XII and John Paul II: that resort to armed force may not be justified even when such a just cause exists. In such a position, the idea of just cause has dwindled to little more than a formal placeholder, and the heavy lifting of deciding whether to resort to force in the service of statecraft has been given over to prudential calculations in which the conditions are tilted against any possibility that force can serve the cause of justice.

This position represents an enormous turnaround relative to classic medieval and early modern just war doctrine. Where has it left us with regard to the idea of just cause?

WHY JUST CAUSE NEEDS REASSESSMENT

There are, in my view, two important reasons why the concept of just cause needs to be reassessed in the current environment. The first is the moral inadequacy of the idea of just cause in its current state in positive international law and its even more woeful state in recent Catholic teaching. The second is that these authoritative contemporary statements of the idea of just cause are founded on an understanding of the international order, the nation-state, and the nature of war that rests on outmoded assumptions.

The Problem of Moral Inadequacy

As we have seen, just war theory in its classic medieval and early modern form defined a place for the moral use of armed force by politically sovereign communities. In the context of this theory, armed force was itself morally neutral; it might be employed for good or ill, according to the context. What just war theory sought to do was to specify the conditions required for the use of force to serve justice.

"In order for a war to be just," as Thomas Aquinas put the matter in stark simplicity, "three things are necessary." First, *sovereignty*—having no earthly superior, according to the medieval writers; also having the ability to defend the rights of one's own political community, according to the addition made by Vitoria—defined whose authority it was necessary to have before such force could be used. The second necessity was *just cause*, which in the classic theory included three justifying rationales for resort to armed force: defense against attack, recovery of something wrongly taken, and the punishment of wrongdoing. It was the responsibility of the sovereign authority to determine whether, in a given case, one or more of these justifying rationales was present. The third necessary condition was that the decision should be undertaken with *right intention*, which was understood positively to be an intent in line with just cause, and negatively to be the avoidance of various kinds of evil motivations. These latter were defined in a passage from Augustine that set the standard: "the desire for harming, the cruelty of avenging, an unruly and implacable animosity, the rage of rebellion, the lust of domination and the like—these are the things to be blamed in war."[44] The sovereign authority's decision regarding resort to force was also to be guided by other prudential concerns, but just war theory in its classic form did not dwell on these; what was necessary for a justified resort to force was the set of three conditions cited by Thomas: sovereign authority, just cause, and right intention.

I have shown how twentieth-century positive international law has sought to restrict the resort to force to the case of defense against aggression, with offensive resort to force denied as a means for resolving inter-state disputes. Under the controverted first-use/second-use distinction, aggression is defined as first use of force regardless of circumstances, while defense becomes second use alone. The classic just war conception of just cause is more comprehensive in the possibilities it anticipates. Defense there includes the possibility of genuine preemption of an attack (subject to the conditions for right intention), as Grotius's discussion makes plain, and it also allows resort to force to recover something wrongly taken and to punish wrongdoing. As I have argued above, in the contemporary usage of states the concept of defense has tended to expand to include uses of force for such reasons, evidence that there remain justifying reasons for the use of force beyond that of defensive response to an armed attack in progress. In effect, the concept of just cause explicitly stated in classic just war theory has come into contemporary international law implicitly, through the back door.

The United Nations Charter, in Chapter 7, reserves to the Security Council certain additional justifications for interventionary uses of force, notably peacekeeping and response to threats to international peace and security. These latter threats are not limited to cases of aggression, and in any case the United Nations is not bound by the "no first use" rule in the face of such threats. So it is possible to argue that so far as this international body is concerned, despite the legal effort to restrict states from employing armed force except in defense against "armed attack," the concept of just cause defined in classic just war theory remains honored.

By its very nature, law cannot render the fine details of moral argument. Its purpose also is different and more narrowly focused: it is a hedge against undesirable behavior. Nonetheless, law bears an important relation to moral concerns, and over time these concerns may emerge in greater fullness through the interpretations attached to the positive law and the behaviors aimed at complying with it.

The roots of international law on war are in the just war tradition, and international law is, in historical perspective, one of the most important carriers of that tradition during the modern period. The effort to limit just cause for resort to force to cases of defense against attack puts into positive-law form only a portion of the idea of just cause inherited from the larger tradition. That restricting effort came into being in a particular context in which the other traditional elements of just cause were understood as being addressed at the level of the international order. The resurgence of those other elements in an expanded concept of defense reflects the failure of the international means that were intended to address them. The question now is how to draw out the whole range of elements recognized in the classic theory so as to clarify their present-day implications for policy and political decision-making. I will return to this in the following section.

Relative to the moral content of the classical theory of just war, the contemporary state of Catholic thought on war is, in my judgment, far more problematical than is international law. For in recent authoritative Catholic teaching, not only has just cause for resort to force by a state been reduced to a defensive response to an attack still in progress (as in positive international law), but even that allowance has been undercut by two innovations in interpreting just war tradition.

The first innovation is identifying the resort to force as itself morally questionable. This is the development that the 1983 statement of the American Catholic bishops terms the "presumption against war." This "presumption" reflects judgments about the nature of war and the motives of states that can be traced to the era of Vatican Council I and that intensified with the development of nuclear weapons.

The second innovation in recent Catholic thought on war is that the *ius ad bellum* priority is given to the place of contingent prudential judgments (namely, the amount of destruction that can be anticipated, whether the situation is genuinely one of last resort, whether

there is a reasonable hope of success), so that resort to force is effectively questioned or denied even when there is admitted just cause.
This entirely inverts the logic of the classic theorists and goes far
toward removing force from the tools of statecraft employable in the
service of justice.

I will argue below that the justification for these prudential judgments is both one-sided and outmoded in the present context, but my
point here is a different one: that this inversion of the logic of the *ius
ad bellum* represents a deep unfaithfulness to the values expressed in
classic just war thought. The classic theorists, among whom those discussed above are benchmark figures, did not approach the question of
war with a presumption against the use of armed force; what motivated them was a *presumption against injustice*. The fundamental rationale was to prevent injustice even at risk to oneself, as shown by the
paradigm from Ambrose about the Christian encountering an armed
bandit who was attacking an innocent traveler. That need to prevent
injustice was what defined the role of the prince as "minister of God"
in the often cited text from Romans 13 (the ruler "is the minister of
God, a revenger to execute wrath" upon the evildoer) that figures
centrally in Thomas Aquinas's comments on the justification of war.

The problem with prudential judgments is not that they are prudential but that they are contingent. For this reason, classic medieval
and early modern just war theory placed the responsibility for the
prudential concerns included in the *ius ad bellum* on the competent
authority who determines whether to resort to armed force. In other
words, these concerns pertain to the function of statecraft; the role of
the moralist is to specify that they must be taken into account, not to
usurp the role of statecraft by specifying how they are to apply, or
what they mean for specific instances or general periods of time.

In contemporary Catholic thought on the *ius ad bellum*, the
assumption on which the analysis depends is the "presumption against
war," the assumption that, in the present age, war may no longer be
employed to remedy "violations of justice." But it was precisely "violations of justice" that the classic just war theorists aimed to address
and remedy. In these two contexts, the prudential concerns of overall
proportionality, last resort, and reasonable hope of success take on different colorations. There is no doubt that the classic just war theorists
were concerned *to right injustices*. By comparison, the logic of recent
Catholic teaching on war seems to leave no doubt that the intent is to

avoid resort to force. This is, I suggest, a cause for concern, unless it is granted in advance that such resort always produces the greatest injustice. I have already shown the link between the development of the idea of the "presumption against war" and the judgments made by critical actors about the nature and motivations of war as they understood them. The question is whether the uses of military force typical of the present day justify such judgments.

The Problem of Outmoded Assumptions

On the basis of the experience of the two world wars and, before that, "national war" as defined in the nineteenth century, positive international law on the resort to war defined its concept of just cause in terms of assumptions about nations, conflict among nations, and the hope of an international order in which such conflict would gradually be eliminated. The understanding of war shaped by this experience was of a totalistic form of conflict in which winning or losing came to have cosmic implications.

At the same time, the victorious powers who brought the United Nations into being, and who assigned themselves permanent places on the Security Council, did not for a minute doubt that the use of military means in a just cause has a central and necessary role in international politics. Accordingly, states were not to avail themselves of military means in an effort to serve their interests in a dispute unless the other party did so first (unlawfully). Here the principal villain is represented to be not the destructiveness of war itself but rather the evil of aggression, defined as first resort to force in the settlement of a dispute between nations. Pointedly, the United Nations Charter reserves the right for the Security Council to authorize resort to force for unspecified threats to international peace and security. Twentieth-century international law thus maintains an understanding of war as a potential instrument for purposeful human activity against injustice, in which both states and the international community have a role.

By contrast, recent Catholic thought has been deeply marked by an understanding of modern war as itself so morally questionable that the ability of human purpose to shape it and use it to serve justice has been all but lost: what remains is the ability to seek to prevent it. As we have seen, two themes stand out: first, that the moral possibility of national purpose has been subverted by the militarism imposed by large military establishments, for which the only cure is disarmament; and second, that the destructiveness of modern weapons, and in particular nuclear weapons, severely restricts and perhaps eliminates the possibility of resort to them as instruments of moral purpose. Neither of these themes holds up as a general descriptive statement either of the nature of contemporary states and statecraft or of the actuality of war once begun. Both are seriously outmoded in the post–Cold War context.

In the first place, the nature of the actual wars that have occurred since the end of the Cold War stands out, not as something whose destructiveness is inexorably beyond human control and whose point far outruns the ends of politics, but as something deeply shaped by human decision-making and expressive of political purpose. These conflicts have been limited ones in different but significant ways; none has ushered in a global holocaust, and none has escalated to all-out use of the military might of the great powers, including nuclear weapons. Nor, indeed, is this only a recent phenomenon. In truth, the face of armed conflict since the end of World War II has been essentially the same as in these post–Cold War conflicts.

This suggests that "modern war" is now this: localized, limited though sharp conflicts in which ethnic or religious differences or local political disputes provide the proximate causes, not totalistic clashes on the model of the two world wars or the feared global nuclear holocaust. The reality of such conflicts has, indeed, been terrible enough; yet the rape of Kuwait, the starvation of civilians in Somalia, and the ethnic massacres in Rwanda and the former Yugoslavia have not exemplified a type of destructiveness different from what was known by Vitoria, Grotius, or their predecessors. (Grotius, after all, lived during the Thirty Years War, arguably the most devastating conflict Europe has ever experienced.) All these conflicts have been condemned by the international community, and each has occasioned action by members of that community to relieve suffering and end the conflict. In these responses, military means belonging to the great powers have been brought to bear in limited rather than totalistic ways, and with varying degrees of success.

This is remarkable in two important respects. The first is that these cases have defined the limits of what various forms of the international community can do. The United Nations has had success at peacekeeping, but other international coalitions have been necessary where peace does not exist or exists only tenuously, as in the cases of the Gulf War and the NATO intervention in Bosnia. The second remarkable element in the way the major powers have employed their military forces in these conflicts is that in doing so they have gone substantially beyond a narrow definition of their national interests to include humanitarian and international-order concerns—just the opposite of what they were expected to do on the model of the state that emphasizes militarism, national chauvinism, and venality.

JUST CAUSE REASSESSESSED: IMPLICATIONS FOR MORAL STATECRAFT

It is apparent that the concept of just cause for resort to force is undergoing significant reinterpretation in the framework of statecraft; but moral doctrine has not yet examined what this implies for just cause in the framework of just war tradition. I turn to this problem in what follows.

The Continuing Power of States

While classic just war theory envisioned the state, under the authority of its sovereign head, as the central actor in the decision whether to employ force to combat injustice, twentieth-century legal and moral thought in the just war tradition has sought to limit the right of individual states to resort to force while reserving a larger latitude to international organizations. For the United Nations Charter and for much moral reflection hostile to the state as well, the latter meant one organization in particular: the United Nations. The right to engage in offensive uses of force, in the sense of military actions across borders, was located here, while other groupings of states, whether formal treaty alliances like NATO and the Warsaw Pact or ad hoc coalitions like that formed in response to Iraq's invasion of Kuwait, were held to the same restrictions as individual states: legitimate resort to armed force only for the purpose of defense.

Moral thought shaped by visions of the militarism, self-interestedness, and venality of states, not to mention internationalists focused on the United Nations as the beginning of a new world order, neglected to take adequate account of a fundamental fact: that real power was not located there but remained with the individual states and in groupings of states for a common purpose. In this sense these efforts to define a form of statecraft in which states play a subordinate role were utopian, imagining a reality that did not exist and degrading the reality that did exist. The relentlessly negative portrayal of the state as an institution both disregarded the positive attributes of the state system and ignored differences in the way specific states were constituted and behaved.

The uncritically positive attitude toward the possibilities of international order, on the other hand, overlooked the fact that the structure of order defined through the United Nations could not stand alone; rather, it depended on viable states in order to function. Further, this attitude toward the United Nations did not take account of the fact that under the conditions of the Cold War, this organization was not able to do even the best it was capable of in living up to the role envisioned for it in the Charter. The end of the Cold War set the United Nations free to act in accord with what the Charter provided: to intervene in conflicts where no peace had been established in order to set right conditions that posed a threat to international peace and security.

Yet paradoxically, its newly achieved freedom to act in this way showed clearly that the United Nations lacks the attributes it needs to do so effectively. It lacks *cohesion*, so that policies and decisions have led to inconstancy on the ground of the conflicts it has addressed. It lacks *sovereignty* in the sense that Vitoria singled out, the power to assert and defend its own rights. It lacks an effective *chain of command* for military forces set in the midst of an ongoing conflict, which means that these forces cannot be an effective arm of international statecraft. These qualities are in fact necessary characteristics of the state as a political institution, and their absence at once shows the limits of the United Nations and the continuing importance of states in the international system. All the deficiencies mentioned are in the first place defects in sovereign authority, but since without such authority there is no entity competent to determine just cause and undertake military action on its behalf, the lack of these qualities undermines the positive-law definition of just cause in which certain rights regarding the use of force are reserved to the Security Council while being denied to states or other groupings of states. In the practical arena, the fiascos in Bosnia and, earlier, in Somalia have brought these problems to light.

Customary Law vs. Positive Law

At the same time, the press of events has produced a nascent *customary law* that preserves the form of extant positive international law while reflecting the continuing rights and responsibilities of states. The customary law proceeds from the fact that viable states possess what the United Nations does not: competent authority to formulate policies and reach decisions regarding the just use of force, to exercise command over such force, and to make assessments of their rights and responsibilities relative to ongoing conflicts even when they have not been party to these conflicts.

Many commentators regard customary international law, based on the collective attitudes and actions of states, as the real international law, rather than that which is written down in positive form, unless the latter is backed up by state attitudes and behavior. So it is especially important, I think, that the crises in Kuwait, Somalia, and the former Yugoslavia have brought into being a process by which the rights of just cause reserved to the United Nations in positive international law have been extended over individual states and coalitions of states, to give them rights to use military force across national borders that the positive-law concept of just cause sought to deny them. These three cases exemplify this extension in different ways. The legal grounding of the response to the invasion and occupation of Kuwait, where the extension first appears, was admittedly mixed. While the coalition's action was carefully defined so as to fit the conditions of Article 51 of the Charter, whereby groups of states are given the right collectively to respond to an ongoing armed attack, Security Council authority—not strictly required under the terms of Article 51—was also sought and obtained for action. Somalia too provides a mixed lesson: the United States and other individual nations contributed forces under the legal authority of the United Nations and in accord with its definition of just cause; yet in the case of the U.S. forces, the chain of command was American, and the United Nations had only an ineffective command authority over the other national forces present. The problem of an effective chain of command carried over into Bosnia, both while the intervention was entirely a U.N. operation and after it became a mixed U.N.-NATO cooperative effort. However, the state of affairs achieved in Bosnia after the Dayton accords carries the development I have described to what may be a new state of equilibrium, in which regional alliances employ interventionary force with the formal authorization of the United Nations and in accord with the just causes reserved to that body, causes going beyond what is allowed such regional alliances by positive international law.

Coalitions as Bearers of Authority

Now, while I have had a good deal to say about the question of authority, these reflections bear simultaneously on the question of just cause, since these two elements of the *ius ad bellum* are closely intertwined. Encapsulated within the development I have sketched is a significant expansion of the *de facto* conception of just cause for leading states and powerful groupings of states able to shape Security Council decisions. Whatever the *de jure* limits on the right of a state or a group of states to engage in the use of force across national boundaries, if Security Council sanction for such action can be obtained, the result is effectively the same as if the states directly possessed that right. This possibility has existed since 1945, but during the Cold War it was limited by the presence of the veto in the Security Council. Now, the logjam of a party-line veto has given way to a situation in which, in practical terms, what is required is that the majority of Security Council members agree to support a particular use of force, while no one permanent member opposes it enough to veto it. This implies that the extension of the just cause idea I have described will take place only with coalitions of nations whose core includes a majority of the permanent Security Council members.

It is notable that both NATO and the coalition formed against Iraq in the Gulf War satisfy this condition. While the latter was an ad hoc grouping of nations for a single purpose, NATO's ongoing institutional existence defined by treaty, common interests of the members, and a half-century history of cooperation gives it a much more significant potential role. NATO was brought into existence in accord with the understanding set out in the United Nations Charter that regional alliances of states could be formed for a defensive purpose. It was thus defined formally by the same highly restricted positive-law conception of just-cause-for-use-of-armed-force that applied to individual states.

The debate over NATO involvement in Bosnia and the gradual growth of that involvement marks a transition away from this conception of NATO's role, and it also marks the coalescence of a new definition of just cause for the use of forces under NATO command. With the replacement of the U.N. peacekeeping forces by a robust NATO force, and with tactical decisions regarding just cause for use of that force in the hands of the NATO chain of command, a state of affairs has been reached that embodies the new conception I have sketched above. The positive legal authority for this force's presence remains that defined by the framework of the U.N. Charter; but the *de facto* authority for the use of force has been delegated to this regional organization, which has been given the power to act within the broader framework of just cause that was earlier denied to it—a framework that includes not only defense of self but also defense of the rights of others.

This development is extremely significant in both political and moral terms: politically, in that it embodies a conception of a political unit greater than the individual state, yet not so utopian as earlier conceptions of world order; morally, in that it embodies both (a) the recognition of a concept of just cause for use of military force that goes beyond the narrow right of self-defense and (b) the extension of this concept to a regional grouping of states.

The United States, because of its post–Cold War preeminence, is positioned to be considerably affected—with both benefits and burdens—by this *de facto* redistribution of the right to resort to force for reasons other than national defense against armed attack. At the same time, the nature of the shift implicitly requires that such decisions be subject to the approval of the other powers that make up the permanent membership of the Security Council and participate in such regional security groupings as NATO or ad hoc coalitions that may be formed in response to particular crises. This suggests that the states involved in such groupings must share more than simply common interests: they must agree that common values are at stake. Thus there seems to me to be a tilt here toward support for broadly recognized rights and humanitarian needs, a point to which I will return below.

The Possibility of Preemption

What this developing *de facto* state of affairs implies for major powers acting in their own spheres of interest, either unilaterally or at the head of regional groupings of states, also seems clear by this point. Whether it is the United States employing military force in the Western Hemisphere (as in Grenada, Panama, and Haiti), or Russia in the Caucasus (as in Chechnya and, more limitedly, elsewhere), or France in its former colonies in central Africa, the restrictive limits of the *de jure* definition of just cause no longer apply—if, indeed, they ever in reality had the force they claimed.

All this bears directly on the possibility for genuinely preemptive uses of force in which there are actions across a national border in response to perceived security threats while those threats are developing, or, more broadly, in response to violations of human rights or other prominent evils that the local authorities either do not address or are unable to deal with. The behavior of states since 1945 has never consistently ratified the effort in Article 2 of the U.N. Charter to disallow cross-border projections of force except after a first military attack has fallen.

Yet there are two new elements in the current scene: first, the recognition that the danger may not be military but may nonetheless threaten national security (e.g., the drug trade, terrorism and other forms of hostile acts by the leadership of a foreign country or with their approval and support); second, the possibility of interventions to correct ills that are not themselves directly or immediately threatening to national security but are major violations of universal values that the local government cannot or has not sought to remedy (indeed, it may itself be the source of the violations). The U.S. intervention in Haiti exemplifies a national action to set right violations of values that had both these characteristics at the same time.

National Interests and Universal Ideals

These last considerations introduce another morally significant element in the developing *de facto* understanding of just cause for use of armed force: that just cause as currently understood in practice may proceed either from concerns of national interest that include but go beyond immediate military threats, or from concern to protect universal values, remedy their violation, and prevent continuing violations. At the same time, the use of military force that is justified in these ways is not the same as that envisioned in the effort to restrict military action to responses to armed attack. This latter conception envisioned military action as the initiation of war between nations, war that might escalate to become total in its means and draw other nations into it so that it became global. While the redefined just cause I have been describing includes this as an extreme possibility, it chiefly has to do with far more restrained and local applications of military force.

Indeed, such applications may be not to make war at all but to encourage the establishment of peace: to separate warring parties, to provide or facilitate delivery of food or medical care, to keep peace while a fractured society rebuilds, and possibly to support such rebuilding not only morally but materially. Above this level but still well below the level of all-out war are uses of military means that might involve interdiction or punishment of organized criminal activities (e.g., U.S. use of air, naval, and military intelligence capabilities against the Latin American drug trade), limited applications of force to discourage and punish aggression (e.g., the use of NATO air and U.N. artillery strikes in Bosnia in the period prior to the signing of the peace accord), or protection of the rights of minorities (e.g., enforcement of the protective zones designed to benefit the Shiite and Kurdish populations in Iraq). Also at this intermediate level are military responses to terrorist activity (e.g., Israel's ongoing military action in southern Lebanon, the U.S. air strike against Libya) and preemptive limited military strikes to remove a threat still in the process of developing (e.g., Israel's use of air power against an Iraqi nuclear reactor capable of producing weapons-grade fissionable material).

Where, in the above mixture of situations, do interests end and ideals begin? I suggest that in the present environment, interests and ideals are not discrete alternatives but mutually supplemental sources for the idea of justice in just cause for resort to armed force, as exemplified by the variety of causes being served in the above cases. Indeed, I would carry this argument further. If the paradigm is that individual states and regional organizations of states may resort to force only in armed self-defense against attack by other armed force, then the argument from national or regional security interests fits it well. But if the paradigm is instead the developing one I have sketched, in which the rights reserved in positive law to the United Nations are exercised in a *de facto* manner by regional organizations and individual states, then not only state interests narrowly conceived but also broadly recognized values must be taken into account.

At this point it may be possible to return to the matter of the skepticism regarding all uses of force in recent Catholic teaching, a skepticism that has tended toward a *de facto* denial of all contemporary resort to armed force under national authority, even when the just cause of self-defense is present. For the understanding of the current state of affairs I have sketched is one much more obviously akin to the situation employed by Ambrose to describe both the responsibility to use force in service of one's neighbor and the limits of such uses of force. The implication is that the denials of the right to resort to force *even when just cause exists* that were put forward in recent papal statements and paralleled in much other recent religious discourse on war do not apply when what is assumed is not a war of nations on the model of the two world wars, or a massively destructive nuclear exchange between the superpowers, but a limited application of force that is in accord with internationally accepted values and takes place with the express or tacit authority of the community of nations, even though national interests may also be served by such action.

Some Conclusions

Generals are often criticized for planning that aims to fight the previous war. Paul Fussell has put the matter more globally: "Everyone fighting a modern war tends to think of it in terms of the last one he knows anything about."[45] Implicit in the argument I have made is that those who have aimed at defining the right of resort to armed force in the modern period have also thought of this right in terms of the last war they know anything about, from the national wars of the nineteenth century to the two world wars of the twentieth. Indeed, even the imagining of war among those who have focused on the destructive potential of nuclear weapons has proceeded from this understanding of war as an all-out, totalistic use of military might. From this reasoning to the effort to limit national resort to armed force to cases of defense, or even to condemn it outright, is not a large step. But in fact the form that contemporary uses of military force have taken is quite different from this, and the relation of national uses of such force to international sanction for the resort to force has developed accordingly.

It has been my thesis that in the contemporary world, the idea of just cause has developed in a way that allows individual states and groupings of states to employ limited force for reasons formerly denied to them, and to address issues that go beyond those formerly held to motivate states. In support of this thesis I have argued from a reading of the world as it exists after the end of the Cold War and from a reading of states and the state system as forces for justice in that world. Not by accident, the picture I have drawn closely matches the assumptions about states, the international order, and permissible uses of armed force found in the foundational just war theorists treated early in this essay. Nor is it accidental that the concept of just cause I have identified for the present state of affairs includes restoring that which has been taken wrongly (including violated rights and universal values), punishment of evil (uses of military means against troublers of international peace and security), and defense against military attacks not only when they are already under way but also while they are still in preparation.

From the perspective of persons who regard states as incurably venal and all uses of force in the modern era as disproportionately destructive, the position I have defined will seem an unwarranted and immoral loosening of strictures against the resort to force. From the perspective of political realism, on the other hand, my argument will seem to have gone too far, taking too much account of moral concerns, international standards, and values. But between these two perspectives lies precisely the territory of just war tradition, an understanding of statecraft in which the use of armed force in the service of justice is both permitted and restrained. That is the conception of just cause I have sought to define and whose implications I have sought to draw out.

2

Competent Authority Revisited

Eugene V. Rostow

As befits a chapter in the moral theology of a universal church built for the ages, the just war tradition rests on an implacable respect for the reality that always limits the possibility of social change: an awareness that trees do not grow to the sky; that men are capable of evil as well as of moral grandeur; and that the societies they build, manage, and destroy are no better. To borrow a phrase from George Weigel, the just war philosophers are idealists without illusions. Since the time of St. Augustine, they have been engaged in an enormously productive crusade against war without being pacifists. They are utopians who have dared to defend the goal of perpetual peace, but have always carefully rendered unto Caesar what was properly his. They are not quixotic utopians who think that because some men have been saints, all men are angels. On the contrary, they fully accept Kant's observation that "out of timber so crooked as that from which man is made, nothing entirely straight can be built."[1] So the influence of the just war tradition on the behavior of princes, their states, and the law

Eugene V. Rostow is Distinguished Research Professor of Law and Diplomacy at the National Defense University in Washington, D.C., and an adjunct scholar at the American Enterprise Institute. His most recent book is *Toward Managed Peace: The National Security Interests of the United States, 1759 to the Present* (Yale University Press, 1993).

they have created has always been limited by the resistance of social forces too powerful to be gainsaid: nationalism, fear, pride, and folly, to name only the most important. Thus in the beginning and for a long time thereafter, the just war philosophers accepted any war declared by a legitimate monarch for any purpose as morally permissible.

Nothing could serve to demonstrate the interplay of these ideas more vividly than the controversy that raged in 1996 about the respective authority of NATO and the United Nations Security Council in authorizing and conducting what was erroneously but officially described as a United Nations "peacekeeping" action in Bosnia. In the special vocabulary of the United Nations, it would be more accurate to identify NATO's Bosnian campaign as an action of collective self-defense carried out entirely under the auspices of NATO and on the "competent authority" of the nations that sent troops to participate in the effort.

What is at stake in this controversy is nothing less than the capacity of the major powers, or a decisive number of them, to see to it that the rules of the U.N. Charter against aggression are effectively enforced. If that is done, one could hope that those rules would become not simply an aspiration and a hope, or no more than a rhetorical pretense, as they are now, but, in fact, the central principle of a world system of public order based on international law.

If the state system chooses to persevere in its decision to rely on NATO and like arrangements of collective self-defense as the primary (and in fact the only available) vehicles through which to vindicate the conception of peace put forward in the United Nations Charter, it should become possible, with another half-century or so of active Western diplomacy, to fulfill the dream of the just war philosophers, which was also President Wilson's dream. If, on the other hand, the states choose to defy reality, as they did during the thirties, and attempt to rely only on the peacekeeping machinery and procedures of the United Nations, Wilson's great experiment will go the way of the League of Nations, leaving humanity to flounder until a new Concert of Europe can emerge to resume the quest for peace through law.

For it cannot be said too often that the possibility of peace requires the concerted influence of the major military powers of the day, backed by their willingness to use force if necessary to attain peace and to maintain it. The nineteenth century was the last time the world has enjoyed such a period of peace. The idea of the Concert of Europe is the indispensable component of the concept of world peace. For the century between the final defeat of Napoleon at Waterloo and the outbreak of World War I in August 1914, the major powers of Europe, under the leadership of Great Britain, achieved a greater and more sustained degree of peace than any of their predecessors since the heyday of the Roman Empire, and any of their successors.

As is now obvious everywhere, the post-Soviet world is not a tranquil Garden of Eden, where peace will prosper simply through the automatic adjustment of the various parts to one another. The state system must have a means of containing the impulses toward war that are bound to arise from time to time, and this stabilizing function can be provided only by the concerted effort of the major states. What is at stake in this controversy, therefore, is nothing less than the possibility that the state system can be managed as a system of peace.

THE JUST WAR TRADITION AS A SOURCE OF LAW

Revisiting the subject of competent authority gives me a convenient vantage point for reviewing the present state of just war doctrine and its prospects as an influence on international life and thus on international law. For I should make it clear at once that I am not an Austinian or any other kind of legal positivist. I do not believe that the norms of law are no more than the commands of a sovereign, and that international law is an illusion because there is no international sovereign to proclaim it.

The United Nations is not a world government. In my view, it is most unlikely to become a world government, despite the thrust of Article 25 of its Charter, which purports to give the Security Council, at least on matters of international peace and security, the power to issue "decisions" that the member states accept as legally binding. Formally, most Security Council resolutions are "recommendations," and the few labeled "decisions" have nonetheless been treated, by and large, as recommendations, designed to stimulate cooperation among the member states, which are consistently viewed by the Charter and by the Security Council as equally sovereign. The Security Council has often sponsored active diplomatic efforts to persuade states to comply with such resolutions, but so far it has stopped short of trying to use force itself or encouraging states to do so in its behalf.

For example, Security Council Resolution 338, adopted by the Security Council on October 22, 1973, immediately after Israel's victory in the Yom Kippur War, *"decides"* that "immediately and concurrently with the ceasefire, negotiations start between the parties concerned under appropriate auspices aimed at establishing a just and durable peace in the Middle East." Despite this categorical Security Council order, no such negotiations began concurrently with the ceasefire, or for many years thereafter. Egypt, the first Arab government to comply with Resolution 338, made peace with Israel in 1977. Jordan made peace with Israel in 1995. Later that year Israel and Syria engaged in negotiations in accordance with Resolution 338, and other Arab states are expected to establish diplomatic relations with Israel if the negotiations between Syria and Israel are successful. Complex multilateral and bilateral negotiations to implement Resolution 338 have followed the conference of 1993 in Madrid and the negotiations in Oslo in 1995.

Law Realistically Defined

One of the most sophisticated, realistic, and balanced definitions of international law I know is Article 38 of the Statute of the International Court of Justice in The Hague, which provides that:

1. The Court, whose function is to decide in accordance with international law such disputes as are submitted to it, shall apply:
     a. international conventions, whether general or particular, establishing rules expressly recognized by the contesting states;
     b. international custom as evidence of a general practice accepted as law;
     c. the general principles of law recognized by civilized nations;
     d. subject to the provisions of Article 59, judicial decisions and the teachings of the most highly qualified publicists of the various nations, as subsidiary means for the determination of rules of law.

2. This provision shall not prejudice the power of the Court to decide a case *ex aequo et bono* [i.e., according to the Court's sense of what is right and good rather than strictly according to the law], if the parties agree thereto.

One of the many virtues of Article 38 is that it defines law as a pattern of state behavior—or rather, as *the* pattern of state behavior deemed right by the community of nations—rather than simply as a collection of precatory rules. Article 38 sharply distinguishes international law from the formulations of legal norms attempted in treaties and the writings of judges, arbitrators, law professors, and other publicists. Such statements are treated as relevant "sources" of law, but not as law itself. A given proposition becomes law only when the states accept it as law and absorb its implications into their behavior. Declaring that the International Court of Justice should not be bound by its decisions as precedents, Article 38, like Article 59, to which it refers, treats the law to be applied by the Court as a continuous process for making fresh decisions about social policy. It focuses attention on the modes of reasoning developed by courts over the centuries as the essential tools lawyers use to discover law emerging from its matrix in social, moral, and intellectual experience. Thus the draftsmen of Article 38 expected law to change from time to time as the sources from which it is drawn change.

Article 38 walks a fine line between two quite different ways of thinking about law. Conceptually, the two schools of thought agree that it is of the essence of sovereignty that a sovereign state cannot be bound by certain propositions as law until it has agreed to treat them as law. They differ, however, in their willingness to infer such consent from custom and practice, from multilateral treaties, and from even less formal evidence of actual consent by the individual state.

Defining Competent Authority

The attempt to define the authority competent to initiate war— that is, "war" as distinguished from banditry, piracy, or kidnapping— and the circumstances under which it should be regarded as moral and legal to do so is an integral part of the history of the state system. Having emerged from the mists of the late Roman Empire, that fragmented system developed in more or less distinct stages from a congeries of small, localized, autonomous communities until it took on its contemporary shape in the seventeenth, eighteenth, and nineteenth centuries in Europe, most particularly after the Congress of Vienna in 1815.

In the beginning, manifestly, the just war philosophers meant by the phrase "competent authority" a monarch vested with sovereign authority "by the grace of God." Gradually, that authority was deemed to have been transferred to the secular modern states, whatever their form of government, so long as they are recognized as functioning states by the international community.

There has always been tension between the prevailing moral code and the practice of war. Throughout history, large and small tribes, cities, and other social units have made war, singly and in alliances, but almost all of them purported also to believe in the Sixth Commandment or its equivalent in other religions: "Thou shalt not kill." All but the most exalted pacifists among them have believed as well, however, that in an imperfect and sometimes evil world, war in self-defense, at least, and wars to help neighbors being attacked are necessary to physical and moral survival, and should therefore be recognized, in the nature of things, as an exception to the prohibition against killing.

Evolution of the Just War Tradition

Out of this tension the doctrine of just war slowly took shape, starting with the writings of St. Augustine and St. Thomas Aquinas. The moral analysis of just war spread even more slowly as a guide to state behavior and finally as a vital source of both positive and customary international law, with the principles of *ius ad bellum* concerned with the initiation of war and those of *ius in bello* governing the conduct of war. Thus the society of nations has struggled since 1919, first with the Covenant of the League of Nations and now with the Charter of the United Nations, both of which, like the rapidly evolving body of international humanitarian law, draw heavily on the just war tradition. These documents pledge the nations to give up what used to be considered their sovereign prerogative to go to war at will for plunder, for sport, for glory, for conquest, or in crusades to spread the true faith by the sword. Both the Covenant and the Charter would confine legitimate or permissible war to the categories of (1) individual or collective self-defense, (2) United Nations "enforcement actions," and (3) assistance to friendly states being attacked.

The just war tradition in its modern formulation stresses four primary propositions: the use of armed force is morally permissible, despite the Sixth Commandment, when (1) it has been authorized by legitimate authority and is carried out by uniformed personnel bearing their arms openly; (2) those armed personnel are part of an organized and disciplined military force controlled by a competent state; (3) it is undertaken only as a reasonable, limited, and proportional response to an illegal act of a forcible character, like an armed attack; and (4) it is carried out by means that are considered humane and that minimize damage to non-combatants, who should not be directly attacked in any event.[2]

When the Age of Discovery began five centuries ago, another exception to the Sixth Commandment was at least tacitly acknowledged. The Christian nations of Europe were deemed morally free to conquer, colonize, and rule the newly discovered lands, provided they encouraged missionary work among the natives. That exception to the prohibition against killing has not lost all its vitality. The major powers of the state system do not yet treat war and the threat of war in the Third World as they treat the threat of war among themselves. Italy's conquest of Ethiopia in 1935, for example, and India's annexation of the surviving Portuguese territories in India during the fifties were not considered sufficiently serious acts of aggression to require a remedial or punitive great-power response of the kind successfully provided for South Korea in 1950 and Kuwait in 1990.

In another form, the same issue has been presented by the tragic conflict in what used to be Yugoslavia. Bosnia, formerly a constituent republic of the federated state of Yugoslavia, declared its independence and was admitted to the United Nations. Nonetheless, for a long time it was denied international protection against aggression by Serbia and Croatia. Was the prolonged delay in an effective response by either the U.N. or NATO to the aggression in the Balkans simply a manifestation of the popular but erroneous view that the Balkans are a semi-barbarous region where it is futile to expect peace, and excessively costly to try to impose it?

The emphasis in the just war doctrine on the authorization of war by competent authority thus reflects one of the principal policy goals of the social and political movements that created the modern state. As political units grew larger and more centralized, under the influence of economic, military, and political pressures, and under the influence as well of monarchs who dreamed of becoming at least regional Leviathans, it became more and more obvious that there could be no stability, no order, and no domestic tranquillity unless the states had a monopoly over the use of force within their realms. The king's sheriffs, the king's courts, and the king's armed forces gradually replaced those of dukes, barons, and bishops.

The same claims of necessity and order supported the policy of treating the states as monopolists of the privilege of making war internationally. Limiting the use of military force to states and their armed forces made possible both domestic and international peace, as states came to agree upon rules for the use of force derived from just war principles, and rules necessary to assure the peaceful cooperation of states within the state system.

THE USE OF FORCE: ONLY BETWEEN STATES?

Since the end of the Second World War in 1945, the most severe challenges to the international law that purports to embody these principles have concerned its strict policy of confining permissible international war to states. Strong voices have urged that international law should recognize that states are no longer the only actors on the global stage. Political movements, churches, multinational corporations, guerrilla groups, trade unions, revolutionary bodies, and universities have become international actors, and the world should realize that the older rules are obsolete. But, despite the zeal and even passion that have been devoted to this plausible thesis, international law shows little if any sign of revolutionary change. The modern state is proving to be a stubborn and resistant institution that continues to be the organizing unit of the world system.

The reason is not hard to see. The state still meets the need that is in fact the first functional necessity of any organized society, the need for what my colleague Myres McDougal calls minimum public order.[3] In an increasingly turbulent and even anarchic world, only states can assure such a degree of order both domestically and internationally. Without such an assurance, mankind will have to confront the hazards of anarchy, a social condition incompatible with civilization. In the past, a condition of anarchy has invariably led to a restoration of order through dictatorship.

Law and the American Civil War

Perhaps the best place to begin to examine this process is in the law purporting to govern the realm of civil war. Before 1945, when the United Nations came into being, the prevailing law was exemplified by the diplomacy of the American Civil War, which, I venture to suggest, still represents the prevailing position of international law.

When the Confederate States of America was organized in 1860–61, its leaders, like the leaders of the Continental Congress eighty-five years earlier, understood that obtaining diplomatic recognition in Europe was their principal political hope, and indispensable to any conceivable strategy for achieving military victory. If they could persuade Britain and France to recognize the Confederacy as a state, then it would be a state in the eyes of international law—a state, that is, and not a rag-tag gang of rebels against the recognized authority of the United States of America. As a recognized state, it would have all the rights, duties, and privileges assured to states by international law. Then, under the laws of neutrality prevailing at the time (and perhaps still prevailing), Britain and other countries could give or sell the Confederates arms, train their soldiers, and perhaps send troops and ships of their own to help the rebellion if they decided to go that far in their desire to weaken the United States as a potential rival. On that footing, the South could realistically have believed it had a real chance of succeeding on the battlefield.

The climax of this struggle was the *Alabama* episode. The Confederacy had sent secret agents to buy arms in Europe. One of those agents had ordered a number of cruisers to be built in England for the Confederate navy, and the *Alabama* was one of those ships. The United States monitored the progress of its construction in a Liverpool shipyard, protesting vigorously and almost daily to the British Foreign Office with all the emphasis at its command. In his final *démarche* on the subject, the American minister in London, Charles Francis Adams, threatened the use of force if the British government failed to prevent the *Alabama* from slipping out of the shipyard onto the high seas. The geographical position of Canada gave that threat particular force.

Under circumstances that still remain murky, the *Alabama* did escape, and it became a disastrously effective commerce raider. Britain later paid the United States what was then considered a very large sum of money as damages awarded by a panel of arbitrators. That is, it was agreed that international law, on pain of heavy damages, required Great Britain to make sure that its territory was not used as the base from which an illegal attack on the United States was mounted.

Thus the classical legal theory of the American Civil War was neat and coherent. It was derived entirely from the proposition that the state is a sovereign entity in the eyes of international law. The first duty of each state, therefore, is to respect the sovereignty of every other state. Thus international force cannot be used to interfere with the territorial integrity or political independence of any state. Residents of a state may rebel against its authority and seek to change it by insurrection or revolution, but international law is not concerned with such events. Legally, rebellions have been considered to concern only the domestic criminal law of the states where they occur. What international law does prohibit is any international use of force to attack a state, either directly or by inciting, fomenting, or aiding a domestic revolution against its government.

(The Nuremberg trials and certain other developments since 1945 require a qualification of this generalization, because the states have begun to apply international law to individuals in both civil and criminal proceedings. After World War II, the victorious Allies established tribunals and sponsored the trials of certain German and Japanese individuals for extreme violations of the laws of war they committed as state officials. Most of them were tried for violating provisions of the Geneva Convention dealing with *ius in bello*, the principles governing the conduct of war—their maltreatment of prisoners of war, for example, or the massacre of civilians. In a few instances the trials were based on a new war crime, the crime of waging aggressive war, deemed to have been established by the Kellogg-Briand Treaty of 1927 and reaffirmed by the universal acceptance of the U.N. Charter. Since that time, in a few cases, particularly in the United States, individuals have been held liable for damages for violating international law in another country—for engaging in official torture, for example.[4])

During the American Civil War, then, the European states were deemed free to sell arms to the United States, or even to help it put down the rebellion if they decided to go that far, but they could not assist the Confederacy in similar ways.

International Law and the Cold War

This principle of international law has been the focal point of intense controversy for the last two generations. Throughout the period of the large-scale and intense Cold War, which began towards the end of World War II, the legal issues considered during the American Civil War never left the agenda of world politics. Inciting civil war and assisting rebels in a civil war were favorite tactics of the Soviet Union as it pursued its policy of expansion between 1944 and 1989. In the late forties, for example, the Soviet Union sent arms and troops into Greece through Bulgaria and Yugoslavia, to be used by the Communist party within Greece in its more and more open attempt to seize control of the Greek state. In Vietnam, Communist attacks by forces that identified themselves as a "liberation army" were a conspicuous feature of North Vietnamese offensives against South Vietnam.

Meanwhile, all over the world, the Soviet Union and its supporters sought political and intellectual support for the proposition that international law should recognize the right of a state to support an insurrection against the authority of another state, so long as the rebellion was being fought in the name of "the self-determination of peoples," "socialism," or some other popular cause. Many books and articles sympathized with this view, and it made some progress in attempted codifications of international law through private or public commissions or other study groups. But in all those forums, the efforts of those who favored the Soviet view failed. What invariably resulted in the final reports of such committees was ambiguity and obfuscation. No state was willing to accept the thesis that its neighbors had a legal right to send military help to an armed rebellion against the state's authority. What resulted was double-talk: a report in which one paragraph proclaimed the absolute protection of all states, large and small, against attacks on their territorial integrity or political independence, but another paragraph recited equally fervent support for the principle of the self-determination of peoples.[5]

The high tide of this effort was recorded in the opinions of the International Court of Justice in *Nicaragua v. United States* (1984 I.C.J. 392 and 1986 I.C.J 14), a suit filed by Nicaragua on April 9, 1984.[6] Nicaragua had been one of the states assisting a radical insurgency against the government of El Salvador. In the exercise of their right of collective self-defense in behalf of El Salvador, the United States and a number of other governments had been helping the Salvadoran government resist the attacks sponsored by Nicaragua and its colleagues. Discouraged by the more and more vigorous attacks on El Salvador mounted and orchestrated by Nicaragua, the United States raised the level of its own participation in the struggle by mining Nicaraguan harbors and by giving military assistance to a rebellious group (the Contras) that was conducting a guerrilla war against the Nicaraguan government.

Nicaragua claimed that the United States had in effect consented to the jurisdiction of the International Court of Justice by virtue of its having accepted compulsory jurisdiction in 1946 under Article 36(2) of the court's statute, reinforced in this case by the provisions of a general Treaty of Friendship, Navigation and Commerce between the United States and Nicaragua, which entered into force in 1956. American acceptance of compulsory jurisdiction under Article 36(2) was withdrawn on October 7, 1985, and American acceptance of the Treaty of Friendship was withdrawn in 1986.

The decision of the court that it had jurisdiction both under Article 36(2) of its statute and under the 1956 treaty has been severely criticized. But for our purposes here the most notable feature of the court's opinions is its decision that U.S. action against Nicaragua went beyond the limits of permissible collective self-defense and amounted, therefore, to a breach of the peace. The court found that Nicaragua had not been guilty of making an "armed attack" on El Salvador, because its shipment of arms to the rebels in that country was not, standing alone, sufficient evidence of a breach of the peace or an aggression. Once the court took that step, its judgment against the United States followed automatically.

Article 51 of the U.N. Charter provides that "nothing in the present Charter shall impair the inherent right of individual or collective self-defense if an armed attack occurs against a member of the United Nations." This passage does not create the right of self-defense but refers to it as an existing right, inherent in sovereignty and fully recognized in customary international law. Before 1945, when the U.N. Charter went into effect, international law did not insist on an actual armed attack before a defensive response could occur. As a major authority on international law remarked in 1914, international law does not require the aggrieved state to wait before using force in self-defense "until it is too late to protect itself."⁷ Moreover, in the customary law of self-defense as it was universally understood prior to 1945, sending arms into another state to support an insurrection was strictly forbidden—indeed, a *casus belli*.

"The Draft Declaration of the Rights and Duties of States, adopted by the International Law Commission in 1949, said that states had a duty 'to refrain from fomenting civil strife in the territory of another state, and to prevent the organization within its territory of activities calculated to foment such civil strife.' " This statement, quoted with approval by Judge Schwebel in his dissenting opinion in the *Nicaragua* case, states the law correctly.⁸ The obligation of each state in this regard is absolute, so long as it knew or should have known about the activities going forward on or from its territory. An offending state need not have been complicit or substantially involved with the activities. It may have been too weak to put down the armed bands or terrorist groups operating from its territories. This was the case in 1818, when the United States was raided from Spanish Florida by a force of Indians, runaway slaves, and irregular soldiers. The United States sent troops into Spanish Florida under General Andrew Jackson to disperse the raiders. And it was the case recently, when Lebanon was used as a base by the P.L.O. for attacks on Israel. Or the host state may not have had time to suppress the armed bands, as was the case in the *Caroline* affair in 1837, where an armed band of enthusiastic supporters of an insurrection in Canada encamped in the United States and crossed the Niagara River in a ship named *Caroline* to join the revolutionaries in Canada. The British sent troops into the United States to break up the guerrilla camp and send the *Caroline* over the Niagara Falls. The same principle was applied in the *Alabama* controversy, when the host state knew about the illegal activities going on within its territory but negligently failed to stop them. In the 1949 *Corfu Channel* case, the International Court of Justice tactfully concluded that while it was not convinced that Albania had laid the mines that damaged several British warships, Albania must have known that mines had been laid in the Corfu Channel, and was therefore liable in damages to Great Britain for having failed to warn of the danger and clear the mines.⁹

The evidence of state practice on this aspect of the problem is overwhelming. The customary international law is epitomized by the universal conviction in 1914 that the government of Serbia was responsible for the incident at Sarajevo, not because it was substantially involved in the terrorist act but because it had failed to repress nation-alist groups conspiring in the cafes of its capital.[10]

Perhaps the most fundamental error in the court's *Nicaragua* opinion appears in paragraph 206, which declares that

> before reaching a conclusion on the nature of prohibited interven-tion, the Court must be satisfied that State practice justifies it. There have been in recent years a number of instances of foreign intervention for the benefit of forces opposed to the government of another State. The Court is not here concerned with the process of decolonization; this question is not in issue in the present case. It has to consider whether there might be indications of a practice illustrative of belief in a kind of general right to intervene, directly or indirectly, with or without armed force, in support of an inter-nal opposition in another state whose cause appeared particularly worthy by reason of the political and moral values with which it was identified. For such a general right to come into existence would involve a fundamental modification of the customary law principle of non-intervention.

Orthodox and reassuring as the main thrust of the paragraph is in its rejection of the Brezhnev Doctrine and other attempts to condone religious, moral, or ideological crusades against states, the implications of the dictum about "decolonization"—that such struggles are excluded from the general rejection of foreign intervention—are far-reaching and disturbing. The International Court itself rejected the argument implied by this dictum in its advisory opinion in the *Namibia* case,[11] where it said that while South Africa had in effect given up the right to keep German South West Africa as a mandate, no one was authorized by the Charter to use force to eject it. And the Security Council has rejected this implied principle repeatedly in a long series of resolutions calling on or ordering the Arab states to make peace with Israel.[12]

THE CRISIS IN THE FORMER YUGOSLAVIA

The slow and tortured emergence of a NATO policy to deal with the crisis that has ravaged the land and the peoples of the former Repub-lic of Yugoslavia since 1991 recalls a comment attributed to Winston

Churchill. During the Second World War, the story goes, a senior British general complained bitterly to Churchill about General Eisenhower. "He can't make up his mind," the British general fumed. "He delays and postpones decisions and actions. It is frustrating beyond endurance." Churchill cut off the general's complaint. "You must understand," he said mildly, "that is how Americans behave. They do the right thing in the end, but not until they have proved that all the alternatives are much worse."

President Clinton's decision in November 1995 to send American ground troops to Bosnia as part of a NATO expeditionary force was a commitment to an action that NATO should have taken in the former Yugoslavia at least three years earlier. If the Western allies had offered the combatants a fair diplomatic solution then, and backed up the offer with visible, ready, and overwhelming NATO forces, including ground troops, the fighting would have stopped; tens of thousands of lives would have been saved, and many more thousands spared the horror of becoming refugees. But it was not to be. When the issue first arose, President Bush said that the conflict did not concern the national interests of the United States. In a sequence that recalls the diplomatic follies of the thirties, the British, French, and Germans followed suit. Americans also said that the dispute, tragic as it was, primarily concerned Europe and that the Europeans should deal with it. In any event, the conflict was a civil war, and not a matter of international concern.

It soon became clear that none of the reasons advanced to justify the decision was tenable. The war was not a civil war, because the world recognized the secession of Croatia, Slovenia, and Bosnia-Herzegovina and admitted them to the United Nations. Serbia and Montenegro formed a single state and claimed the name "Yugoslavia." Although that action has not been formally recognized, Serbia-Montenegro is treated *de facto* as a state and has participated as a leading belligerent in the war. The efforts of the Security Council and of an Ad Hoc Diplomatic Contact Group appointed by the European Community to find a peaceful solution to the conflict have proved unavailing. Toward the end of 1995, the leading powers began to realize that they had been indulging in illusion. This brutal and costly war was proving to be a seriously destabilizing breach of the general peace in and near Europe.

Article 2(7) of the United Nations Charter states, "Nothing contained in the present Charter shall authorize the United Nations to intervene in matters which are essentially within the domestic jurisdiction of any state or shall require the Members to submit such matters to settlement under the present Charter; but this principle shall not prejudice the application of enforcement measures under Chapter 7 [the chapter entitled "Action With Respect to Threats to the Peace, Breaches of the Peace, and Acts of Aggression"]." More and more experts began to recall that this provision of the charter does not deny the Security Council jurisdiction over all events occurring within a state that would normally be within the domestic jurisdiction of that state.

The law cannot be otherwise. The Charter was ratified in 1945, just as the world was beginning to learn about the Holocaust and the Gulag Archipelago, and the world piously said, "Never again." Of course the atrocities of the war in ex-Yugoslavia are a matter of international concern, and of themselves fully justify international intervention. International law has always acknowledged a right of humanitarian intervention under such circumstances. And Article 2 (7) of the U.N. Charter by referring to Chapter 7 specifically contemplates that the Security Council may find such events a breach of international peace. The Charter ratified under these circumstances can hardly be interpreted to deny the United Nations the authority to intervene against a new Hitler or a new Stalin.

One by one, the arguments put forward to justify the failure of the Western allies to preserve the peace in the Balkans were revealed as empty, or worse. The Balkan War is not a civil war but an international war, started by Serbian (and Croatian) aggression against independent states. The national interests of the United States and all the other members of NATO were therefore engaged from the start. As President Bush said at the time of the Persian Gulf War, with regard to Iraq's aggression against Kuwait, "We have all learned in this terrible century that aggression cannot be allowed to stand." This proposition constitutes the first element in any realistic definition of the national interest of the United States and all other nations. In the case of the Persian Gulf, the proposition was upheld not only by Congress and the President but also by overwhelming popular majorities revealed in public opinion polls.

NATO vs. the Security Council

The conflict in Bosnia has another dimension relevant to the issues we are considering. From the point of view of international law, and of the just war tradition more generally, which authority is competent to authorize the NATO intervention in Bosnia announced by President Clinton in November 1995: the North Atlantic Council, which is the governing body of NATO, or the United Nations Security Council? The Russian government took the position that it would cooperate with the NATO forces only if their intervention was specifically approved, and presumably then monitored and supervised, by the U.N. Security Council. A Security Council blessing was obtained for the Allied forces that fought the war in the Persian Gulf in 1990 and 1991. The same procedure was used in initiating the Korean War in 1950. The idea has considerable support in the U.S. Congress and elsewhere as legally unnecessary but politically comforting, and strategically harmless.

It is important to reject this popular argument root and branch, and to make it clear that Security Council resolutions are not necessary to authorize states to exercise their right of self-defense. To accept the practice as obligatory would gravely threaten the security of every nation. In effect, such a practice would annul what may be the last surviving remnant of state sovereignty—the inherent right of states to defend themselves and to have friendly states cooperate with them in the process of self-defense, guaranteed by Article 51 of the U.N. Charter. To require Security Council approval of actions like the NATO intervention in Bosnia would give the permanent members of the Security Council a veto power over any other country's exercise of its right of self-defense.

This is not what the Charter intended, nor does it correspond to the uniform practice of states and of the Security Council since 1945 in situations involving states' exercise of their right of self-defense. The language of the Charter is clear, and the practice of states is equally clear. What the Charter posits and must be interpreted to provide is that its norms against breaches of the peace can be enforced by either of two equally legal and equally legitimate procedures: (1) direct enforcement by the Security Council itself under Article 43 of the Charter, through the armed forces of member states assigned to the Security Council for the purpose, or (2) exercise by an aggrieved state or states of what Article 51 calls the "inherent right of individual or collective self-defense."

The procedure of Article 43 is the chief change the U.N. Charter made in the Covenant of the League of Nations. The article obliges U.N. members to "undertake to make available to the Security Council . . . armed forces, assistance, and facilities, including rights of passage, for the purpose of maintaining international peace and security." It was designed to remedy what was perceived to be the major weakness of the League Covenant, and to make it possible for the U.N. to develop effective multilateral methods for enforcing peace. Yet the draftsmen of the U.N. Charter never lost sight of the failure of the League, and they realized that the procedure they so bravely proposed might fail as well. They therefore decided to retain the full right of self-defense under customary international law as reinsurance against the possibility that for one reason or another the procedure of Article 43 would not work. It was generally expected in 1945, however, that the Article 43 procedure would be the normal method used by the Security Council whenever the peace was seriously threatened. That expectation turned out to be unrealistic. In fact, the procedure of Article 43 has never been used at all.

The International Court of Justice has ruled that the Charter plan for direct enforcement of the Charter by earmarked national military forces is not the only way the Security Council can act to keep the peace.[13] The Council's primary tools for carrying out that responsibility are persuasion, adjudication, mediation, and conciliation. However, the Charter gives the Council the authority to go beyond diplomacy across the full spectrum of military and economic coercion when it deems such action necessary to the goal of peace. Its peacekeeping authority is comprehensive and expansive.

In Article 53, the Charter notes that the Security Council may call on the regional "arrangements or agencies" provided for in Article 52 to cooperate with it in peace-enforcement actions but that such agencies may not undertake enforcement actions without Security Council approval. The United States has always taken the view that NATO is not a regional organization—such as the Organization of American States—as identified in Chapter 8 (i.e., "Regional Arrangements," Articles 52-54) of the Charter. NATO is primarily a military alliance, a combination formed to provide collective self-defense for its members.

Initially, its reach was limited to the territories of its members plus parts of the adjoining seas—what was called the treaty area. The Allies recognized in the Harmel Report of 1967 that their security could be threatened by events occurring outside the treaty area. Two subsequent sessions of NATO's Council, one in Oslo and the other at Gleneagles in Scotland, declared that the function of the Alliance was to protect security and peace in the entire Euro-Atlantic region.

As has already been noted, the Security Council has never attempted to act under Articles 42 (enabling the Council to use "air, sea, or land forces . . . to maintain or restore international peace") and 43. For years it was assumed that the pressures and tensions of the Cold War alone had paralyzed the Security Council as a peace-enforcement agency. Since the dissolution of the Soviet Union, however, it has become clear that the causes of the Security Council's paralysis lie much deeper. The requirement of great-power unanimity among the permanent members presents an obstacle for which there is no obvious remedy. As an astute student of the subject once commented, the Security Council now offers the world a grim choice between "true community of power"—i.e., great-power unanimity—"and anarchy."[14] The U.N. could not exist without the great-power veto. But it cannot become an effective instrument for enforcing peace so long as the veto exists. Great-power unanimity can never be taken for granted, and no state can prudently base its security policy on the expectation that this unanimity will materialize in a crisis that affects it directly.

The machinery for direct peace-enforcement action by the Security Council has never been established. There are no special agreements between the Council and member states about the formation of forces. On the contrary, in its two attempts at peacekeeping that most closely resemble the peace-enforcement model of Article 43— the Korean War, which began in 1950, and the Persian Gulf War of 1990-91—the Security Council carefully avoided mandatory language that might have sought to transform its resolutions from precatory "recommendations" into legally binding "decisions," and it made no attempt to establish genuinely collective control over the military operations carried on in its name. The campaigns in Korea and the Persian Gulf must therefore be classified as actions of collective self-defense, not United Nations "enforcement measures."[15]

The "Peacekeeping" Model

The wide discretion of the Security Council in seeking to establish or restore peace has led during the last forty years to the development of what are often called "traditional U.N. peacekeeping actions," as distinguished from U.N. "peace enforcement" measures like those authorized by Articles 42 and 43 of the Charter. These "peacekeeping" forces of the U.N. are lightly armed, and are deployed in areas of combat only with the consent of the host country. It was hoped that the presence of such neutral forces interposed between combatants would help to maintain a ceasefire or an armistice agreement after it had been made, and thus establish an atmosphere favorable to negotiations for peace.

Dag Hammarskjöld, the brilliant and rather mystical second secretary general of the U.N., and Lester Pearson, an outstanding Canadian foreign minister, were the major architects of the "peacekeeping" plan. During the Suez crisis of 1956-57, Hammarskjöld was absorbed with preventing the entire U.N. agenda from being swept away in the Cold War. The first peacekeeping force was the 1957 United Nations Emergency Force (UNEF), whose mission was to stand between Israeli and Arab forces after a ceasefire had been achieved in the Suez War of 1956-57.

From the beginning the UNEF peacekeeping model has resulted in friction, and sometimes in combat, when one of the hostile parties resists the policing activities of the peacekeepers. The peacekeepers are instructed to confine their mission to peaceful and neutral functions, principally observation and policing, and to fire only to protect themselves or their mission. However, the natural reaction of soldiers under fire is to strike back. Thus in the U.N. Congo expedition of 1960-64, which the International Court of Justice said was not a "peace enforcement measure,"[16] U.N. peacekeepers were actively resisted by the forces of the Congolese province of Katanga, which had declared its independence. The U.N. peacekeepers, hard pressed, finally took matters into their own hands (probably in violation of their orders), defeated the forces opposing them, and restored the government of Congo to power.[17]

Under Article 51 of the U.N. Charter, victims can exercise their "inherent" right of self-defense "until the Security Council has taken the measures necessary to maintain international peace and security."

Clearly, the right of self-defense is not suspended when the Security Council takes note of a conflict simply by putting it on the Council's docket. Nor can it be said that the Security Council has earned exclusive jurisdiction over the Balkan tragedy by its nearly four years of futile, inadequate, and wrong-headed effort to resolve that conflict.

The Council can supersede an effort of collective self-defense only by taking adequate and effective action to enforce the peace, and by "deciding" that the campaign of self-defense has become a breach of the peace. Such a vote could, of course, be adopted by the Security Council only with the concurrence of all its permanent members; that is, the "great power veto" would be applicable. The Security Council can assert its primacy as the peace-enforcing authority under the Charter only by taking action of this kind, which it tried to do in 1956 during the Suez crisis, only to be defeated by British and French vetos.

Recognizing the central role of self-defense in the quest for peace will become more urgent by the day, as the world comes to realize that Article 43 of the Charter is a dead letter that cannot and should not be revived. The assumption on which Article 43 rests is untenable for the reason given by Kant in his essay on "Perpetual Peace." Supranational sovereignty is not in keeping with the peoples' idea "of the law of nations,"[18] Kant wrote—that is, not in keeping with their commitment to the principle of national sovereignty protected by law. It does not follow, however, that the Wilsonian quest for peace is futile. The quest for peace must continue, but on a more realistic legal footing, one compatible with the nature of the state system as it has evolved historically.

The diplomatic experience of the Concert of Europe during the nineteenth century, as well as the success of the Western Allies' policy of containing the expansion of the Soviet Union between 1947 and 1989, should persuade timid statesmen that the task, formidable as it is, is not impossible. These precedents, supplemented by the example of what has been done by way of collective self-defense in the wars in Korea and the Persian Gulf, should be enough to animate a program for enforcing the U.N. Charter that is capable of succeeding where the League of Nations and the U.N. Security Council have so abjectly failed.

Some are attached to the idea of requiring Security Council approval of campaigns of self-defense as a compromise between the strict Charter peace-enforcement method of Article 43 and the customary law of collective self-defense. In effect, they would extend Article 53, precluding regional organizations from taking peace-enforcement measures without Security Council approval, to Article 51, upholding exercise of the right of self-defense without Security Council action: they would expressly require Security Council approval before campaigns of individual or collective self-defense could be begun. But the price of such a compromise is too high for it to be seriously considered. The right of self-defense is too deeply imbedded in the modern mind to be abandoned or qualified.

Hopes for the Rule of Law

In his book *Visions of World Order* (1986), Professor Julius Stone of the University of New South Wales reached similar conclusions about the capacity of the Security Council to fulfill its role as an effective enforcer of the peace. I shall quote at some length from this final, reflective book of a long and distinguished scholarly career. By 1962 (the year of the Cuban Missile Crisis), Stone wrote,

> it was . . . already clear that any early hope of replacing the international balance of nuclear terror by "the rule of law," on the model of successful national societies, was vain. One reason was that states and especially great powers could not find judges in whom they could all trust sufficiently to agree in advance to accept their compulsory jurisdiction in all future disputes. They have also been unable to find such trustworthy executive authorities with effective means of enforcing international law and judicial decisions under it. Behind this lack of trust is the flat refusal of most states, great and small alike, most of the time, to have enforced against them anyone's version of international law except their own. This refusal rests, over and beyond the arrogance of sovereignty, on the inadequacy of the settled content of international law, on the absence of an efficient legislature to make it more adequate, and on the dearth of human leadership at a level of integrity to which Moscow and Washington, not to speak of Peking, Paris, London, Bonn, and the rest, would be willing to entrust their destiny and even survival.
>
> A second reason was that this reality of every state's traditional claim to be the sole judge in its own cause could not be banished even by the awesome realities of threatened nuclear destruction.

Even if the stockpiles of nuclear weapons were not of their present "overkill" dimensions on both sides, the risk of such destruction could not be removed except by stripping both sides of these weapons, and keeping them stripped. And this latter would imply stripping them also of all other weapons of major violence. The alternative of endowing some Olympian "international" violence authority with stockpiles of such weapons, clearly superior to either Moscow's and Washington's (and any combination of them), must obviously be ruled out. First, an authority that states would trust to this extent is not to be found; second, it would be impossible ever to be sure that the "international" nuclear endowment was superior enough to prevail without the threat to use it. But that very threat would return us to the risk of nuclear destruction which we are seeking to escape.

Pejoration or name-calling by one side against the other cannot help this situation. Nor is it changed by those who prematurely conjure the risk of destruction into certainty, conclude that any alternative is preferable to this, and forthwith call upon their own state unilaterally to abandon its weapons. Better red than dead! Yet, even if we assumed that such unilateral submission was necessary for survival, we could not be sure that it would   be   effective for that purpose! The assumption of survival ignores the new and increased dangers in which unilateral nuclear disarmament would itself involve the state concerned. And, for example, in the United Kingdom, it would ignore the fact that unilateral disarmament by one state would not end the nuclear confrontation in which each aligned state—whatever its own armaments—may become embroiled.

Third, the hope fostered by the Nuremberg trials that individuals, at any rate, can be made amenable to the rule of law and thus deterred from "aggressive warmaking" also proved oversanguine. This is not only because of the difficulties of defining and identifying aggression between states, except in the rare case where a paranoid leader like Hitler lays out in advance the objects of his military adventure. I have shown in my *Conflict Through Consensus: United Nations Approaches to Aggression* (Baltimore, 1977) the persistence of these difficulties even after the U.N. General Assembly promulgated its supposed definition in 1974. And events since, such as the hostilities in the Persian Gulf, Afghanistan, Lebanon, and Grenada, confirmed this persistence. But even had these difficulties been overcome, the hope of preventing war by deterring national leaders from "aggression" was . . . dim if not desperate. For insofar as we can scarcely expect to try such leaders until after the end of the war, or expect victorious states to allow their own leaders to be tried, only leaders of defeated states would be under deterrent threat. What future national leaders would be deterred from, therefore, was not so much waging a war as losing one. The effect, then, is that once tension in the relations of states moves beyond a certain point, the threat of criminal punishment may actually accelerate resort to war. For leaders of both sides may conclude that they had better act to ensure their side's victory. It sadly accords with this that the number of wars of substantial scale between 1945 and 1980 already exceeded one hundred and thirty, and with a duration (end to end, as it were) of two hundred fifty years during an actual historical span of only thirty-five years.

Fourth, as I also observed in *Quest for Survival*, not only was the use of criminal penalties to deter individuals from initiating wars of aggression thus problematical. It was often almost as difficult for international law to prevent an aggressor state from acquiring legal rights by virtue of its wrongdoing. Thus if, as some advocated, that law were to attempt to deprive an aggressor state that had occupied its victim's territory of the legal rights of a belligerent, the aggressor almost certainly would respond by denying the complementary rights of the inhabitants against himself. The penalty would then fall mainly on the local inhabitants, or other innocent third parties. And so, too, with breaches of war law. These do not, as has sometimes been proposed, result in the suspension of all benefits of the wrongdoing state under war law. For there again the wrongdoing state's response would usually be to spread wider the range of innocent persons injured by violations. The sanctions that international law attempts to use are more limited. As to individual wrongdoing soldiers, their fate on capture is in theory "at the discretion" of the aggrieved belligerent, though in modern practice he may try them for breaches of war law. As against a culprit state, the law accords rights of retaliation and (in due course) of compensation to the victim state. Of course, claims for compensation, like similarly instinctive demands for victorious aggressor states to be stripped of the fruits of victory, presuppose that international law can find some way of defeating every aggressor-victor at the moment of his victory. It remains a tragic truth that international law does not have such power nor the means of acquiring it. If we forced it into such a quixotic design against victorious states, we would doom this law to a mothlike existence, fluttering ever helplessly into the destructive flame of state power.[19]

Some advance another reason for requiring a Security Council vote to approve NATO's Bosnian expedition, whether it can be considered legally necessary or not. They feel uneasy about the basic idea of Article 51: that, in the end, states have an inherent right—a right of sovereignty—to decide for themselves when and how to fight for their security. Those who take this view point out that no one should be a judge in his own case, and find it morally preferable to have a third-party judgment to give a kind of legitimacy to the enterprise. They recognize that under the Charter, the Security Council would still have the last word in the argument, because it has the theoretical power to find that the campaign of self-defense has gone too far and has become in itself a breach of the peace. The point is meaningless, they say, because where permanent members of the Security Council are involved, as they are in Bosnia, the Security Council cannot adopt any such practice because of the great-power veto and what it represents.

There are two fatal objections to this line of reasoning. First, it is plausible to claim that the Security Council of the United Nations should be treated as the ultimate guardian of the soul of the state system, the only body that could possibly give an authoritative verdict on the morality of using force. But seventy years of experience with the Council of the League of Nations and its successor, the United Nations Security Council, offers no ground for optimism or even hope about the capacity of the Security Council to make such decisions consistently and rationally.

The objection to accepting the practice of requiring Security Council approval of any exercise of the right of self-defense is, however, much more fundamental than this. National feeling is still much too strong to make such a policy acceptable to the states or the peoples of the world. While the idea of the United Nations is very powerful everywhere, that sentiment is not strong enough to lead states to abandon their right of self-defense, which philosophers and theologians of all religious traditions have found to be morally impregnable as part of the law of nature.

3

Just War in a New Era of Military Affairs

A. J. Bacevich

Ours is an age in which any untoward development becomes a crisis, the slightest departure from the ordinary is tagged historic, and the mere glimmer of novelty is heralded as revolutionary. Such semantic extravagance is not especially conducive to clear thinking about the real moral and ethical issues posed by change.

The rapid and momentous change in military affairs now under way fairly burst upon the public consciousness at the time of the Persian Gulf War. It manifested itself above all in the dazzling "systems" that figured prominently—or at least appeared to figure prominently—in the victory over Iraq: stealth aircraft, anti-ballistic missiles, an array of "smart" munitions, and above all an integrated architecture of command and control. Embodied in hardware such as surveillance satellites, the Global Positioning System, JSTARS and AWACS aircraft, and Aegis warships, American superiority in Command, Control,

---

A. J. Bacevich is executive director of the Foreign Policy Institute at the Paul H. Nitze School of Advanced International Studies, Johns Hopkins University, in Washington, D.C. He is the author of *Diplomat in Khaki: Major General Frank Ross McCoy and American Foreign Policy, 1898-1949* (1989).

Communications, and Intelligence (C3I)—the product of a concerted effort to tap the military potential of microelectronics—not only exposed the vulnerabilities of Saddam Hussein's old-style arsenal but rendered it all but irrelevant.

To many observers, these technologies suggested that the United States had achieved a level of military superiority without precedent in modern history. To others, Desert Storm was less a demonstration of capabilities fully developed than a tantalizing hint of what was yet to come. Extrapolating from the experience of the Persian Gulf, analysts identified four major capabilities that make up this remarkable advance in military prowess, none of them altogether in hand, but each within reach for a wealthy and technologically advanced nation. Those capabilities are:

- near perfect real-time intelligence available to commanders at all levels ("a transparent battlefield");
- extremely accurate means of target acquisition, independent of range and immune to countermeasures;
- technologically enhanced methods of command enabling forces to operate "inside the decision cycle" of their opponent, reacting more quickly than he and rendering his actions meaningless ("information dominance");
- highly lethal munitions capable of hitting targets over extended distances in any conditions while producing minimal collateral damage ("long-range precision strike").

Welcoming the Revolution

As interpreted by a cadre of imaginative defense experts in the United States and elsewhere, these capabilities suggest the dawn of a radically different era in military history. Hardly had the Gulf War ended when these experts began competing vigorously to identify that conflict's salient "lessons." Even more vigorously, they have labored to fit those lessons into a larger theoretical framework. So far there is no consensus even on what to call the phenomenon; among the names in use are Military Technical Revolution, Revolution in Military Affairs, and Revolution in Security Affairs.

Whatever the label, non-expert opinion in the United States has been virtually unanimous in welcoming this "revolution." Whether viewed as a rightful dividend for the national treasure invested throughout the Cold War, attributed to American ingenuity, or interpreted as one more affirmation of divine favor, the spectacular new military dominance enjoyed by the United States has been applauded across the domestic political spectrum, by doves no less than by hawks.

Why the universally positive response? There are at least three related reasons.

First, with the Soviet Union now reduced to a bad memory, the United States has no rivals capable in the near term of challenging its monopoly in this new way of war. And, seldom doubting our own benevolence, we find it easy to assume that American possession of that monopoly serves the interests of the world at large.

Second, we have persuaded ourselves that the high-tech combat displayed in the Persian Gulf has restored to the concept of force the political utility it lost after Hiroshima. When it comes to policing the world—restoring order, stemming catastrophe, disciplining evildoers, rescuing victims of oppression—the Left no less than the Right now considers military superiority an eminently useful possession.

Third, least noted but arguably the most significant, we see in the military revolution heralded by Desert Storm a means to escape from a moral quandary that has dogged us since the onset of the Cold War. Aspiring to be both global hegemon and righteous democracy, the United States has struggled with the dilemma of using the vast power at its disposal while still satisfying self-imposed requirements that it act in a morally defensible manner. In the Persian Gulf we seemed to glimpse a solution to this dilemma. In other words, underlying America's delight with the outcome of the Gulf War and punctuating the widespread certainty that the war marked a turning point in history was a moral subtext. Desert Storm was satisfying not only because it was a decisive victory won at surprisingly low cost, but also because the enterprise was unbesmirched by ethical ambiguity. "We went halfway around the world," President George Bush told a joint session of Congress on March 6, 1991, "to do what is moral, just, and right."[1] That assurance was precisely what Americans longed to hear.

Just War and the Gulf War

The just war tradition enjoyed a revival in the debates preceding the actual liberation of Kuwait, and despite the contrary predictions of various ethicists and moral theologians, Desert Storm neatly met the criteria both for *ius ad bellum* and for *ius in bello.* That is, according to the common-sense judgment of most Americans, the *decision* to use force against Iraq was morally justified and the *manner* in which American forces fought was morally appropriate.

This latter point is especially important. With military briefers and television analysts celebrating the surgical accuracy and carefully calibrated effects of American weapons, U.S. operations in the Persian Gulf seemed to exceed all previous standards in adhering to the requirements of proportionality and discrimination, the classic *ius in bello* criteria. As a result, Desert Storm proceeded to its happy conclusion with few of the moral controversies that had marred virtually every other large-scale use of American force since 1945: collateral damage was kept to a minimum, civilian casualties were few, and operations were promptly terminated as soon as military objectives appeared to be within reach.

Thus, besides demonstrating a stunning capacity to project power, the revolutionary new style of warfare heralded by Desert Storm also suggested that the United States had discovered a military-technical solution to the dichotomy implicit in its identity as democratic superpower. This military revolution would enable Americans to satisfy their yearning to believe themselves virtuous even as they exercised commanding influence across the globe.

Yet this is a dual illusion. On the military side, events since Desert Storm have already outlined the limits of U.S. military superiority as an instrument of policy. The promised new world order will come only at enormous cost, if at all. At the moment, the American people show little sustained willingness to pay that cost.

In the moral realm, too, the military revolution is likely to be problematic. Even a high-tech military offers no easy escape from the moral ambiguities that remain the lot of an imperial democracy. The expectation that Desert Storm has endowed the United States with the capacity to dominate world events without soiling itself in the process only sets Americans up for painful disappointments. Given the extent to which policy in the post–Cold War world is beholden to public opinion, those disappointments will have important political ramifications.

TWENTIETH-CENTURY MILITARY REVOLUTIONS

How revolutionary is the current revolution? Despite all the expert commentary, it remains ill defined. How deep and how far does change reach? Has Desert Storm established the paradigm to which warfare in the twenty-first century will adhere? Or was that brief, showy conflict simply the final triumphant turn of a superannuated mode of warfare that is giving way to something radically different? Do the wondrous technologies displayed in the Gulf signify simply a change in the tools of war, or, as some contend, are they transforming the very nature of human conflict? Or, a third alternative, is change in the realm of military affairs proceeding as a subset of broader and ultimately more decisive social, political, and scientific developments?

These are the preliminary questions that must be considered before we draw any conclusions about the moral implications of modern military technologies. A brief look at sea power in the twentieth century—a story of multiple, interrelated revolutions—may help to illustrate the point.

The Emergence of Dreadnoughts

The first of this century's upheavals in naval affairs occurred in 1906, when Great Britain launched the first in a new class of very fast, heavily armored, all-big-gun battleships. In the eyes of naval experts then and since, *Dreadnought* transformed naval warfare. In a single stroke, every other capital ship afloat—and that included every other battleship in the Royal Navy—was rendered obsolete.

Historians cite *Dreadnought* as a prime example of military revolution. But what did this revolution accomplish? Britain's technological innovation added fuel to an existing arms race, as each of the industrialized powers—not least the United States—hurried to acquire *Dreadnought*-type warships for its own navy. Yet the new ship's impact on reigning concepts of sea power was negligible. If anything, the powerful new class of warship reinforced the naval orthodoxy of the day: *Dreadnought* seemed the ideal instrument for applying the precepts of sea power developed by the influential American naval officer and publicist Alfred Thayer Mahan—yet these precepts derived from Mahan's study of naval history *in the days of sail*. In that sense, though marking an impressive advance in naval technology, *Dreadnought* served primarily to affirm rather than to subvert the accepted rules of the game. Posing no threat to the recognized conventions of naval warfare, the revolution inspired by *Dreadnought* in 1906 had little impact on the definition of what constituted moral or immoral conduct when fighting at sea. From a moral perspective, it was immaterial.

In fact, however, certain of the assumptions underlying those conventions—specifically the Mahanian notion that a dominant battle line of heavily armed surface ships offered the key to both command of the sea and world power—were shaky at best. Within a decade this became apparent as war of epic proportions engulfed Europe.

In determining that war's outcome, the squadrons of massive dreadnoughts, built at such enormous expense, figured only marginally. In a brutal conflict that lasted over four years, the main British and German fleets met only once in battle, in an inconclusive action off Jutland in 1916. For the most part they sat out the war, warily eyeing each other from anchorages on opposite sides of the North Sea. According to Winston Churchill, the admiral commanding Britain's Grand Fleet at Scapa Flow "was the only man on either side who could lose the war in an afternoon."[2] Yet such a back-handed testimonial amounted to acknowledgment of an embarrassing fact that Churchill was loath to admit outright: in the vast and desperate struggle of World War I, the military instrument that epitomized the power of the Empire, and into which Britain had poured such treasure, remained essentially on the sidelines. Perhaps through recklessness or miscalculation the commander of the Grand Fleet could lose the war, but all his mighty dreadnoughts made precious little contribution to winning it.

The Undersea Revolution

But to conclude from the relative inactivity of the main British and German battle fleets that maritime matters were unimportant to the conduct of the war would be a great error. On the contrary, both sides understood that the ability of the Allies to sustain their armies in France hinged on the Royal Navy's control of the world's sea lanes. As has so often happened in warfare, comparative disadvantage served as spur to innovation. Overmatched in the race to build battleships, Germany was compelled to explore unorthodox ways of turning the Allies' maritime flank.

This imperative gave birth to a second revolution in naval affairs: undersea warfare. With the aim of severing the enemy's strategic lines of communications—especially Allied trade with the Americas—Germany revived and radically transformed the tradition of commerce raiding. Both Allies and neutrals such as the United States denounced the U-boat campaign as barbaric. Certainly, in its "unrestricted" form, it was ruthless. It was also highly effective—until the Royal Navy (supported from early 1917 on by the Americans) suspended the further construction of battlewagons and poured resources into the fledgling science of anti-submarine warfare.

Although undertaken reluctantly by the naval establishments, this shift signified a transformation of naval warfare that cut far deeper than the revolution wrought by *Dreadnought*. Operationally, the U-boat redefined the concept of "battle" at sea. Strategically, it suggested ways of bringing sea power to bear more decisively than through the classic fleet actions envisioned by the disciples of Mahan. Both of these developments had profound moral implications. In the context of the just war tradition, submarine warfare posed a particular challenge to the principle of discrimination, both in the narrow sense of declaring merchant ships (often carrying noncombatants) to be fair game for attack without warning and in the broader sense of enticing military planners to consider campaigns designed to bring the enemy civilian populace slowly "to its knees."

The Naval Air Revolution

Yet even if further reaching than *Dreadnought*, the U-boat revolution was itself transitional, superseded in short order by a third even more fundamental transformation in naval affairs. This was the revolution in naval air.

No sooner had World War I ended than the Mahanians attempted to put the undersea genie back in the bottle. The Allies stripped the

German navy of its U-boats and by treaty prohibited Germany from acquiring new ones. Old-line officers in the victorious navies scrapped their anti-submarine fleets and directed their energies once again to perfecting the dreadnought, designing a new generation with even larger caliber guns and heavier armor. But most of this was retrograde nonsense, naval nostalgia swathed in armor plate, teak, and gunpowder.

Within the navies of the advanced nations—but especially those of the United States and Imperial Japan—reform-minded officers pursued a new vision that would shatter that nostalgia, ending once and for all the battleship's reign as the standard for measuring maritime power. Their goal was as bold as it was straightforward: to harness air power to naval power in ways that would create a sea-based weapon of unprecedented flexibility and effectiveness.

The immediate product of this vision was the aircraft carrier, wielded with spectacular success by the United States Navy in the next great world war. Yet to conceive of this revolution as simply one of developing the techniques of carrier aviation is to understate its true significance. Not content with the Mahanian goal of securing "command of the sea," the architects of this revolution sought to project naval power well beyond the sea. The naval air pioneers aimed to eradicate the boundary between war on land and war at sea, between the traditional role of armies and that of navies. Thus, for example, having broken the back of the Imperial Navy, American naval officers at the end of World War II were quick to claim a share in the climactic air campaigns that pummeled the Japanese home islands and the Japanese government into submission—the kind of mission to which U.S. Navy carrier task forces would return in subsequent conflicts such as Korea and Vietnam.

Yet technological opportunity alone does not suffice to explain the resourcefulness that the United States showed in seizing upon the potential of naval air power. This was a military revolution that had economic, cultural, intellectual, and even psychological roots. In the decades leading up to World War II, American society had developed an ardent disposition toward air power.[3] Moreover, the remarkable American capacity for large-scale research and production, for the diffusion of technology on a grand scale, and for what would later be called systems integration all made the United States ideally suited to transform the airplane from a newfangled contraption to the preeminent instrument for waging total war.

The moral implications of this expanded application of naval power were large. Even if not explicitly intended to terrorize civilians, carrier-based attacks against the enemy's "vital centers" inflicted some—at times extensive—injury to civilians and damage to non-military facilities. Whatever the intentions of planners or air crews, such collateral damage was an all but inevitable by-product of the large-scale use of air power from the 1940s through the 1960s. Perhaps the efforts to exploit the potential of carrier aviation to the fullest did not foster a deliberate disregard for the claims of *ius in bello*. At a minimum, however, they encouraged an indifference or insensitivity to the moral issues implicit in the free-wheeling use of the air weapon. One result of this process was to mutilate the principle of noncombatant immunity to the point that it became nearly unrecognizable.

Yet for all the glamour of carrier operations, the ultimate expression of the naval air revolution—and the initiative posing the largest challenge to the just war tradition—lay not in manned aircraft but in nuclear-tipped guided missiles. By the late 1950s, U.S. development of the submarine-launched ballistic missile (SLBM) carried the revolution in naval air to its Cold War–driven conclusion: holding Russian cities hostage to guarantee retention by the United States of a retaliatory capability that the Soviet Union was powerless to disarm. Beginning with Polaris—to be followed later by Poseidon and Trident—the SLBM transformed the meaning of capital ship. The Polaris submarine was the first major naval combatant whose weapons were designed exclusively to attack land targets rather than ships.[4] More importantly, it was an instrument of war explicitly intended to obliterate noncombatants on a massive scale—to go the U-boat one better and bring a nation to its knees virtually in an instant. In the logic of deterrence, the SLBM's indiscriminate destructive power was its primary military virtue. In the context of the just war tradition, that military virtue was a moral nightmare.

MORAL PROSPECTS FOR THE COMING CENTURY

What do these three interlocking naval revolutions suggest to us about the ethical implications of today's ongoing transformation in military affairs? Above all, the naval experience of the century now drawing to a close alerts us to the prospect that the century to come will bring not one military revolution but several. We would therefore be foolish to expect the determination of what is morally permissible in war to occur in relation to a single authoritative standard of military practice. As with naval warfare during the century now coming to a close, the product of multiple revolutions will be not moral clarity, but deepening moral complexity.

Like Great Britain at the end of the nineteenth century, the United States at the end of the twentieth is a dominant world power with an interest above all in perpetuating that dominance. The existing order—the distribution of wealth and influence, the basic rules governing the game of world politics—suits us, and we are committed to its preservation. Like the British a century ago, as an integral part of our strategy to maintain that order, we have invested heavily to create a defense establishment that assures our success in a certain kind of war. Indeed, in our efforts to acquire a decisive military edge, we have spared no expense. Having done so, many Americans—including most serving officers—are loath to entertain any suggestion that the model of warfare forming the conceptual basis of that investment might be of limited utility.

Like Great Britain in 1906, which was eager to define the naval revolution as beginning and ending with *Dreadnought*, the United States today is highly susceptible to self-deception. Americans have a compelling interest in suppressing developments that might undermine the global status quo. We desire to define the military revolution in terms best suited to sustaining the paradigm of warfare with which we are most comfortable and within which the American lead appears to be unassailable. Indeed, as was the case with *Dreadnought*, the very purpose of a **Military Technical Revolution** (one of the terms being given to today's military revolution) is to fend off more radical change likely to subvert the existing order. The Royal Navy conceived of *Dreadnought* with an eye toward insuring that Britain's next naval war would be fought like Trafalgar, and with an identical outcome. Similarly, for many Americans today, the allure of a military revolution is its seeming guarantee that future conflicts will be fought like Desert Storm: brief, decisive, successful, and in terms of American lives lost, relatively cheap.

To be sure, such a narrowly conceived revolution is especially conducive to the application of traditional just war criteria. Indeed, if the transformation presently under way is merely technical—a change in the means of waging war but not in the nature of war—then it may revitalize conventions that have provided the traditional basis for regulating conflict: that wars are properly fought between opposing armies rather than by insurgents, irregulars, or terrorists; that the nation-state retains a monopoly over the means of violence and that the use of force remains illegitimate except when directed by responsible political authority; and that the principle of noncombatant immunity is sacrosanct rather than being waivable at the convenience of belligerents. Surely a defense establishment that has mastered the capabilities to which the American military presently aspires—the ability to "see" everything throughout the battlefield, to target with precision, to strike with unprecedented accuracy, great lethality, and minimal collateral damage—is especially well positioned to adhere to just war principles such as proportionality and discrimination. Thus the style of warfare presaged by Desert Storm holds the promise of enabling the United States both to sustain its status as reigning superpower and to congratulate itself on wielding its power in a way consistent with traditional moral teachings.[5]

Uncooperative Enemies, Unconventional Methods

Yet however much the United States might seek to define the military revolution in terms to suit itself, future adversaries are unlikely to cooperate.[6] Like the German navy of World War I—stymied by British superiority in dreadnoughts—those disadvantaged by the existing rules will devise new rules more amenable to their interests. While Americans dazzle themselves with the latest military application of advanced technologies, America's challengers will seek ways of rendering that technology superfluous. Toward that end, they will have a powerful incentive to undertake a genuine **Revolution in Military Affairs**, recasting the terms of conflict in ways that play to their strengths and exploit our vulnerabilities. Alas, as the Vietnam War above all would suggest, those vulnerabilities are all too apparent.

This prospect of a true Revolution in Military Affairs is not without its moral complications. By jettisoning the established conventions governing armed conflict, such a revolution is likely to move into murky terrain: people's war, subversion, terror, and banditry. The past is rich with examples of the efficacy of such methods. And the brief military history of the post–Cold War era—featuring the likes of General Mohammed Farah Aidid, Sheik Omar Abdel Rahman, the masked *commandantes* of Chiapas, the suicide bombers of Hamas, and the perpetrators of the attack on Khobar Towers—suggests that the relevance of those examples has not been lost on those who reject America's view of how the world should work. Unhampered by the squeamishness or scruples of our own post-Clausewitzian elites, these neo-Clausewitzians are eager to revive old ways of employing force to subvert the status quo, adopting selected new technologies that make it possible for ever smaller groups of perpetrators to inflict ever larger amounts of mayhem. In the future, such unconventional methods could become more effective still if combined with means drawn from the opposite end of the spectrum of warfare: weapons of mass destruction such as portable nuclear devices or highly virulent bacterial agents.

For those who would adhere to the just war tradition, unconventional warfare—and the countermeasures it invites—has always posed enormous difficulties. Inevitably in such conflicts, the distinction between combatants and noncombatants becomes blurred. Force is employed, not to achieve standard military objectives such as the destruction of the enemy's army or the capture of key terrain, but to intimidate political authorities, capture media attention, or foster an environment of insecurity. As a result, considerations such as discrimination and proportionality quickly go by the board. Often, this is the case not only with those who instigate war using unconventional methods but also among the forces that must defend against such methods.[7]

Unfortunately, when Americans employ the language of morality to disparage unconventional war, their critique does not come across as entirely disinterested. It can readily be perceived as self-serving— much as was British criticism of the U-boat campaign while Britain was engaged in a more traditional (and therefore permissible) blockade of German ports. To the world beyond our borders, it may appear that Americans are asserting a double standard, denouncing the bomb placed in a parking garage (to which the United States may be particularly vulnerable) as reprehensible while deeming the disabling of an urban electrical grid by remote missile attack (which the United States is uniquely equipped to launch) altogether acceptable. In an era of great upheaval in military affairs, U.S. efforts to assert such moral distinctions are unlikely to be persuasive. Indeed, nothing is more likely to discredit just war teachings in the eyes of others than the perception that they are being employed not to ameliorate the effects of war itself but as a prop for American hegemony.

A More Fundamental Transformation

Of course, the foregoing analysis presumes that the military revolution can be "captured," that either the United States or some other nation or group of nations can determine its shape or direction. It also implicitly assumes that the overall political and social context in which conflict occurs will remain static.

Such assumptions are likely to be false. To postulate that the military revolution will manifest itself either in terms of the Desert Storm paradigm or as "dirty wars" that arise in reaction to the U.S. superiority in high-tech conventional warfare is to disregard evidence of an even more fundamental transformation afoot—much as the attention claimed first by *Dreadnought* and then by the U-boat impeded recognition of the air revolution that would subsume them both. That more fundamental transformation—an emerging **Revolution in Security Affairs**—could well emerge as a result of developments in several quarters: political, economic, and social. Although not strictly military in origin or content, it would impinge broadly on the conduct of national security affairs.

To hazard a description of this revolution is to engage in speculation. There are no "cases" to use for illustration. Nonetheless, certain political, economic, and social trends already in evidence suggest the basis of a rough outline. For example, *political* developments pointing toward radical change in security affairs include the following:

■ ever-increasing constraints on sovereignty and on the freedom of action enjoyed by the individual nation-state;

■ the eclipse of nationalism (crucial as the basis for rallying popular support for war in modern societies) by ethnic, religious, or regional loyalties; among intellectuals, a growing penchant for national self-flagellation, manifested in American intellectual circles as multiculturalism;

- the shift of the world's geopolitical center of gravity from the North Atlantic region to Asia, combined with the extinguishing of the imperial afterglow that during the post-war era permitted Western countries to exert influence beyond their means.[8]

Economic developments likely to shape an emerging Revolution in Security Affairs include:

- fierce and relentless economic competition combined with accelerating interdependence, rendering national self-sufficiency an impossibility;
- in advanced societies, growing reliance on a hugely expensive and fragile network-based infrastructure;
- increasing resentment throughout the underdeveloped world, generating threats of massive and politically explosive migration should demands for the redress of an unequal and unjust order continue to go ignored.

Finally, *social and cultural* trends likely to influence the Revolution in Security Affairs would include the following:

- media penetration of all aspects of public affairs, discrediting traditional elites as self-serving and corrupt and stimulating the spread of populism;
- growing sensitivity to the so-called global agenda, particularly to the imperative of policies that protect the environment and respond to the demands of women;
- extreme reluctance on the part of low-birthrate nations (notably the United States) to suffer casualties in pursuit of political objectives that seem unrelated to the nation's welfare.

The Prospect of Virtual War

To cite these trends is not to endorse them. To the extent that the foregoing smacks of a prescription for a Global Village directed by debellicized administrators who work for the United Nations or the World Trade Organization, worry excessively about depletion of the ozone layer, and are burdened with guilt over the sins of Western imperialism, it contains elements that many will find objectionable. Nevertheless, some such combination of macro-trends falls well within the realm of plausibility and would have profound implications for the nature and conduct of warfare.

Indeed, such a Revolution in Security Affairs would in all likelihood see the rise of an altogether new form of conflict: "virtual war." Conflicts of this sort would be undeclared, continuous, and conducted not by specially empowered and culturally distinctive "warriors" but by computer-wielding technicians. In virtual war, terms such as "military objectives" or "military targets" would lose much of their meaning. "Battle" as such—the violent collision of opposing military forces—would be seen as counterproductive. Instead, conflict would be all but indistinguishable from economic competition. The aim of parties undertaking virtual war (not necessarily nations but contingent coalitions bound by a momentary convergence of interests rather than by common ideology or values) would be not to achieve decisive victory but to secure marginal advantage at minimal cost and minimal risk to the global structure. Rather than massive physical destruction, the preferred means of achieving the purposes of a "campaign" would be the precise disabling stroke—or the threat of such a stroke—that could disrupt high-value networks critical to the smooth functioning of society.

How would the moral criteria embodied in the just war tradition apply to an era of virtual war? Such conflicts would pose daunting new questions with regard to such concepts as discrimination and proportionality. When conflict no longer pits soldier against soldier, what is the basis for distinguishing between combatants and noncombatants? If force is employed in precisely measured electronic dollops directed, for example, at briefly disrupting an adversary's financial system—incremental pain for incremental gain—how is it possible to assess whether a proposed action satisfies the criterion of proportionality?

I do not mean to suggest by all this that all future wars will be virtual wars. The world will not see outright eradication of the more traditional forms of combat any time soon. Rather, my point is that, as with naval warfare in the first decades of this century, the new millennium is likely to feature not one single military revolution but several, overlapping with, feeding on, and competing against one another. That is the tangled reality that awaits us.

For Americans to imagine that the world's only superpower can dictate the legitimacy of one preferred model of military practice while ruling out others is folly. Such expectations are an invitation to smugness and overconfidence, and as such a recipe for political disaster.

Such hubris also conceals a profoundly dangerous moral snare: the delusion that technique alone has enabled the United States to liberate itself from the tragic and often horrifying legacy of warfare in this century. That delusion gives rise to a second to which Americans are peculiarly susceptible: that they are uniquely endowed with an obligation and authority to impart their designs to the world at large.

Military prowess alone, no matter how prodigious, cannot compensate for the lack of a coherent strategy. For a people who hunger for rectitude even as they aspire—however furtively—to something like global mastery, neither does military prowess offer a short cut to a clear conscience. That fact is one that no revolution, however radical, can alter. Yet it is a fact that Americans today—gripped by their vision of perpetual military supremacy—seem all too inclined to overlook.

PART TWO

When Should We Intervene?

4

NBC-Armed Rogues: Is There a Moral Case for Preemption?

Brad Roberts

In May 1996, Secretary of Defense William J. Perry declared that a new chemical-weapons facility in the desert of Libya "will not be allowed to begin production," implying that the United States would use military force to secure this promise.[1] Would such an action seem right, not only to Americans but to citizens and opinion-makers in other countries? Would it *be* right, which is to say defensible in moral terms?

The long-running debate over what to do about Libya's chemical-weapons program is symptomatic of a larger problem: what to do—if anything—about the emergence of a number of states that flout agreed norms of state behavior, both domestic and international; that use and threaten to use force to coerce those who resist their ambitions; and that seek to acquire arsenals of nuclear, biological, or

Brad Roberts is an analyst at the Institute for Defense Analyses, in Washington, D.C., and an adjunct professor at George Washington University. He previously was the editor of *The Washington Quarterly* at the Center for Strategic and International Studies. He is the author of *Weapons Proliferation and World Order After the Cold War* (Rotterdam: Kluwer, 1996). The views expressed here are his own.

chemical (NBC) weapons to abet these purposes. These are the "rogue" or "backlash" states identified in 1994 by then National Security Advisor Anthony Lake.[2] Perry's statement about Libya reflects the view of many, inside and outside the U.S. government, that preemptive military strikes on the mass-destruction weaponry of such states are essential both for the security of their neighbors and for the interests of the international community.

When policy-makers in Washington and other capitals debate whether or not, or how, to strike preemptively, the choices are highly contentious. Both action and inaction set precedents with long-term consequences. Doing what national-interest calculations call for is not always doing what is right by the hearts and minds of the American people or its friends and allies.

What does moral reflection contribute to the policy debate about preemption? In particular, what does the just war tradition instruct about the value of the different choices?[3] Can there be a moral case— indeed, a moral imperative—for preemption, in addition to a national-interest or legalistic case? In what follows I will offer some speculative answers to these questions. I will begin by reviewing the ethical considerations that typically shape the policy debate about preemption: (1) Is the action undertaken as a last resort? (2) Does it have a reasonable chance of success? (3) Will the action be proportional to the threat being removed? Each will be evaluated in light of the specific attributes of NBC threats. The chapter will go on to explore two further considerations. First, self-defense: When and how can preemption be justified as an essential act of self-protection? And second, competent authority: What political legitimacy is needed to establish the authority to make preemptive strikes?

This review of criteria illuminates the various ways in which the specific NBC dimension of the targeted threat shapes ethical considerations associated with preemption. Two conclusions stand out from this review. One is that in some important places the just war tradition stops a bit short. Thus some further elaboration of the tradition seems warranted on the basis of the new strategic realities created by proliferators armed with weapons of mass destruction. The other conclusion is that tradition imposes some obligations on policy that are not typically appreciated in the policy world. An act of preemption cannot be deemed just simply if it meets the first three criteria stated above. The requirements posed by the self-defense and competent-authority criteria cannot be overlooked. Meeting those requirements, moreover, proves to be more complicated than might be expected, given certain attributes of the problem under discussion here.

This leads to a third and more general conclusion, one that is hardly surprising: A moral case for preemption is possible—even a moral imperative in some cases—but only under certain specific conditions. This chapter evaluates a range of scenarios in which preemption may or may not be justified. It concludes with an assessment of the moral obligations that would follow a preemptive strike.

Why is it important for the policy-maker to think more fully through the moral context of preemption? It is not simply a matter of making preemption more palatable to an American public reluctant to use force for reasons of national interest. Rather, the answer has to do with the particular historical moment, defined by two factors. One is the emergence of the United States as "the world's only super-power"—as a state with unparalleled military power leading an international system in which most of the other states of the world participate as willing partners. The other is the ongoing diffusion of technologies and materials that can be used to produce nuclear, biological, and chemical weapons. If the United States fails to use its power in ways that others will accept as just, a terrible backlash could result. Cooperation could weaken, U.S. leadership could be delegitimized, and weapons could proliferate much more broadly. The future stability of international affairs and the moral framework of American action are thus inextricably intertwined.[4]

THREE PRUDENTIAL CONSIDERATIONS

Just war concepts are hardly new to the policy debate about when and how to use military force. The memoirs of public officials along with public statements of the moment reveal a good deal of concern and often debate about whether particular military actions will be just, and will be perceived as just by the American public and the international community. Policy-makers typically focus on three just war criteria: Can the proposed use of force be defended as a *last resort* effort, after all other means to manage the problem have been tried and failed? Is there a *reasonable chance of success*? And will the action have an effect *proportionate* to the problem it is aimed at solving? When the military act in question is a preemptive strike against the NBC arsenals of rogue states, these criteria require especially careful analysis, largely because the risks and possible consequences loom larger than in many other types of military action.

1. Last Resort

The last-resort criterion is generally understood to require that military action shall not be undertaken unless all other means have been tried and have failed; war-making, after all, should not be the first or preferred course of action in dealing with the war-mongering behavior of a potential aggressor. In fact, the moral requirement is a bit more subtle. Just war thinking does not require that every conceivable alternative course of action be exhausted. As Michael Walzer has argued, "taken literally . . . 'last resort' would make war morally impossible. For we can never reach lastness, or we can never know that we have reached it."[5] The moral obligation requires an assessment of all means available to meet a particular threat—economic, political, and military—and, of those deemed *sufficient* to do so, a preference for means other than war.

In the 1993 debate over preemptive military strikes against the nuclear assets of North Korea, Tokyo and Beijing were unpersuaded that this criterion had been met. Both believed that the United States was looking too readily to military solutions when the problem might still be susceptible to political and economic management. The Libyan chemical facility still fails to meet this criterion in the eyes of many countries; they are more impressed by the history of enmity between Washington and Muammar Qaddafi than by Washington's efforts to use other means at its disposal, such as a trade embargo or legal prosecution, to suppress the Libyan chemical-weapons program.

But the requirement that military action be taken only in last resort does not mean that military action must be forestalled until it cannot be successful (or can succeed only at far higher cost). In Bosnia, for example, the decision of the NATO allies to use force only in last resort contributed to a widening of the war and a substantial increase in human suffering—the just war tradition would arguably have required a narrow interpretation of the "last resort" criterion and an earlier intervention.[6] Particularly when rogue regimes and weapons of mass destruction are a part of the threat calculus, the last-resort criterion should probably be subject to a quite narrow interpretation. Economic sanctions may take months or years to have an effect (and indeed, their likelihood of success is hotly debated). In contrast, weapons programs may quickly reach maturity once a confrontation begins to take shape. Given what is now known about Iraq's pre-war unconventional-weapons programs, for example, it is clear that in just a few additional months of sanctions aimed at pressuring Saddam Hussein to withdraw his army from Kuwait, Iraq's nuclear program would have produced one or two weapons while its biological program could have geared up to a very substantial level of production and weaponization. Moreover, where arsenals already exist, deferring a preemptive strike may induce an aggressor to disperse his weapons and give him the time to do so, greatly reducing the likelihood that preemption will eliminate them. In both scenarios, buying time could cost lives, literally hundreds of thousands of them.

2. Reasonable Chance of Success

This criterion requires that military actions not be undertaken unless they offer a meaningful prospect of eliminating the threat against which they are targeted. The just war tradition dictates that suffering be minimized. Again, the requirement is a bit more subtle than generally conceived. It requires not simply eliminating the threat but restoring a peace that has been disordered by the threat.

If a preemptive strike fails to eliminate an aggressor's nuclear weapons and motivates retaliation, those weapons may be unleashed, causing the loss of a great many lives. The North Korean case, for example, failed to meet the reasonable-chance-of-success criterion because there was little certainty of the number of nuclear weapons produced there, of their location in a massive network of underground storage and transfer facilities, and of North Korea's capacity to use biological and chemical weapons to attack the South even if it were stripped of its nuclear weapons. The Libyan case presents similar considerations.

The difficulty presented by the reasonable-success criterion is magnified by the fact that many NBC assets are located in underground facilities that are very hard to attack successfully. In the case of the Libyan plant, for example, some administration statements have indicated that it might not be possible to destroy the plant without resort to nuclear weapons. This would undoubtedly raise questions of proportionality. Even if the United States acquires some reliable means other than nuclear weapons to destroy hardened underground facilities, gaining high-confidence intelligence about the location of such facilities or other weapon deployment sites may prove extremely difficult.

But "success" in this criterion need not mean perfect success. A preemptive strike that eliminates some but not all of an aggressor's NBC weapons could have a variety of benefits. It might induce greater caution and more conservative behavior by removing any doubt the aggressor might have entertained about the ability or will of the United States to meet his challenges. It might also leave the aggressor with so few weapons and delivery systems that they could readily be defeated by active and passive defensive measures, thus rendering his NBC weapons essentially irrelevant to any direct battlefield confrontation he might initiate.

3. Proportionality

The proportionality criterion is generally understood to require that the minimum necessary force be used. The just war tradition dictates that suffering be minimized, particularly the suffering of noncombatants, and military actions that cause more casualties than they prevent can hardly be deemed just. But once again, the precise requirements of the tradition are a bit more subtle. The proportionality criterion puts two obligations on those who would use force: regarding *ius in bello* (what it is right to do in using force), it requires that only minimum force consistent with the aim be used; and regarding *ius ad bellum* (when it is right to resort to force), it requires that the overall costs of action be less substantial than the costs of inaction. Will the good to be achieved by the resort to violence outweigh the damage to be done, both to individuals and to the community of nations?

With regard to *ius in bello*, it would seem at first glance that virtually any preemption of an aggressor's use of NBC weapons should pass the proportionality test—preventing the use of weapons of mass destruction should by definition save the lives of hundreds of thousands if not millions of people, in exchange for the much smaller number of lives that might be lost in the preemptive strike. The North Korean case failed to meet this test, however, because preemptive military action by the United States was seen as likely to precipitate a broader war on the Korean peninsula, one initiated by Pyongyang in response to U.S. actions. Even if stripped of its nuclear weapons, North Korea would possess a formidable capability to destroy South Korea's military and economic infrastructure and to hold Seoul hostage. In contrast, an attack on the Libyan chemical-weapons facility would be unlikely to pose these difficulties and could more easily meet the proportionality requirement.

With regard to *ius ad bellum,* the proportionality of preemption is clouded by a number of factors. Even if preemption successfully prevents the aggressor's use of those weapons, the cost of that thwarted aggression cannot be known—certainly not publicly proven. The United States would find itself in the position of tallying *actual* casualties caused by its actions against casualties that the aggressor *might* have caused had he not been stopped. This would undoubtedly lead to debate about whether the aggressor would indeed have used his weapons as the United States believed he would. It is important to note that most NBC arsenals have been used not militarily but politically, to coerce a potential adversary to make an important concession (either to do or to refrain from doing something). The costs of this "use" of NBC weapons cannot readily be compared with the costs of preemptive military attack upon them. But such comparisons are necessary in the moral world. The potential coercive use of NBC arsenals does provide a moral basis for preemption, insofar at it is necessary to repel injury or to punish evil. From the perspective of the just war tradition, this moral claim is valid whether or not coercion has been openly backed by military threats. Appeasement, after all, has typically emboldened assertive leaders. Sometimes it has fueled acts of aggression that have produced many casualties and have been reversed only at high cost.

These three criteria draw on both *ius ad bellum* and *ius in bello* dimensions of the just war tradition. They present a substantial set of moral requirements for dealing with NBC-armed rogue states. But they are only the beginning of the story. They do not reflect a comprehensive reading of what that tradition requires of military action. They are in fact what one moral philosopher has termed "contingent prudential judgments."[7] Two prior criteria must be satisfied: the requirements that any use of force be in self-defense, and that any use of force be authorized by a competent authority.

PREEMPTION AND SELF-DEFENSE

Moral philosophy establishes that wars of self-defense are just, whereas wars of aggression are not. But there has long been a healthy debate about precisely what constitutes a war of self-defense. A scholar of just war in the mid-sixteenth century wrote, "There is a single and only just cause for commencing a war . . . namely, wrong received."[8] In our day Michael Walzer has argued, "Nothing but aggression can justify war. . . . There must actually have been a wrong, and it must actually have been received (or its receipt must be, as it were, only minutes away). Nothing else warrants the use of force in international society."[9] In the debate about preemption, the crucial issue is in those "minutes away": how proximate must the threat of the use of those weapons be? Does the just war tradition require waiting until the very last minute?

As James Turner Johnson has argued, much contemporary Catholic thought on war echoes this very circumscribed right to self-defense— "a defensive response to an attack still in progress."[10] Johnson attributes this way of thinking primarily to the Church's rejection of war as a viable instrument of order and peace under virtually any circumstances, and especially in the nuclear era.

A survey of other perspectives, both contemporary and historical, suggests that this circumscribed view is not universally held. Hugo Grotius wrote in 1625 that "the first just cause of war . . . is an injury, which even though not actually committed, threatens our persons or our property."[11] To safeguard against wars of aggression, Grotius emphasized that it was essential to be certain about the enemy's intent to attack. Elihu Root said in 1914 that international law did not require the aggrieved state to wait before using force in self-defense "until it is too late to protect itself."[12] Writing in 1977, Michael Walzer argued that "states can rightfully defend themselves against violence that is imminent but not actual." However, Walzer rejects boastful ranting, arms races, and hostile acts short of war as legitimate bases of preemption, arguing that "injury must be 'offered' in some material sense as well."[13]

The United Nations Charter incorporates competing notions. In its Chapter 7, special rights are reserved for the Security Council to use force in response to threats to international peace and security; those threats are not specifically limited to instances of outright aggression.

On the other hand, Article 51 of the Charter, which affirms the right of self-defense "if an armed attack occurs," is generally interpreted to forbid claims of self-defense *except* in cases of armed attack.[14]

International law restricts the right of states to resort to the offensive use of force in preemptive modes. As Johnson notes, "Under the controverted first-use/second-use distinction, aggression is defined as the first use of force regardless of circumstances, while defense becomes second use alone."[15]

This distinction is controverted for the simple reason that aggression does not usually begin, and injury is not usually "offered," when the first weapons are fired. Hot wars are usually but one phase of a competition of interest and power. In relations among states in an anarchic system, competition is inevitable. But it is usually pursued with "soft power," namely political and economic means, rather than the harder forms. War itself is frequently the culmination of a failure of other means to coerce, dissuade, or compel others. As Clausewitz noted, the aggressor is often peace-loving, and it is his resistant victim who causes war to erupt: "A conqueror is always a lover of peace (as Bonaparte always asserted of himself); he would like to make his entry into our state unopposed; in order to prevent this, we must choose war."[16]

War-Making vs. Preemption

Other than the mechanistic and unreliable use of the first-use/second-use distinction, what criteria can be used to distinguish illegitimate acts of war-making from legitimate acts of preemption? Walzer offers some useful commentary on this point:

> The line between legitimate and illegitimate first strikes is not going to be drawn at the point of imminent attack but at the point of sufficient threat. That phrase is necessarily vague. I mean it to cover three things: a manifest intent to injure, a degree of active preparation that makes that intent a positive danger, and a general situation in which waiting, or doing anything other than fighting, greatly magnifies the risk. . . . Instead of previous signs of rapacity and ambition, current and particular signs are required; instead of an "augmentation of power," actual preparation for war; instead of the refusal of future securities, the intensification of present dangers.[17]

Walzer and others also emphasize the importance of illegal actions by the prospective aggressor, which is to say actions that abrogate specific legal undertakings of the state or that contravene accepted principles of international law.

The acquisition of weapons of mass destruction might fit many of these criteria quite well—these are actions that can confirm an intent to injure, create a positive danger, and raise the risks of waiting. Their dispersal in time of crisis would certainly signal preparation for war. But to acquire such weapons and to prepare for their use is not the same as what Walzer calls "actual preparation for war" or "the intensification of present dangers"—these are qualities that have to do with the nature of the regime itself. As George Weigel has argued:

> Iraqi and North Korean nuclear-weapons programs do not exist in a historical vacuum. They are the expressions of evil, real-world political intentions whose character has been made plain over many years. Precisely for the same reason that we do not think about preemptive action against Britain and France, we can, without collapsing into the moral vulgarities of Realpolitik, consider proportionate and discriminate preemptive action against Iraq and North Korea.[18]

Rogue regimes have already established their aggressive intent—this is the essence of their characterization as "rogue" or "backlash." Their acquisition of NBC weapons is yet another confirmation of that intent. The moral obligation that falls upon them is to conform to established norms of interstate behavior. The moral obligation that falls on their potential victims is to protect themselves. But, given the particular nature of NBC weapons, such protection may be extremely costly if it must await the first blow with those weapons.

Threats to Peace and Order

Moreover, rogue regimes generally threaten not just the immediate sovereignty of their neighbors but the order that is the foundation of long-term sovereignty. They may pose threats to regional peace. For example, had Saddam Hussein been able to use his weapons of mass destruction to secure aggression with conventional weapons in the Middle East, and thus to emerge as a regional hegemon, there would have been significant repercussions for other states in the region—not only those whom he might seek to coerce to do his bidding, such as Egypt or Turkey, but those whom he might seek to defeat or destroy, such as Iran or Israel. In the Far East, were North Korea to prove successful in using its NBC capabilities to coerce the great powers into taking steps that compromised South Korea's safety and well-being, power relations in the region would undergo a period of deeply unsettling realignment, perhaps leading others in the region to acquire NBC weapons of their own.

Rogue regimes may also pose threats to the global order. If an NBC-armed rogue were able to challenge a major commitment or interest of one of the established nuclear powers, and thereby cause that power to back down and appease, others could draw the conclusion that the security guarantees of the great powers—and especially the United States—and the already limited promise of collective security are paper tigers. Similarly, the acquisition of weapons of mass destruction in contravention of existing legal undertakings, such as the Nuclear Non-Proliferation Treaty or the Biological and Toxin Weapons Convention, could lead to an unraveling of the international effort to control the proliferation of such weapons. That could prove highly damaging to international security. Many states have the capability to build NBC weapons but for the moment are uninterested in doing so. The actions of an NBC-armed rogue could lead to the wildfire-like building of mass-destruction arsenals in regions in conflict and in regions now free of such weapons. Such far-reaching changes in the distribution of power and in the credibility of the major powers would be likely to erode sharply the international processes and institutions that for the moment at least are the foundation of international order. These changes could eviscerate the norms and principles of the U.N. Charter, if not lead to their eclipse by new norms antithetical to the interests of justice and peace.

To put it differently: in the international system that exists today, many small and medium-sized states depend upon international norms and collective mechanisms to compensate for their own modest capabilities to provide for their own security. Even the great powers experience a great deal of economic interdependence. Therefore, defending the stability of the system is in the national interest of many states. The world-order argument thus creates an additional moral justification for preemption. Protecting world order is long-term self-defense.

This way of thinking about the just-cause criterion contrasts with the narrow view of self-defense now in vogue. But it is in fact consistent with other elements of the just war traditions, elements that have been eclipsed by the emphasis on defense against aggression. Two other criteria have traditionally been used to define justifiable defensive wars: those aimed at the recovery of something wrongfully taken, and those aimed at the punishment of evil.[19] According to Johnson, in this way of thinking about just cause, just wars were those required to establish a just political and social order among states, "an order that was necessary for the presence of peace."[20] Such a view of war is well ingrained in the balance-of-power school of international politics. In the nineteenth century, for example, Britain viewed war as necessary to maintain a status quo in Europe that made possible the progress of liberty and thus increased the chances for zones of peace built on shared commercial and social interests.

This view of what can justify war predates the Industrial Revolution and the emergence in the twentieth century of total war, i.e., war that mobilizes all the resources of a society to defeat if not annihilate an enemy society similarly mobilized. Of course, wars of complete annihilation are not unknown in history, but technical and scientific sophistication has brought them to a new scale and immediacy. The view of war as a legitimate instrument of peace has lost favor in the Catholic Church not least because of this transformation of war, leading many to conclude that no war could pass the prudential tests cited above.[21]

Two Weaknesses in the Debate

This line of argument helps to expose the two basic weaknesses in the way the moral debate about the use of force draws upon the just war tradition. One relates to collective self-defense. Although the tradition posits the right of states to act in collective self-defense, the moral debate focuses almost exclusively on wars between two states—the aggressor and the aggrieved. In the international system of the late twentieth century, states coexist with multilateral institutions, transnational processes, global norms, and an international community. Aggression threatens interests far larger than those of the sovereignty of a given state. If aggression between states were permitted to return as a common mode of behavior, societies on every continent would pay a price. This suggests that in the moral calculation, the value of defeating an aggressive regime and thereby perhaps deterring similar ones must be added to the values of protecting the national sovereignty of individual states.

The second basic weakness relates to the nuclear revolution in international affairs. The moral debate on nuclear weapons is locked in a time now passed. In the memorable debate on the nuclear bomb in the early 1980s, the U.S. Catholic bishops by and large deemed unjust both the means and the ends of nuclear war, arguing that there is virtually no imaginable real-world circumstance in which the use of nuclear weapons could be satisfied as just *in bello*; the Vatican did accept the possibility of a just nuclear peace, albeit reluctantly.[22] Although arguments will long continue, there is much to suggest that the peace secured in the Cold War and the victory that brought its end have much to do with nuclear weapons. The point here is that most of the moral philosophizing on matters nuclear is held hostage to this era now past—an era when nuclear war was a matter of East-West brinkmanship and global armageddon.

In the post–Cold War era, wars and threats by rogue states armed with nuclear weapons pose new questions. The particular issue from the point of view of this paper is that preemption entails the risk of nuclear confrontation—but not armageddon. If the preemptive strike is not successful in eliminating an aggressor's NBC weapons, and he opts to use them in reply, preemption would have unleashed a terrible chain of events. Wars such as this may or may not prove to be massively destructive, depending on the choices made by the aggressor and the character of the arsenals and delivery systems available to him, as well as the choices made by the United States about how to reply (and its defensive and offensive capabilities). No rogue has the nuclear capacity to annihilate a major power, although each major power has the capacity to annihilate a rogue. Limited nuclear wars of the kind long dismissed in the Cold War are now a matter requiring serious reflection. The United States must consider whether or how to use nuclear weapons in meeting the aggression of such states, not simply in deterrence or for national survival, but for larger purposes of international order. This new agenda permits no easy answers.

Some have seen an escape from the dilemmas of U.S. nuclear use in increased reliance on conventional rather than nuclear means to carry out attacks of strategic significance. The exceptional technical ability of the U.S. military to employ military force discriminately and to use conventional weaponry in precision strikes has fueled a perception that the United States has minimized, to the extent possible, the costs to noncombatants and the risks to anyone other than the soldiers and military infrastructure of the state being struck preemptively. This may make it easier to justify attacks on the NBC arsenals of rogue states.

The overwhelming military power in the hands of the United States does make it easier to threaten attacks. But reliance on overwhelming power and on military actions that impose essentially no cost in American lives raises proportionality questions of its own—questions that troubled senior U.S. policy-makers on the last day of Desert Storm as they considered the reported savagery of the "highway to death." Moreover, conventional preemption may not prevent an aggressor from using his unconventional weapons. The United States may then feel compelled to use its own nuclear weapons, whether for reasons of proportionality (so as not to suffer huge casualties in observing a nuclear taboo already broken by the aggressor) or for punishment (to establish the point that aggression with nuclear weapons is intolerable). In sum, conventional options are unlikely to eliminate nuclear dilemmas.

PREEMPTION AND COMPETENT AUTHORITY

The second criterion for the just use of force that must be met *before* considerations of last resort, proportionality, and reasonable chance of success is that the decision to go to war must be made by a competent authority. The purpose of this requirement is to limit the right to make war to sovereign entities, thereby denying it to individuals or groups whose use of violence is not constrained by the dictates of international society and international law.

The competent-authority requirement is most easily met in wars between two sovereign nations. It is also met in wars of cooperative self-defense, albeit less directly. Moral philosophy permits states not only to act in self-defense but to make common cause in self-defense with others. Thus, under the rule that an attack on one is an attack on all, even a nation not directly attacked by an aggressor's first acts of war has a just cause to undertake military actions in reply.

But in the scenarios considered here, a particular difficulty emerges. Does the United States have the necessary authority to undertake pre-emptive strikes against rogue states that have not first made military attacks on it? This is in one sense a trite question: the United States is, after all, a sovereign entity. But in another sense it is more profound: if it is not the party immediately threatened by a rogue's NBC weapons, and if it is not in a formal alliance with such a party, by what means is its authority deemed legitimate? The cause may be just, but what makes it America's fight?

The United States faces a real dilemma in establishing its authority in this regard: if it arrogates to itself the right to determine when and how to strike at nations it considers outside the law, it may be judged as having put itself above the law. The United States finds itself, after all, in a peculiar historical moment. As the world's dominant military, economic, and political power, it has been cast in the role of primary defender of the global status quo—of the existing balance of global power and of the institutions it has labored to put in place to promote global stability, prosperity, and liberty. As the defender of the status quo, it has a special stake in turning back the aggressions and deterring the potential aggressions of rogue nations. The concern that the United States not put itself above the law is particularly evident among its closest allies, for their partnership with the United States is based on a belief in its benign use of power and on the legitimacy it enjoys within their societies as a steward of common interests. Both of these qualifications would be eroded by acts outside the law.

As A. J. Bacevich has argued: "Like Great Britain at the end of the nineteenth century, the United States at the end of the twentieth is a dominant world power with an interest above all in perpetuating that dominance. The existing order—the distribution of wealth and influence, the basic rules governing the game of world politics—suits us, and we are committed to its preservation."[23] To be sure, there are some fundamental differences between the system of today, in which the United States *is dominant*, and one *dominated by* the United States. Other nations have joined with it in building the current rules and institutions of order, and they remain free to seek an alternative order. Today, the vast majority of states side with the United States in its commitment to the status quo, so long as this permits them the opportunity to make evolutionary changes in ways that promote justice, peace, and prosperity. The genuine challengers to the status quo are few and far between, though many states aspire to improve their lot, which means not only gains in well-being or political status but also enhanced security. Because the so-called status quo has a certain promise of such goals, it is a status quo of unique and unprecedented character.

But this does not eliminate the moral issue for the United States as the primary beneficiary and defender of this status quo. How does it distinguish morally between preemptive actions with a world-order purpose and those that, though wrapped in world-order rhetoric, are in the service of primarily U.S. interests?

Supports for Authority

One answer might be for the United States to seek endorsement by the U.N. Security Council of a decision to strike preemptively. There could be many practical reasons not to consider such a move, not least the warning to the rogue state likely to be given by such an action, which might induce it to disperse its weapons and perhaps to use them before losing them. But the focus here is on establishing just authority. As Eugene Rostow has observed, it is not obligatory for a state exercising its right to self-defense to seek U.N. approval;[24] moreover, the Security Council has the legal authority to act not merely to uphold the right of self-defense but in reply to threats of whatever kind to international peace and security. But the Security Council lacks the moral authority to act as a sovereign. It lacks competent authority in two ways: absence of public accountability, and absence of a command-and-control system for the use of force.[25]

An alternative answer to the competent-authority dilemma might be to stimulate creation of a broad international coalition to carry out, and support, preemptive action. The moral benefit of this approach would be to attach American power and actions to a broad base of international sovereignty.

But this too poses problems. From a practical point of view, it is likely to prove very difficult to assemble such a coalition—preemption is a notoriously unpopular measure, and every hint that the United States might be considering a preemptive attack generates strong reactions among allies as well as potential adversaries. Moreover, it is not clear that this would solve the moral dilemma. As Walzer has argued, "when the world divides radically into those who bomb and those who are bombed, it becomes morally problematic even if the bombing in this or that instance is justifiable."[26]

A third approach would be to rely on unilateral action by the United States in the context of a strong moral argument. Such a case might build on its right to self-defense—after all, the United States seems to be a likely target of weapons possessed by leaders who believe the United States to be the primary defender of a corrupt status quo. It might also draw on the moral duty to help others. And the U.S. case would also have to draw on the obligations of a security guarantor that fall on it as a permanent member of the Security Council—after all, the NBC capabilities of the rogue pose a threat to the interests of international peace and stability.

In fact, the United States has begun to make this latter case. Anthony Lake's original characterization of the rogue-state problem was careful to look beyond the weapons programs of the named states to their flagrant disregard for basic norms of international society, including principally their regular reliance on violence to maintain domestic power and to coerce, if not invade and defeat, their neighbors. Lake thus was careful to frame a normative context for addressing the rogue-state problem that went beyond the national-interest arguments about military capability and power.[27]

This normative framework may provide an international context in which U.S. actions are legitimized. It seems unlikely to establish the United States as a competent authority in a moral sense, however, as the expression of this normative framework is a series of multilateral treaties and institutions that by definition distribute rights and authority through the international system. Unilateral action by the United States in support of those norms would be inconsistent with its commitment to the mechanisms that embody those norms. Moreover, so long as the United States finds itself isolated in making the case that certain states are rogues, any military actions based on this moral case will be open to the charge that they are merely national-interest actions hidden under the rubric of world-order interests. In fact, the Clinton administration's characterization of this set of states as rogues, and its subsequent policies to isolate them and undertake counterproliferation preparations for possible military action against their NBC weapons, are much criticized, not least by U.S. friends and allies abroad who see such actions as an effort to put the United States above or outside the law.[28]

The particular problem with this approach is that the United States sometimes acts in defense of interests that it but not others see as common, or in defense of norms that it asserts but others do not support. For example, in the mid-1980s the United States tried to make a moral case for preemptive attacks on Libya based on the latter's chemical-weapons production activities at Rabta, a case that was politically flawed by the fact that the United States was itself a possessor of chemical weapons and was at the time engaged in the production of such weapons. Even some U.S. allies questioned the moral basis of what appeared to be a punitive if not vengeful act. Similarly, in 1996 the U.S. case for preemption of Libyan chemical plants was weakened by the United States' own continued possession of chemical weapons and its reluctance to ratify the Chemical Weapons Convention. To be sure, there are fundamental differences between the "regimes" in Washington and Tripoli or Baghdad; but the isolation of the United States on these issues underscores how inconsequential those moral differences have proven to be politically.

This review suggests that there is no easy answer to the competent-authority requirement of the just war tradition in the current historical moment. Policy-makers will logically be drawn to the argument that if each approach is inadequate, the best approach is to do all three in combination. Making a clear normative argument, while also building a coalition and seeking a U.N. mandate, would help to satisfy many citizens that preemptive action meets the basic moral requirement of political legitimacy. But whether it would also satisfy moral philosophers is another question. This leads to a conclusion analogous to that in the discussion of self-defense: contemporary moral reasoning based on the just war tradition has not taken into account the moral requirements of a changing world.

Assessing the U.N.'s Authority

But within the tradition there are some touchstones for the path ahead. The emphasis should be on a critique of the moral authority of the Security Council. As noted above, such a critique rests on two key points: the absence of public accountability, and the absence of a command-and-control system for the use of force. Are these in fact the appropriate criteria by which to assess the competent authority of the U.N. to endorse preemptive action?

The Security Council does reflect a certain type of accountability. The Council is accountable to the principles that guide its actions, to the states that are its members, and thus indirectly to the citizens of those states. The indirect nature of its democratic credentials is analogous to that of the U.S. president in the days when he was put into office by the process of indirect election that was the Electoral College, before the electors were bound by the popular vote. The Council's capacity to use power is, moreover, subject to a number of checks and balances. In a global political system of states, what higher moral authority can exist than the collective will of nations?

The U.N. itself does not of course possess full sovereignty. But it does have certain clearly identified, and clearly circumscribed, areas of authority. One is the Security Council's right to authorize the use of force to defend peace and security. For this purpose, it does not have the command-and-control system of a state. But it does have such a system appropriate to its particular role—a system that weaves together national command with multilateral institutions and processes. This too is subject to checks and balances. Its capacity to use force is thus limited to ad hoc circumstances, with the use of borrowed forces under charters granted by state members. The command and control flows from those who are directly responsible in the system.

Moreover, the U.N. embodies an agreed set of norms within the international community about behaviors within and among states that are either appropriate or inappropriate. To be sure, some states ignore the U.N. Charter (though ever fewer, as democracy takes hold in many parts of the world). And to be sure, there are fundamental political divisions within the organization. But it does reflect a consensus-based global normative structure. It is the only institution that aspires to represent the interests of the whole community of nations, and thus the only one with strong moral authority in purporting to defend those interests. Its most powerful members assume special obligations in their role as guarantors of international peace and security on the Security Council, though how they fulfill those duties—and how well they do so—is hotly contested.

The point here is not that the U.N. is sufficiently like a state to establish its sovereignty. Rather, it has a certain moral authority sufficient to the competent-authority requirement. The U.N. can provide the normative framework for actions by a state or group of states in defense of world-order interests. The U.N. is essential, not because it is supranational and "above" its member states, but because its normative attributes redress the competent-authority shortfall.

Invoking the U.N.'s Authority

But how is that authority invoked and operationalized? The moral authority of the U.N. would most clearly be engaged if the General Assembly, the Secretary General, and the Security Council unanimously agreed that a particular threat to world order was so egregious as to require preemptive military action. Such unanimity is of course highly unlikely. Political division implies that the U.N. will not reliably be able to act in times of crisis and will find it difficult to cope with questions of preemption. But the absence of unanimity is not necessarily a moral deficiency, as ethical issues are not determined in popularity contests.

On preemption, the Council possesses the authority to authorize such actions, given its special responsibilities, and the Charter legalizes the associated actions. But whether the competent-authority requirement also requires the assent of the Council for each and every act of preemption by a permanent member for world-order purposes is doubtful. In those cases where prior approval is sought from the Council, the moral requirement probably does not even necessitate an affirmative vote from the Council. To veto a just act is not to rob the act of its justness. General and broad reinforcement of this duty could help to bolster the moral case for specific acts of preemption.

Establishing the competent authority of a world-order defense argument would seem to require more than reliance on the Security Council, however. After all, many states see the Council itself as symptomatic of an *unjust* world order. The Council's authority is hotly contested by many who see it as an anachronism of a world war now a half century past, and as a body dominated by "the world's only super-power," whose use of power is unfettered and whose singular ability to mobilize the U.N. deprives the Security Council of a meaningful role beyond one that serves U.S. interests.[29] The moral authority of the Council can be buttressed only by addressing these concerns.

A footnote to this discussion of competent authority is in order. The competent-authority requirement is intended to bolster the role of sovereigns in international affairs. Under international law, sovereignty has become virtually sacrosanct. But while all states may be equal before the law, all sovereigns do not possess the same degree or type of sovereignty. This ambiguity may have been tenable at a time when the purpose of just war thinking was to codify war as a right of states, but it seems ever less acceptable. A dictator who holds power by the ruthless use of repression, torture, extortion, and murder cannot be equated morally with leaders somehow representing the will of the body politic. Why should he have equal legitimacy in waging war, especially if he is also making war on his own people? Sovereignty requires consent for its proper exercise. Such consent should be an increasingly important measure of sovereignty in an age in which widespread industrialization and technical innovation are putting massively destructive weapons and long-range delivery systems into the hands of more and more individuals or regimes whose grip on power derives from force, not popular will.

WHEN IS PREEMPTION JUST?

There can, then, be no blanket reply to the question, Is there a moral case for preemption? Some acts of preemption will be deemed just, others unjust. For yet others, some elements of a moral case will be present, others absent.

The strongest moral case for U.S. preemption exists under the following conditions: (1) an aggressor has actually threatened to use his NBC weapons, has taken steps to ready the means to do so, and has specifically threatened the United States (including its territory, citizens, or military forces); (2) those NBC weapons have been built in violation of international law; (3) the aggressor's threatened actions invoke larger questions about the credibility of security guarantees or the balance of power within a region; (4) the president has secured the approval of the U.S. Congress; and (5) the United States has secured the backing of the U.N. Security Council and any relevant regional organization. The prudential tests of last resort, proportionality, and reasonable chance of success must also be met.

The weakest case for preemption exists when: (1) a state has made no NBC threats and has no prior behavior of aggression; (2) those weapons are permitted under international law (because the state is not a party to the relevant treaties); (3) the preemption is the culmination of a worsening bilateral relationship with the United States, driven by a loss of objectivity in Washington; and (4) U.S. actions have been condemned by the U.N. or opposed by the Security Council. Even if the intended strike meets all the prudential tests, it cannot be accepted as just under these conditions.

In the middle are a range of scenarios with mixed ethical configurations, drawing on the following factors: Threatened attacks on U.S. allies establish the same moral case as threatened attacks on the United States. Threats that generate Security Council agreement and action should also establish a credible moral case, even where those threats are to international order and not merely to the sovereignty of a particular state. Threats that call into question U.S. security guarantees, even if not formal alliances, also offer less strong but credible moral cases. Preemptive attacks in response not to explicit threats but to implicit intentions as perceived in NBC weapons programs offer a less strong moral case, unless backed by other signals of aggressive intent.

This is not to argue that all acts of military preemption by the United States require approval by others if they are to be just. Rather, preemptions conceived by the United States as necessary to defend world-order interests, rather than those deemed necessary because of alliance guarantees or more discrete and specific national interests, require a normative framework that the United States alone cannot provide in its "unipolar moment."[30]

MORAL OBLIGATIONS FOLLOWING PREEMPTION

The just war tradition also imposes obligations in the aftermath of military action. One is the requirement to make a moral case for the action that has been undertaken. As Weigel has argued, "the presumption is always for peace, and the burden of moral reasoning lies with those who argue for the justness of a particular resort to war."[31]

Justice requires a clear explication of the moral reasoning that led to the chosen course of action. Especially in an era when many countries, both adversaries and allies, fear a hegemonic United States that puts itself above the law in defending its perceived national-security interests, it is incumbent upon the United States to establish that its actions are consistent not merely with the letter of the law but also with the spirit of justice and peace that underpins it. Making this case would help to heal the domestic divisions likely to be caused by preemptive military attack. It would also help to reassure those in other countries who might interpret U.S. preemption as signaling a more bellicose America more likely to intervene abroad.

Making the moral case for a world-order act means making the case to the world community, which of course encompasses many different cultures and ethical traditions. A moral case that draws only on the just war tradition of Westerners and Christians may be rejected by others as cultural imperialism. Moral philosophers face a critical challenge in building up a dialogue across cultures, one that gives them common terms of reference even if not common traditions. There are many obvious differences among cultures and ethical traditions, especially on questions of war. But because problems of war, peace, and justice are universal, there is good reason to believe that beneath the apparent cultural differences are some fundamental commonalities.[32]

A second moral obligation after a preemptive strike is to alleviate the suffering caused by U.S. actions. This may not be practical in cases where a regime that is antithetical to U.S. interests remains firmly entrenched, especially if it exploits the public-relations value of U.S.-inflicted casualties. But it may be practical where preemption leads to the collapse of the regime, or at least to the emergence of new political forces within the targeted country that would accept U.S. humanitarian assistance. Especially in those cases where preemption of nuclear attack leads to acts of retribution by the targeted country, perhaps with remaining nuclear or biological weapons, the United States will have a moral obligation beyond what it might normally feel to help minimize and redress human suffering.

A third requirement is to make a just settlement of the issues in dispute. If U.S. action is deemed necessary to recover something wrongfully taken or to punish evil, then its post-strike actions must work toward those ends.

Concluding Observations

In summary, there is a moral case for preemption, but it is not quite as tidy as policy-makers might desire. The just war tradition puts a number of obligations on policy. Preemption must meet the three basic prudential requirements (last resort, reasonable chance of success, proportionality). But it must first meet the requirements that the action be in self-defense and be authorized by competent authority. Not all contemplated acts of preemption are likely to meet all these criteria. It is not clear that every one must be met for an act to be just.

The latter two requirements (self-defense, competent authority) pose particular difficulties today. The current historical moment is characterized by the simultaneous appearance of two unprecedented factors: (1) broad international diffusion of the technical competence to inflict mass destruction, and (2) a unipolar international order in which the United States finds itself cast as the defender of a status quo. This implies not least that the United States must use its power in ways that others will accept as just; otherwise a terrible backlash could result.

The particular difficulties posed today are as follows. First, the self-defense requirement is too narrow in a world in which the security of so many depends upon the orderliness of the system; defending that order must have a moral quality analogous to that of defending the sovereignty of individual parts, but that quality is not well established in moral theory. Moreover, the self-defense requirement engages nuclear arguments rooted in an era now past. Addressing these problems requires returning to the nuclear debate, but in the light of current strategic realities, and then reconnecting moral debate to that part of the just war tradition that accepts war as an instrument of order under certain conditions.

Second, the competent-authority requirement is rooted in an era long past. Today policy-makers must cope with overlapping national and international institutions and sovereignties, and with world-order problems that transcend the interests of individual states. Addressing this problem requires formulating principles by which just war criteria can be satisfied by international institutions. The logical focal point is the U.N.—especially the Security Council. The potential moral legitimacy of actions endorsed by the U.N. is high, but its own weak legitimacy suggests how difficult this task will be.

Two final observations, the first on the disjunction between moral philosophy and international law on preemption. As noted earlier, international law has had the effect over time of progressively narrowing the legal recourse to war. Moral philosophy has not similarly constrained the just recourse to war. If law exists to serve justice, what is the authority of law that is inconsistent with moral reasoning? The law should permit what justice requires. Moreover, how does a nation that does not want to be above the law act in ways that moral reasoning requires? A world in which the only legal recourse to self-defense is in retaliation for an aggressor's first strike is a world that has legalized the coercive use of weapons arsenals and has made more likely the operational use of those weapons by those not constrained by moral reasoning or even the purposes of state. How tolerable is this when the weapons in question are weapons of mass destruction?

The second observation relates to the contribution of just war thinking to world-order politics. The problem of war has naturally attracted a great deal of ethical debate. But the behavior of states in modes other than warfare has attracted less attention from the moral philosophers. Moreover, the record reflects little or no effort to look beyond the ethical debate about the behavior of states to the normative attributes of world order. We think we know what just wars are, but we are a lot less clear about just statecraft. We think we know that the order the United States seeks to defend and/or lead is a good one, but we are a lot less clear about the criteria and reasoning sufficient to this claim.

Moral philosophy could make a substantial contribution to the construction of a more just and peaceful world for the next century if it would direct more energy to such questions. At the very least, such a dialogue should help to clarify the moral duties that fall upon the United States in its special historical moment and help it to see more clearly when and how to use its power, and when not to.

5

Humanitarian Intervention: From Concept to Reality

John Langan, S.J.

H umanitarian intervention is an uneasy compound notion, with
elements that have very different connections. "Humanitarian"
brings us into a world of universal concerns and of causes (in the
Wilsonian rather than the Aristotelian sense). Today some will regard
it as a species-ist and restricted notion, while others may view it with
suspicion as an echo of progressive piety in a world of anarchic and
brutal conflict. But "humanitarian" is generally brought into discussions of international politics to express a worthy and indeed compelling concern, a value that appeals across divisions of ethnicity and
race, of interest and alliance, of ideology and religion, of class and
gender, to evoke compassionate responses to suffering and injustice.

At the same time, "humanitarian" and its linguistic relatives are less
direct than most of our moral language; they apply to a wide variety

John Langan, **S.J.**, is Rose Kennedy Professor of Christian Ethics in
the Kennedy Institute of Ethics at Georgetown University, Washington, D.C. He is the editor or co-editor of seven books, including *The
Nuclear Dilemma and the Just War Tradition* (1986) and a collection of
the addresses of Joseph Cardinal Bernardin on ethics and public life
(forthcoming, spring 1998).

of situations involving many moral issues and points of view. These terms invoke standards that are initially presented to us in more direct language. They are seen in contrast, for instance, to such terms as "cruel," "barbaric," or "savage." Or they are clarified through more descriptive terms such as "compassionate," "generous," "sensitive," or "merciful." The notion of humanitarian action or response, because it is less direct, more abstract or second-order, brings with it certain questions about reasons and motives that more specific notions would usually begin to answer. We are more likely to wonder why a person or an organization acts out of humanitarian considerations, or to speculate that humanitarian justifications may conceal other motives and interests.

"Intervention" has, in comparison, a more jagged and complex profile. In the first place, it implies a departure from the customary course of events. Intervention is *something extraordinary*. Second, this departure from the normal pattern *comes from outside*: some agents or forces come into a setting in which the normal pattern prevails in a way that threatens to overturn or reverse that pattern. Third, because of this contrast between the setting, with its normal patterns of action and expectation, and the agent or force coming from outside, there will inevitably be *a tension* between the values and rules associated with the normal patterns and the values and rules connected with the pattern-altering actions.

Whether surgical or economic, political or military, intervention normally raises questions of justification and authority. Who decides when an intervention is necessary? What objectives make an intervention morally right? What set of norms ought to prevail in this situation where conflict is not merely possible but highly likely? These questions are likely to be especially pointed when the intervention is military, that is, when it involves using or threatening to use force and inflicting grave harm, even death, on human beings. Then the notion of humanitarian intervention seems not merely composite but also paradoxical, since it offers us the prospect of taking some human lives in order to preserve others.

Let us use this highly general conception of humanitarian intervention as a basis for moral reflection about some of the policy choices that the United States is likely to face in this post–Cold War era. My hope is that this will help us keep in mind some fundamental features of humanitarian intervention that are often obscured when we take up a specifically legal point of view or become involved in choosing among particular policy options.

EXAMINING INTERVENTION

The extraordinary, pattern-breaking character of intervention is taken as fundamental in the way international law understands intervention: it regards intervention as a violation of state sovereignty, an effort to override the authority of a state by inserting military forces responsible to other powers. Each intervention, however much it may fit into currently dominant patterns of international behavior (such as the Soviet Union's applications of the Brezhnev Doctrine), constitutes a departure from a fundamental norm of international order, namely, the principle of non-intervention. That principle is a corollary of the notion of state sovereignty, an attribute possessed equally by all states.

Military intervention is the central concern of traditional formulations of the principle of non-intervention, but the increasing complexity and subtlety of interactions among states and their populations mean that it is possible for one state to exert serious pressure on another without sending troops. There can be economic intervention as well as diplomatic and political intervention, and intervention can also take the form of omissions (e.g., embargoes and boycotts) that disrupt the normal flow of communications and commerce. Intervention can be overt, with the intervening government taking responsibility for the actions it carries out or subsidizes or endorses; or it can be covert, with the intervening government unwilling to acknowledge its involvement in operations that may be of dubious legal status at home as well as in the targeted country. The form and the legal status of intervention will also depend to some extent on the perceived legitimacy of the sovereignty involved.

It is necessary to keep referring to the "normal" pattern of interaction between states, since almost any major decision by a government can affect enterprises and organizations in other states. If intervention were thought of in purely military terms, then many of the ways in which states can exert pressure upon other states would be left unexamined. If it were thought of as simply any action by a government and its agents that had some effect upon another state, then we would have an overly broad and in fact useless notion of intervention.

Insistence on the pattern-breaking character of intervention should not, however, be taken to imply that the prior situation was stable or orderly. On the contrary, when intervention begins to strike observers or neighboring states as necessary or useful, the country in question will usually be in a bad way, often a catastrophically bad way (e.g., Rwanda, Somalia, Uganda, Cambodia, Bosnia). The bonds of community will have been grievously disrupted; deeds that breed hatred and provoke downward spiraling cycles of revenge and violence will have been done. This has not always been the case. In the past, powers that were intent on opportunities for imperial expansion or assertion of their presence have been willing to draw sweeping conclusions from reports of comparatively minor disturbances or internal difficulties. The memories and shadows of imperialism, whether Western or Soviet, do not fade easily, nor should they. But in our day, intervention is much more likely to be unduly late than to be premature.

The standard scenario at present is that the country in trouble may actually be in a normal condition from the standpoint of international law: that is, there are no aggressive or intervening alien forces on its territory. But its government is likely to be subject to serious internal challenges and to be failing to maintain security for its citizens or for some substantial group of them. The plausibility of intervention presupposes that the state in question is in a condition of crisis; if there is not a crisis, the primary justification for intervention, and for the overriding of sovereignty that it entails, is absent.

Intervention cannot itself become a normal situation, though it may be a necessary step if normality is to be attained. The abnormal character of intervention, at least in a post-imperial world, means it must be limited in scope and duration so that the sovereignty of the troubled state is not extinguished. Even while an intervention is going on, there is always good reason to keep it limited and to show respect for the values, laws, and practices of the local community. The scope of the intervention should be limited by the legitimate and morally justifiable objectives of the intervening parties; normally these objectives will not and should not include transforming the suffering society and its fundamental institutions and cultural system, even when these are seriously flawed and even when they have played some part in bringing about the catastrophe (e.g., the clan system in Somalia).

We should recall that the principal successful effort at cultural transformation in an interventionist mode was carried on by the Allies in Germany and Japan after 1945. This occurred in the aftermath of an extraordinarily destructive war of aggression launched by those two states, which for a time effectively forfeited their sovereignty. We shall look further into the similarities and differences between intervention and war later; here it is sufficient to note that this important experiment does not count against the general limitations we would urge on interventions.

Internal-External Tensions

The second general feature of intervention we noted is that it involves the entry of some person or group or force from outside. In international cases, this person or group or force lacks a pre-established right to be where it is and to do what it does; it needs justification and authorization if its actions are to be legally and morally acceptable. Where military force is used, the need for moral justification is particularly important. The fact that intervention is done by outsiders opens it to the charge of being improper interference not only with the sovereignty of a state but also with the self-determination of a community. This point carries particular weight in an age that repudiates imperialism.

It might seem that the external character of the intervenor improves the likelihood that a dispute will be resolved in an impartial and just way. The effort to avoid plausible charges of partisanship does sometimes influence choices about which states are asked to participate in interventions and which states are excluded. But the stance of impartiality is difficult to maintain when one side (most likely the locally dominant group) resists the intervention, or when one side benefits by receiving significant protection that would not otherwise have been available to it.

There are, of course, three interlocked issues here: first, whether the intervening force does carry on its authorized activities in an impartial way; second, whether policy that includes these activities will be impartial in its impact on the contending parties; and third, whether local contestants *believe* the intervening parties are acting in an impartial way. In many situations, however, the intervenor will have no effective concern for impartiality; it will already have made serious commitments to one or more of the contending parties. Participants will then understand the intervention as an entering in on one side of a local conflict by powers that were originally external to the conflict but now have their own reasons for getting involved.

Intervention can in fact be conceived in two quite different ways: first, as a coming between two adversaries, which is closer to the Latin *intervenire*, to come between; second, as a joining in on one side, where the intervenor does not attempt to come between the adversaries. Despite the desirability of impartiality, it would be a mistake to conclude that the first type of intervention is always morally superior to the second. Vietnam was justified in conceiving the task of its intervention in Cambodia as removing the Pol Pot regime; to see its task merely as standing between that regime and its victims and opponents would not have been right. But if the intervenors believe that a contending group may have a continuing claim to function either as a sovereign state or as the representatives of an enduring minority group, then the intervenors should want to keep at least some elements of an impartial stance in the way they treat that party, even if its leader or members have behaved very badly in the course of the local conflict. This, it seems to me, is a relevant consideration for the form and spirit of NATO intervention in the Bosnian conflict.

The external character of the intervenors points in two directions. In the first place, it raises questions about what their motives actually are, whether their motives match their public professions. These are inescapable questions in an age of ideological suspicion and political realism. But it also raises questions about whether the issues and interests at stake for the intervening parties will sustain the weight of their commitment and will enable them to bear the burdens and costs of the intervention. These questions are particularly salient in the current American debates over interventions in areas where the primary interests and security needs of the United States do not obviously require the involvement of U.S. military forces.

Intervention During the Cold War

The Cold War provided a rationale for massive extensions of the area of U.S. strategic interest, well beyond the Caribbean and Western Europe and portions of the Western Pacific, which had all been established as areas of special U.S. concern before 1941. Areas that were close to vulnerable allies, and areas caught up in national liberation struggles in which the contending parties both looked for external support, came to be included within the scope of U.S. concern. The entire world came to be seen as providing opportunities for Communist or Soviet penetration, and in the international agon that was the Cold War it was comparatively easy to conceive the whole encounter of ideologies, military alliances, and economic systems as a global zero-sum game. What they win, we lose. The reality of international political life was always more complex than this simple but comprehensive model allowed, not least because the alliance systems themselves were not monolithic and because the Sino-Soviet split made it impossible to identify Communism solely with the policy of the Soviet Union.

But, given Americans' deep apprehension about the Soviet threat and about the prospects for Marxist takeovers in vast stretches of the Third World, it was nearly always possible, at least until the midpoint of the Vietnam War, to put together a politically persuasive argument in favor of intervention—sometimes overt, sometimes covert—on the side of those threatened by Marxist forces. Even after the quagmire in Vietnam, the Reagan administration was able to draw on considerable support for an actively anti-Marxist agenda in Central America, which is, admittedly, an area of special concern even for those historically inclined to construe U.S. security interests in rather narrow terms. Both Americans (elites and public opinion) and local contending parties tended to link these local struggles with the Marxist and anti-Marxist formulations of the grand historical drama centered on the technologically advanced and expansive society of the West. These interpretations provided a ready base, both political and intellectual, for moral arguments according to which intervention in a local conflict was required precisely because of that conflict's relation to the global conflict. The result was a strong interventionist bias among those who regarded the struggle against Marxism for the preservation of free societies as the moral substance of American foreign policy.

Now the Marxist adversary—or at least the one Marxist adversary with the capacity and the inclination to engage in a global struggle threatening capitalism from the shores of Florida to the Fulda Gap and from the Nile delta to the Mekong valley—has disappeared from the stage of world politics. Therefore, the links between local conflicts and the security interests of the United States, now understood not as the leader of a global coalition but as a particular country, are much harder to establish and do not support a comprehensive interventionist program. A link might be developed, for instance, in a way that would support the Clinton administration's deployment of U.S. forces in Haiti on the grounds that uncontrolled flows of refugees will have immediate negative effects on south Florida; but such a line of argument, if we look at it from the side of the objective that is proposed, actually makes the case for an effective government rather than a humane one, that is, for a government that may or may not respect human rights but is in effective control of the movements of its population.

Given the absence of the global framework of Cold War policymaking, it is likely that nothing more than specific ad hoc arguments for and against intervention can be developed. These arguments will be vulnerable to shifts in public attention. People are much more likely to announce that they have heard enough about Bosnia and don't want to discuss it any longer than they were to say this about Berlin or Cuba, where the Soviet Union and the United States were seen to be in serious confrontation.

A Rationale for Intervention

Correlative to the affirmation that the intervening parties are external to the local conflict is the affirmation that the conflict is external to them. Their participation is optional. The local conflict is not their conflict. So there is a need to consider what reasons might persuade them to become participants rather than disapproving bystanders or opportunists looking to gain from the misfortunes of others.

Let us speak directly of Americans, since in the world of today it is they who will have to carry most of the risks and costs of intervening. These factors that might persuade them to intervene seem to me to be of two sorts. First are the arguments that a particular local conflict, because of factors specific to it (such as its location, the possession and likely use of nuclear or chemical weapons by one or more of the parties, serious impact on the interests or even the survival of a major U.S. ally), is likely to cause significant damage to U.S. security. Given the comparative isolation of the United States and its distance from states that may currently want to threaten it (Libya, Iraq, North Korea, Iran), arguments of this kind are unlikely to sustain a comprehensive interventionist program or one that will meet the humanitarian needs of populations menaced by the collapse of unstable states, though they may be used to justify limited strikes against rogue states.

Second are the more general arguments that the United States (as well as other powers that share its regard for the values of liberal, democratic capitalism and its opposition to racism, aggressive nationalism, and totalitarianism) should intervene in response to human-rights violations when these are sufficiently grave. These arguments have a strong initial appeal to those who are committed to the legal structures and the moral ideals associated with the establishment of the United Nations, as well as to those who responded so hopefully to the human-rights initiatives of the Carter administration. They suffer from two difficulties.

In the first place, such arguments are usually vague about why the United States should respond to violations of human rights in country X, with which the United States may have no history of significant interaction. They usually dwell on the horrendous conditions within the country that is being torn apart by the local conflict, without specifying why the United States can be said to have special obligations toward this country. If successful, these arguments establish a general obligation for human beings and their governments to come to the aid of the victims of grave human-rights violations. The incompleteness of the arguments does not establish, of course, that the United States does *not* have an obligation to rescue or protect such victims, any more than noting the fact that others tell lies would free me from an obligation to tell the truth.

The second difficulty with these arguments is that, if successful and if taken in isolation, they prove too much. In early 1996, for instance, they could have established a U.S. obligation to intervene to correct abuses in North Korea, Myanmar, Indonesia, Iran, Iraq, Afghanistan, Syria, Saudi Arabia, Sudan, Somalia, Zaire, Kenya, Nigeria, Liberia, Peru, Colombia, Mexico, Guatemala, Turkey, Georgia, Russia, and China. In all these places there was either ongoing bloodshed or repression according to entrenched patterns that the current regime showed little or no willingness to alter. This, of course, leaves aside the many countries where human-rights abuses occur from time to time, where they are rooted in certain aspects of the local culture, and where they are often concealed by the police and the authorities. Even the most zealous advocates of human-rights interventionism have rarely looked at the consequences of universalizing a prescription to intervene to correct such abuses (though they customarily bring forward universalist considerations in urging people to take action in support of their favored causes, such as South Africa, Chile under Pinochet, and China).

Even the most energetic Wilsonian and the most buoyant Carterite would find excessive the prospect of intervening to set all these wrongs right. And it is perhaps true that only the pedantic and the pettifogging (i.e., philosophers and lawyers) would worry about such a demand for comprehensive moral integrity and compassion. Nearly everyone recognizes, with either relief or regret, that such a program of universal interventionism would both damage many other necessary concerns and exceed the capabilities of the United States and any partners whom it might attract to aspects of such a program. In the days of the Cold War, it was comparatively easy to restrain such purist proposals by reminding people of the stakes in the struggle with the Soviet Union and of the likelihood that if Soviets were to prevail either regionally or globally, the net outcome for human rights would be seriously negative. At the present time, we lack a persuasive or generally agreed on set of considerations to replace the constraints on universal interventionism that flowed from the strategic facts of the Cold War.

From a moral standpoint, it is clearly not enough to point to the current unwillingness of the American public or the American military to undertake such missions, or to the dangers of unpopularity and failure for political and military leaders. Such considerations are obviously important in the conduct of political life and in the process of national-security decision-making. They do not, however, enable us to answer the inevitable questions about whether the great American public or the current interpreters of its will may not be wrong, may not be in reality victims of self-deception, sloth, cowardice, and selfishness. We badly need a set of principles to guide us as we decide when and where to intervene, at a time when it is compellingly clear that we cannot intervene in every situation where the need for rescue and the innocence of the victims are poignantly manifest and broadcast.

More Than a Principle of Rescue

There is no plausible way of connecting principles to cases so that U.S. and multilateral assistance would be provided for all and only those countries with the most massive violations of human rights, or with the highest number of people in jeopardy should law and order break down, or should a tyrannical or genocidal government come to power. Rather, we have to recognize several things: that the resources (political, military, economic, and intellectual) we can bring to correcting internal problems in other states are limited; that the situations in which we may be asked to intervene present differing problems and opportunities; that not all the factors pointing to the legitimacy and necessity of intervention will be matched by factors establishing its feasibility and the likelihood of a beneficial outcome; and that the negative impact of intervention on other important concerns of U.S. foreign policy that have considerable moral weight (e.g., nuclear non-proliferation, alliance relationships, stable financial and trade relationships) may be quite serious.

The result is that we cannot elaborate an intervention policy for the United States simply by taking catastrophic situations on a case-by-case basis and asking whether it is possible to remedy them. An account of the morality of humanitarian intervention requires far more than simply applying a principle of rescue to differing situations or even balancing a principle of rescue with a principle affirming the value of sovereignty. That moral account has to include the major elements of policy-making on the global scale and the U.S. position as the sole surviving superpower in a world in which power and possibilities of violent action are distributed in new and often disturbing ways.

A slightly different way of making substantially the same point is to say that what the United States does by way of humanitarian intervention sends an important message about the weight we accord to different values and about the character of our leadership. This is not simply a message about whether we are "caring" (interventionist) or "selfish and uncaring" (non-interventionist). Think about what message we would have sent by intervening in Chechnya or even by being supportively involved with the secessionist movement there. This was not a live policy option, and so people generally did not express opinions about it. But it is clear that such a policy would have seemed to show that the United States was careless about angering a power that still had nuclear weapons and considerable (though disorganized and locally ineffective) military power. It would have shown a disregard for long-range consequences as well as for immediate dangers; it would have been imprudent in the highest degree. To say this is not to suggest that what the Russian government and military did in repressing the rebellion was not itself short-sighted and grievously wrong, involving massive violations of human rights and an attack of near genocidal proportions.

The duty to rescue by means of forceful humanitarian intervention clearly cannot be treated as absolute, however horrifying the scenes of destruction portrayed by the media and however base the cause invoked to justify the atrocities. At the same time, to turn humanitarian intervention into a right that governments may exercise or not, depending on their policy orientation and the preferences of the electorate, seems to minimize the gravity of the problem presented by genocide and by states that collapse into savage anarchy. There can, of course, be no duty for other states to do things that, in the judgment of prudent and experienced persons, will do nothing to ameliorate these catastrophic situations and may in fact make them worse. But as we look at such situations, it seems only right that we should feel the desire to help and that governments should find ways to make such desires effective.

Governments should also be ready to educate the public on the complex factors that will, in many cases, make intervention ineffective. An interventionist policy driven by an altogether appropriate public indignation and sympathy needs the information and the prudence that regional expertise, cross-cultural understanding, careful intelligence work, and patient diplomacy in their different ways can provide. An interventionist policy that does not include the hard intellectual work necessary to understand the local and regional context of the problems it is attempting to confront is not worthy of respect. An interventionist policy that does not also recognize the inevitable risks, costs, burdens, and sufferings of intervention and is not willing to carry them when necessary is an essentially adolescent response to a world whose intractability will defeat even the most fervent moral dreams. We need not approach these difficulties in the grandiose and romantic spirit of President John F. Kennedy's inaugural; but those who would intervene need an appropriate combination of courage, generosity of spirit, and sober realism.

TOWARD A MORALITY OF INTERVENTION

What I have said so far has had to do largely with the subjective disposition of those who would, in reaction to the horrors of the outer world, use force to aid the victims of war, tyranny, and racism. But the harder questions arise about the conditions in that outer world that create a *duty* to intervene for humanitarian ends. To what factors should we pay particular attention as we attempt to develop what might be called the casuistry of intervention? I can do no more than make a few suggestions. I offer these as one who is strongly committed to the norms of the just war tradition governing the use of force and who is interested in developing that tradition in response to the dilemmas of contemporary warfare and diplomacy.

First, timing is crucially important. This applies both to humanitarian intervention itself and to threats of intervention. It is quite plausible to think that the war in Bosnia might have been prevented or considerably reduced in scale had the Western powers been able to agree on a concerted policy against Serb expansionism at an early point in the dissolution of Yugoslavia, and had they been willing to make clear their readiness to use force against those who would attempt to settle boundaries by force in defiance of the Helsinki agreement. It is also plausible to think that once the war began, the costs of intervention, especially casualties taken by the intervening forces, would have been prohibitively high, and that intervention became a plausible option only after the Bosnian Serbs had lost control of the Krajina and western Bosnia and after the participants in the conflict had reached an equilibrium of exhaustion. The question of timing is even more important when the catastrophe to be prevented is the work not of organized armies or even of guerrilla formations but of local militants who are intermingled with the victim population. As the case of Rwanda illustrates, once the bloodshed begins, since it is effectively localized and not dependent on sophisticated technologies that can be seized or shut down, to separate murderers and victims in a timely fashion will not be possible.

If these points are correct, at least generally if not in all particulars, then it will be necessary to rethink the standard way of interpreting the requirement in just war theorizing that the use of force be a last resort, after all other measures have been tried and found wanting. There has always been some indeterminacy about how to ascertain this, both because of the open-ended character of the notion of alternatives and because of the contrary-to-fact hypotheticals that have to be established to show that force or war is indeed the last resort. In some cases, principally those involving overt aggression by one state against another, it is not hard to show that the alternatives to force are no longer relevant. But as the cases of Bosnia and Rwanda indicate, large numbers of lives may already have been lost. States can collapse quickly, and the fault lines of civil war can rapidly tear apart the order imposed by previous imperial or federal regimes. Therefore a serious case can be made for encouraging a forward stance on the possibility of humanitarian intervention. Obviously, such a stance will not mean much unless it is taken as credible by the various players in the crisis; and that means there must be a genuine willingness to use force on the part of those who would intervene.

Second, great care must be taken to observe *the norm of proportionality*. The prime moral rationale for overriding considerations of sovereignty and for undertaking the burdens of intervention is to protect the lives and basic rights of the innocent. Intervention scenarios, both at the planning stage and during implementation, have to aim at minimizing the loss of noncombatant life.

Third, the other major focus in humanitarian intervention is *the preservation of a politically significant community* of persons. This community may be the object of prejudice and hatred; it may be a party in a contest for power or in a civil war; it may be defined in ethnic or religious or ideological terms. Its adversaries may attempt to eradicate it (the Holocaust), to remove it from the territories that they control (ethnic cleansing), to terrorize it into submission by indiscriminate slaughter (Rwanda), to deprive it of access to the basic infrastructure and commodities necessary to sustain the life of the community (Sudan, perhaps Somalia). Humanitarian catastrophes generally occur when there is either a collapse of or a violent challenge to the established political authority.

The issues of a civil war or of a war of secession are political issues. Humanitarian intervention is unlikely to be able to establish a lasting settlement unless the lines of the settlement reflect the balance of political and military forces. It should not be assumed that the secessionists or rebels are always morally justified; in some cases they will merely have had less opportunity to display their own variety of violent disregard for human dignity. But there may come a point in the conflict between parties, ethnic groups, or religious groups in which one or more of the parties decides that, in order to protect its own continuity, its survival, its hold on power, its communal values, it is ready to extirpate another community. It then goes beyond killing warriors, assassinating leaders, and seizing territory to attacking unarmed prisoners, civilians, women, children, and cultural and religious monuments. It determines that "they" must never be allowed to "pollute" or threaten or rule over its people and their descendants. The essential elements of this process were masterfully laid out by Thucydides in his account in Book I of the revolution on Corcyra at the beginning of the Peloponnesian War.

Similarly, patterns of human-rights violations should not be treated as justifying humanitarian intervention in themselves. This holds true even when the violations are entrenched and pervasive, as they have invariably been in totalitarian regimes and as they customarily are in racist regimes, such as the apartheid regime in South Africa. The reason for not considering intervention is not that what these regimes do is all right but that much greater harm would come from attempting to remove these abuses by an external use of force. What is being proposed as a morally concerned form of humanitarian intervention turns out to be a thinly disguised form of war aimed at altering the behavior of a sovereign state that is in control of its territory and of the apparatus of order within it. Forcible rectification of human-rights abuses in such circumstances is very likely to violate the principle of proportionality and to produce death and suffering beyond what repressive regimes normally inflict.

But when a repressive regime turns genocidal against a politically significant community, then there is in my mind a good cause for humanitarian intervention. If the genocidal state is very powerful, we are confronted with the prospect of a major war. It is uncertain whether the Allies would have undertaken such a war to rescue the Jewish people and the other communities targeted by Nazi Germany; when the Nazis moved from anti-Semitic persecution and discrimination to the actual implementation of the Final Solution, Britain and

Russia were already at war with them. The issue was veiled from full public awareness. But if we set aside concerns about the reliability of reports about what was going on in concentration camps and on the Eastern Front, there can, I think, be little doubt that humanitarian intervention would have been morally justified, even though the distinction between it and war would have been a legal and moral nicety. I suggest that coming to this resolution on the question of possible responses to the Holocaust should be one test for an adequate casuistry of these matters.

Humanitarian intervention should be seen, then, primarily as an effort to protect politically endangered communities from extirpation. It differs from humanitarian action to rescue people and communities from natural disasters and from the police activity of governments that endeavor to assure the security of their citizens and visitors in the circumstances of ordinary life. Because these endangered communities are embedded within sovereign states, humanitarian intervention involves an overriding of the claims of sovereignty. It attempts to interpose the moral authority of one or more states and of military forces supplied by them in an effort to establish basic standards of civility and humanity, standards that are at risk when groups struggle with one another for power and when some of these groups are the objects of systemic hatred and suspicion.

Humanitarian intervention should be conducted in a way that affirms the values central to the just war tradition of thinking about the exercise of force. Still, some modification of specific norms of the tradition does seem to be called for.

6

Complex Humanitarian Emergencies and Moral Choice

Andrew Natsios

Perhaps the most distasteful of the many moral choices forced upon policy-makers during the fifty years of the Cold War was whether to embrace and sustain pro-Western, anti-Communist regimes that were at the same time squalid, corrupt, and abusive towards their own people. The customary justification for this support was that the greater end of restraining Soviet expansionism required it. And indeed, the expansion of the Soviet system in itself, even apart from any *realpolitik* calculation, should have offended the moral sensibility of anyone familiar with the systematic atrocities committed by Communist regimes against their own people for much of this century.

In the early days of the post–Cold War era, some policy-makers no doubt dreamed that such morally ambiguous choices would no longer present themselves. Unfortunately, if anything the post–Cold War

Andrew Natsios is vice president of World Vision U.S. He served with the U.S. Agency for International Development (AID) from 1989 to 1993, first as director of Foreign Disaster Assistance and then as assistant administrator for the Bureau of Food and Humanitarian Assistance. The views expressed here are his own and not necessarily those of World Vision.

world has given rise to more moral ambiguity, not less. Policy-makers have been confronted with a set of troubling ethical issues brought on by a rising tide of ethnic and tribal conflict and the consequent failure of states. What I shall try to do in this essay is to define "complex humanitarian emergencies" (a term relief managers began using in 1990), analyze the institutional mechanisms for responding to them, and explore some of the ethical choices facing policy-makers as they deal with these grave problems.

The complex humanitarian emergency may be defined by five characteristics:

1. Ethnic, religious, or tribal conflict that includes widespread atrocities against the civilian population.

2. The failure or deterioration of government authority, including the wholesale destruction of infrastructure, breakdown of public order and public services, and decline in the influence of the central government in the life of the society. (At least three countries have had no national government for five or more years now: Liberia, Somalia, and Afghanistan. A half dozen more have a government in name only, where the central government exercises little or no influence outside the capital city.)

3. Macro-economic collapse, including hyper-inflation, depression-level unemployment, the failure of markets, and double-digit declines in family income and in the gross national product.

4. Widespread food insecurity leading to high levels of severe malnutrition and starvation, sometimes accompanied by a public-health emergency with epidemics of communicable diseases, conditions that translate into high death rates.

5. Massive population movements of internally displaced people and refugees, where sometimes up to half or two-thirds of the population are driven from their homes for periods as long as four or five years.

These conditions cause a national crisis that is greater than the sum of its parts. They interact in insidious ways and do enormous damage to the fragile social and economic structure of developing countries. Complex humanitarian emergencies destroy the coping mechanisms people have developed over time for dealing with adversity, and thus are particularly deadly. Wars do not necessarily evolve into complex emergencies. For instance, the German defeat and occupation of France during World War II produced only a few of these conditions.

While life was oppressive and terrible atrocities certainly took place, a complex humanitarian emergency did not occur in France during the German occupation.

A study by the Office of Foreign Disaster Assistance in the Agency for International Development (USAID) found that the number of complex emergencies increased from an annual average of five during the period 1978-85 to fourteen in 1989. In 1996 there were twenty-three.[1]

Complex humanitarian emergencies present both humanitarian and political challenges to policy-makers. In those twenty-three complex emergencies in 1996, nearly 40 million people were at risk of death from violence, epidemics, or starvation. That situation should prick the conscience of moral philosophers and geostrategists alike. The American value system attaches great value to each individual human life; policy-makers simply cannot ignore the potential death of 40 million people.[2]

These emergencies also present immense political challenges to policy-makers. The chaos they cause is not contained by national boundaries. Whole regions have been destabilized by complex emergencies. Witness the effect of the Bosnian civil war on Kosovo, Macedonia, Serbia, and Croatia. The Sudanese civil war spilled over into Eritrea, Ethiopia, Kenya, and Uganda. Such situations are also expensive; in 1995, the U.S. government spent over a billion dollars to respond to the humanitarian needs created by these emergencies.[3] The long-term damage they cause to the infrastructure and economic productivity of a country is enormous. Perhaps most troubling for the policy-maker, they have quite unpredictable outcomes. In geopolitically sensitive regions of central importance to U.S. policy interests, this unpredictability is in itself a reason to pay closer attention to these emergencies and to engage in more rigorous analysis of them.

The more recent debates on these crises have tended to contrive a dichotomy between humanitarian/ethical and political/geostrategic considerations. Notwithstanding Michael Mandelbaum's clever description of foreign policy as social work,[4] this dichotomy reduces a set of complex issues to a simple formula that is of little analytical use in the debate over the design of U.S. policy. Humanitarian assistance has moral and political implications that are not easily separated from each other, just as geostrategic policy considerations have moral and humanitarian implications. Even the preeminent modern exponent of the *realpolitik* school of international relations, Henry Kissinger, admits that unjust international orders, however much they may maintain an equilibrium of power, are not ultimately sustainable.[5]

It is unlikely that the public in a democracy, particularly one with as rich and powerful a religious tradition as the United States, will allow its leaders to conduct foreign policy without reference to moral and ethical norms, however they may be defined. This applies not only to the *limitations* placed on policy-makers by ethical norms but also to the *expectations* of positive action to deal with a foreign crisis. If a major famine were to occur in a region that is of little political, economic, or military significance to the United States, the American people would nevertheless expect their government to provide assistance. However much some policy analysts may wish to dismiss complex humanitarian emergencies as the business of social work, they cannot do so.

The U.N., the U.S., and Other Actors

In the first few years after the end of the Cold War, the advocates of a strong United Nations believed that this was finally to be that institution's hour. The paralyzing rivalries of the Cold War were past, and a new robust multilateralism was to be the order of the day. But in most of the complex humanitarian emergencies of the 1990s, U.N. enthusiasts have been sadly disappointed by the institution's incapacity. Its sporadic moments of glory have a common characteristic: all were led, even if behind the scenes, by the great powers—specifically, by the United States.

The U.N.'s incapacity should not have been surprising. To begin with, the great powers have not wanted a strong U.N., believing that it would constrain their conduct of foreign policy. Developing countries also, while wanting access to the resources of U.N. agencies, saw the world body as a potential threat to their sovereignty and a thinly disguised agent for advancing great-power interests. Few member states have sought to create within the U.N. the robust institutions needed to carry out policy, or the personnel system needed to staff such institutions. For example, nothing like either the American foreign service or military personnel system exists in any part of the U.N. It was after all these two systems, despite their imperfections, that recruited, trained, promoted, and rewarded the men and women who led America to victory in the Cold War. The notion that the U.N. secretary general and a few undersecretaries can change the institution without profound changes in the personnel system is greatly mistaken. The overarching problem with the U.N. is that the political constraints under which it operates prevent any serious effort at reform.

In the near or medium term, the U.N. is unlikely to achieve the institutional energy or capacity needed to lead international responses to complex emergencies. This would be true even if sustained support for a major reform effort miraculously appeared from the great powers and others. Reforms can certainly improve matters, but improvement will never be enough. By nature, the more complex and culturally diverse the interests represented in any institution, the more ponderous its decision-making process and the less effective its structure. The U.N. is unlikely to achieve the financial independence it needs to do its work. It does not have its own sources of revenue; it is not a state with the power to tax. The discussions about creating an on-call force for U.N. military interventions beg the logistical question—especially the matter of personnel airlift—that drives any combat operation. Where will the U.N. get this capacity, one that is as important as the troops themselves?

The U.N. agencies and the divisions of the U.N. Secretariat are notoriously resistant to central direction or unified strategy. The secretary general does not have the institutional authority to impose discipline on what is essentially a feudal authority structure.

This does not mean that the United Nations is irrelevant in complex emergencies. Some of its agencies provide important services in such situations, and the Security Council has been an important forum for creating the international consensus needed for intervention. But in the end we must conclude that in its structure, personnel systems, revenue sources, and military capability, the U.N. falls far short of what it needs to do its job.

Alternatives to U.N. Leadership

If the U.N. is not up to the task, then who or what is? The European countries (and their institutional manifestation in the European Union) and Japan do have the financial resources, competent public-sector bureaucracies, and (in the case of the Europeans) the military force to provide this leadership. What they lack is political will and unity of effort. Leadership of the effort to deal with the crisis in Bosnia was left to the Europeans, with distressing results. Not until the United States assumed responsibility in late 1995 did the crisis have any chance of being resolved.

The European Union (EU) may someday evolve into an institution capable of providing this leadership. But so far the European governments have continued to keep their diplomatic resources (held in their national capitals), military resources (in NATO), and financial resources (in the European Union) separate from one another. The EU does have greater financial resources available to it than the United States, particularly as the isolationist impulse manifests itself in Washington. NATO made a limited demonstration of its military capacity in Bosnia, but only a limited one. Its fifty years of preparation for war have never truly been tested on the battlefield.

That leaves the United States as the only serious contender for the role of providing the leadership needed to respond to complex humanitarian emergencies. The United States has several resources all the other actors lack: (1) a policy coordination process that can bring together diplomatic, military, and humanitarian resources with a focused strategy and an institutionally strong chief executive; (2) vast political and diplomatic clout; and (3) powerful military-airlift and other logistical capacities. This does not mean that the United States should police the world for any sign of suffering or abuse. Neither the world nor the American public would stand for that. It does mean that the United States must provide the bulk of the officer cadre to lead humanitarian interventions, while other countries contribute more in the way of troops and money. Leadership—institutional, political, diplomatic, and strategic—is what is most needed, and only the U.S. government can fill that void.

This is not to say that such a role is necessarily *desirable*. Why should the United States care enough to assume this daunting task?

I think an answer can be given on political as well as humanitarian grounds. Part of America's influence in the world derives from the moral force implicit in its leadership. We are perceived by other countries to act in ways that strike out beyond what a narrowly construed national self-interest demands. The sum of our foreign policy is greater than its geopolitical parts. This moral resolution was an important part of our ability during the Cold War to create the West-ern alliance and during the Gulf War to bring together the coalition forces to free Kuwait. It is a not insubstantial part of how we as a nation are able to influence world affairs. To stand by and watch mass starvation while arguing that it is someone else's duty to deal with it would damage our standing in the world geopolitically.

Beyond Wilsonian Idealism

What form should this moral dimension of foreign policy properly take? First, the United States should avoid trying to right all wrongs, settle all disputes, end all injustice, and otherwise engage in a crusade to make the world safe for democracy and righteousness. American political leaders have spent much time in the past three decades rescuing foreign policy from the mischief and naïveté of Wilsonian idealism. Those who led that rescue effort were not unsupportive of the moral dimension of U.S. policy and our duty to deal with crises that may be outside our geostrategic interests. In my opinion, Richard Nixon, Henry Kissinger, Ronald Reagan, and George Bush advanced the humanitarian agenda much further than either the Carter or the Clinton administrations: witness Nixon's intervention in the Biafran civil war, Reagan's efforts to expose the atrocities in Uganda and Mozambique, and Bush's interventions in Somalia, northern Iraq, and a half dozen civil wars in Africa.

In place of both Wilsonian idealism and *realpolitik*, the United States should consider a vigorous leadership role informed by several principles:

1. The United States should use its diplomatic influence, military-airlift and other logistical ability, and humanitarian-assistance programs to organize the international community—sometimes through the U.N., sometimes outside it—to prevent widespread atrocities (e.g., Bosnia), genocide (e.g., Rwanda), or famine (e.g., Somalia). I hasten to add that this would continue a long tradition of American leader-ship in humanitarian work, adapting it to the particular challenges of today's world. As in the past, other countries would be called on to join the effort, but the United States would assume the role of leader.

2. The United States should not support egregious violators of human rights or governments that deliberately starve their own

people. A distinction should be made between levels of human-rights abuses. As Jeane Kirkpatrick pointed out, a qualitative distinction exists between totalitarian and authoritarian regimes.[6] Violating a person's right to a fair trial and committing genocide are both human-rights abuses, but they are of a profoundly different character. The United States cannot guarantee the former outside its own borders; the latter it can, as a matter of policy, actively oppose.

3. While the United States cannot solve all the world's problems, through its leadership, application of resources, and moral authority it can make the world a little more civilized and decent, so that the genocides, famines, and ethnic-cleansing campaigns of this century are not repeated in the next.

The proposition that the United States ought to support—or in some cases lead—efforts to stop famine, genocide, and mass atrocities is supported by recent history. In Rwanda, between half a million and a million Tutsis along with some Hutu moderates were massacred in four months during 1996; the Hutu military and militias methodically hunted them down and killed them in what was one of the most terrible acts of savagery in this century. There was a U.N. peacekeeping force of several thousand troops already posted to the country. Under the provisions of Chapter 7 of the U.N. Charter ("Action With Respect to Threats to the Peace, Breaches of the Peace, and Acts of Aggression"), the U.N. could have intervened aggressively to stop the genocide and protect noncombatants, had the Security Council authorized it. Instead, the United States and other countries voted on April 21, 1994, to *withdraw* the force instead of expanding its mandate. The U.S. defense was that the situation did not meet the conditions of the Presidential Review Directive recently signed by President Clinton to guide U.S. policy on U.N. peacekeeping operations.

Here was a case in which no U.S. ground troops were needed. Later, Senegal and France, followed by several other African countries, offered to send their troops to Rwanda to create a safe zone and asked the United States to provide armored personnel carriers, trucks, and logistical support to airlift their troops to the area. The United States agreed, then proceeded to drag its feet so that it was four months before any of the equipment and support arrived—too late to stop the genocide. If the human-rights policy of the U.S. government does not include stopping genocide, it is hollow indeed. It will be generations before Rwanda recovers from the devastation.

ETHICAL DILEMMAS OF COMPLEX EMERGENCIES

Two sorts of ethical constraints are involved in deciding how to respond to complex humanitarian emergencies: we must avoid doing wrong, and we must do positive good. We can make geostrategic decisions fully constrained by a set of moral norms that render certain calculations unacceptable—that is, we can avoid doing wrong—without necessarily doing any positive good. U.S. decision-makers can, without doing wrong, operate within a general policy framework in which the United States pursues its own self-interest, narrowly defined by the promotion of commerce, the protection of American citizens abroad, balance-of-power calculations, and the response to security threats abroad. There is nothing inherently wrong with a nation's pursuit of its own narrowly defined interests.

But U.S. foreign policy ought to do more. We should deliberately design policy to do good. Humanitarian assistance and military and diplomatic intervention in complex emergencies that are of little or no geostrategic interest to the United States are attempts to do good. These interventions have had mixed results. Some, such as the interventions in Mozambique and northern Iraq, have been successful. Somalia was a success if judged by the more limited objectives of the original intervention in December 1992, which were to end the famine, reduce death rates, and restore a marginal level of self-sufficiency to Somali society. Bosnia may also be a success, though that remains to be seen. Others have not been so successful. In Rwanda, Burundi, Liberia, Sudan, and Afghanistan, robust humanitarian-relief interventions were not matched by military or diplomatic efforts at resolution.

These complex emergencies provide a rich set of examples of ethical dilemmas facing emergency managers and policy-makers. Such dilemmas seem to be occurring with increasing frequency. What follows will be an attempt, not to produce a comprehensive framework for decision-making, but to deal with *some* ethical questions.

1. Should the U.S. government provide life-saving humanitarian assistance or long-term developmental assistance to countries with brutal governments when that assistance may prolong the governments' existence? Is it ethically permissible to allow the death of innocent people as a necessary step toward a justifiable political end?

Food has long been a weapon of war. It is used to buy the support of neutral groups and pay soldiers for their loyalty, and it is withheld to kill off adversaries. President Reagan theoretically settled the policy debate during the Ethiopian famine when he erected a wall between humanitarian assistance and geopolitical calculations. In what should have become known as the Reagan Doctrine, he argued that a hungry child knows no politics. The Ethiopian government at the time was a Marxist dictatorship, perhaps the most brutal and barbaric in Africa. Its leader, Mengistu Haile Mariam, was for good reason called the Stalin of Africa. Mengistu executed tens of thousands, refused to acknowledge a famine in 1984 that led to the death of a million people, sent tens and perhaps hundreds of thousands of teenage boys to their deaths in a civil war in which he refused to negotiate seriously with the rebels until he was near defeat, and forcibly resettled millions of unwilling highland people to lowlands where hundreds of thousands died of disease and hunger even apart from the drought-induced famine. His continuation in office was a clear and present danger to the Ethiopian people—indeed to the existence of the country itself.

Famines are politically destabilizing wherever they occur, and the 1984-85 famine could have toppled Mengistu from office just as the 1973-74 famine under Emperor Haile Selassie was one cause of his overthrow. Unfortunately, famine did not bring down Mengistu. Several attempts to overthrow him did take place, but he remained in power until the victory of the rebel forces in the spring of 1991 forced him to flee the country and seek asylum in Zimbabwe, where he remains. (What repeatedly saved him was the East German–designed system of dual, independent secret-police organizations that ensured that everyone was always under surveillance, even the police themselves.)

A more recent example of this ethical dilemma is the food crisis in North Korea. Three factors have led to the crisis: (1) the lack of agricultural land in a largely mountainous country; (2) the agricultural policies of the central government over the past fifty years, including forced collectivization of agriculture, the over-use of chemical fertilizers and over-cultivation of marginal land, the absence of investment in agricultural research, and the absence of a market economy and its incentives for production; and (3) two natural disasters in 1995— severe hail storms and massive flooding—that destroyed crops and croplands, and a severe drought in 1997. A full-scale famine struck North Korea in 1997; estimates are that as many as 120,000 people died of starvation in 1996, in the early phase of the famine.

The Clinton administration, in some confusing policy acrobatics, seems to have suggested at various points that U.S. food aid be conditional on North Korean acceptance of four-power talks among the United States, China, North Korea, and South Korea—talks that President Clinton had proposed. Though their position has never been entirely clear, it does appear that the Clinton administration is attempting to rescind the Reagan doctrine on famine. For its part, Congress has not encouraged the Administration to transcend political considerations. Four members of the House who typically support robust U.S. foreign-assistance programs (Congressmen Gilman, Beureter, Hamilton, and Roberts) have insisted that four conditions be met in order for North Korea to receive food assistance. The humanitarian pledge of support that the United States made to the U.N.'s World Food Program for North Korea could only be characterized as token until July 1997, where it finally relented after a good deal of public and media pressure and pledged a significant amount of food.

In the case of Ethiopia, the failure to send food early in the famine resulted in the death of perhaps a million people. It is apparent that any instability caused by the Ethiopian famine would have resulted in some but not serious disturbance to American geopolitical interests. Perhaps the only consequence to U.S. interests would have been the destabilization of the Sudanese government owing to the massive movement of refugees from Ethiopia into Sudan, at the time a faithful U.S. ally in the region. It is unclear whether the Mengistu regime would have been overthrown because of pressure caused by the famine had the rebel forces not succeeded; I think it unlikely.

In the case of North Korea, the geopolitical interests of the United States are clearly involved. That country's capacity to produce weapons of mass destruction, its threatening posture toward South Korea, its border with and ties to China, the size of its armed forces (the third largest in Asia), and its ties to other rogue states make North Korea of great geostrategic interest. Famine there will have unpredictable results. It is unlikely to lead to the collapse of the government. However, people facing famine move to where they think food is available, and there has been an increase in population movements into China. There might also be some movement into South Korea. A hungry country, particularly when armed with such a large military force, can be a destabilizing force. Add to this North Korea's distorted view of the world and its exaggerated sense of the threat from the outside and the result is a dangerously unsettling situation.

In such cases, one of the principal arguments against aid used by skeptics is that the military will divert the food for its own use. But when starvation actually takes place, the military always has the resources to ensure its own survival. I know of no instance where there has been widespread starvation among the military in a dictatorship (absent combat conditions where supply lines have been disrupted). In a command-and-control economy, the military typically gets access to the cream of the crop at harvest time. The North Korean military maintains stocks of food for its one-million-man army that are separate from civilian supplies.

While serving as the senior humanitarian relief officer in USAID during the Bush administration I struggled with the dilemma of whether it is ethically permissible to stop food deliveries during a famine when massive diversions are taking place and the intended recipients are not getting the bulk of the food aid, or when the government is interfering with food delivery for political purposes. This happened in Somalia, Sudan, and Angola. In the case of Sudan, the U.S. government diverted an ocean freighter full of food during the 1991 drought when the Sudanese government confiscated all U.S. government grain stocks in the country after finally acknowledging that a major drought was under way. We believed that the Sudanese government would not have distributed that food on the basis of need. Within a week the Sudanese government released the U.S. government food stocks, and deliveries resumed. A similar thing happened in Angola in 1991, during the civil war. We had no diplomatic relations with Angola's government at the time and indeed were trying to defeat it on the battlefield by supporting the rebel movement known as UNITA. When the government violated an access agreement allowing us to feed both sides in the civil war, USAID diverted a shipment of food that was on its way to the government side. Within a week the government relented, and food deliveries resumed.

Was it ethically permissible to stop food shipments under these circumstances? While the offending governments did choose to act quickly to mend their ways, they could have refused to do so. In the cases of Sudan and Angola, we had a reasonable degree of assurance that the food being sent would not be delivered properly to those in need. Using food as a weapon in order to assure access to those who desperately need it seems to me to be ethically defensible.

In most countries famine kills, in predictable order, children under five, lactating mothers, and elderly people. These groups are the weakest and most vulnerable. If the famine is particularly severe, adult men and women will die, too, but usually last. More people die in rural areas than in urban areas where the elites live. The poor die first because they do not have family assets to sell in order to buy food on the markets, where food prices are grossly inflated (in a market economy). In summary, then, the most vulnerable, most politically insignificant die first. Those who die are not the ones responsible for their government's objectionable policies. What political purpose can be served by allowing them to die by denying them food assistance?

Even if the famine would result in the overthrow of these abusive governments, is it ethically permissible to allow innocent people to die in order to accomplish this morally desirable outcome? No. People's lives cannot be treated as a means to an end: they are ends in themselves. All human life has God-given value. Once it is lost, it is not recoverable after the political objective has been achieved. Moreover, while the expectation that a famine will cause the downfall of a government is supported by some historical evidence, that result is never assured.

2. Should the U.S. government provide long-term developmental assistance when that assistance may prolong the existence of a brutal and repressive government?

The difference between disaster relief and development assistance is more ambiguous in practice than the terms imply. If people are hungry enough they will eat the seeds for the next planting season. If seed is not distributed, people will require food aid again even if there is no drought, since there will be no harvest. Typically, then, during a famine, relief agencies will distribute seeds and tools to farmers to plant the next crop. Humanitarian agencies refer to this as developmental relief. Another example: humanitarian agencies reduce high child mortality rates in developing countries through a series of interventions integrated into what are called child survival projects. The purpose of these projects is to save lives, though no disaster or emergency of the usual kind exists.

From the perspective of ethical norms, the distinction to be made in the conduct of foreign policy between disaster relief interventions and developmental interventions ought to be this: interventions that save human lives, whether they are called relief or developmental, should be separated from those that raise the standard of living. These latter interventions may be ethically postponed as a matter of policy in order to avoid strengthening abusive or brutal governments.

3. Is it ethically defensible to impose economic sanctions on repressive or abusive regimes in order to pressure them to mend their ways—or in order to hasten their collapse—if a probable ancillary effect would be to increase child mortality rates or jeopardize the food supply for at-risk population groups?

Economic sanctions as an instrument of foreign policy are not new. The League of Nations imposed a limited form of them on Italy after Mussolini invaded Ethiopia in 1935, with little effect. Britain and France raced to see which of them could rescind the sanctions first, while Hitler ignored the sanctions and continued to ship coal to Italy. If anything, the ineffectiveness of the League's sanctions encouraged more aggression by Germany and Italy.[7] Since the end of the Cold War, economic sanctions have been imposed in three complex humanitarian emergencies; the sanctions were intended to express the outrage of the international community against human-rights abuses in Haiti, Iraq (here there were other offenses as well), and Bosnia (by Serbia). (The U.N. also imposed weak and ineffective sanctions on the Sudan government for its abuse of its own population in the ongoing civil war.) These regimes—with the partial exception of Serbia— were authoritarian and were immune to popular pressures. While in all three cases medicine and food were exempted from the sanctions, these exemptions only partially mitigated human suffering.

Alone, sanctions appear to be a blunt and ineffective instrument of policy, if their purpose is to change the behavior of the regime. They are blunt in that they cannot be directed at the regime itself; instead, they make life miserable for the poor and pauperize the middle class, who have little power and limited coping capacity for dealing with the decline in their living standards, while the elites who control the levers of political power are relatively immune to the consequences of sanctions. The elites can move themselves and their assets outside the country easily, and they frequently enrich themselves within the country through black-market trading made profitable by the shortages.

Moreover, sanctions are inconsistently enforced depending on the interest neighboring states have in complying with them. When combined with diplomatic and military interventions, sanctions can have some effect, but it is not decisive. They are frequently used as a symbolic measure, despite their ineffectiveness, to indicate international disgust with abusive regimes where the great powers do not wish to take more aggressive military or diplomatic measures. Perhaps most significantly, the same sanctions regime applied to different economic systems can have very different results. In the case of a poor country of animal-herders and subsistence farmers, with few urban poor and few imports or exports, sanctions may have only a limited effect on the poor. And in a country with many expatriates who send back a lot of money to their families, the effect of sanctions will be substantially diminished. But in Haiti, where 50,000 factory workers in urban areas had to be laid off after the final set of most aggressive sanctions were imposed, sanctions probably increased the child mortality rates and devastated the Haitian working class.

Both liberals and conservatives selectively endorse and oppose sanctions on ideological grounds. Conservatives opposed sanctions against South Africa while liberals insisted on them. Liberals, many of whom opposed the U.S.-led action to liberate Kuwait, now believe that the sanctions against Iraq are too onerous and should be lifted. It is instructive that few groups, liberal or conservative, have condemned the sanctions against Serbia on moral grounds, though some have questioned their credibility, given their ineffectiveness (because of violations by neighboring countries) and given the West's diplomatic and military paralysis until late 1995 in dealing with Serbian aggression. It is clear that the sanctions against Serbia have cut per capita income in half and increased the level of misery among the poor. But moral outrage over economic sanctions seems to be selectively applied, according to how onerous one finds the regime.

Economic sanctions can be defended on moral grounds if certain conditions are present. If the structure of the economy of the targeted country would inherently limit their effects on the poor (e.g., most of the poor are farmers; there are few urban poor dependent on the cash economy), or if food and medicine are exempt from sanctions and are fairly and widely distributed, or if family money from abroad is widely available to the at-risk population, then the sanctions could be justified. If a set of sanctions could be designed that did not appreciably increase food insecurity, damage life-saving health-care systems, or increase mortality rates, those sanctions would be morally defensible. The ethical test ought to be the effect on the at-risk population. The problem, of course, is that reality is far more muddled than these neat paradigms. Seldom is comprehensive information on the probable impact of sanctions available to policy-makers before the sanctions are imposed.

One other factor significantly complicates any moral judgment of sanctions as an instrument of foreign policy: the behavior of the regime. In the case of Iraq, for five years, until the summer of 1996, Saddam Hussein refused to use the provision of the U.N. sanctions regime that permits the sale of Iraqi oil by the U.N. in order to enable Iraq to (1) provide humanitarian assistance to its own people and (2) make war reparations to Kuwait. The Hussein regime objected to U.N. control of the funds and to the reparations provision; the regime cared little what the human cost of its policies might be for its own population.

4. Should the U.S. government allocate humanitarian relief assistance—which of course is not unlimited—to areas of geostrategic interest or solely on the basis of human need?

Larry Minear and Tom Weiss in their book *Mercy Under Fire* suggest distribution according to the principle of proportionality:

> The . . . principle is that humanitarian action should correspond to the degree of suffering, wherever it occurs. From a humanitarian standpoint, the idea that human life is equally precious everywhere in the world seems self-evident. In practice, however, the world's humanitarian system has great difficulty putting flesh on that proposition.[8]

While their point is well taken and should be the starting point for any analysis of the moral implications of policy decisions on allocation, the point cannot stand alone. Subordinate principles need to be considered as well:

■ Should the principle of proportionality—that "humanitarian action should correspond to the degree of suffering"—consider the absolute *number* of people at risk or the portion of the population at risk? That is, if the percentage of the population suffering is higher in one country than in another where the absolute number of people suffering is greater, how should the principle be applied?

■ It is not always useful to measure the intensity of response by budget levels, food-aid tonnages, and relief supplies distributed. Some societies have a greater indigenous coping capacity than others, which means they require less assistance. Certainly the capacity of the government is a critical factor: India is much more capable of dealing with a major famine than, say, Zaire.

■ The accessibility of the population at risk should be a critical factor. Some of the worst suffering in the world has been in remote areas of central Sudan in the Nuba Mountains, where the central government is conducting an ethnic-cleansing campaign of unspeakable ferocity and where tens of thousands of women and children have been sold into slavery.[9] The area is inaccessible to humanitarian relief agencies because of the Sudanese government's restrictions on travel, exceptionally poor transportation routes, and military maneuvers that make working there very dangerous. It would be futile to allocate resources to this area since they could not be distributed.

■ The diversion of relief supplies by military and militia units in civil wars has, on occasion, reached such a high level that the relief effort has done little to reduce human suffering and reduce mortality rates. In fact, diverted relief supplies have been used to purchase more weapons, a circumstance that must affect any moral judgments on where to direct such supplies. If the insecurity in a complex humanitarian emergency is so general and relief efforts so vulnerable, then humanitarian assistance may have the effect of exacerbating the conflict. This was the case in Somalia before the U.S. intervention in December 1991. Humanitarian assistance should not be committed in a complex humanitarian emergency if the bulk of the assistance cannot be expected to get to the people in need and if the level of violence would appreciably increase as a result of diversions.

In summary, then, the general principle would be: humanitarian assistance should be allocated on the basis of proportionality, tempered by the principles of (a) the coping capacity of the society itself, (b) accessibility of the at-risk population, and (c) security of the distribution of supplies.

One final caveat to the rule of proportionality: Humanitarian assistance is more effective, obviously, when it is combined with military and political interventions that deal comprehensively with the causes of the complex humanitarian emergency. Thus humanitarian intervention is more likely to be successful in Bosnia, with NATO troops present to enforce the political settlement the three parties agreed to in 1995, than in, say, the Great Lakes region of Africa, where there is no regional political settlement. Equal distribution of humanitarian assistance in these two places could mean the failure of the Bosnia peace accords from want of sufficient resources for reconstruction. A morally defensible argument can be made to invest greater resources in areas where there is greater hope for a permanent settlement. This does not mean that the Great Lakes region should be starved to feed Bosnia, only that application of the rule of proportionality should not be untempered by the political and military prospects for peace.

Concluding Observations

The post–Cold War world presents challenges to policy-makers of a very different sort than those the United States faced earlier in this century. While the response to complex humanitarian emergencies should not be the dominant concern of foreign policy, especially in regions of the world of little geostrategic importance to U.S. interests, policy-makers must focus some of their attention on these crises because of their destructiveness, their unpredictability, and the profound moral dilemmas they create. With over 40 million lives at risk from famine, disease, or violence, for policy-makers to neglect these complex emergencies is morally unacceptable. American foreign policy, while it should avoid Wilsonian visions of a new world, should not ignore the moral imperatives implicit in policy choices. Wilsonian idealism and Metternichian *realpolitik* are not the only choices as a framework for U.S. policy.

That policy should state as a principle that famine, genocide, and widespread atrocities cannot be used by states against their own citizens or by one ethnic or religious group against another, just as the precedents of the U.N. Charter and of international reaction to Iraq's invasion of Kuwait show that they are not to be used by one country against another. The United States as a matter of policy should take the lead in the international community to see to it that these horrible practices do not taint the human community in the next century. This is not to suggest that the United States should strike out against all injustices wherever they exist, only that the internationally accepted minimum common denominator of human decency should be raised enough to make these three evils—genocide, the political use of famine, and widespread atrocities—unacceptable in the future.

Complex humanitarian emergencies, chaotic and destructive as they are, undermine the natural coping mechanisms people use to survive in difficult times. Therefore policy-makers need to be particularly careful about what pressure they put on the contestants in a conflict to settle their differences. The moral implications of these interventions are made more urgent by the inherent weakness of people living through the humanitarian emergency. This is true whether the interventions be (1) economic sanctions, (2) the use of food aid, relief assistance, or sustainable development programs as a bargaining tool in negotiations, or (3) the denial of relief to a country suffering a humanitarian emergency but governed by a ruthless regime. In all these cases the moral justification rests on one fundamental proposition: ends do not justify means when the means require the death of innocent people to achieve a political end.

But while the principle is stated easily enough, its application is difficult. Circumstances will determine whether or not an intervention in a particular situation will kill innocent people. Even more difficult for policy-makers is the attempt to predict, in chaotic circumstances, what the consequences will be of economic sanctions, or relief, or developmental assistance. Yet the moral consequences, however difficult to assess, should be part of the decision whether to intervene or not.

7

Somalia and the Problems
of Doing Good

A Perspective From the State Department

John R. Bolton

During the Cold War, Somalia's location on the Horn of Africa made it a focal point of superpower attention, as the navies of the United States and the Soviet Union vied for control of its vital harbors and nearby sea lanes. Alliances shifted as political developments in East Africa and the Middle East brought different regimes with different objectives to power in the various countries in the region. Although the United States and other Western donors had programs of economic assistance in place after Somalia became aligned against post-Selassie, Marxist Ethiopia, the military dimension of the Somali-American relationship was clearly predominant. Somalia's economic conditions were precarious, but they had been so for many years, and they raised no concerns substantially different from those in

John R. Bolton is senior vice-president of the American Enterprise Institute, Washington, D.C. During the Bush administration he served as Assistant Secretary of State for International Organization Affairs. His article "Wrong Turn in Somalia" appeared in *Foreign Affairs*, January/February 1994.

numerous other developing countries whose long-term prospects seemed perennially bleak.

Somalia first came up on the U.S. Department of State's "big" radar screen (that is to say, outside the Africa Bureau) in late 1991 and early 1992. At that time, fighting among Somalian factions in the wake of the overthrow of dictator Siad Barre had made the delivery of humanitarian assistance more and more risky. American assistance, provided through the U.S. Agency for International Development (USAID) and private relief organizations, raised no major policy issues. But as the situation in Somalia appeared to worsen, international discussion of possible responses grew.

During discussions in early 1992 of the appropriate United Nations role, members of the Non-Aligned Movement pressed for a larger political involvement for the U.N. Secretariat in attempting to mediate among the several Somali factions. They argued that the factions and their warlord leaders were caught in a cycle of violence from which they could be extricated only by external intervention, without which a humanitarian tragedy would develop. The appropriateness of a U.N. role in delivering humanitarian assistance through the pertinent U.N. agencies, and through non-governmental organizations (NGOs) and other traditional bilateral and multilateral channels of relief, was not debated at all but simply assumed.

In the spring of 1992, security for both Somalis and foreign relief workers continued to deteriorate, and calls for inserting some kind of U.N. military presence into Somalia began to increase. Relief supplies were then being distributed in Somalia under the watchful eyes of armed thugs, loosely characterized as "civilian guards," who extracted significant amounts of the supplies from NGOs as the price of their "guard" services. (So embarrassed were the NGOs by this very successful bribery by street thieves that their accounting entries for these payments listed "technical services," giving rise to the popular term for the thugs and their armed jeeps, "technicals.")

FROM HUMANITARIAN TO POLITICAL

A very small group of us at the State Department had qualms about a major U.N. political (as distinguished from humanitarian) role because the internal Somalian dispute did not then appear to constitute a threat to "international peace and security," as required by the U.N. Charter. As tragic as the situation in Somalia might become, we believed that the scope of the Security Council's jurisdiction was carefully defined in the Charter, and we had no intention of allowing it to be expanded. Other channels, including the Organization of African Unity (OAU) and the Organization of the Islamic Conference (OIC), as well as bilateral efforts at mediation, were more suitable for any international involvement in the domestic Somali quarrel. In any event, it was up to the Somali leaders—many of whom seemed to believe that outside involvement could be used to bolster their own political-military position—to make more serious efforts to come to a political agreement.

By contrast, Boutros Boutros-Ghali, the newly installed secretary general of the U.N., pressed hard for an expansive U.N. political role. Considering his equally emphatic views on the sanctions regime in place against Libya for complicity in the bombing of Pan Am 103, we believed at the time that Boutros-Ghali's interest was largely attributable to Somalia's proximity (geographic and religious) to his country, Egypt. Indeed, his own career had involved extensive dealings in the Horn of Africa, and he seemed to view Somalia as a potential test case of his tenure as U.N. secretary general. However, Boutros-Ghali increasingly came to see Somalia as the counterpoint to European concentration on the emerging humanitarian issues in Bosnia-Herzogovina. His inclinations were buttressed by some relief and human-rights organizations that, as a matter of their own policy, desired a more interventionist role not only in the domestic affairs of Somalia but elsewhere around the world.

Toward a U.N. Guard Force

Despite some opposition within the Department of State, those who were not inclined toward a larger U.N. neocolonial role prevailed in arguing for a U.N. "guard force" to accompany the humanitarian relief effort, modeled along the lines of the guard force associated with "Operation Provide Comfort" in northern Iraq. Such a force, as established by the Security Council, could provide a limited amount of protection for the relief effort, but it was not intended to have its own political mandate in what all still agreed was an essentially internal civil conflict. In standard U.N. parlance, the force was called UNOSOM, for U.N. Operation in Somalia.

In the prevailing U.S. view, no issue of international peace and security existed that would warrant either the authorization of force by the Security Council or the need to establish an international peacekeeping force. This latter was especially true, in that none of the conditions under which U.N. peacekeeping forces had previously been created was then present in Somalia. There was no real agreement among the parties to the disputes on issues such as truce or ceasefire (indeed, it was hard even to know who the parties were at any given moment), there was certainly no consent by all the parties to a U.N. deployment, and there was no agreement among members of the Security Council what the mandate of a U.N. peacekeeping force would be. Historically, the Security Council had resisted the creation of peacekeeping forces for situations in which there was no peace to keep. While all prior U.N. deployments had been in situations that were at least equally dangerous militarily, all had occurred in a political context that gave some assurance that the mission was neither endless nor hopeless. A context of this sort did not then exist in Somalia.

In some of the early deliberations, Under Secretary General James Jonah (one of two such officials assigned to international political matters within the U.N. Secretariat) argued for the deployment of a small (fifty-man) unarmed U.N. contingent of military observers. These observers, rather than an armed infantry battalion of approximately 500, which was the original projected force level for the U.N. guards, would monitor a hoped-for ceasefire among the Somali factions. During this period, it should be noted, not only were the warlords still at one another's throats, but the capital, Mogadishu, was rife with bandits not controlled by any of the factions. Jonah's argument turned the originally conceived protection mission on its head, because a fifty-man observer mission could not defend even itself, let alone the widely dispersed humanitarian relief personnel. His goal, however, may have been a more subtle one: to turn a guard-for-humanitarian-relief force with no political connotation into a "force" with an overtly political mandate.

From the U.S. perspective, the guard-force approach had another advantage over the peacekeeping-force approach. Costs of a guard force would be assessed to the United States at its regular U.N. budget share (25 per cent) rather than at the peacekeeping level (then just over 31 per cent). Secretary of State James A. Baker approved of the American position, including the budgetary aspects. Indeed, his main interest when the budget issue was first raised with him was why his department was lagging in its efforts to reduce the U.S. peacekeeping assessment level to the regular budget assessment level. Especially in light of the subsequent controversies surrounding the U.N. budget and the status of U.S. contributions thereto, these Somali-related budget discussions can be seen in hindsight to be much more than mere bean-counting exercises, a criticism that was made at the time by some NGOs.

It soon became clear that the real impetus for the deployment of military personnel was the Secretary General's insistence that the U.N. treat Somalia on a kind of parity with the disintegrating Yugoslavia. To do otherwise, many Third World countries argued in chorus, would demonstrate the Security Council's racist bias, its excessive concern for civil tragedy in Europe compared to civil tragedy in Africa. In an action not untypical of the State Department at work, where bending to often-hard-to-identify "international opinion" is a fine art, the United States eventually acquiesced in Resolution 751, which the Security Council adopted on April 24, 1992, authorizing deployment of the military observers.

Shortly thereafter, Mohammed Farah Aideed, one of the leading warlords, reversed his earlier acceptance in principle of the deployment of U.N. peacekeepers. One of the leaders of his United Somali Congress, Mohammed Abdi, was quoted as saying that armed U.N. soldiers would be killed "for their boots and berets," and that the U.N. had best deploy coffins along with the troops. Mohammed Sahnoun, the U.N. mediator appointed by the Secretary General, met repeatedly with Aideed but was unable to persuade him to change his mind again and accept U.N. peacekeepers. Nonetheless, by late May, food and other humanitarian supplies were being offloaded without incident in Mogadishu, and were apparently being distributed in a relatively even-handed fashion. Unfortunately, Sahnoun and Jonah were engaged in a serious turf conflict within the U.N. Secretariat, with periodic threats by Sahnoun to resign.

A U.N. Armed Presence

In early June, the situation turned again. Aideed's forces controlling the Mogadishu airport were stealing literally tons of Red Cross medicines and food from the U.N. World Food Program. The fifty hapless U.N. military observers finally arrived in Mogadishu in late July. Meanwhile, pressure continued for deployment of the infantry battalion, now identified as being contributed from Pakistan. The Pakistanis had won this dubious distinction as an Islamic country, and because none of the traditional troop-contributing countries were rushing forward to offer troops. Even those that were still considering the possibility, such as the Belgians and the Canadians, were asking to be airlifted in by the United States.

Nonetheless, in an exercise in unreality, the Security Council on August 28, 1992, approved Resolution 775 acceding to Boutros-Ghali's request to increase the U.N. armed presence from 500 (not yet there—the Pakistani battalion was still in Pakistan) to 3,500 men. Two of the unarmed U.N. monitors and three Somali guards were killed a few days later in a raid in Mogadishu, during which the attackers stole twenty-five trucks, 300 tons of food, and all of the World Food Program's available fuel supplies. Many thought the raids had been organized by Ali Mahdi, Aideed's chief warlord opponent, to dramatize the lack of security and thus to draw in additional U.N. forces to help tip the balance of power against Aideed.

A unilateral American military airlift of humanitarian assistance, staged out of Kenya and using leftover Desert Storm supplies and transport already in the region, had begun in late August. Undertaken without any significant policy consideration, this airlift represented a logistical decision rather than a major new initiative.

The bulk of the Pakistani battalion was finally deployed by the end of September. Sahnoun, the U.N. mediator, continued his efforts to convince local Somali leaders to accept the further deployment of U.N. peacekeepers outside of Mogadishu, including a Belgian battalion in the south (in Chismayu) and a Canadian battalion in the northeast (in Bossasso). The fourth of the four geographical regions that U.N. assessment teams had identified was the northwest (in Berbera), and here Sahnoun met with the least success. While these discussions were under way, however, the Pakistani battalion found itself pinned down defending part of the Mogadishu airport, and shortly thereafter it had to hire local guards from the Hwadle subclan to protect it against threatened reprisals by the still unhappy Aideed. These U.N. negotiations further infuriated Aideed.

In the United States, congressional interest had by this point intensified only marginally. It was largely confined to bipartisan urging by Senators Kassebaum and Simon to expedite the deployment of UNOSOM, the U.N. force.

The internal U.N. turf fight continued to rage. By this time, Sahnoun had conceptualized a "two-track" approach to Somalia. During an October 12-13 (1992) U.N.-sponsored conference in Geneva, Sahnoun advocated pursuing simultaneously the provision of humanitarian assistance and political reconciliation among the Somali factions. By contrast, Boutros-Ghali and Jonah had come to believe that the humanitarian problem had to be stabilized before negotiations aimed at real national reconciliation had any prospect of succeeding. Not surprisingly, the Somali factions read these internal Secretariat splits, made public by Sahnoun in his open criticism of the Secretary General, in light of their own widely divergent interests. This almost ensured that little progress would be made on the political front.

By November, another kind of turf fight was also raging, between the humanitarians of the world and the U.N. Secretariat. The Under Secretary General for Peacekeeping, Marrack Goulding, continued to argue that UNOSOM should be treated as a traditional U.N. force, relying on the consent of the parties. It was neither mandated nor equipped by the Security Council to fight its way ashore in Somalia, nor to distribute relief supplies at the point of a bayonet. But the humanitarians were unwilling to accept this. With increasingly loud voices they argued that the U.N. should use force to stabilize and pacify Somalia. Aideed was complicating matters still further by opposing the deployment of Belgian, Canadian, and Egyptian peacekeepers. He threatened armed resistance and "unprecedented bloodshed" if the deployment proceeded.

The Americans Decide to Act

It was at this point—early- to mid-November 1992—that some in the State Department and on the staff of the National Security Council first began to advocate seriously the large-scale use of force, including American troops, in Somalia. These were career foreign-service officers (some in the civil service, because of State's hybrid structure), up to and including Under Secretary of State Frank Wisner. Many had never been at all involved with U.N. peacekeeping operations. They were frustrated with the slow pace of U.N. operations and with the political complexity of the situation in Somalia, and they feared the effects of inaction on the Somalian people. Increasingly they felt that the "international community" was making itself look bad in the media by not doing more. Having just seen a graphic demonstration in northern Iraq of the Pentagon's ability to provide massive amounts of humanitarian aid in a chaotic situation in a remarkably short time, the Somalia interventionists thought that they had an easy example to follow, and that a Somalia expedition would probably take only four months. Calls for international action were increasing, and there was considerable discussion of what could be done to expedite the previously agreed upon deployment of U.N. forces.

I was then Assistant Secretary of State for International Organization Affairs. Having concluded that U.S. military intervention was not the correct approach, I had earlier sent Acting Secretary of State Lawrence Eagleburger and Under Secretary Wisner a memorandum headed "Somalia: Easier To Get Into Than To Get Out Of." There were a host of unanswered questions about such an undertaking, not least of which was how the United States could justify a major role in Somalia but not in Liberia, Bosnia, or other countries on a long and growing list where internal order was breaking down.

In addition, what the State Department interventionists missed were the political-military differences from the post–Gulf War situation, where the only real military force in Iraq, Saddam Hussein's army, had just suffered a massive military defeat and was effectively excluded from the intended area of operations. In Somalia, by contrast, armed contingents were everywhere, engaged in a very basic and very brutal political and military struggle.

Moreover, the State interventionists saw the always expected "handover" of a U.S.-led operation to the U.N. as both inevitable and desirable. It was, they thought, a way to involve the United States more directly and significantly in a U.N. peace operation than ever before. To their minds, this would be an entirely positive development, one that some considered long overdue. By contrast, at least a few others in the State Department still believed that the most prudent course for the United States, and for the other four permanent members of the Security Council, was generally not to participate in U.N. peacekeeping operations, in order to maintain detachment in their judgments about such operations. As the tragedy of Marine Colonel Higgins (assigned to the U.N. Truce Supervisory Organization) in Lebanon had only recently demonstrated, U.S. personnel wearing blue helmets made particularly attractive targets. Some of us were not interested in creating a more target-rich environment.

Options for the President

There really was no coherent State view by November 20, the date of a critical meeting of the "Deputies Committee," a group of U.S. officials that met frequently at the White House or by secure teleconference to engage in what could fairly be called "crisis management" activities in a wide variety of situations. At that meeting, the Pentagon argued vigorously for essentially an American military takeover of the entire relief effort. The Department of Defense wanted to create a military coalition outside the U.N., using at least a full division of American forces as its core. The proposal had been authorized by Colin Powell, chairman of the Joint Chiefs of Staff.

Unlike virtually all U.N. peacekeeping operations, where force was a last resort, to be used by the peacekeepers only in self-defense, the Pentagon asserted from the outset that force and the threat to use it were central to their humanitarian relief strategy. While the military hoped to conduct the effort peacefully, they stressed that they would be prepared to use "harsh" and "punishing" force against the slightest interference—from any party—with their mission of delivering relief supplies. No one at State could really explain this new Defense position, though some speculated that the Pentagon saw Somalia as more like Grenada than like Iraq, i.e., an easy "win."

The Deputies Committee agreed to draft an options paper for the President, with essentially three options:

1. "stay the course," but push the U.N. harder (my preference);

2. propose a bigger U.N. peacekeeping force with major U.S. participation (Wisner's preference); or

3. send a U.S.-led military force prepared for combat if necessary (Powell's preference).

Not untypically, the consensus of the Deputies Committee was something between options one and two, albeit very close to two.

Once again, however, the State Department was surprised to learn from Acting Secretary Eagleburger, after a meeting with President Bush on the morning of November 25 (the day before Thanksgiving), that "we are more or less at option three." Powell later that day characterized the Pentagon mission to Wisner as "more than the United States simply coming in with trucks, but less than pacification and occupation." U.S. forces would secure ports, airports, roads, and distribution centers to allow food and other supplies to flow through, with helicopter gunships at the ready to pay calls on the headquarters of any troublemakers.

Eagleburger called Secretary General Boutros-Ghali to request a meeting that afternoon, and he and I flew to New York to deliver the President's surprising decision. Eagleburger made it plain, however, that the President also wanted Boutros-Ghali's support, and that he wanted the entire U.S.-led operation conducted under the authority of a Security Council resolution, much as Operation Desert Storm had been. The Secretary General concurred with President Bush's decision, and the requisite Security Council authorization was obtained in due course. Thus was the American intervention in Somalia launched.

POLICY LESSONS

This brief survey of roughly one year of Bush-administration decision-making suggests a number of important lessons, some more on the theoretical level, some more operational, but all of interest to moralists and philosophers as well as to policy-makers. I will mention six.

■ As the political/humanitarian crisis began to develop, the U.S. government at its highest levels really knew and cared little about Somalia. While East Africa experts certainly were aware of the deteriorating political situation in 1990-91, and of the consequent economic hardships as the country descended into chaos after the fall of Siad Barre, this knowledge simply did not initially penetrate the highest levels of policy-making at the Department of State. A collapse into virtual anarchy was occurring at approximately the same time in Liberia and Sudan as well, and these situations too failed to register on the big radar screens on the State Department's seventh floor.

Although some in the NGO community and some Third World leaders argued that this inattention was simply a product of the ill-concealed racism of American society, a more logical explanation was that Somalia's internal difficulties implicated no vital U.S. national interests. Moreover, its troubles set off no alarms within a significant domestic political constituency that might have generated attention even before the arrival in Somalia of the CNN cameras. Before any-one concludes that the lack of attention at State was racist, it should be stressed that, apart from some members with oversight on matters African, congressional attention was completely lacking also. A better conclusion than racism is the more understandable fact—and more obvious, if harder for some to admit—that after the end of the Cold War, Somalia had ceased to be important in Washington's calculations, while Sudan and Liberia had never even made it that high.

■ Whether for good reasons or bad, the "CNN curve" did reach Somalia in a major way, one that graduate schools of journalism and of international relations will study for some time to come. Contrary to the received wisdom, however, the television coverage did not force a policy decision, only policy-level attention at the State Department. Moreover, especially in wartime or humanitarian emer-gencies, the camera can show only current happenings, not root causes, and certainly not solutions. Media attention can thus narrow and distort the public perception of a crisis, and this may hinder prospects for a long-term solution, or even shorter-range measures that might have sufficed but for the glare of television lights.

■ The humanitarian crisis in Somalia arose at a time when many observers, in the United States and abroad, had fundamentally misread the lessons of the U.N.'s role in the Persian Gulf Crisis and the impor-tant, but limited, successes of Security Council action in Namibia, Central America, and Afghanistan. These observers concluded that the Council's escape from Cold War gridlock necessarily meant that it now was more or less able to undertake the responsibilities envisaged by the founders of the U.N. in 1945. They concluded further that those who opposed a vigorous role for the U.N. in world affairs either failed to understand this transformation or were isolationist or mean-spirited.

This analysis was wrong in multiple respects. One fundamental mis-reading of the Security Council's role in the military aspects of the Gulf Crisis was that U.N. operations could now be safely launched into areas beyond traditional peacekeeping, as defined above. Whether described as "peace enforcement" or "humanitarian intervention" or something else, such operations entailed a U.N. force that was willing and able to fight, not just one that would separate belligerents or observe ceasefires. This, however, member governments were really not ready for. Moreover, advocates of peace enforcement were never able to explain how "dying in the service of the United Nations" for purely humanitarian reasons would ever gain much political appeal in the capitals of most U.N. members, particularly the Security Council's five permanent members.

Moreover, Somalia, whatever its human tragedy, was by no means a crisis that threatened international peace and security, the threshold mark of the Security Council's jurisdiction. Thus, while the United States was unwilling—or unable—to resist an early U.N. role in Somalia, a long and deepening U.N. role was never likely to command widespread majority support. Nor should it, given the carefully circumscribed role laid out for the Security Council in the U.N. Charter.

■ Lack of familiarity with the U.N. and its limitations drove ambitious State Department policy-makers to propose American involvement that would not have been taken seriously just a few years before. The U.N.'s limitations would have led inevitably to a limiting and scaling down of the U.N. presence, as occurred in 1994. What happened in the fall of 1992 with the creation of a major unilateral U.S. involvement, however, was a more fundamental mistake about the use of American force for humanitarian purposes.

Those in the State Department who advocated the expansive role of military force for humanitarian purposes stressed that they conceived of the operation as distinctly limited in time and scope. Any suggestion of the "Q" word was rejected as alarmist because the advocates of a military mission knew full well the evocative power of the "quagmire" possibility. What the State warriors missed, however, was the inevitable involvement of a large military force in questions well beyond the simply humanitarian.

Their further dilemma stemmed from the fact that there were no bright lines they could draw in Somalia. There was no even arguable American national interest at stake. Therefore there were no benchmarks, no criteria for evaluation, no measures by which to judge when the time had come to go, especially against the unending arguments of the humanitarian NGO community for a continued American presence. Many of these groups wanted a U.S. policy of "nation-building" right from the start, and saw the initial massive U.S. military involvement as the way to get Washington's attention in a major way. Once the Americans were in, the NGOs knew well it would be hard for them to get out, and they knew it better than the humanitarian neo-imperialists at State. That is why I had argued against intervention in the first place.

■ From the perspective of national foreign-policy decision-making, the Somalia mission was utopian from the start. The deliberations inside State and the National Security Council had an otherworldly aspect that is difficult to describe after the fact. Had the Somali operation been conducted entirely by political appointees, it would have been criticized for its lack of grounding in the realities of Somalia in particular and Africa in general. We would have heard about the importance of relying on experienced professionals who knew the territory, who could bring their experience to bear in mature, cautious, and non-political ways, rather than on inexperienced political appointees whose decisions were motivated by crass considerations of domestic American politics.

In fact, however, virtually all those involved in the decision-making at State were career officers, at the most senior and responsible levels in both the foreign service and the civil service. But although some had experience in Middle Eastern affairs, almost none were "Africa hands." Moreover, the State interventionists together had had almost no experience with the U.N. in recent years. Even so, their principal mistake was neither lack of experience nor even lack of judgment. Rather, their failing was in attempting to adapt the world and U.S. policy to idealized and untested models, rather than to define U.S. interests and then pursue them. Other nations were not in the lead; nor did the State interventionists take cues on policy from the ubiquitous journalists; nor were they were misled or misdirected by NGOs or U.N. officials. They undertook their policies entirely on their own, convinced that they could accomplish larger objectives than merely feeding the starving Somalis. In a sense, "nation-building" in a truly utopian sense was what the Bush administration (or large parts of it) was up to, and Somalia was merely the first available arena in which the game was to be played.

■ Sad to say, one of the most basic questions that future humanitarian operations will have to face is the proper relationship between military force and the provision of aid. Traditionally, NGOs have resisted association with military forces, especially those of the parties to a dispute, arguing that such association would "politicize" the delivery of assistance. They had agreed to close working relationships during Operation Provide Comfort in northern Iraq in part because they understood that only a massive U.S. military effort could preclude disaster for the Kurdish refugees. Unspoken publicly, but much on the minds of some NGOs, was the belief that the United States had caused the Kurdish refugee problem either by starting the war against Iraq or by finishing it without deposing Saddam Hussein. Accordingly, under either variation, military involvement by the United States to help mitigate a problem it had "caused" seemed appropriate.

Somalia most significantly departed from the traditional relief model because of the use of the "technicals," although the humanitarian NGOs were exceedingly unwilling to admit this deviation from the norm. Once the use of the technicals was accepted practice, however, it was not much of a leap to argue for U.N. (i.e., foreign) guards in lieu of the dangerously disorganized locals. The U.S.-led military coalition and its successor U.N. operation (UNOSOM II) were simply further steps down the road to the consolidation of humanitarian operations and military force. While such militarization may not have been inevitable, the process in Somalia was certainly far different from the very outset.

Looking Ahead

In addition to policy lessons, of course, we are also entitled to draw some larger conclusions from the Somalia experience. Unfortunately, the Clinton administration was either unable or unwilling to reach these conclusions before it plunged full tilt into "assertive multilateralism" and "nation-building." Although sorely tempted to revisit the terribly flawed Clinton excursion around the Horn of Africa, I will instead try to look somewhat further ahead.

Leaving aside the manifold operational questions, the basic issues posed by Somalia concern the willingness and ability of the "international community" to act as stewards (or "nannies") in countries where normal civil institutions have collapsed, and the propriety of doing so.

The U.S. experience in Somalia has apparently left us with no philosophical inhibitions about "neo-colonialist" enterprises, no fears that the "international community" will find us "imperialist" or "hegemonistic." The subsequent intervention in Haiti proves that. The real debate over the propriety of massive civil intervention is an internal American debate over the use of American lives and resources, as the example of Haiti once again proves conclusively.

The best prediction is that such interventions in the future will be rare, because the general American level of willingness is quite low. This disinclination stems not from any lack of humanitarian spirit but rather from the painful realization of the high probability of futility. Picking the right faction in Lebanon's civil war in the 1980s, "moderates" in Iran, "democratic" Kurds in Iraq, "good" warlords in Somalia, or "progressive" forces in Chechnya is simply not something that diplomats in the paneled offices of the seventh floor of the State Department are adept at doing. Absent a demonstrable U.S. national interest in supporting one side or the other—which is hard to find in all these cases after the end of the Cold War—American willingness to intervene will be justifiably low.

This hesitancy is also caused by a frank assessment of ability. While the U.S. military capability in Somalia was never used to full effect, there is no doubt what the casualty tolls would have been had the original plan of inflicting "harsh" and "punishing" force actually been implemented. But there is simply no disputing the U.S. military's unparalleled logistical capability to distribute humanitarian aid on short notice in emergencies, especially compared to the capability of international agencies and NGOs. In Haiti, the military faced no real threat and fully performed the military mission it was "given." In Bosnia, the military face very real threats, which are likely to remain only potential until the U.S. withdrawal, thus permitting the U.S. administration to say that the military fully performed its assigned responsibilities. These experiences certainly contrast with those of U.N. forces in Bosnia and Russian troops in Chechnya. Even America's most powerful allies could project only a pale shadow of force without extensive use of the infrastructure built and maintained by the United States.

The real question of ability, however, is not the ability of the military but the ability of even the best-motivated outsiders to engage in "nation-building." Ultimately, the only long-run policy with any hope of success is "Somalia for the Somalians." Thus I conclude from the U.S. perspective that humanitarian assistance should either be (1) distributed in a non-political fashion, in the original, long-time policy of most NGOs, or (2) withheld (as in the case of Iraq) where the ruling regime cannot be trusted to allow the non-political (or, at least, not anti-American) use of the assistance. To supply humanitarian assistance as part of a larger political policy not based on identifiable U.S. interests is likely to result in the same failure seen by the unfortunate country of Somalia. And to do so risks creating an even larger disinclination to be involved abroad than we already see in the United States.

8

Somalia and the Problems
of Doing Good

A Perspective From the Defense Department

Alberto R. Coll

O n December 4, 1992, President George Bush, recently defeated
in his bid for reelection by Arkansas governor Bill Clinton,
announced his decision to send over 20,000 U.S. troops to Somalia.
The purpose of this large military force was to insure that large
amounts of food being donated to the Somali people by the international community would reach their intended beneficiaries. There
was widespread fear among international relief organizations and the
United Nations that a great many Somalis were on the verge of starving to death. The country was wracked by civil war, and the various
rival clans struggling for power were keeping much of the international aid from reaching its destination. Unless military force was used
to reopen seaports, roads, and the main airport at Mogadishu, and to
convoy the food supplies throughout the country, the famine was sure

---

Alberto R. Coll is professor of strategy and policy at the U.S. Naval
War College in Newport, Rhode Island. From 1990 to 1993 he
served as Principal Deputy Assistant Secretary of Defense (Special
Operations and Low-Intensity Conflict).

to take a devastating toll. The President's decision to use American military force for such a worthwhile objective was widely applauded within the United States and around the world. Thus began "Operation Restore Hope."

The President's decision to send U.S. troops to Somalia was surprising to those who during the previous two years had in vain urged the Administration to intervene in places more important to the United States than Somalia. In the spring of 1991, for example, Saddam Hussein, then staggering from the destruction of most of his army in Operation Desert Storm, had begun to massacre thousands of rebellious Shiites and Kurds. Despite repeated pleas for help, the United States did not move against Saddam for several weeks. When it finally intervened, it did no more than impose a ban on Iraqi military aircraft in southern Iraq and establish a protected zone in the Kurdish region.

A few months later, as the war in the former Yugoslavia broke out in full fury, the United States also refused to intervene. By the late spring of 1992, all of Europe was concerned about the Serbian military onslaught against Croatia and the Shiite regions of Bosnia-Herzegovina, and such distinguished critics as former British prime minister Margaret Thatcher and former U.S. secretary of state George Shultz were urging vigorous American political and military efforts to end the conflict before it did further damage to European stability. But the Bush administration took the position that this was a crisis beyond the capacity of U.S. power to resolve at a reasonable cost, and that it was up to the Europeans to take the lead in resolving it. In the summer and fall of that year, candidate Bill Clinton made much of the President's inaction as illustrative of his alleged passivity and moral insensitivity.

THE BUSH ADMINISTRATION: TAKING A STAND

Why, then, did President Bush decide to intervene in Somalia? During the Cold War, Somalia had been of some importance to the United States because of its geographical position astride the Horn of Africa, bordering both the Red Sea and the Indian Ocean. As the Soviets consolidated their hold over Ethiopia in the late 1970s, their relationship with Somali dictator Siad Barre deteriorated. In 1977, much to the elation of the United States, Barre expelled all Soviet advisors, and in 1980 he offered the U.S. Navy use of the port of Berbera in exchange for arms and financial aid. Washington also received another indirect benefit: Barre continued to support the Eritrean secessionist guerrillas, who were creating serious difficulties for the Soviet-supported Ethiopian regime.

Barre's overthrow in January 1991 coincided with the end of the Cold War. For a short time, Somalia seemed to disappear from the map of America's strategic interests. Various factions struggled to gain control, and the country became engulfed in a bloody civil war. By late 1991 the war had begun to disrupt the country's food production. Famine was beginning to develop. By early 1992 conditions had become so serious that the United Nations, along with a host of inter-national non–governmental organizations (NGOs), was carrying out a massive famine relief effort. In the United States, newspapers and the ubiquitous Cable News Network (CNN) were carrying daily stories showing dramatic images of starving children with bloated bellies and emaciated bodies. By the summer, the death count had passed 200,000 and was rising.[1]

On August 15, shortly before the Republican National Conven-tion, President Bush, then trailing Bill Clinton in the polls by a wide margin, decided to step up U.S. support for the famine relief efforts of the United Nations and various international charitable organiza-tions. The United States would increase the amount of food it was donating, and would provide different kinds of technical and logisti-cal support to ensure that the food was widely distributed once it reached Somalia.

Coping With Chaos

The new measures, however, turned out to be insufficient to stop the famine. The key problem was Somalia's political and military chaos. Central governmental authority had ceased to exist, and the country had broken up into a series of fiefdoms controlled by rival warlords. Getting food shipments to various parts of the country required massive bribes to secure the permission of the roving militias and armed groups in control of the territories through which the food had to pass. In many cases the warlords obstructed the shipments, trying to seize the food for their army's use, or for sale on the black market, or simply in order to deny it to their enemies. In addition, there were the infrastructure problems. The civil war had taken a severe toll on the country's roads and bridges, and the ports and the major airport at the capital of Mogadishu were often shut down as a result of military violence.

Although the volume of food entering the country rose from 20,000 to 37,000 metric tons per month between September and November, the proportion of donated food reaching those in need declined from 60 to 20 per cent.[2] The United Nations warned that unless more drastic measures were taken, many Somalis would die within the next six months. In Washington, a number of officials began to ponder whether a U.S. military intervention might be the best step to take, given the scale of the problem.

Shortly after his defeat by Bill Clinton on November 6, George Bush began to turn his full attention to Somalia. The outgoing chief executive wanted to end his presidency on a high note. Foreign policy had always been his *forte,* and he intended before leaving office to complete a major arms-control accord with Russia that would remind the world and future historians of his key contribution, as he saw it, to ending the Cold War. The U.N.'s energetic secretary general, Boutros Boutros-Ghali, had made it clear to the President that he wanted to see the United Nations mount a major effort, with substantial American military support, to break the logjam of food distribution in Somalia.

During the second week of November, the President instructed his senior advisors to prepare a set of policy options for dealing with the Somalian crisis. That Thanksgiving, as CNN continued its coverage of the famine, George and Barbara Bush along with their large family were deeply moved as they watched images of starving Somali children. The President had already decided that the United States must act vigorously and disinterestedly to help. Certainly it should be possible to bring American power to bear to end the famine and save innocent lives, all of it at a reasonable cost to the United States.

Differing Views at the Pentagon

At the Pentagon, word had arrived in mid-November that the President was serious about a military intervention in Somalia. The main question was what form it should take, and on this there were differences of opinion between the military and civilians. The military were led by the chairman of the Joint Chiefs of Staff, the formidable General Colin Powell. Born in Brooklyn of Jamaican immigrant parents, Powell had risen by dint of hard work and unparalleled political skills to become the first African-American to occupy the highest post in the U.S. military. As with many other Vietnam veterans, his service in that disastrous war had been the key experience shaping his professional outlook. The chief lessons Powell had carried from Vietnam were the need to avoid entangling the military in wars that had no popular support, and the requirement that, if the military *was* sent to war, it should be sent with all the strength necessary to win decisively and quickly.

In the year following the 1991 war against Iraq, Powell had capitalized on that renowned success of arms to institutionalize his views through what became known in the Pentagon as the Powell Doctrine. It was a restatement of the earlier Weinberger Doctrine (1984), which Powell had helped to draft for President Reagan's secretary of defense, Caspar Weinberger, in his capacity as Weinberger's military assistant. The Powell Doctrine stated that the United States should employ combat troops only if vital American interests were at stake, if it could achieve a clear-cut victory, and if military power would be used with "overwhelming force." While the war against Iraq was an example of this use, a "humanitarian intervention" in the murky political complexities of Somalia was not, and for months Powell and his senior staff had been quietly lobbying against a U.S. military intervention.

Over on the civilian side, the outlook was somewhat different. The principal policy advisor to Secretary of Defense Richard Cheney was Paul Wolfowitz, a bright thinker and skilled bureaucratic player who, out of intellectual conviction, kept his focus on what he considered the key strategic problems facing the United States in late 1992: strengthening NATO at a difficult time of uncertainty over the alliance's future and increasing disagreements over Bosnia, encouraging Russia and Ukraine to reduce their nuclear arsenals while maintaining tight control over them, and keeping a set of assorted dangerous regional troublemakers such as Iraq, Iran, and North Korea in check. There was no place for Somalia in Under Secretary Wolfowitz's set of priorities. When word arrived that the White House expected imminent serious action on Somalia, Wolfowitz passed the tasking to two offices in his staff: the Deputy Assistant Secretary of

Defense for International Security Affairs, Africa (ISA-Africa), and the Assistant Secretary of Defense for Special Operations and Low-Intensity Conflict (SOLIC). In the large bureaucratic battles of late 1991 and early 1992 over future U.S. military strategy and force structure, these two offices had been largely on the sidelines. Now their hour had come.

While SOLIC had repeatedly been a strong advocate of using American special-operations forces in various parts of the world on missions of broad military support to U.S. diplomacy, the position it took regarding Somalia was surprisingly conservative. Somalia was not an important U.S. interest; therefore any commitment of resources should be limited. If U.S. troops had to be used in a humanitarian intervention, they should be used in support of a broader U.N. operation in which the United Nations, not the United States, would bear the risks and pay any political costs that might accrue. A high-profile military intervention with the United States in the lead was inappropriate, given Somalia's low ranking among American strategic priorities.

Ironically, it was General Powell who did the most to sink SOLIC's proposed policy option and insure that the U.S. intervention in Somalia would be a solo effort. If the U.S. military was to be involved in Somalia—and the politically sensitive general knew that George Bush had decided as much—it would come as close to the "overwhelming force" model favored by Powell as possible. The notion of placing American combat forces under U.N. command was distasteful to Powell, who justifiably had little confidence in the United Nations' ability to perform military operations competently, much less to safeguard American lives as well as a U.S. command would do. For Powell, unlike the civilians at SOLIC, Somalia was an all-or-nothing affair: either the United States should not intervene (the general's preference), or it should intervene on a large scale so as to accomplish its mission as bloodlessly and as quickly as possible, and then get out. Powell's view was shared by General Joseph Hoar, commander-in-chief of the Central Command, who would have overall responsibility for directing the military intervention.

Within the Pentagon, Powell's standing was so high, his political capital so large, that his victory in the bureaucratic battle over the shape of the Somalia intervention came as no surprise to anyone. The general enjoyed the well-earned confidence of both the Secretary of Defense and the President, the latter having become particularly appreciative of his counsel. The die was cast.

The massive U.S. force began to land on the beaches of Somalia on December 9, under the incongruous glare of the lights of television cameras. As the troops were landing, the Bush administration went out of its way to indicate that this was a limited humanitarian intervention. The Americans were there to feed the starving. They would make sure that the food reached the hungry. Once they accomplished this, they would be withdrawn, and the mission would be turned over to the United Nations. In comments to journalists, National Security Advisor Brent Scowcroft hinted that he expected that some of the U.S. troops involved would be returning home by January 21, the date of President-elect Clinton's inauguration, or shortly thereafter. Although Defense Secretary Cheney and General Powell distanced themselves from any such optimistic assessments, they too insisted that this would be a mission limited in both scope and duration.

International and domestic support for Bush's decision was overwhelming, and included the strong endorsement of President-elect Clinton and the Congressional Black Caucus. Yet there were a few dissenting voices, though at the time no one paid much attention to them. On December 1, several days before the intervention began, the U.S. ambassador to Kenya, Smith Hempstone, a seasoned observer of African affairs, sent Washington a long cable opposing the intervention. Once the United States had stepped into the morass of the Somali civil war, he warned, extricating itself would be difficult. In somewhat injudicious language that had the unfortunate effect of lessening the power of his arguments, Hempstone wrote that Somalia would prove to be "a tar baby" that the United States would be unable to hand over to someone else. Elsewhere, one of America's most celebrated students of foreign affairs, George F. Kennan, wrote in his diary on December 9 that the Somalia operation would turn out to be "a dreadful error of American policy."[3] Had Kennan published his gloomy reflections instead of keeping them to himself, he would have seemed like a modern-day Scrooge to the American people and the First Family, all of whom were greatly cheered that Christmas by the images of young American soldiers diligently alleviating the hunger of millions of Somalis.

THE CLINTON ADMINISTRATION:
ESCALATION AND WITHDRAWAL

When Bill Clinton took the oath of office on the steps of the Capitol on January 21, 1993, the humanitarian mission was not over, and the process of bringing the troops home had not begun. Indeed, American troop strength reached its peak of 25,000 that month. The process of clearing the political and physical obstacles to the relief effort and distributing the food supplies was taking longer than anticipated. Yet success, measured by the number of Somalis being fed and the quickly receding prospects for mass famine, was at hand.

By late February it was clear that the mission, as narrowly defined initially, was about to end. At this point policy discussions in Washington became complicated. The Clinton administration was divided as to what to do next. On the one hand, the senior military leadership, including General Powell, believed that the United States should withdraw as quickly as possible and hand over the reins to UNOSOM (U.N. Operation in Somalia) II, the United Nations force then being assembled for the purpose of restoring some political stability to Somalia. According to this viewpoint, U.S. troops remaining in Somalia after the handover to the United Nations should be few in number and should play a supporting rather than a leading role.

On the opposite side of the debate were a growing number of political appointees in the State and Defense departments, supported by the career Africa experts at the State Department and large segments of the liberal establishment press, all of whom believed that now that the U.S. military was in Somalia, it should go beyond the narrow task of feeding the starving and engage in a substantial degree of "nation-building"—reconstructing Somalia's shattered political and economic infrastructure. It would be a great pity, if not an outright tragedy, if the United States, having already spent a lot of money and political energy alleviating the famine, were to leave Somalia without addressing some of the root causes of the instability and violence that had brought about the famine in the first place. Only after Somalia was on a course toward political reconciliation and economic stability, according to this view, would the United Nations be capable of taking over the task of reconstruction from the United States.

It is important to point out that even though the advocates of immediate withdrawal seemed to carry the day—the United States handed over its mission to the U.N. force on May 4—the underlying sentiment that favored a more thoroughgoing American involvement in Somalia's internal political and economic affairs than the Bush administration had ever contemplated remained an immensely powerful force in shaping subsequent U.S. policy. Indeed, this sentiment was to guide all efforts by the Clinton administration as it worked to support the U.N. undertaking from May on.

An Ambitious U.N. Agenda

Right after it took over from the Americans, UNOSOM II ran into problems for a number of reasons. First, its political objectives were both highly ambitious and ill defined. In late March the U.N. Security Council, with the full support of the Clinton administration, passed Resolution 814 setting forth the mandate of UNOSOM II. Its goals were no less than:

> . . . the economic rehabilitation of Somalia . . . to help the people of Somalia to promote and advance political reconciliation, through broad participation by all sectors of Somali society, and the reestablishment of national and regional institutions and civil administration in the entire country . . . the restoration and maintenance of peace, stability and law and order . . . [and the creation] of conditions under which Somali civil society may have a role, at every level, in the process of political reconciliation and in the formulation and realization of rehabilitation and reconstruction programmes.[4]

Given the giant scale of Somalia's political and economic troubles, and the almost feudal condition of its institutions, not even the most ardent advocates of "nation-building" could agree on the precise point at which UNOSOM II could consider that it had achieved success. Promoting Somalia's transition toward political reconciliation was a case in point. Did this objective, hazily defined as it was, encompass merely the end of hostilities between warring factions in the country? Or did it also embrace reviving the old system of clan assemblies, in the hope that it would produce a national leadership acceptable to most Somalis? How far should UNOSOM II interfere in all these processes? How should it relate to the warlords, most of whom saw themselves as representing large clans and therefore entitled to a large share of power, if not the preeminent position of political power in the country? Should UNOSOM II simply prevent any renewed outbreaks of large-scale violence, or should it go further and disarm the warlords, by force if necessary? Although similar quandaries confronted the U.N. mission in the economic field, it was in the political and military arena that UNOSOM II was most vulnerable to incoherence.

The Clinton administration did not attempt to clarify the objectives. In its internal debates—dominated by those who wanted to see Somalia reconstructed—and in its policy guidelines for supporting UNOSOM II, the Administration showed an equal degree of conceptual confusion.

Second, in addition to objectives that were at best unclear and at worst overly ambitious, UNOSOM II faced a gap between its goals and the military and economic resources to implement them. The sums of money pledged by U.N. members, large as they were, were insufficient for the enormous task at hand. Militarily, the force was far weaker than the American contingent had been, and it was hobbled by the typical problems facing U.N. military operations: an awkward command structure, with a multiplicity of national sub-commands below the UNOSOM II command level, and sharp disagreements among members about objectives and strategy. To these were added substantial shortfalls in mobility and heavy firepower. All these problems were particularly worrisome given the U.N. force's ambitious agenda and the likelihood that to implement it, the force might have to take on some of the warlords, a number of whom were heavily armed, had years of military experience, and knew the country's terrain well.

During the three months of their preliminary mission, the Americans had avoided conflict with the warlords by combining their superior and unquestionable military strength with a wise policy of talking and negotiating with the warlords whenever any difficulties arose. The U.S. commander on the ground, Marine General Robert Johnston, was a veteran of the ill-fated 1983 Beirut "peacekeeping" mission. So was his political counterpart, Ambassador Robert Oakley, the U.S. Special Envoy to Somalia. They both were determined not to get the United States entangled in Somalia's civil war, and to avoid any appearance of favoring one faction over another. Given that their objective was simply to feed the starving, the Americans' policy made sense; it was a replay of the old Teddy Roosevelt adage, "Speak softly and carry a big stick." Perhaps inadvertently, and certainly unavoidably, in view of its limited resources and broad agenda, UNOSOM II soon started to move in the opposite direction: it began uttering rather ambitious rhetoric while carrying an obviously inadequate stick.

Enter Aideed

The presence and agenda of UNOSOM II soon were perceived as a threat by some of the warlords, especially those strong enough to hope that, with the U.N. force out of the way, they could gain power. Notable among these was Mohammed Farah Aideed, a shrewd Somali politician who had spent considerable time in the United States and had served as Somalia's ambassador to India during the Siad Barre regime. In 1990, Aideed had taken up arms against Barre, and of all the warlords he had been the most effective militarily in helping to push the dictator out of the country and defeat his efforts to return. Aideed considered himself entitled to lead the country and had amassed substantial military forces in areas outside the capital, Mogadishu, as well as a large following of armed supporters in the city. Aideed calculated, with good reason, that the further UNOSOM II succeeded in implementing its ambitious "nation-building" agenda, the less likely he would be to gain control of the country and the greater the risk that some of his rivals would do so. In May 1993 he launched a virulent nationalist political campaign designed to persuade Somalis that UNOSOM II was bent on returning Somalia to colonial status, and that it was time for the U.N. forces, including its small number of Americans, to depart.

In response to the inflammatory rhetoric emanating from Aideed's radio station, "Radio Mogadishu," UNOSOM II decided to shut down the station. Before doing so, it notified Aideed that it would send teams of peacekeepers to inspect several of his weapons storage sites. On June 5, a team of Pakistanis, after inspecting the storage site located at the radio station, was attacked by Aideed's militia, the SNA. The violence soon spread into a city-wide rampage that left twenty-four Pakistani soldiers dead and scores injured. There was now a direct military conflict under way between UNOSOM II and the country's most powerful warlord.

At this point a prominent retired U.S. Navy admiral, serving (as a private citizen) as Special Representative of the U.N. Secretary General to Somalia, began to play a role that was to enmesh the United

States further in UNOSOM II's growing difficulties. Admiral Jonathan Howe had served his country with great distinction as a naval officer for three decades. His previous post before the UNOSOM II job had been none other than Deputy National Security Advisor to the President, a highly sensitive job in which he was closely involved in the Bush administration's decision to intervene. Widely known as a "hard charger" who got things done when no one else could, Howe was extremely well connected in Washington throughout the civilian and military bureaucracies. Shortly after taking the UNOSOM II job with the full blessing of the Clinton administration in the spring of 1993, he began to use his extensive connections, and his intricate knowledge of America's military capabilities, to lobby for a more vigorous involvement in Somalia in support of the troubled U.N. operation. Senior officials at the highest levels in the National Security Council, the State Department, and the Pentagon received frequent calls from Howe at all hours of the day and night requesting more U.S. resources for the U.N. force.

By late June, with two dozen Pakistani soldiers dead, Aideed in full open defiance, and his supporters roaming through the streets of Mogadishu, it was clear to Howe that UNOSOM II was in danger of collapsing unless the United States acted energetically to prop it up. Howe also worried that the contingent of American forces remaining in Somalia was becoming increasingly vulnerable to the spreading violence and might suffer an attack from Aideed similar to the one that had cost the Pakistanis many casualties. On June 17, after a bloody melee between Aideed's militia and UNOSOM II forces, Howe forsook whatever possibilities might have remained for negotiations with Aideed by issuing a warrant for his arrest and offering a $25,000 bounty for his capture. He also began to ask persistently that the United States send the famed Delta force to Somalia to help UNOSOM II capture Aideed. Delta is a highly classified, superbly trained U.S. special counterterrorist unit, possibly the finest of its kind in the world.

Howe's request met with considerable ambivalence in the Pentagon. While the senior special-forces commanders were eager to see Delta sent into action, General Powell and much of the Joint Staff were leery of the considerable political and military risks involved. On the civilian side, the SOLIC (Special Operations and Low-Intensity Conflict) office of the Defense Department once again counseled restraint, reminding senior decision-makers that Delta was a lethal and powerful military instrument and suggesting that it was inappropriate for this case, given the political uncertainties of Somalia and the limited nature of U.S. interests at stake there.

The successor to Paul Wolfowitz as Under Secretary for Policy, Ambassador Frank Wisner, agreed for the time being with SOLIC's assessment that Delta should not be sent, even though he had been pushing for months for a more activist U.S. effort in Somalia. A brilliant Foreign Service officer who had served as ambassador to Egypt and later as an undersecretary of state, Wisner had moved over to the Pentagon in late January 1993 with an activist agenda. He was a strong believer in U.S. engagement in the Third World and in the value of the United Nations to U.S. interests in the post–Cold War world. Wisner came from a highly educated and cosmopolitan family, his father having gained renown in the OSS during the Second World War. As a young Foreign Service officer, he served in Vietnam alongside Anthony Lake, who was now President Clinton's National Security Advisor. Unlike many of his contemporaries, while in Vietnam he gained a good deal of respect for the American military, particularly the Special Forces.

Wisner was one of the senior Washington officials whom Howe contacted regularly from his Mogadishu post. While Wisner was reticent to back the use of the Delta force to hunt down Aideed, he agreed with Howe on the need for more active American political and military support for UNOSOM II. As early as April, he had been mulling over the use of U.S. special-operations forces to help disarm the warlords and destroy some of their large weapons stockpiles. By late June, he was warning the somewhat indecisive Secretary of Defense, Les Aspin, that the failure of the United Nations in Somalia would deal a severe blow to America's national interest. The U.N.'s future as a useful peacekeeping organization was at stake. Failure in Somalia would spell an end to U.S. efforts to use the United Nations in crises that, though not significant enough to merit direct American involvement, were nevertheless important enough to require active resolution.

The month of July saw unremitting escalation of the military conflict between UNOSOM II and Aideed, with the United States using its small but powerful contingent remaining in Somalia—the Quick Reaction Force—in increasingly heavier strikes against Aideed as part of the Clinton administration's strategy to bolster the U.N. force. A major threshold was crossed on July 12 when the Quick Reaction Force, without any warning, carried out a devastating raid against Aideed's command post. The helicopter gunships fired sixteen missiles into the compound, killing a number of prominent Aideed supporters and SNA leaders. The International Committee of the Red Cross put the Somali casualty figures at 54 killed and 161 wounded.[5] In the wake of the raid, a top aide to Aideed warned that "there was no more United Nations, only Americans. If you could kill Americans, it would start problems in America directly."[6]

Searching for Aideed

Following several SNA attacks in early August that killed several American soldiers, President Clinton on August 22 secretly ordered the Delta force, augmented by the equally legendary Army Rangers, to Somalia. Another Rubicon had been crossed. The United States had decided to stake its international reputation and the credibility of its elite military forces in a direct challenge to a minor Third World warlord. There was high confidence in Washington that Aideed would be the loser in this gambit.

During the subsequent six weeks, Somalia turned out to be an eerie replay of the Vietnam tragedy on a minor scale. The United States was unable to translate its overwhelming technological superiority over Aideed's ragtag forces into either a military or a political victory. With impressive skill and daring, the special forces searched for Aideed constantly, but he always managed to stay a step ahead of them. His numerous sympathizers kept him well informed of the special forces' movements. He avoided radio communication to prevent interception of his messages.

The special forces never captured him. An intelligent man who, unlike Saddam Hussein, knew the United States well, Aideed figured that the foreign intruders might tire of the whole enterprise if he could raise the political costs just a bit. After all, precisely because Somalia was not important to the United States, a few well-placed blows might induce the Americans to give up.

By now, the U.S. Congress, including many Democrats, had become restless with the inconclusive and increasingly escalating Somalia operation. Besides, the President, still only eight months in office, seemed uninterested in foreign policy and uncomfortable with its details, thereby providing a tempting target for his Republican adversaries. As congressional opposition began to mount, a number of thoughtful critics on and outside Capitol Hill began to ask whether the Administration had any exit strategy for Somalia, any notion of when or under what conditions it was prepared to bring America's involvement to an end.

The Administration's responses to these queries were less than reassuring. The President and his Secretary of Defense argued that the situation was improving, that the United States could not be seen as retreating, and that it would be able to fulfill its mission and bring its forces home in the near future. Revealing how little he understood what the U.S. forces were doing, or perhaps in a deliberate effort to tap into the American people's humanitarian impulse even at the cost of misleading them, the President kept insisting that the central purpose of the U.S. forces was to feed the hungry, even though by then the famine had been over for several months.

On October 3, tragedy struck. A special-forces team swooped down by helicopter on a Mogadishu building to arrest several prominent Aideed lieutenants who were in hiding. In a few minutes, the special forces rounded up the suspects and were ready to carry them away, the operation apparently a success. But word had spread quickly, and hundreds of armed Aided sympathizers began to gather around the building, firing their weapons at the Americans. The battle lasted for several hours, during which the Rangers killed more than 300 of Aideed's militiamen and wounded some 1,000. Unfortunately, the casualties included a large number of women and children caught in the crossfire. The besieged American team was rescued eventually, but not before losing eighteen soldiers. Like the Tet offensive of 1968, the battle was a military victory but a political defeat.

Pandemonium broke out in Washington. A beleaguered Secretary of Defense, called to testify immediately before a congressional committee, set off a firestorm of outrage when, in an uncharacteristic outburst of humility, he asked the congressmen their opinion of what U.S. policy toward Somalia should be. To make matters worse, some Pentagon sources leaked the news that several weeks earlier the U.S. field commander in Somalia, General Montgomery, had requested heavy armored vehicles to protect the American forces, but that Aspin had turned down the request because of concerns that sending the heavy equipment might alarm Congress unduly by feeding suspicions about further escalation.

In fairness to the Secretary, it must be said that none of his military advisors at the Pentagon, including General Powell, had been particularly adamant about the need for the vehicles. They had not given him an accurate idea of the serious risk to which the U.S. forces were exposed in Mogadishu, and thus it was understandable that he had decided the matter as he did. Now that a debacle was in the making, not one of Les Aspin's advisors—for that matter not even his superior—stepped in to his rescue. He was allowed to twist slowly under heavy congressional and media fire, the clear scapegoat for a disaster to which many others had contributed aplenty. To his credit, Aspin took most of the blame on himself, unfair as that may have been. With his credibility and reputation in tatters, he was to resign a few months later from the job to which he had aspired all his life, and in which he had lasted less than eleven months. He would die, a broken man, less than two years later.

A few days later, President Clinton, eager to cut his mounting political losses, announced that the United States would withdraw its military forces from Somalia within a few months. No preconditions were attached. Two weeks later, UNOSOM II opened negotiations with Aideed. By the spring of 1994 the United States had withdrawn most of its remaining forces, and the other states participating in the U.N. force also had begun to pull out their troops. Surrounded by cheering throngs of supporters, Aideed entered Mogadishu triumphantly on May 20, 1994. The last U.N. forces left the country, under protection of the U.S. military, in March 1995.

WAS IT WORTH IT?

From the U.S. perspective, after some $2 billion spent on military operations alone, exclusive of the non-military aid donated to Somalia, and a total of 30 Americans dead and another 175 wounded, was it worth it? The answers to this question run across a wide spectrum of opinion. At one end are the interest-driven realists and at the other the values-driven globalists.

The Interest-Driven Realists

The argument from this group is that no matter how powerful the United States is, and no matter how broad and global its interests are, both its economic and its political resources are still limited, and therefore it needs to choose carefully where and to what extent it becomes involved in the crises dotting the globe today. The significant sums of money that the Defense Department spent on Somalia came out of some other account in its budget; some important program had to be downgraded or sacrificed altogether, some significant investment neglected or postponed, to pay for the Somali intervention.

Similarly, the political resources of the U.S. government are limited, as are the reservoirs of public support for foreign commitments. The enormous amounts of time, energy, intellectual focus, and political capital that the President and his top diplomatic and military advisors spent on Somalia came at the expense of other critical issues, some of them of greater relevance to the well-being and security of the American people. Given limited resources and multiple demands, the United States has to be tough-minded as it chooses among competing priorities. Somalia should have been ranked low on the list. It is true that the American people were disturbed by the reports of the spreading famine, but not so much as to demand that the government intervene to stop it. Even though the President received wide popular support when he decided to intervene, there is no evidence that a failure to do so would have led to strong public disapproval outside the Beltway.

Furthermore, even if some form of intervention had been agreed upon, its scope, duration, and the size of the forces involved needed to be measured also in the context of the limited U.S. interests at stake and the potential costs and risks involved. Unlike the 1991 Operation Blue Angel, in which the U.S. military, with the full support of the Bangladesh government, had extended humanitarian assistance to that country in the aftermath of a devastating cyclone, this was not an unopposed humanitarian intervention. In Somalia there was a full-blown civil war among heavily armed factions, and the intervention ran the risk of opposition by some of those factions, especially as it engaged more deeply in "nation-building" missions.

Among interest-driven realists, especially those outside the isolationist or neo-isolationist camp, many have what I would call an interest-driven "domino theory" of international precedent and consequences. They realize that isolated events and actions can have strategic consequences far beyond their original narrow context. This is why, in foreign policy and defense, they tend to favor the exercise of American strength and resolve as long as the U.S. interests at stake are significant. A tough stance on behalf of American interests in country X will affect perceptions of U.S. credibility and strength in country Z and many more besides. A show of weakness in one place will embolden U.S. adversaries elsewhere.

On the whole, interest-driven realists are skeptical of humanitarian interventions, especially those involving high costs and risks in places of marginal strategic importance to the United States. Lest we see these realists as bereft of a moral compass, they point out that selectivity in choosing whether to intervene, the weighing of costs and risks, and an appreciation of the nation's limited resources in a world of multiple dangers are all morally worthwhile concerns. Moreover, they warn, costly interventions in places of limited value to the United States wind up leaving the American public with a sour taste about international commitments, thereby imperiling future public support for action in places that really matter, whether Kuwait, Korea, or Bosnia.

As their final trump card, the realists like to point to the apparently inexhaustible reservoir of humanitarian crises around the world and the seemingly arbitrary choice of Somalia. Why not Sudan, where people also were dying from hunger? Why Haiti and not Cuba? Is it morally appropriate to allow Cable News Network to influence America's choices of strategic priorities? These are legitimate questions in a world of seemingly limitless human suffering and limited resources.

The Values-Driven Globalists

At the other end of the spectrum in the debate over Somalia, most of those whom we might call values-driven globalists think they are as aware of the realities of power politics and as concerned about promoting U.S. national interests as the interest-driven realists. The key differences are, first, their broader conception of the national interest in the light of contemporary global economic and political interdependence, and second, a values-driven "domino theory" of precedent and consequences. The globalists' viewpoint has been expressed forcefully by Chester Crocker:

> President Bush was right—politically, strategically, and ethically— to launch Operation Restore Hope, and President Clinton was right to support his decision. The judgment that U.S. forces could and should stop humanitarian disaster in Somalia was a proper assertion of global leadership. . . . As the end of the century nears, it is surely wise that we and others broaden our understanding of national interest to include consideration of interests related to global order (sanctity of borders, extension of the Nuclear Non-proliferation Treaty) and global standards (avoiding genocide, mass humanitarian catastrophe).[7]

Values-driven globalists focus on the degree to which the well-being and security of the United States are tied to a certain kind of benign international order. They would agree with the realists that this order needs American military power at its foundation, but it also depends for its health and vibrancy on global institutions of cooperation, including the United Nations, and the strengthening of shared international legal and moral norms that provide some restraints on state behavior. The spread of civil war and mass famine, even in a small country such as Somalia, could not be written off as a tragic but ultimately inconsequential event. To allow it to continue would have had repercussions beyond the purely humanitarian tragedy. It would have contributed further to the overall deterioration of Africa. Moreover, once the United Nations intervened, a U.S. refusal to support the operation would have led to U.N. failure and thereby would have undermined that organization's credibility.

In keeping with their values-driven "domino theory" of precedent and consequences, globalists argue that allowing extreme suffering and degradation in a place like Somalia has its costs, imperceptible as these might seem to the realists. International passivity in the face of gross human suffering and violations of human rights in one particular place contributes to a generalized loss of respect for life and human dignity in the world as a whole. International society, morality, and basic decency form one whole fabric. A tear in one place affects the quality and strength of the fabric everywhere else, and though obviously not all tears are of the same kind, we should repair all tears whenever feasible. It is interesting to note that the just war tradition has recognized these global communitarian links to which the globalists pay so much attention. In his sixteenth-century treatise *The Indies*, for example, Francisco de Vitoria argued that human-rights violations in one country affected everyone else in that all persons are part of the same larger human society spanning the whole world.

Globalists argue that, given the United States' enormous resources, aid to Somalia and support for the U.N. intervention was a reasonable, feasible course of action. The fact that the intervention eventually became resented by many Somalis and perceived by most Americans as a fiasco does not erase several fundamental realities. First, thanks to American leadership, the famine ended and many Somali lives were saved, though a serious study has shown that by the time the Marines began to land in December the famine had peaked, and the total number of lives saved by the intervention may have been as low as 10,000.[8] Second, in spite of the affair's ambiguous ending, Somalia did not revert to civil war. Although it does not enjoy a stable or peaceful domestic political climate today, the country is out of the worst throes of the internal strife that almost destroyed it. Economically, Somalia also has a long way to go, but its agricultural production is considerably above 1991-92 levels.

On balance, a modicum of order and well-being was restored to a corner of Africa. All these achievements justify the entire operation, in the globalists' eyes, despite the tragic loss of American lives, the financial cost to the Defense Department, the mistakes made along the way by all parties, and the incomplete and anti-climactic ending. To the degree that Somalia's corner of Africa is a slightly more orderly place today, and the international system has one fewer point of chaos, the benefits to the United States of the Somalia intervention, though indirect, were not insubstantial.

Finally, the globalists have an answer for the realists' question, Why Somalia? There may have been even more serious crises elsewhere, but there were practical opportunities to act in Somalia, and so it was appropriate and useful to step in even if it meant giving less attention to other humanitarian emergencies. We face similar dilemmas in our personal lives and in domestic policy. The fact that we are unable to assist all the deserving poor to the fullest extent of their needs does not prevent us from engaging in some forms of charity. Our choice of those charities is shaped by circumstances that are largely accidental if not arbitrary; yet no one would argue that it would be better not to give to any charity at all than to give to some on the basis of less than fully systematic reasons.

Concluding Observations

The substantive debate between the *interest-driven realists* and the *values-driven globalists,* and among those at various points between these two poles of opinion, will not be settled soon. In the Somalia intervention, good intentions were mixed with miscalculations in roughly equal proportions to produce an outcome that was as full of ambiguities and failures as of undeniable achievements. The United States started out its mission with high confidence that it could do some good at low cost, without becoming entangled in Somalia's conflict. As the humanitarian effort proceeded successfully, American officials and their U.N. counterparts fell to the temptation of expanding the missions in order to address Somalia's wider political and economic problems.

This was the fateful step. For in expanding the mission to include the country's wholesale political and economic reconstruction, they put themselves on a collision course with powerful Somali forces that had a different vision of where the country should go. The error of expanding the mission was compounded when, after encountering resistance from such forces, notably Aideed, they proceeded to underestimate them and to forsake compromise in favor of all-out war. Although grossly outmatched technologically, Aideed fought this war skillfully, mindful that, as long as he could evade capture and continue killing American soldiers, it would not be long before the Americans gave up, given Somalia's unimportance to the United States.

In the end, the United States did some good, but not without incurring significant economic, political, and human costs. What started out as an effort to demonstrate American global leadership wound up leaving the United States embarrassed and humiliated. Clausewitz's warning that "in war even the seemingly most simple things turn out to be not so simple" is as applicable to the use of military force in humanitarian interventions as to the larger conflicts with which we usually associate these somber words.

9

The Duty to Intervene:
Ethics and the Varieties of
Humanitarian Intervention

Drew Christiansen, S.J., and Gerard F. Powers

[H]umanitarian intervention [is] obligatory where the survival of
populations and entire ethnic groups is seriously compromised.
This is a duty for nations and the international community.
—Pope John Paul II, 1992[1]

Since the end of the Cold War, ethicists, policy-makers, international
lawyers, and others have renewed a long-standing debate over the
legitimacy of humanitarian intervention. The urgency of this debate
is evident in the proliferation of such interventions in recent years:
establishment of the U.N. protective area in northern Iraq, the use of
military force to back up relief programs in Somalia, the protection of
refugees and their safe havens in Bosnia, the West African peacekeeping effort in Liberia and the U.S. rescue of expatriates and Liberian
leaders from that country, U.N. action in response to the genocide in
Rwanda, and, finally, the U.N.-backed U.S. intervention in Haiti.

Drew Christiansen, S.J., is former director of the Office of International Justice and Peace at the United States Catholic Conference.
Gerard F. Powers has been a foreign-policy advisor to the USCC
since 1987. The two are co-editors of *Peacemaking: Moral and Policy
Challenges for a New World* (USCC, 1994).

This essay is not intended to add to the already voluminous literature on the issues raised by humanitarian intervention for traditional notions of statecraft. These issues include: how do we reconcile intervention with the principles of non-intervention and state sovereignty, what constitutes just cause for intervention, and who has the right to intervene.[2] Rather, our objectives are: (1) to help clarify the rather amorphous category of "humanitarian intervention" by surveying the diverse forms it takes; (2) to comment on the pertinence to humanitarian intervention of just war criteria; (3) to examine a variable that has received relatively little attention, namely, the question of legitimate *means* in humanitarian intervention; and (4) to propose that the fit between means and ends in humanitarian interventions is key to determining their moral validity. Once it is clear that just cause and legitimate authority exist for humanitarian intervention, a wide spectrum of means can be used to achieve a similarly wide spectrum of ends. These means range from non-violent acts, such as the unauthorized distribution over many years of emergency relief in southern Sudan, to the NATO bombing of Bosnian-Serb positions to protect safe havens after the fall of Srebrenica in 1995.

Our hypothesis differs in three ways from standard approaches to distinguishing types of humanitarian intervention. First, it assumes two things: that a moral assessment of humanitarian intervention should not be limited to military types of intervention but should also include non-coercive measures and coercive measures short of military force; and that a moral assessment should also distinguish among different kinds of military intervention. Second, these different kinds of intervention suggest the need for different thresholds, or just causes, for intervention, with a high threshold (e.g., genocide, enslavement, widespread starvation) for military interventions that entail war-fighting but lower thresholds (e.g., widespread human-rights abuses, undemocratic regime) for less forceful interventions. Third, while many lawyers, ethicists, and policy-makers struggle to formulate a threshold for humanitarian intervention and then find themselves uncomfortable about the elastic use others make of the threshold, our focus on types of intervention suggests a more casuistic, case-by-case moral evaluation, one that involves calibrating means to the various ends being pursued.

For example, a case can be made that third parties may employ economic sanctions to oppose a government's widespread, but not massive, abuse of the human rights of its own nationals, but that it would be inappropriate for third parties to use *military* force to the same end. Similarly, the use of limited force may be appropriate to protect refugees or to provide humanitarian aid in a civil conflict, but not to restore democracy in the aftermath of a coup. In short, while the criteria of just cause and legitimate authority remain of vital importance, whether the means to be employed are appropriate to achieve legitimate objectives will be a decisive factor in concluding whether a particular type of intervention is morally justified. This focus on the relation between means and ends suggests a *composite moral judgment* in which other just war criteria (last resort, probability of success, proportionality, and discrimination) also remain relevant.

In what follows we will first delineate three major types of humanitarian intervention. Next we will make the case for using a just war form of moral reasoning, in the context of a cosmopolitan political ethic, to evaluate these three types. The bulk of our discussion will then focus on specific ways in which means and ends are decisive for determining the morality of humanitarian interventions.

THREE TYPES OF HUMANITARIAN INTERVENTION

For the purpose of argument, we shall take humanitarian intervention to be: (a) a use or threat of non-violent diplomatic or substantial humanitarian activity, economic or political coercion, or military force, (b) by a state, collection of states, or international organization(s) (governmental and non-governmental), (c) in a way that impinges on the receiving state's sovereignty, (d) on behalf of the population within that state, (e) in response to genocide, mass suffering, or widespread human-rights abuses (f) caused by aggression, a failed state, or systemic injustice. Some of these provisions may seem too broad, others too narrow. Let the formulation stand as our best assessment of what qualifies both experientially and morally as a humanitarian intervention.

The most common way of distinguishing among interventions looks at *the evils* that the intervention attempts to correct. Numerous justifications have been offered for recent cases of humanitarian intervention. Bosnia and Rwanda involved genocide. Somalia was a case of preventing mass starvation attributable to a failed state, and Sudan, of mitigating the effects of civil war. Interventions in northern Iraq,

Bosnia, Haiti, and Rwanda were justified, at least in part, as responses to refugee crises. The restoration of democracy was the overt reason for the early involvement of the Organization of American States in Haiti, and it has been a component in the resolution of conflict, under U.N. auspices, in Cambodia and Bosnia.

Another way to distinguish among interventions is to consider *the cause* of the humanitarian crisis. Is the genocide, mass killing, or refugee crisis engineered by a totalitarian regime, as in the case of the Khmer Rouge in Cambodia, or is it connected to ethnic-nationalist conflict, as in Bosnia? Is the widespread starvation a byproduct of civil war between contending political authorities, as in Sudan or Ethiopia, or a symptom of the anarchy associated with a failed state, as in Somalia or Liberia? Does a military coup take place in a country with strong prospects for democracy, or is it a symptom of a lack of democratic traditions and culture? These diverse causes affect whether and how the international community can and should respond to a particular humanitarian crisis, and also the prospects for success.

A third distinction looks at *the ends,* or specific objectives, of an intervention. In Rwanda and Bosnia, genocide justified intervention, but the objective of intervention was not to stop or reverse the genocide. Rather, in Rwanda, objectives were limited to caring for refugees and prosecuting war criminals. In Bosnia, in addition to these two objectives, the international community sought to provide minimal protection to civilian populations, to contain the conflict while a political solution was found, and, after the Dayton Accords, to help implement the accords and create the conditions for post-war economic and political reconstruction. In Somalia, the objective initially was to feed starving populations but later was expanded to include a minimal effort at nation-building. In Haiti, the objective was to restore an elected government to power and to stop refugee flows, again with a minimal commitment to nation-building. Distinguishing among objectives helps determine whether an intervention is an adequate response to the humanitarian crisis that justified it, the extent to which it impinges on a state's sovereignty, and its feasibility.

A final morally salient distinction looks at whether *the means* of intervention are non-violent, coercive short of military force, or military. Let us look briefly at these three types of means as a way of classifying interventions.

1. Non-Violent Interventions

On this end of the spectrum there are at least three sorts of interventions: diplomatic, humanitarian (relief), and civil or legal (e.g., the sending of human-rights monitors and election monitors). These interventions can make use of a range of resources, including military, but they do not involve coercion or the use of force.

Diplomatic interventions include ordinary diplomatic representations, negotiations, mediations, and extraordinary declarations and resolutions. These differ from other diplomatic activities in that they are directed at preventing or resolving a serious humanitarian crisis by influencing the internal political dynamics of a country.

Non-violent *humanitarian* activities include emergency relief for refugees or other affected populations and reconstruction programs. Some of these are undertaken by private relief agencies or non-governmental organizations (NGOs), and some by international organizations, such as the United Nations High Commissioner for Refugees or the International Committee of the Red Cross. They often rely on logistical and other forms of assistance from military units, as in Operation Provide Comfort in northern Iraq. This field of activities can be a muddle of jurisdictions, since it includes both non-governmental organizations and officially recognized organizations with special international status. The humanitarian activities may have the official approval of the nominal state power or may take place without that approval, as in Sudan and Ethiopia.

Non-violent *civil and legal* measures include the creation of war-crimes tribunals, as for Bosnia and Rwanda, the assignment of human-rights and election monitors, and the commissioning of police and judicial training units. The latter, as in El Salvador, Cambodia, and Haiti, are usually international representatives operating with the explicit permission of the local government in the completion of a peace process. Human-rights and election monitors, both official and unofficial, represent an exceptional international presence in the internal workings of nations. They therefore involve, to varying degrees, an attenuation of the principle of non-interference and belong to the category of intervention. Human-rights monitors in particular, and especially non-governmental human-rights monitors, may be positioned between a government and its people. The intervention of these independent actors is often impelled by a cosmopolitan ethic that is inclined to dismiss the moral difficulties with intervention. Without these NGO efforts, however, the state system is likely to neglect rights abuses and impending humanitarian crises until they represent a threat to peace or order among states, such as that presented by large refugee flows.

War-crimes tribunals are an important form of intervention because they reinforce international humanitarian norms and introduce an element of justice into a situation of grave injustice. They can be an important step in the process of reconciliation between deeply divided communities.

2. Coercive Diplomacy and Sanctions

Among the forms of coercive diplomacy that may qualify as humanitarian intervention, the pre-eminent one is economic sanctions. Others would include suspension of aid, denial of credit, boycotting of international events such as sports competitions, suspension from international organizations, and imposition of arms embargoes. Coercive diplomacy aims to penalize the offending state for its violation of international norms and to force a change in government behavior.

Coercive diplomacy represents the first serious test for the proposal that there are different thresholds for different sorts of humanitarian interventions. It provides an expanded set of options for dealing with humanitarian crises that are not susceptible to purely non-violent or diplomatic measures, yet do not rise to the level that would justify military intervention. In other words, it offers a way to improve the likelihood of success while ensuring that the means of intervention are proportionate to the evil to be corrected.

Thus, for example, it may be appropriate to use economic sanctions to influence a government to alter a regime based on systematic violations of human rights, such as the South African regime under apartheid, or to effect change in a military government that engages in significant and widespread, though not massive, violations of human rights, such as the Cedras government in Haiti. In neither case would it have been justifiable to go to war to change the regime.

3. Military Options

Military forms of intervention that have been used or contemplated in recent years range from lightly armed peacekeeping missions to massive military intervention in a war-fighting posture.[3] Traditional *peacekeeping* uses military forces to monitor ceasefires, as in Croatia, or to help implement a peace settlement, as in Bosnia. Peacekeepers usually are inserted once the fighting has stopped, with the consent of the warring parties, to monitor ceasefire lines and oversee demilitarization. The troops normally use force only to defend themselves. *Protective engagement* (or *active defense*) uses troops to establish safe havens, protect aid convoys and refugee columns, and help stimulate a peace settlement while strife continues. It could also include the use of troops and international police in a post-conflict situation, using force, if necessary, to protect returning refugees, to prevent further "ethnic cleansing," and to ensure peaceful elections, as in Bosnia and Haiti.

If peacekeeping and protective engagement may be seen as variations of international policing, the other two forms of military intervention involve at least the willingness to engage in large-scale war-fighting. *Deterrence* uses military deployments to dissuade those who are contemplating violence. The U.N. Force in Macedonia provides such a trip-wire, deterring both outside aggression and internal ethnic violence. In 1996 the U.N. considered for a time the deployment of a rapid-reaction force near Burundi in an effort to deter an explosion of genocidal violence there. Finally, at the upper range of armed intervention for humanitarian reasons is *peace enforcement*. Peace enforcement involves a full-scale military invasion to resolve a humanitarian crisis by imposing a solution, as the United States threatened to do in Haiti in 1994. This term technically applies to enforcement measures under Chapter 7 of the U.N. Charter, which deals with U.N. responses to breaches of the peace and acts of aggression. Desert Storm in Iraq is an example. But the same types of interventions may take place outside the Charter framework. Two such examples are the Indian incursion into East Pakistan and the Tanzanian involvement in ending Uganda's civil war.[4]

Typology of Humanitarian Intervention

Justifications:
Genocide
Mass starvation
Human-rights abuses
Refugee crisis
Undemocratic regime

Cause of Crisis:
Repression by
totalitarian regime
Civil war/ethnic conflict
Failed state
Interstate conflict

Objectives:
Replace offending government
Rebuild political/economic/
social order
Contain conflict
Encourage a political settlement
Protect civilian populations
Provide humanitarian aid
Vindicate justice

Means:
A. Non-violent:
Diplomacy
Humanitarian relief
Civil/legal measures

B. Coercive:
Diplomacy
Arms embargoes
Economic sanctions

C. Military:
Peacekeeping
Protective engagement
Deterrence
Peace enforcement

A Case for Just War Reasoning

This classification of humanitarian interventions along a continuum of means and ends raises a preliminary question: Is a just war style of moral reasoning germane to actions that either do not include the overt use of force or employ force in only a policing rather than a war-fighting mode? Some would say that just war criteria apply only to means akin to war-fighting, or, more strictly, only in cases of war between states.

We would like to argue for a broader application of the just war tradition, or, more precisely, for the use of a just war style of thinking in the moral analysis of both non-coercive and coercive measures, whether by governments or by NGOs, that count as interventions into the internal lives of states. This style of thinking is more broadly applicable than is sometimes supposed. In the first place, just war thought has evolved to fit varying circumstances and varying outlooks on the role of force in the exercise of public authority. The age of Augustine and those of Aquinas and Vitoria differed in the kinds of problems they had to address, in their understandings of the theological premises and political ethics underlying just war thought, and in the elaboration and application of just war criteria.

Today, similarly, such developments as the expanded use of economic sanctions by the United Nations demand that we expand just war analysis beyond traditional uses of military force. Economic sanctions, though sometimes an alternative to war, as in the case of Serbia, can equally well be a prosecution of war by other means, as in the case of the U.N. sanctions against Iraq.

Furthermore, economic sanctions raise some of the same questions, albeit at a different level, that are presented by the recourse to war: questions of just cause, legitimate authority, civilian immunity, proportionality, probability of success, and so on. Whether or not explicit appeal is made to just war precedents, as statecraft evolves the same kind of considerations will need to be raised about policies made to deal with other forms of conflict.

A continuum of means and ends, however, also takes us from the subdued conflict of a sanctions regime into the range of non-violent measures. Even strictly humanitarian undertakings that assume no military protection, such as Operation Lifeline Sudan or relief programs in Liberia, may nonetheless need to address a set of questions akin to the just war criteria. What is the threshold for ignoring state sovereignty in order to bring aid to affected civilians in a civil conflict? By what authority do aid agencies "intervene" in civil conflicts? Are there points beyond which aid ought not to be given because of its unintended negative effects? A consortium of aid agencies struggled with such issues before returning to Liberia after the collapse of a ceasefire there in 1996.[5] Aid agencies faced similar questions with regard to the conflict in Zaire in 1997.[6]

We would contend, therefore, that the style of reasoning characteristic of just war thinking should not be restricted to armed conflict between nations or military forms of humanitarian intervention. While the humanitarian interventions of the last several years may require adaptations not found in literature dealing with armed conflict, the kinds of issues raised, the tests to be met, and the moral distinctions to be drawn will bear a sufficient family resemblance to traditional just war analyses to be taken as a contemporary variation on that centuries-old theme.

Just War and the Cosmopolitan Political Ethic

Humanitarian intervention presents an additional feature that favors employing a just war type of thinking along a continuum of means and ends: it emerges out of a cosmopolitan political context in which the rights of persons (and communities) have a greater value than in traditional state-centered approaches to just war. Humanitarian intervention characteristically is undertaken on behalf of individuals or groups who are victims of failed states, of so-called rogue governments, or of belligerents in a civil war. In practice, such interventions are actually a mix of cosmopolitan and state-centered considerations. The cosmopolitan political ethic with its high valuation of individual rights presses toward action on behalf of victimized peoples and temporarily sets aside the prerogatives of state sovereignty. The state-centered political ethic tends to hold to non-intervention as long as possible, often as much from reluctance to increase the level of violence and from assessments of the likelihood of success as from traditional state interests. It is, of course, the cosmopolitan political ethic and the value it places on human life independent of the state that gives rise to the contemporary phenomenon of intervention by outside parties for humanitarian reasons.

Just war reasoning has always been situated in a broader political ethic, stipulating the nature of authority, its sources, prerogatives, and limits. So today, just war reasoning must be situated in a political ethic that, by comparison with the Westphalian state model that preceded it, is more cosmopolitan, more inclined to protect individual rights, less inclined to ignore the failure or inability of governments to protect those rights and ensure the survival of their people.

In this respect, the teaching of *Pacem in Terris* (Peace on Earth), the 1963 encyclical letter of Pope John XXIII, is instructive.[7] In many ways, *Pacem in Terris* is the charter of contemporary Catholic teaching on political ethics. It is the most extensive and comprehensive document in the body of Catholic social teaching on the topic. The logic of the encyclical is that the end of government is to protect the common good, defined as the promotion, protection, and safeguarding of human rights.[8] In a move that anticipates the politics of humanitarian intervention, Pope John XXIII concluded that, when governments fail in their responsibility to protect human rights, then not only are their acts illegitimate but it falls to other public authorities to supply that protection.[9]

Pope John Paul II has taken the teaching even further, arguing that in extreme cases, like genocide, there is "a duty to intervene."[10] Pope John Paul's profession of the duty of states and the international community to intervene is especially noteworthy in that he has generally taken a highly restrictive view of the use of force. He makes it clear that Catholic teaching still insists on the obligation to defend justice and the common good, understood in terms of the rights of persons and communities, at the same time that it strictly construes just cause for resort to force, limiting it to defense against ongoing aggression.[11]

In this regard, it is salutary to remember that Christian just war thinking arose in the cosmopolitan context of the late Roman Empire, where public authority was not divided among nation states with frequently competing interests. In addition, in a largely Christian empire, the justification for the use of force was the demand of charity that public authority defend the innocent.[12] These two historical factors explain, in part at least, why much Christian just war thinking, and particularly that of the Vatican, has sometimes seemed more accepting of humanitarian intervention than has the thinking of other international actors or international-relations theorists.

Accordingly, if the political ethic of contemporary Catholic social teaching, as well as Vatican practice, can be seen as one paradigm of a cosmopolitan political ethic, the application of just war reasoning to humanitarian intervention is not just a matter of extending just war analysis to a special class of cases. It is, rather, an appropriate use of the method in the context of a broader political ethic. For a cosmopolitan political ethic grants only conditional legitimacy to states, gives primacy to human rights and welfare, and finds in the defense of those rights a compelling reason for intervention, including, at times, the limited uses of force.

Setting a High Threshold

Without qualification, this argument for using a just war type of analysis in the context of a cosmopolitan ethic could end up justifying what the U.S. Catholic bishops have called "endless wars of altruism."[13] As the Pope makes clear in his call for humanitarian intervention, however, sovereignty and non-interference retain their value as fundamental principles of international affairs because they are essential to uphold the fundamental freedom and equality of states. Therefore a state's sovereignty may not be overridden except in exceptional circumstances.[14]

As a matter of practical and prudential morality, there are several reasons for setting a high threshold for humanitarian intervention. First, a low threshold would provide pretexts for illegitimate meddling by regional and global powers in the affairs of weaker states. As the U.S. bishops point out, "effective mechanisms must be developed to ensure that humanitarian intervention is an authentic act of international solidarity and not a cloak for great power dominance, as it sometimes has been in the past."[15]

Second, the potential number of occasions for such intervention also argues for setting the threshold at a high level. The community of nations has a difficult time deciding on action even in cases of mass murder, genocide, and "ethnic cleansing." To lower the threshold for intervention would be to squander needed moral capital.

Third, as evidenced by the sluggish response first to Rwanda and then to Burundi, the resources and will for frequent interventions are simply lacking. Rarely would individual states have the capacity to intervene effectively. As for multilateral institutions, they currently lack the capacity to intervene in the comprehensive and long-term ways that are usually necessary to achieve lasting results, and they are unlikely to be able to generate the necessary political will.

Fourth, the conflicts in which intervention is most easily justified, such as genocide in Rwanda, are often those least susceptible to outside influence. To be sure, an "ancient hatreds" explanation may misdiagnose the cause of a particular conflict and serve as an excuse for international inaction. But some conflicts are intractable, leaving little room for effective intervention. The problems in implementing the civilian aspects of the Dayton Accords in Bosnia-Herzegovina (e.g., elections, right of return of refugees) are just one example of how difficult it is, even with a massive use of international troops and other resources, to alter the political, social, and cultural dynamics that generated the humanitarian crisis.

Fifth, given these local dynamics, it is very difficult to intervene in a way that is impartial and does not embroil the intervenor in local political disputes.[16] Interventions that lack, or are perceived to lack, impartiality risk not only exacerbating the local conflict but also bringing the international community into disrepute.

Finally, the way the international community intervenes, even if relatively impartial, can bring discredit to itself. In Somalia and Bosnia, this happened when armed action by military forces under U.N. auspices resulted in civilian casualties. In Rwanda and Bosnia, it occurred because the international forces that had been deployed failed to prevent atrocities and human-rights abuses from taking place all around them.

These practical concerns about the actual implementation of a cosmopolitan ethic's approach to humanitarian intervention lead to a revised theory of sovereignty that would maintain the presumption for non-intervention but, in exceptional circumstances, would not only tolerate but even demand humanitarian intervention. Ultimately, this intervention, though impelled by a cosmopolitan ethic, would serve state-centered conceptions of sovereignty, because it would restore a situation in which the purposes of state sovereignty, notably protection of basic human rights and promotion of the common good, could be fulfilled. The aim is to make sovereignty work, not abolish it.

HUMANITARIAN INTERVENTION: MAKING A COMPOSITE MORAL JUDGMENT

Even if there is consensus that a just war style of reasoning applies to non-military types of intervention, and that a revised theory of sovereignty can be found to justify certain humanitarian interventions, a major task remains for any moral analysis. The U.S. Catholic bishops, like many others, have noted that a revised model of statecraft in which humanitarian intervention is more acceptable, even obligatory, requires a clearer delineation of criteria for intervention.[17] The task is not just to clarify *why* intervention is justified (just cause) but, perhaps more difficult and more necessary, better to define *when* and *how* to intervene. For all three questions are part of the composite moral judgment about particular humanitarian interventions.

In most of the current cases in which humanitarian intervention is considered, the debate is less about whether there is just cause or legitimate authority for intervention and more about what kinds of intervention could succeed, be proportionate, and be accomplished with means consistent with the humanitarian objectives. The purposes for which interventions are carried out generally point to the moral justifications; by themselves, however, such purposes do not offer sufficient reason to intervene. They provide the motive but not a full assessment of what counts as a valid moral reason.

A full assessment requires giving special attention to how the problem to be addressed, the specific ends or goals, and the means used to carry them out relate to one another. For example, if the purpose is to protect refugees, the intervenors can do this by providing asylum, establishing temporary cross-border camps or safe havens, or bringing a war to an end. Once they choose one of these goals, they must choose the means they will use: e.g., human-rights monitors, impartial peacekeepers, armed guards, or international troops with a mandate for active defense. Each set of options requires a careful assessment of need, feasibility, cost, and adequacy to the task. In Bosnia, where the purpose seemed clear and morally appropriate (protecting refugees and preventing new refugee flows), the specific policy goal (establishing safe havens) was not achieved, in part because of morally inadequate implementation. Multiple U.N. mandates, evasions of responsibility, a lack of adequate resources, and questionable strategies, such as the studied impartiality of peacekeepers, all contributed to a moral failure. Hence, a composite judgment of the morality of a particular intervention may be very different from a judgment based primarily on the morality of the justification for intervention.

Means, Ends, and Sovereignty

In making a composite moral judgment, the first point to consider is the extent to which various ends and means actually interfere in the internal affairs of a state, and whether that interference is consistent with the underlying justification for humanitarian intervention. That is, are the goals and means consistent with the moral basis for intervention? Are they designed to enable the intervenors to substitute temporarily for local authorities in upholding the purposes of sovereignty, i.e., in safeguarding human rights and the common good?

In general, *non-violent* means do not penalize a state's offensive behavior, except with loss of face and some (usually minor or temporary) diminution of authority over its people. *Coercive* and *military* means, with the exception of traditional forms of peacekeeping, do penalize the offending government or limit its authority in certain areas. In cases of protective engagement or active defense, intervenors interpose themselves between governments or rival factions and the threatened population; in cases of peace enforcement, they may impose terms on the offending authorities, or they may oust authorities in order to rescue a victim population.

While increased uses of force usually mean greater infringements on sovereignty (and/or autonomy), sometimes the reverse is true. For example, the diplomatic pressures and threat of renewed sanctions that forced Radovan Karadzic from power in the self-declared Serb Republic of Bosnia were a greater infringement on the republic's autonomy than the earlier deployment of U.N. forces to protect aid convoys.

The key question is always whether the intervention is intended and designed to restore the basic human rights and the conditions for community that are the *raison d'être* of sovereignty and non-intervention.[18] A moral analysis must carefully assess the extent to which particular types of intervention actually infringe on (or enhance) a nation's political and territorial integrity as this relates to its capacity to uphold fundamental human rights and promote the common good.

The Presumption in Favor of Non-Violence

In Vatican statements on humanitarian intervention, considerable attention is given to diplomatic and other non-military forms. When military means are endorsed, it is for limited purposes, such as enforcing economic sanctions or a "no-fly" zone, escorting aid convoys, or deterring violence through the mere presence of international forces, as in Macedonia. This approach reflects a strong presumption that, as in conflicts between states, non-violent means are preferable to military means in humanitarian intervention.[19]

This presumption in favor of non-violence requires some examination in light of experience. To begin with, we need to acknowledge the growth of attitudes favoring non-violent remedies to political conflicts.[20] The acceptability of such approaches has to do in part with the success of the mostly non-violent overthrow of authoritarian governments in the 1980s in the Philippines and in Central and Eastern Europe. The growth of democratic regimes and the reluctance of governments to risk lives in a foreign cause have also contributed to a reluctance to use force. So, too, have the theological convictions of religious leaders, such as Pope John Paul II, who played an exceptional role in the non-violent transformation of Eastern Europe.[21] Finally, the political difficulties in assembling and maintaining a consensus of nations in favor of coercive diplomacy or some form of military intervention also tend to drive the international community to search for diplomatic and civil alternatives to the use of military force.

At the same time, whether non-violence is principled or pragmatic, we need to ask where its limits may be found. Are there situations, such as genocide in Rwanda, where diplomatic persuasion will be unlikely to work because there is no political center, or centers of responsibility are dispersed? Are there regimes, such as Iraq, for which experience shows that diplomacy, to be effective, must be backed by some level of force? While humanitarian intervention, like just war thinking, ought to preserve a preference for non-violent means, there is a need to identify the limits of diplomatic and other non-violent interventions.[22]

The intermediate arena of action—coercive measures short of military force—also requires more attention by moralists. Such measures involve moral perplexities akin to those at issue in the use of military means.[23] Economic sanctions, for example, may be either an alternative to war or another form of war, depending upon how they are used. As a tool to pressure an offending state to comply with internationally recognized norms, economic sanctions offer several advantages. They provide an alternative to the use of force as a means of addressing unacceptable state behavior. Even as they increase pressure on a regime, sanctions normally do not infringe on the political and territorial integrity of a state to the same extent as the use of force.

As an alternative to force, sanctions enable governments to proportion their response to offensive acts that would not justify more coercive measures. And when properly targeted so as not to do irreparable harm to civilian populations, sanctions can meet the test of civilian immunity, the moral duty not to harm innocents.[24] Of course, where sanctions would do real harm to an innocent population and do little to influence the policy of an offending regime, then the sanctioning parties must consider whether to move to the use of force or to rescind sanctions and—this is the more likely and usually morally preferable scenario—return to other less coercive means.

The effect, then, of the presumption in favor of non-violence is to establish a high standard for moving from non-violent and coercive measures to the active use of force. We would limit forceful interventions to cases of genocide, mass starvation, or similar mass suffering, where the survival of significant segments of a population is at risk. Humanitarian intervention could still be justified in other cases, such as widespread human-rights abuses and the subversion of democracy, but the means would be limited to non-violent measures, coercive measures short of force, and use of the military in a policing capacity.

Relating Means and Ends

While a presumption in favor of non-violent means raises the threshold for justifying forceful humanitarian intervention, the legitimacy of intervention in a particular case will rest mainly on a proper assessment of the interconnected issues of (1) last resort, (2) probability of success, (3) proportionality, and (4) discrimination.[25] All these highlight in different ways the need, once intervention is deemed justified, to define goals adequate to the humanitarian task at hand and to select appropriate means to achieve these goals.

The criterion of last resort brings up two important points about these situations. First, the internal political crisis that generates a need for humanitarian intervention usually involves a lengthy incubation period. Would-be intervenors will more easily meet the last-resort criterion if they have tried, through early warning and preventive diplomacy, to anticipate crises and prevent them from developing into full-blown emergencies. Second, once a humanitarian emergency exists, the last-resort criterion will recede in importance. In Iraqi

Kurdistan, Somalia, Bosnia, Haiti, Rwanda, and Burundi, there was little doubt that non-violent or coercive measures short of military force either had not succeeded or would not succeed in resolving the humanitarian crisis. In fact, the last-resort question raised by these cases is not so much whether force was used prematurely as whether a gradualist approach of trying and exhausting non-military remedies only made the situation worse, increasing the necessity of a large-scale military intervention once force was used.[26] In Bosnia, for example, if instead of pursuing endless negotiations, an arms embargo, economic sanctions, and limited peacekeeping measures, the intervening parties had deployed international troops early in 1992 with a mandate to help protect the political and territorial integrity of this newly recognized state, they might have prevented much bloodshed and achieved their goal at much less cost.

Probability of success and proportionality are closely related. The means employed must have a reasonable probability of achieving legitimate objectives without causing harm disproportionate to the good to be achieved. In Rwanda, Somalia, and Bosnia, the immensity of the humanitarian catastrophe suggests that rather robust means would have been proportionate. Yet the criterion of probability of success presents a major challenge in such situations. Those who are skeptical of humanitarian intervention correctly point out that international intervention, no matter how massive, has a limited capacity to promote a lasting and just peace, given the ancient hatreds and internecine conflicts that are often involved.[27] Prospects for success are further impeded by the daunting long-term need to rebuild economic, social, and political life. Even in Haiti, the more limited task of restoring a democratically elected government to power is not easily done by outsiders, given the country's political and economic divisions and its lack of democratic traditions and institutions. Michael Walzer argues that "[a] state is self-determining even if its citizens struggle and fail to establish free institutions, but it has been deprived of self-determination if such institutions are established by an intrusive neighbor."[28] Although Walzer underestimates the ability of outside forces to help establish the conditions for democracy, his basic point—that ultimately national futures will be determined by internal struggles—counsels a healthy dose of humility and reticence when the international community aspires to rebuild failed or deeply divided nations. The issue is not so much whether there is a right to try to do so as whether it is feasible.

Unfortunately, this realistic assessment of whether outsiders can do much to deal with the deep roots of humanitarian crises too often degenerates into a self-fulfilling conviction of impotence. This conviction can serve as a convenient mask for indifference. True, ancient hatreds do not disappear once outsiders arrive on the scene to set things right, and democracy cannot be imposed from outside; but in an interdependent world the international community *can* have a significant influence on the future direction of a country, using the panoply of tools now at its disposal. The international community is quite adept at dealing with the humanitarian symptoms of civil war or failed states, as it did in saving hundreds of thousands from starvation in Somalia and keeping a similar number alive in Bosnia. More needs to be done to develop its capacity to intervene in a more comprehensive and effective way, including providing surrogate political authority—as did the U.N. in Cambodia and the European Union in Mostar, Bosnia—to help rebuild functioning governments, societies, and economies in strife-torn countries. But even with more limited interventions, outsiders can do much to support the establishment of a just and lasting peace. Whether by defending safe havens, monitoring human-rights abuses, prosecuting war criminals, helping to implement a peace settlement, or overseeing elections, the international community can make the difference between the success and failure of local efforts.[29]

Gathering Will and Resources

Recent experience shows that prospects for successful humanitarian interventions depend in large part on whether the prospective intervenors are able to garner the political will and the resources necessary to achieve realistic goals.[30] In part because of the perceived intractability of conflicts and in part because of a lack of political will to take the necessary risks and to commit the necessary resources, the international community has either defined its humanitarian objectives too narrowly or taken half-hearted measures that could not possibly achieve the stated purposes of intervention. In some cases, too narrowly defined interventions (e.g., the provision of humanitarian aid) or mandates without resources (e.g., the declaration of safe havens) have had more to do with masking indecisiveness, indifference, or a desire to limit international commitments than with seriously trying to resolve the humanitarian crisis.[31]

Again, the safe havens established in Bosnia are indicative of this problem. By mid–1992, "ethnic cleansing" had created a refugee crisis that had overwhelmed asylum and relief systems. Moreover, the barbarity of the siege of Sarajevo and other cities intensified pressure to intervene. The U.N. declared a half dozen cities safe havens but did not provide the means necessary to protect them. The U.S. Catholic bishops, with a strong commitment both to civilian immunity in wartime and to the care of refugees, urged stronger measures to ensure the success of the safe havens, including the use of an active defense (as opposed to a reactive one) to protect them.[32] In doing so, the bishops fully understood they were passing from peacekeeping to a limited use of force. They did so because in this war of "ethnic cleansing" it had become evident that civilians, rather than being occasional casualties of war, were themselves the targets of the war. The mere deployment of U.N. troops in a low-level, reactive mode had done little to improve civilian protection. Moreover, the restricted numbers of those troops as well as the overlapping mandate for peacekeeping restricted commanders to an impartial style that resulted in more and more demoralizing compromises with the aggressors.

Acknowledging the moral permissibility of defense of refugees and civilian populations meant the bishops understood that the Bosnian conflict had come to the point where only an active military engagement had probability of success in protecting civilians from Serb attack. Also implied in their judgment was the assessment that this step would be proportionate to the risk of an expanded or intensified war it might provoke. Of course, no such limited protection was afforded, and, faced with the failure of the peacekeeping model, NATO opted for an intense, though brief, air campaign in July 1995.[33]

Thus the moral standing of safe havens depended, as in just war analyses of tactics, on assessment of the means necessary to achieve an appropriate objective. To be sure, the fact that safe havens would not work under "impartial" peacekeepers was not fully clear from the beginning. But it should not have taken the fall of Srebrenica to prove that the means were inadequate to the task.[34] This failure of will to do what was necessary to achieve legitimate humanitarian objectives had repercussions beyond Bosnia. Such debacles impede the development of international enforcement mechanisms insofar as the United Nations, NATO, or other multilateral bodies are brought into disrepute or come to be considered impotent.

If Bosnia represents a case where the *probability-of-success* criterion suggested the need to use robust means more likely to achieve humanitarian objectives, Cambodia, Bosnia, and Haiti show how the *proportionality* criterion can place necessary restraints on humanitarian interventions.

In one set of cases, proportionality concerns restrict humanitarian impulses insofar as intervention could internationalize, and thus escalate or widen, a conflict. This was the case in Cambodia in the late 1970s, where intervention by outside powers to stop the genocide could have had disastrous and disproportionate consequences given the way the country was intimately tied up in Cold War conflicts. Even without the Cold War straightjacket, strong and effective international intervention in Bosnia always risked a wider regional conflict, as well as deepening rifts between the major powers. This risk of widening a conflict often counsels restraint in humanitarian interventions.

In a second set of cases, the humanitarian objectives themselves place restraints on intervention. In Haiti, ending violations of human rights and restoring a democratically elected government justified diplomatic interventions and targeted economic sanctions, but the use of force would have been disproportionate, especially given the remote possibility of lasting success in a nation with no history of democracy. The use of force would have been even less proportionate if weighed against the goal of stopping refugee flows to the United States.

Even under cosmopolitan political theories, then, there are degrees of injustice and humanitarian suffering that can be tolerated as long as a variety of other initiatives have been and continue to be tried, because the potential risks for armed conflict are too great or the stakes are too small.

The Duty Toward Civilians

A final consideration needs mention: the importance of *ius in bello* concerns in assessing humanitarian intervention. The civilian suffering caused by U.N. military actions against Aideed in Somalia and U.N.-imposed sanctions against Serbia and Haiti highlights the importance of using humanitarian means to pursue humanitarian goals. "We must be wary," according to the U.S. bishops, "that the outstretched hand of peace is not turned into an iron fist of war."[35] The dilemma is that the means that are needed to succeed, and that may be proportionate to the good to be achieved, may also seem to contradict the humanitarian purposes of the intervention. For this reason, it might be appropriate to impose a stricter standard for assessing discrimination and proportionality in cases of humanitarian intervention than in wars of self-defense between states.

Another question arises, however, one not addressed in standard just war analysis: To what degree do those intervening for humanitarian purposes have a *duty* to take appropriate measures to defend the innocent? Obviously, there can be a duty to act in a particular situation only if the intervenor has the capacity to do so without excessive risk to himself. The moral issue becomes salient, however, when the pattern of interventions indicates a lack of balance between concern for the risks to intervenors and concern for the survival or basic rights of the population on whose behalf intervention was justified in the first place. The priority too often has been to limit mandates to protecting the troops while permitting them to do little more than monitor the atrocities taking place around them. The problem is not that the troops lack courage or commitment. It is that the leaders are unwilling to define ambitious enough objectives, to commit adequate resources, and to assume necessary risks. Owing in part to fear of losing domestic potential support for intervention, potential intervenors may be excessively concerned about avoiding casualties (the Somalia Syndrome) and not getting stuck in a quagmire (the Vietnam Syndrome). Consequently, in Bosnia, international peacekeepers rarely acted to defend civilians against attack during the war. And despite a massive military presence to implement the Dayton Accords, as of late 1997 international troops and police have studiously avoided, with a few exceptions, opportunities to arrest war criminals, and have done little to stop ongoing "ethnic cleansing" or to facilitate the right of refugees to return to their homes in areas where they would be a minority.

The failure to act to save lives is less problematic than the indiscriminate taking of life in war, but it is problematic nonetheless. If *ought* implies *can*, so also *can* implies *ought*. The irresolute rescuers' sins of omission have become a vexing moral problem of humanitarian intervention.

An Overall Assessment

This review of some of the practical moral considerations in implementing a right or duty of humanitarian intervention leads us to some summary remarks about the special challenges posed by the three main types of humanitarian intervention: non-violent, coercive short of military, and military.

The obvious moral advantage of *non-violent* forms of intervention is that they avoid the potential negative consequences of coercive and military measures, thereby better ensuring that humanitarian ends are matched by humanitarian means. That advantage, combined with the lesser infringement of sovereignty associated with most (though not all) non-violent measures, allows for a lowering of the threshold (i.e., an expansion of just cause) for legitimate humanitarian interventions.

The moral challenge for non-violent measures is set by the criteria of last resort and probability of success. Cases where humanitarian intervention is most needed are often those where the gradualist approach of diplomacy and other non-violent measures involves tolerating, sometimes even prolonging, widespread suffering and postponing inevitable military intervention. In some cases, a first resort to coercive or limited military measures may forestall the outbreak or spread of conflict before it reaches genocidal proportions. Non-violent measures that are ineffective or deal only with the symptoms of a humanitarian crisis may do little more than bring the concept and practitioners of humanitarian intervention into disrepute.

On the other end of the spectrum of means, *military* measures often seem the only feasible way to stop grave humanitarian crises. Oftentimes, non-military means simply do not suffice in the face of genocide, starvation, enslavement, and even widespread human-rights abuses.

Yet military means can be the bluntest of instruments, whose deadly consequences can too easily blur the distinction between Good Samaritan and war criminal. Given the risks of self-interested military intervention by major powers under the guise of humanitarianism, the threshold for such interventions should generally be high, but this threshold may be lowered to accommodate interventions that are more like policing and less like war-fighting. Military intervention may be more likely to succeed in stanching the killing and dying, but any resulting peace will be only temporary unless military means are combined with massive and long-term non-military efforts to restore a functioning political, economic, and social order.

The middle type of humanitarian intervention—*coercive* measures like sanctions—incorporates both the advantages and the disadvantages of the other two types. To the extent that such measures are targeted to avoid unwarranted civilian suffering and are imposed as an alternative to force, they are more likely than military intervention to be humanitarian in means as well as ends. At the same time, they usually offer a greater possibility of success than non-violent measures. Yet economic sanctions and other forms of non-military coercion can be blunt instruments, even more blunt at times than military force, while they suffer from all the problems of a gradualist, non-violent approach.

Concluding Observations

As contrasted with the Westphalian state system, the current world order is marked by a modified state ethic more and more influenced by cosmopolitan considerations of human rights and individual welfare. This modification of the state system is evident in the increasing incidence of humanitarian intervention by national, international, and non-governmental actors. While in a traditional state-centered political ethic, humanitarian intervention would be exceedingly rare, in the cosmopolitan ethic guiding churches, human-rights agencies, and humanitarian relief agencies, as well as in the modified state ethic evolving in international organizations, there is an increasing awareness of what Pope John Paul II has called a "duty to intervene" when whole populations are at risk. It is appropriate to use just war reasoning to define why, when, and how to exercise this duty in an international system that combines cosmpolitan and state-oriented elements. To do so is not just a matter of extending the just war analysis to a special class of cases but rather is an appropriate use of the method in the context of a broader political ethic.

We propose that the moral validity of humanitarian interventions depends on a complex judgment of several criteria, with the emphasis less on just causes or legitimate authority for intervention (though these do not lose their importance) and more on probability of success, the proportion of the means to the good to be achieved (or the evil corrected), and *ius in bello* considerations such as civilian immunity. The practical moral task is to draw harder linkages between standard justifications for humanitarian intervention—acts that shock the conscience of humankind, such as genocide and enslavement—and the specific objectives to be attained and means to be utilized. This emphasis on the when and how, rather than the why, makes sense in a world that is currently in the experimental stage of developing the institutions, processes, techniques, and political will necessary to realize the more cosmopolitan goals underlying humanitarian intervention.

We have found it most helpful, therefore, to distinguish among types of humanitarian intervention according to the means used: non-violent, coercive, and military. Most effective and legitimate humanitarian interventions will probably be some combination of these three types. The presumptions in favor of non-violent means and a high threshold for humanitarian intervention must always be tested in light of the complex realities of a particular case. Sweeping moral judgments about humanitarian intervention are not possible, for each case requires a difficult prudential judgment about how the just war criteria apply. In such cases, since they involve a number of contingent issues, clear lines are harder to draw than in cases where just cause and legitimate authority are the principal bases for moral decision-making.

But some general observations are possible. Moving from non-violent to coercive means and from coercive means to military force involves significant moral hurdles. We would favor limiting the use of armed force in a war-fighting mode to cases of genocide or mass killing (or dying); armed force would not be used to restore or promote democracy or to prevent widespread (but not massive) human-rights violations. In the latter cases, however, non-violent methods or coercive means short of the use of force may be permissible, provided other relevant ethical standards, particularly humanitarian provision in the case of comprehensive sanctions, are satisfied.

In the end, whether appropriate means are used will in large part be determined by whether the international community is committed to finding a lasting solution to the humanitarian crises that justify intervention. So far, that level of commitment has been notable for its absence.

10

Weinberger Triumphant: Seeking Certainty in an Uncertain World

Robert Kagan

At a time of free-wheeling debate over when, where, and how the United States ought to use force in overseas conflicts, a time when the Clinton administration's interventions in Haiti and Bosnia have drawn sustained attack from both Republican and Democratic critics, there has nevertheless been a growing consensus around some important principles of intervention. Many policy-makers and analysts seem to agree on the need for a set of *a priori* guidelines to determine when and how the United States should get into, and out of, foreign involvements. A yearning for precision and predictability in the making of foreign policy has been manifest, and both the Clinton administration and its many critics have responded with ever more detailed models and blueprints.

In a speech in March 1996, for instance, then National Security Adviser Anthony Lake listed seven circumstances that, alone or in

---

Robert Kagan is Alexander Hamilton Fellow at the American University, Washington, D.C., and a contributing editor of *The Weekly Standard*. He held State Department posts from 1984 to 1988.

combination, could warrant the use of American military force; these ranged from defense against attacks on the United States or its allies to such "humanitarian" missions as combating famine and countering gross abuses of human rights. Not all threats to these "interests" necessarily require an American response, Lake argued. But as a guide to action, he suggested a rudimentary calculus whereby "the greater the number and the weight of the interests in play, the greater the likelihood that we will use force—once all peaceful means have been tried and failed . . . and once we have measured a mission's benefits against its costs, in both human and financial terms."[1]

As for the nature and conduct of the missions, Lake attempted another taxonomy. Sometimes a "selective but substantial use of force" might be more appropriate than a "massive use." Sometimes threatening the use of force, when the threat is backed up by the will to carry it out, could be as effective as "actually using it." On the hot topic of the day, "exit strategy," Lake argued that "when it comes to deterring external aggression—as in the Persian Gulf or the Korean Peninsula—or fighting wars in defense of our most vital security interests, a more open-ended commitment is necessary." But in the case of the more common, limited tasks of the present era, the Bosnias, Haitis, and Somalias, Lake argued, "tightly tailored missions and sharp withdrawal deadlines" had to be "the norm." "Before we send our troops into a foreign country, we should know how and when we're going to get them out."

"Not specific enough"—that was the judgment of a Heritage Foundation report published two months after Lake's speech, charging Lake and the Clinton administration with failing to set forth sufficiently "selective" criteria for intervention.[2] In a discussion that well articulated and elaborated the view held by many Republicans, the report listed five criteria for determining "when, where, whether, and how the U.S. military should conduct military interventions." It called for another "set of criteria" for determining "when and in what capacity the U.S. will participate in multilateral military operations through coalitions, alliances, and other structures such as the United Nations." In addition, it called for a strict "prioritization of national interests and national security interests," and a clear "methodology" for discriminating among three categories of interests: "vital national interests," "important national interests," and "marginal interests."

The Heritage report also declared that any mission must have military goals that are "clearly defined, decisive, attainable, and sustainable." Finally, it insisted that all these sets of criteria, prioritizations, methodologies, and assurances of success should be codified in a "National Security Strategy" that the President would have to submit annually to Congress.[3]

Business ought to be booming these days for soothsayers and oracles specializing in affairs of state, or at least for their modern equivalents, the political scientists, international-relations experts, and military planners. Not for many centuries have statesmen demanded so much insight into the future, so much certainty about cause and effect in human affairs, so many immutable guidelines to behavior. Or, at least, not for many centuries have they made such a pretense of trying to base their actions on such divinations of the future. In ancient Greece, generals sometimes sought guidance from the oracle at Delphi before deciding whether or not to engage in battle. The high priestesses at Delphi spoke a drug-induced gibberish that had to be translated and interpreted, however, and it was remarkable how often the interpretation of the gibberish seemed to suit the predilections of the inquirer.

That ancient Greek tradition provides an apt metaphor for our present craze for certainty. Attempts to predict the future generally produce gibberish that remarkably often provides its interpreters with justification for doing or not doing what they wanted or didn't want to do in the first place.

The Weinberger Doctrine

The search on all sides of the political spectrum for ever more precise criteria for intervention abroad represents a surprising triumph of the Weinberger Doctrine more than a decade and a half after Caspar Weinberger, then Secretary of Defense, first laid out his own guiding principles. Widely disparaged at the time by then Secretary of State George Shultz and many others for appearing to proscribe the use of force in all but the most immediate situations of national peril, the Weinberger Doctrine, with corollaries and emendations contributed later by General Colin Powell and, as we have seen, by Anthony Lake, has become the reigning intellectual construct of the post–Cold War era—honored in the breach by the Clinton administration, and in the observance by the administration's critics. It has been modified, honed, expanded, made more subtle and complex. Yet its essential principles have remained the same: to avoid involvement in limited wars for limited objectives; to keep U.S. powder dry for the biggest strategic challenges—like that once posed by the Soviet Union; and, if involvement in lesser conflicts proves unavoidable, to seek to "tailor" missions that are brief and easily concluded, to insist on goals that are tightly circumscribed, and to avoid what has come to be called "mission creep," that is, the unanticipated expansion of objectives in response to unanticipated developments.

The triumph of the Weinberger Doctrine, and the concomitant demand for predictability, comes at a time when the world is probably more uncertain and international events more unpredictable than they have been for fifty years, a time when our faith in the predictability of human actions and reactions ought to be at a low ebb. This increased unpredictability is attributable not to a change in humanity but to a change in the structure of international relations.

During the Cold War, when the two superpowers dominated world affairs in what the political scientists like to call a system of "tight bipolarity," smaller powers with their own local ambitions and difficulties were generally constrained from making the kind of trouble that required superpower intervention. And while we should not oversimplify the past—the Cold War era, after all, had its share of conflicts in "gray areas," one of which, Vietnam, became the United States' most disastrous war—nevertheless there is little doubt that American "grand strategy" and the lesser strategies and tactics needed to carry it out were more easily comprehended. Because the United States faced a single adversary, and because the two superpowers very quickly worked out a rough *modus vivendi*, with some clear boundaries and a set of rules for how their competition would be conducted, there was a measure of predictability in international affairs.

It is no surprise that the field of international relations—with its predictive aspirations—thrived as an academic discipline in the Cold War. So much of foreign policy seemed to revolve around rational calculations of binary threats and deterrence, which in turn involved mathematical formulas concerning the kill ratios and circle-area probabilities of nuclear weapons. Foreign-policy analysts could perhaps be forgiven for increasingly coming to believe that relations among peoples and nations were susceptible to the same kinds of measurements and predictions as relations among their weapons of mass destruction, and that with sophisticated enough models and the computers to run them on, political science might begin to predict and prescribe the interactions among states fairly reliably.

They were mistaken, of course. The predictions of the model-builders and the international-relations experts managed to miss entirely the single most important development of that era—the collapse and retreat of the Soviet Union. And even before the ending of the Cold War did such damage to the reputation of international-relations theory, the discipline had been subjected to increasing outside criticism and suffered from many internal doubts as the promise of models and equations proved more and more hollow.

As even the so-called hard sciences began to accept the limitations of their disciplines and to entertain notions of unpredictability and "chaos," the once grand aspirations of "soft" political science, social science, and international relations diminished considerably. Most scholars inside and outside these fields increasingly came to agree with historian John Lewis Gaddis's judgment that there was inevitably going to be a "large class of phenomena for which prediction will never be possible, for the simple reason that to build a model capable of simulating subjects of this sort, one would have to replicate the subject itself."[4] One such category of phenomena was the behavior of people and especially the interactions among large groups of people, including the relations among states and the conduct of conflicts between them.

Clausewitz vs. Jomini

Accepting the severe limits to prediction and therefore prescription in human affairs, and particularly in military conflicts, constituted a giant step forward—into the nineteenth century. For it was, after all, more than a century ago that Karl von Clausewitz introduced the notions of "friction" and the "fog of war" into the study of international conflict. Drawing attention to the imprecision and unpredictability that suffuse combat and, indeed, all human struggles,

Clausewitz placed special emphasis on such human and immeasurable qualities as emotions and passions, and thus accepted the mammoth problem inherent in any search for eternal principles for understanding and guiding human action and behavior. He recognized the tension that must necessarily exist between theory or "ideal type" and the messier specifics of reality.

Clausewitz thus refuted the notion, as popular in his own day as in ours, that scientific laws govern warfare. His work stood opposed to the theories of Antoine-Henri Jomini, who premised his study of war on the conviction that "all strategy is controlled by invariable scientific principles," and to the theories of the British general and military theorist Henry Lloyd, who insisted that the art of war rested on "certain and fixed principles, which are by their nature invariable."[5] Clausewitz searched hard for general principles that could guide statesmen and strategists in avoiding, planning for, and conducting war, and he met with greater success at this than anyone before or since. Nevertheless he held firmly to the conviction that "a theory of action should not lay down rules."[6]

Near the close of this present century, we ought again to be moving toward Clausewitzian complexities and away from Jominian certainties. Yet while scholarship in the academy has indeed been deemphasizing models, predictions, and "rules" of human behavior, elsewhere—in the halls of Congress, in the corridors of the Pentagon, in the conference rooms of policy analysts—the quest for certainties and rigid guidelines has not only persisted but accelerated. Weinberger's disciples have been undaunted by the fact that the collapse of the Soviet empire ushered in an era much less predictable than the Cold War had been. Thus, while the Heritage Foundation report acknowledges, for instance, that the "new world disorder" presents to statesmen a "volatile and unpredictable international arena that does not lend itself to conceptual or strategic clarity," this has been no deterrent to the search for certainty.[7] On the contrary, the heightened unpredictability is said to make it all the more necessary to develop a "concrete set of policy guidelines for when and how to use American military forces abroad."[8]

There is, of course, more than an intellectual failure in evidence here. The insistence on predictability in an inherently unpredictable world is a form of escapism. And today's proponents of the Weinberger Doctrine and its variants have indeed been seeking an escape from the type of world created in the aftermath of the Cold War and from the role that the United States seems required to play in it.

Principles of Avoidance

The Weinberger Doctrine and its descendants have always aimed primarily at avoidance. Weinberger's principles, after all, were born of past failures and designed to avoid future ones. They reflected the American military's understandable insistence that it never again become engaged in a disastrous, losing affair like the war in Vietnam. And Weinberger enunciated them largely in response to the debacle in Lebanon in 1983, where more than 200 U.S. Marines lost their lives to a terrorist car bomb. The thrust of Weinberger's doctrine was simply, "Never again." And the principles he set forth tried to answer the question, "Never again what?"

What Weinberger meant was no more limited wars or military interventions for limited objectives. The first of his six principles was that the United States "should not commit forces to combat overseas unless the particular engagement or occasion is deemed vital to our national interest or that of our allies." The second was that "if we decide it is necessary to put combat troops into a given situation, we should do so . . . with the clear intention of winning."

There was no need to read the remaining four points. The first two alone precluded almost every imaginable kind of conflict except a full-scale conventional war between great powers. As George Shultz later complained, "in the face of terrorism"—which was the hot topic of 1984—"or any other of the wide variety of complex, unclear, gray-area dangers facing us in the contemporary world, [Weinberger's] was a counsel of inaction." Shultz noted that the Weinberger Doctrine "would have stopped us dead in our tracks on Grenada."[9]

What neither Shultz nor Weinberger could have foreseen was that the Grenadas would soon become the rule, not the exception. The end of the Cold War, the end of "tight bipolarity," the emergence of long-simmering conflicts that had been suppressed by the superpower confrontation, have all left the United States with primary responsibility for maintenance of the present fairly benign world order. And while political warfare has broken out over assigning "blame" to one administration or another for engaging in limited wars for limited ends, a less partisan view would recognize in American behavior since 1990 a trend that transcends parties and presidents.

The first post–Cold War limited war, after all, was the invasion of Panama, an elaborately staged kidnapping of a despised dictator who was neither a Soviet ally nor a threat to America's "vital national interests." Then came the Gulf War, which Colin Powell, keeper of the flame of the Weinberger Doctrine, initially opposed as not meeting the test. After that came the quintessential "humanitarian mission," the intervention in Somalia, which for some reason Powell not only approved but actively promoted. The later missions undertaken by the Clinton administration—in Haiti and Bosnia—followed an existing pattern, therefore, and, contrary to the view of Michael Mandelbaum, broke no new ground as international "social work."[10]

"Grand Strategy" Today

Under the circumstances of the post–Cold War world, in which neither a Republican nor a Democratic president has been able to avoid engagement in such limited wars, the application of Weinberger principles can only be understood as a vigorous attempt to use theory as an escape from the messy realities. Like it or not, American "grand strategy" in the post–Cold War world has come to resemble the containment policy that foreign-policy "realists" and many military planners found so disturbingly vague during the Cold War. In defense of a world order that greatly benefits the United States, we are forced once again to be able to respond with force, as George Kennan put it fifty years ago, "at a series of constantly shifting geographical and political points." In such circumstances, the demand for fixed targets, for clearly delineated gradations of "vital," "important," and "marginal" interests, for strict rules of behavior, can be tantamount to rejection of the grand strategy itself.

Many military planners and strategic thinkers will complain that this "grand strategy" is too vague and provides an insufficient map for American behavior. But that is the way it is with most grand strategies. As Paul Kennedy has noted, "grand strategy can never be exact or foreordained." It is "full of imponderables and unforeseen 'frictions.' It is not a mathematical science in the Jominian tradition, but an art in the Clausewitzian sense—and a difficult art at that, since it operates at various levels, political, strategic, operational, tactical, all interacting with each other to advance (or retard) the primary aim."[11]

The Weinberger Doctrine and its variants have expressed the discomfort with these uncertainties felt by many in American military circles. As one military analyst has put it, "when it comes to being engaged in any undertaking where political objectives are hazy, public support only tepid, the prospects for a rapid decision remote, and the risk of substantial casualties high, service opinion is unanimous: count us out."[12] A popular article by Charles J. Dunlap, Jr., entitled "The Origins of the Military Coup of 2012" offered a deliberately exaggerated warning of what could happen if the U.S. military were pushed too many times into these "untraditional" roles.[13]

Obviously, military leaders would prefer the most straightforward missions, where military objectives match political objectives, and where the likelihood of success is high and the dangers of high casualties low—where the goal is "winning" rather than maintaining. Equally obvious, however, is the difficulty of limiting our interventions to such circumstances. Clausewitz, the intellectual godfather of the principle of matching military ends with political ends, nevertheless realized that the two could not always be identical. In some cases, he wrote, "the political objective will not provide a suitable military objective. In that event, another military objective must be adopted that will serve the political purpose."[14]

Clausewitz knew, too, that in limited wars, the goal might not be easily described as "winning." A military had to be willing to carry out its operations in pursuit of "hazy" objectives. Since there can be "no question of a *purely military* evaluation of a great strategic issue, nor of a purely military scheme to solve it," sometimes military leaders have to accept the employment of limited means to achieve limited ends—something that General Powell, for instance, has notably refused to accept.[15] Clausewitz recognized that the military could not always fight the kinds of wars it wanted to fight, that, as Lord Kitchener once said, it might be necessary to conduct war "as we must, not as we should like."

The Price of Certainty-Seeking

The price we are paying for our insistence on greater certainties than life allows is high. Most of the interventions of the post–Cold

War era have come in regions and conflicts where our "vital interests" were not thought to lie. When Elliott Abrams and others recommended a special operation to snatch General Noriega in the mid-eighties, military leaders like Admiral William Crowe and General Colin Powell were opposed, not seeing any vital interest in unseating the general when the Panama Canal wasn't threatened. A couple of years later, the United States sent 10,000 troops to Panama to remove Noriega, though the canal was no more threatened in 1989 than it had been in 1986. Most Republicans have opposed U.S. military involvement in Bosnia, as well, yet it is doubtful whether George Bush in a second term would have been any more able to avoid deeper involvement than President Clinton was.

In Panama, in Haiti, and in Bosnia, moreover, it seems clear in retrospect that a willingness to undertake more limited but firm interventions early on could have obviated the need for much larger interventions later. In 1992, for instance, President Bush probably had the necessary credibility after the Gulf War to cow the Serbs into limiting their ambitions through the threat or use of air power alone. According to former Secretary of State James Baker, all plans for such limited use of force were blocked by Powell and Secretary of Defense Richard Cheney, both of whom feared that any involvement would "put us on a slippery slope leading to greater military involvement down the line."[16] In the end, however, the unwillingness to involve the United States militarily led to exactly that outcome—in Bosnia and in Haiti, as well as in Panama. In these cases, application of the Weinberger Doctrine probably made large interventions more, not less, likely.

A second unfortunate consequence of the new mood can be seen in Bosnia. The Clinton administration, having eschewed Weinberger's principles in going into Bosnia with 20,000 troops, has nevertheless tried to abide by some variant of the Weinberger Doctrine while in Bosnia. In a supreme effort to avoid "mission creep" or "another Somalia" in the former Yugoslavia, the military mission in Bosnia has so far been constrained from doing what may be necessary to accomplish the political objectives of U.S. involvement. The force that Secretary of Defense William Perry once described as "the meanest dog in town" dares not detain the war criminals on all sides who have the power and the motive to destroy the peace that U.S.

intervention made possible. In the interest of creating as much pre-dictability as possible, and in a profound reversal of Clausewitz's first principle, the political goals are being subordinated to the military. Our "grand strategy" is being undermined by our "exit strategy."

If the "grand strategy" of the United States today is to maintain the current beneficial world order, we will need to accept some of the dangers and difficulties, both practical and intellectual, that this entails. Although the United States possesses no empire, it is engaged in something like "empire management." The task should not be too much for us; it is certainly nothing like fighting and winning two world wars and the Cold War. But it does require some adjustment of our way of looking at the world's problems. As the great military historian John Keegan wrote not long ago, both Britain and France, "old imperial powers with a long experience of combating disorder in violent areas of the world," avoided the kind of "all-or-nothing approach" inherent in the Weinberger and Powell doctrines. "In North Africa and in India they were accustomed to dealing with armed dissidents always ready to go to war when weakness or the chance of advantage was scented." They "did not hope for total victory. They accepted the wickedness of the world and sought to contain it by a whole spectrum of means, including . . . threat and punishment."[17]

Keegan's is a typical old-world criticism of new-world idealism, and indeed it is one of the virtues of Americans that they are less willing than the Europeans or British to live side by side with wickedness. On the other hand, Keegan's argument provides a useful antidote to the kind of criticism made by Mandelbaum and others, who indict recent interventions for having produced results that are "provisional, fragile, and reversible."[18] What in human affairs is not "provisional and reversible"? Even the Gulf War, to many a classic instance of the Weinberger Doctrine employed most successfully, did not produce an irreversible result. The United States may have to remain on guard against a resurgence of Iraqi belligerence for another decade or more. There are few real exits in this world, and few permanent solutions, even after the most convincing of military victories.

The resurgence of the Weinberger Doctrine in the present era not only violates fundamental Clausewitzian tenets, therefore, but violates common sense as well. The demand for immutable principles and rigid guidelines for intervention is more than foolish—it is dangerous. It is as if someone with only a very dim flashlight who was preparing to travel through a dark tunnel full of sharp objects insisted on preparing in advance a course from which he refused to deviate. There is no reliable calculus for making foreign-policy decisions in advance, much less a way of knowing how things will turn out once the decision is made. That is why we employ statesmen to guide us through the darkness as time and circumstances dictate.

PART THREE

Can Democracies Fight Terrorism?

11

Terrorism and Just War Doctrine

Anthony Clark Arend

When classic just war theory developed, the world consisted of a variety of political entities—kingdoms, principalities, empires, and the like. With the passage of time, however, the territorial state emerged as the primary political unit, and writers in this tradition began to apply just war doctrine exclusively to the behavior of states. Today, the vast corpus of just war writings deals with questions about the permissibility of the recourse to force *by states* (the principles of *ius ad bellum*) and the conduct of hostilities *by states* (the principles of *ius in bello*).[1]

Since the Second World War, however, the world has witnessed the emergence of a number of non-state actors on the international stage. Among these actors are terrorist groups. Over the last several decades, the Palestine Liberation Organization, the Hezbollah, the Irish Republican Army, the Abu Nidal Group, the Red Brigade, the Red Army,

Anthony Clark Arend is an associate professor of government at Georgetown University, Washington, D.C. He wishes to thank William V. O'Brien, emeritus professor of government at Georgetown, for his ongoing support and inspiration. The author also thanks Robert J. Beck of the University of Virginia, with whom he has collaborated in examining terrorism and the use of force; their article on the subject is identified in note 2 of this essay.

223

and numerous other groups have used force against a variety of state and non-state targets. Their activities have elicited forcible responses by states—the United States and Israel, in particular.[2] Yet because these groups are not states and operate quite differently from states, it is unclear just how the principles of contemporary just war doctrine would apply to states attempting to counter these terrorist groups.

My purpose here is to attempt to find out—that is, to apply contemporary just war doctrine to state efforts to respond to terrorist actions. Parts one and two will explore the traditional *ius ad bellum* and *ius in bello* principles in relation to terrorism, and part three will offer several recommendations for making just war doctrine more applicable to the terrorist threat.

IUS AD BELLUM AND TERRORISM

Classic just war doctrine was most concerned about when a political entity could justly undertake the use of force.[3] Plato and Aristotle, Augustine and Aquinas, and others searched for specific criteria that could be used to determine when war was justly entered into, and modern just war theorists have continued to use and refine these criteria. Today, while there is no single set that all just war theorists use, six elements figure in most contemporary discussions of *ius ad bellum*: competent authority, just cause, right intention, last resort, probability of success, and proportionality.

1. Competent Authority

To be justly undertaken, a war or other use of force must be initiated by a legitimate authority. As Aquinas explained, "[a] private individual may not declare war. . . ."[4] Instead, "since responsibility for public affairs is entrusted to the rul[ers], it is they who are charged with the defence of the city, realm, or province."[5] In the world of today, the notion of competent authority has generally been understood to mean that *states* can declare or otherwise initiate hostilities. Whether any entity other than a state has the authority to do so is less clear. Given the historic support within the just war tradition for "just revolution," there seems to be reason to think that certain *revolutionary groups* may constitute competent authority.[6] But just what criteria such a group would need to meet remains unclear.[7] It would also seem logical to conclude that *the United Nations* can be considered a competent authority, given the authority vested in it by states. As states ratified the United Nations Charter, they did so with the understanding that the Charter empowered the Security Council to authorize the use of force when the Council determined that there was a threat to the peace, breach of the peace, or act of aggression.[8]

When the concept of competent authority is applied to the use of force against terrorists, on the surface it seems to provide no particular difficulty. Clearly, states are the entities that respond to terrorists, and states are the competent authorities *par excellence*. On closer examination, however, the situation is a bit murkier. In recent discussions of competent authority, scholars have explored precisely who or what body within a state is empowered to authorize the use of force. Can the American president do so alone? Or must Congress, which under the Constitution has the authority to "declare war," be involved in the decision? Virtually all scholars would argue that when the United States is under direct attack, the president can use force without the consent of Congress. But beyond that, scholars and public officials differ considerably on the circumstances under which the president can use force without congressional approval.

This problem is especially acute with respect to terrorism and its unconventional methods of warfare. Terrorists do not generally wear military uniforms and engage in overt attacks across international borders. It is not to be expected that a terrorist group will march across the U.S.–Mexican border with flags flying. Instead, terrorists will attack military and diplomatic installations abroad, take hostages, and kill civilians. Under American constitutional law, it is not clear whether the president has the authority to respond forcibly without the consent of Congress. The War Powers Resolution provides that the president can introduce troops into hostilities only "pursuant to (1) a declaration of war, (2) specific statutory authorization, or (3) a national emergency created by attack upon the United States, its territories or possessions, or its armed forces."[9] It does not provide for the use of force in response to actions against U.S. nationals abroad. Yet presidents have certainly asserted such a right. In 1985, for example, Ronald Reagan unilaterally authorized force to bring down an Egyptian aircraft carrying terrorists allegedly involved in the *Achille Lauro* highjacking.[10]

2. Just Cause

The second criterion, just cause, can be divided into (a) the substance of the cause and (b) comparative justice.

a. The Substance of the Cause. Every just war theorist—from the most ancient to the most recent—has asserted that for war to be properly undertaken, there must be a substantive just cause, some legitimate reason for going to war. A state cannot simply declare war. Underlying this concept is a critical element of just war doctrine: there is always a presumption against the recourse to force. As the National Conference of Catholic Bishops has observed, "just-war teaching has evolved . . . as an effort to prevent war; only if war cannot be rationally avoided, does the teaching then seek to restrict and reduce its horrors."[11] It does this, they explain, "by establishing a set of rigorous conditions which must be met if the decision to go to war is to be morally permissible."[12] Especially today, they continue, "such decision . . . requires extraordinarily strong reasons for overriding the presumption *in favor of peace* and *against war*."[13]

But while just war theorists agree that there must be a just cause, they do not agree on exactly what qualifies as a substantive just cause. Augustine wrote in the broadest of terms, explaining that "those wars are generally defined as just which avenge some wrong, when a nation or a state is to be punished for having failed to make amends for the wrong done, or to restore what has been taken unjustly."[14] More recently, James Childress has refined this concept of substantive just cause by narrowing it to three circumstances: "to protect the innocent from unjust attack," "to restore rights wrongfully denied," and "to re-establish a just order."[15]

Regarding the first of these circumstances there is universal agreement. All just war theorists would assert that a state can use force in the event of an armed attack. Indeed, Article 51 of the United Nations Charter guarantees states a *legal* right to "individual or collective self-defense if an armed attack occurs."[16] But the precise meaning of "armed attack" is unclear, especially in regard to terrorism. When does a terrorist action constitute an armed attack? Must it occur in the territory of the aggrieved state? Must it be of a particular intensity? Would an isolated terrorist action amount to an armed attack, or would it have to be part of an ongoing effort? Would the *threat* of an armed attack be sufficient? In other words, could a state justly engage in preemptive or anticipatory self-defense?

More problems arise with the second category of Childress's understanding of substantive just cause, the use of force "to restore rights wrongfully denied." In general just war discussions, scholars would probably take this to mean that force can be used in the face of genocide or other massive human-rights violations. With respect to state actions, a government that engages in genocide or other systematic abuses of the rights of its citizens may be liable to forcible intervention. Indeed, a growing body of literature discusses circumstances under which a "humanitarian" intervention can be justly undertaken.[17] But how the concept of humanitarian intervention would translate to terrorist activity is uncertain. If terrorists were killing or torturing innocents on a massive scale or taking large numbers of people hostage, that action would probably be equivalent to genocide by a state. But what if a terrorist group were causing a group of people to live in great fear for their lives, without actually doing physical harm on a large scale—could such a "reign of terror" give rise to a just intervention? Could a state argue that the mere presence of some terrorist groups poses such a threat to the indigenous population that a forcible action would be justified?

Finally, there are also difficulties with Childress's third category, that force can be justly undertaken "to re-establish a just order." What is a "just order," and when would terrorists violate it? Over the past several years, non-state actors of a variety of sorts have caused a tremendous degree of instability in states. In Lebanon, Somalia, the former Yugoslavia, Liberia, and Sierra Leone, for example, such actors have prevented the centralized government from exercising effective control over large portions of the state's territory. Would such a case justify intervention? Could it be argued that force is necessary "to preserve," in the words of the U.S. Catholic bishops, "conditions necessary for decent human existence"?[18]

b. Comparative Justice. It is not enough that a state have a substantive just cause for force: it must also satisfy the requirement of comparative justice. While scholars differ on its meaning, this requirement seems to acknowledge that while all parties to a dispute may have substantive just causes, not all such causes justify the resort to force. As the American bishops conceive of comparative justice, the issue is twofold: "which side is sufficiently 'right' in a dispute, and are the values at stake critical enough to override the presumption against war?"[19] In other words, for a state to use force, its "just cause" should be better than its opponent's and must be worth the "violence, destruction, suffering, and death"[20] caused by war.

Here I will take the first aspect of the bishops' definition of comparative justice—which side is sufficiently "right"?—to reflect a proper understanding of that concept. The latter aspect—is the just cause worth the evil to be produced in the war?—can, I believe, be subsumed under the concept of proportionality and will be discussed later.

To apply the requirement of comparative justice to terrorism may seem at first to produce an extremely undesirable result. Typically, terrorist groups are motivated by legitimate causes. The Irish Republican Army has fought against the British for its "unjust occupation" of Northern Ireland. For years, the PLO challenged Israeli possession of the West Bank, the Golan Heights, and other territories. An observer might be inclined to conclude that comparative justice was indeed on the side of these groups. But terrorism introduces another factor into the calculation. What is abhorrent about terrorism is not the cause for which it is acting but the nature of the act. While certain terrorist groups may indeed have legitimate reasons for desiring change in the status quo, the methods of terrorism are in and of themselves impermissible. Targeting innocent civilians and other non-combatants, taking hostages, killing and torturing prisoners of war—these are completely unacceptable violations of the concept of *ius in bello*.

This aspect of terrorism introduces an important challenge to just war doctrine. How can we evaluate the comparative-justice requirement when the methods of one party are clearly unjust from the perspective of *ius in bello*?

3. Right Intention

Aristotle, one of the earliest proponents of the notion of the just war, explained that the ultimate purpose of war must be to establish peace. Just wars are to be fought out of a desire for charity and peace.[21] The purpose is not to obliterate an enemy but to end the aberrant behavior that has breached the peace. As Augustine noted, "the desire to hurt, the cruelty of vendetta, the stern and implacable spirit, arrogance in victory, the thirst for power, and all that is similar, all these are justly condemned in war."[22] Accordingly, revenge, hatred, and the demonization of the enemy have no place in a just war.[23]

This requirement of *ius ad bellum* is one of the most difficult in a conventional war.[24] It is a rare war in which the enemy is not portrayed as evil and the notion of revenge is not present—think of the American propaganda about the Germans and the Japanese during the Second World War. And for terrorist actions, the problem is even greater. Given the tactics of terrorist groups and their often fanatic ideology, it is quite easy to vilify them beyond reason. Moreover, because their deeds engender international outrage, the desire for punishment or revenge sometimes seems to be the main motivation for forcible response.

4. Last Resort

Hostilities should commence only after peaceful alternatives have been explored. There is, however, some disagreement among just war commentators as to how much effort should be expended on exploring these other methods of dispute resolution. The American bishops, for example, state that "all peaceful alternatives must have been exhausted,"[25] while William V. O'Brien notes that "all reasonable efforts to avoid it [war] while protecting the just cause should be tried."[26] The latter approach, requiring all "reasonable" efforts at avoidance, seems to make the most sense. In any conflict, an observer could always argue that there was "one more" alternative that had not been explored.

But even if we understand this criterion as requiring that we exhaust all reasonably peaceful remedies, terrorism raises special difficulties. In conventional international conflict, there are established diplomatic channels and international organizations that have states as parties. Such institutions provide clear methods for pursuing peaceful settlement and non-violent sanctions. Before the Gulf War, for example, the United States and its allies pursued traditional diplomacy and various multilateral methods available through the United Nations. Such methods are not formally available with terrorist groups. They do not have diplomatic missions in the traditional sense and are normally not members of international organizations, and they are not readily susceptible to economic sanctions and other non-violent pressures. As a consequence, it is unclear how a state could reasonably be said to have exhausted peaceful methods of dispute resolution in dealing with terrorists. Furthermore, efforts to establish any form of official contact may be seen as granting a legitimacy to the terrorist group that would help its cause. Israel's reluctance to negotiate with the PLO stemmed in part from this fear.

5. *Probability of Success*

A state should engage in the use of force only if the action is likely to succeed. As the American bishops note, the purpose of this requirement "is to prevent irrational resort to force or hopeless resistance when the outcome of either will clearly be disproportionate or futile."[27] But, they continue, "the determination includes a recognition that at times defense of key values, even against great odds, may be a 'proportionate' witness."[28]

But how is success defined when this criterion is applied to terrorism? In a standard war, success means the aggression is ended, or the territory is returned, or the status quo ante is reestablished. But does success against terrorism mean the ending of a particular series of terrorist acts? The capture or death of all the terrorists? Because of the tenacity of terrorists, success can often be elusive. How many years should a state fight against a PLO or an IRA?

6. *Proportionality*

While this criterion is also present in *ius in bello* calculations, as a *ius ad bellum* category proportionality means that "the damage to be inflicted and the costs incurred by war must be proportionate to the good expected by taking up arms."[29] Are the just causes sufficient to outweigh the injustices of war? Needless to say, this can be a perplexing calculation. It is difficult to anticipate the full consequences of a war. The tragedy far outstretches the number of persons killed or injured and the amount of property damage. War can destroy entire cultures and break the spirit of nations.[30]

In regard to terrorist actions, the requirement of proportionality does not seem to pose any more problems that it does in conventional international conflict; it may even present fewer. First, since terrorist groups do not have full authority and control over a territory, it could be contended that force against them would have less significant long-term consequences than force against a state. Second, it also seems logical to assume that the type of force used against terrorists is likely to be less destructive than the force necessary to combat state actors.

IUS IN BELLO AND TERRORISM

Once a state has properly undertaken to use force, once it has satisfied the requirements of *ius ad bellum*, the conflict must then meet the *ius in bello* requirements in order to be considered just.[31] Over the years, two *in bello* criteria have emerged: proportionality and discrimination.

1. Proportionality

Here the requirement is that the means used in war be proportionate to the ends to be achieved. This means two things. First, any given use of force must be proportionate to the military end sought in that particular case. For example, if the military objective in a battle can be achieved by destroying the communications center of a particular unit, then only the amount of force necessary to accomplish that task should be used. Anything beyond that would be considered disproportionate and, thus, impermissible. Second, proportionality means that, as William V. O'Brien puts it, a military action "must be proportionate in the context of the grand strategic and moral ends of the war."[32] In his book on Israel's conflict with the PLO, O'Brien notes that "an action might be justified in purely military terms at the tactical or strategic level, but not justified as part of a total pattern of behavior when viewed from the standpoint of the grand strategic ends of the war."[33] Specific uses of force must be proportionate not only in context but also to the overall goals of the general conflict.

Proportionality seems more difficult to apply at the tactical level of terrorism than at the grand strategic level. This is because at the specific case level, proportionality has frequently been understood to mean that the response to a specific terrorist act must be at roughly the same level of force as the act itself.[34] Oscar Schachter, for example, has observed that from a legal perspective, "the U.N. Security Council in several cases, most involving Israel, has judged proportionality by comparing the response on a quantitative basis to the *single attack* which preceded it."[35] This approach has been called "tit-for-tat proportionality."[36] The difficulty with it is that it could lead to a vicious cycle of terrorist acts and equivalent responses without any real progress toward ending the series of acts.

When the problem of terrorism is viewed through the lens of the broader goals, however, another approach to proportionality becomes plausible. This is what has been called the "eye-for-a-tooth" approach or "deterrent proportionality."[37] As O'Brien has explained, "counterterror measures should be proportionate to the purposes of counterterror and defense, viewed in the total context of hostilities as well as the broader political–military strategic context."[38] Accordingly, "the

referent of proportionality" is "the overall pattern of past and projected acts."[39] Under this approach, a state responding to a terrorist act
would be able to use force not just proportionate to that single act but
proportionate to the terrorists' accumulated past acts and anticipated
future acts. This approach makes a great deal of sense in light of the
peculiar problem of terrorism; yet it is not universally accepted.

2. Discrimination

The principle of discrimination "prohibits direct intentional attacks
on noncombatants and nonmilitary targets."[40] Needless to say, all these
terms—"direct intentional attack," "noncombatants," and "nonmilitary targets"—have inspired debate.[41] This is especially true with
regard to nuclear-weapons use and targeting.[42] Leaving aside these
general debates, let us consider difficulties that the principle of discrimination presents for counterterrorism efforts.

A basic element of discrimination is that innocent civilians are
not to be attacked or targeted. In a conventional war, military personnel are clearly identifiable. They wear uniforms, use military vehicles, and stay in military installations. Terrorists are not nearly so easy
to identify. They do not necessarily wear uniforms or live in military
compounds. They are, in fact, civilians. But they are not innocent
civilians. Hence, one of the greatest difficulties is figuring out exactly
who the guilty parties are. The matter becomes even more complicated because terrorists frequently use innocent civilians and normally
immune targets—such as hospitals and churches—as covers. A terrorist group may have its headquarters in the middle of a crowded city,
where innocent people go about their daily activities. How can any
targeting policy that complies with the requirement of discrimination
be established in such conditions?

TERRORISM AND JUST WAR: RECOMMENDATIONS

Given the particular difficulties that terrorism poses for contemporary just war doctrine, I would like to make some recommendations
regarding application of the *ius ad bellum* and *ius in bello* principles.
These recommendations seek to preserve the spirit of just war
thinking while responding to the specific challenges that terrorism
presents.

The Principles of Ius ad Bellum

1. *Competent Authority.* The real question here is whether under domestic constitutional arrangements it should be easier to use force against terrorists than to engage in conventional war. My recommendation is that more freedom should be given to the executive of a state—the president of the United States in particular—to respond to terrorism. Short, quick actions against terrorist targets should be permitted. Without this type of accommodation, it could be very difficult to intervene in a timely fashion to prevent future terrorism.

2. *Just Cause.* First, regarding *substantive just cause*:

Under traditional just war doctrine, *self-defense* is the most obvious just cause. But how this applies to terrorism is somewhat unclear. I suggest that terrorist actions be regarded as an armed attack, engendering the right of self-defense, under the following circumstances.[43] First, a terrorist attack against targets within a particular state should be considered tantamount to an armed attack. If, for example, terrorists blew up New York's World Trade Center, that would constitute an attack upon the United States. Second, a terrorist attack against state targets abroad—such as embassies and military bases—should be regarded as an armed attack. If terrorist groups attacked an American military base in Germany, the United States could use force in self- defense to respond to that act. Third, significant attacks upon the citizens of a state who are outside that state's territory should be regarded as an attack upon that state. This is harder to specify. Certainly, an isolated action against a few citizens abroad is tragic, but does it amount to an armed attack that would engender the right of forcible response? My own sense is that only when such acts are of significant proportion should they be considered an armed attack. Of course, "significant" is open to varying interpretations; but I believe that this criterion can be a starting point.

Must a state experience an act of terrorism before using force, or can it act preemptively to prevent such an act? Many scholars hold that under contemporary international law, states maintain a right of *anticipatory self-defense.*[44] Traditionally, however, the right can be asserted only if the state (1) can show necessity and (2) responds proportionately. In other words, the state must first demonstrate that if it does not respond immediately an attack will occur, and its response must be proportionate to the threatened attack.

I believe that these same criteria can be applied to anticipatory self-defense to preempt terrorist actions. If a state can show that an armed attack, as defined above, is imminent, and if it responds proportionately, such actions should be considered permissible.

As for *terrorist "genocide"*: Most just war theorists would assert that if a state engages in genocide or similar massive violations of human rights, another state can intervene justly to prevent further human suffering. I strongly suggest that this concept of "humanitarian intervention" be applied to terrorist actions. If a terrorist group is involved in wide-scale killings and terrorizing, an outside state should be able to intervene justly even if it or its citizens are not directly affected. If, for example, a terrorist group in the Sudan is murdering hundreds of innocent civilians, the United States would have a substantive just cause to intervene.

Concerning the second category of just cause, *comparative justice*:

While it is clear that terrorists may indeed have just motivations for their actions, their methods are fundamentally unjust. I recommend that the methods employed by the terrorist be part of the comparative-justice calculation. Even if a group is pursuing a valid cause, if it uses indiscriminate killings, torture, hostage-taking, and other such abhorrent methods, those actions should tip the balance against the terrorists.

3. Right Intention. Any use of force—even for a just cause—tends to be accompanied with a vilification of the enemy and a desire for revenge. This tendency is especially strong in response to actions by terrorists. I believe, however, that the same strict standard of right intention must also be applied to terrorists. While it is always proper to acknowledge an evil deed as evil, terrorists are human beings who must be dealt with out of charity. The purpose of using force against them must be to end their abhorrent actions, not to exact revenge. While it is of course impossible to change the hearts of decision-makers who respond to terrorists, at the very least just war theorists should condemn rhetoric that savors of revenge.

4. Last Resort. This *ius ad bellum* requirement poses a particular problem for counterterrorist actions because the normal diplomatic channels available to states do not exist for terrorist groups. While states understandably wish not to legitimize the terrorist group through negotiations, the presumption against the use of force requires a good-faith exploration of peaceful alternatives. I am not suggesting that compromises should be struck with terrorists that would be fundamentally unjust, or that states should engage in negotiations if to do so would enhance the terrorists' status. Rather, I am suggesting that states should not immediately assume that only forcible methods exist. They should make an effort to determine if any other methods would secure a just result. It may very well be that in virtually all cases, the problems of attempting to pursue such alternatives would greatly outweigh the cost of forcible action. Nonetheless, the examination of these non-forcible options should still be undertaken. It is a fundamental tenet of just war thinking that force is not to be chosen without an exploration of other options.

5. *Probability of Success.* Another difficulty with counterterror actions is how to define success. What would be a successful forcible action against terrorists? I recommend that success be defined as the elimination of the terrorist threat. This may not mean the capture of all members of a particular terrorist group, but rather the effective ending of the terrorist actions.

This goal is unlikely to be achieved by force alone, since force does not deal with the underlying causes of the terrorism—a desire for territory, a desire to participate in the political system, and the like. While states should not accede to terrorist "demands," they must give some consideration to addressing the underlying causes if they are to succeed in eradicating the terrorist threat.

The Principles of Ius in Bello

1. *Proportionality.* Some would argue that each specific forcible response to terrorists must be directly proportionate to the proximate terrorist act. Given the nature of terrorism, however, I recommend adoption of the "deterrent proportionality" approach discussed above, according to which a state may respond in a manner proportionate to the accumulated past acts of the terrorists and their anticipated future acts. While this approach clearly introduces a greater element of subjectivity than the "tit-for-tat" approach, it is more suited to prevention of further terrorist actions.

2. *Discrimination.* Once a determination has been made that it is permissible to use force to respond to terrorism, against what targets

can a state act? This is a very difficult question, given the differences between terrorists and conventional warriors. In keeping with the importance of the principle of discrimination, I offer a couple of recommendations, aware that the precise targets will vary depending upon circumstances.[45] First, a clearly identifiable terrorist camp or training facility would be a legitimate target. Second, if the terrorists are being supported by another state, military assets in that state would be legitimate targets. Thus, if it were clearly established that Libya was providing a great deal of support to a particular terrorist group, Libyan weapons and military installations would be legitimate targets.

To conclude: While the nature of terrorists and terrorist actions raises a number of critical challenges for just war doctrine, that doctrine offers a great deal of guidance for counterterror operations. It is my hope that the observations presented here will help to illuminate this guidance.

12

Counterterrorism and Democratic Values

An American Practitioner's Experience

Oliver Revell

Although I spent thirty years in the FBI, my first experience with terrorism was as a Marine officer in 1962, when my squadron was deployed to Oxford, Mississippi, to deal with the Ku Klux Klan and other radical segregationists opposing the integration of the University of Mississippi. We were sent to support the U.S. marshals enforcing the integration order of the federal court in the James Meredith case. The country was faced with the threat of a domestic group actually carrying out violent actions against the U.S. government. As a Marine officer I was also deployed to Cuba to deal with some of the activities of the Cuban revolution and its spawning of revolutionary movements and terrorist activities throughout the Caribbean and South America. So early in my professional life I

Oliver Revell served in the FBI from 1964 to 1994. From 1985 to 1991 he was the Associate Deputy Director in charge of the investigative, intelligence, counterterrorism, and international programs. He currently is the president of Revell Group International, global business and security consultants in Dallas, Texas.

started becoming involved in combating activities related to the use of violence for political purposes—i.e., terrorism.

Most of my early FBI career was spent in organized crime investigation, but in Kansas City in 1964-65 I did deal with a group that grew out of the American Nazi party, namely, the Minutemen. The Minutemen were organized around a particular political philosophy— a heinous one, but still based on political beliefs—and the use of force and violence to carry out that philosophy. I also dealt with some activities of the Ku Klux Klan, which at the time was still very prominent in that part of the country. Later, in Philadelphia, I dealt with a black hate group called the Revolutionary Action Movement (RAM), and with the Black Panther party. So I had some front-line experience with domestic groups that espoused the use of force and violence to achieve their political goals. Later, as acting agent in charge of the FBI's Chicago office, I had to deal with Puerto Rican groups such as the FALN, a political movement that by and large had taken up terrorism as its principal tactic in its efforts to force its agenda on the society at large.

In 1980, I became assistant director in charge of the Criminal Investigative Division of the FBI, which had responsibility for all criminal investigations, including those connected with terrorism. At that time, the United States was suffering approximately 100–120 terrorist incidents per year. People think the World Trade Center and Oklahoma City were the first acts of terrorism in the United States, but we have a very short collective memory. During the early 1980s the FBI was still attempting to deal with violence associated with the black-power movement, the civil-rights movement, and the anti-war movement. Some Puerto Rican organizations were carrying out the most acts of terrorism. Remnants of the Weather Underground were also still active in committing terrorist acts, including murder, assassination, and bombings. Terrorists were operating right here in Washington—placing a bomb in the Capitol building and at the naval base in the Potomac Basin. There were groups targeting the infrastructure of the United States, carrying out bombings against power stations and communication centers. And there were groups aiming at the military structure—recruit centers, depots, and so forth.

The Breakdown of Intelligence-Gathering

In the FBI we were trying to cope with the effects of one of the frequent purges that go on in our government. During the 1960s and 1970s there had been no consensus in this country on how to deal with the anti-war movement and with the more radical elements of the civil-rights movement. The Executive branch of the government had taken certain actions that had not been by consensus. They had been essentially presidential decisions. Some of the tactics used would today be considered illegal; at the time they were not illegal, but they perhaps were unwise. In seeking to determine who was behind certain movements and groups that carried out violent acts, the FBI and military intelligence, as well as the CIA, had engaged in such improper activities as wiretaps and surreptitious entries. In most of the world today, including Britain, France, and Germany, these types of intelligence-seeking activities can still be authorized by executive order of the government. In the United States they cannot, and in my view they should not be. But at the time they were.

In the mid-seventies, Watergate and the turmoil it brought to our political system had led to a series of hearings by the Church (Senate) and Pike (House) investigatory committees. The intelligence components of the U.S. government were highly criticized for some of the things they had done during this period, particularly for spying upon individuals and groups that, though radical, were not a threat to the nation's existence. There was no consensus in the body politic on the extent to which the domestic law-enforcement and intelligence services could be used to investigate the causes, structure and membership of groups that, in fact, made use of systemic violence.

While the criticism that arose out of the Church and Pike hearings was primarily directed at the CIA, the FBI got its share, especially for a very ill-considered program called COINTELPRO. This program had adopted counterintelligence methods meant to be used against a foreign power for use against domestic groups. In COINTELPRO the FBI had used extra-legal tactics to determine who was behind certain movements and what they were involved in. After this became known, the Bureau was quite traumatized about its proper role and about the legal use of executive authority to combat domestic terrorism.

In the late 1970s, the FBI practically shut down its entire domestic security operation. It was dealing with specific criminal acts after the fact only; it did virtually no collection or analysis of intelligence prior to the commission of a violent act by some politically motivated organization.

The Rebuilding of Intelligence-Gathering

By 1980, the level of these incidents had risen to the point where we at the FBI believed we had to become proactive again, but very carefully and under a set of guidelines that we had participated in designing. These guidelines, called the Attorney General's Guidelines, were intended not only to tell us the limitations of our authority but also to sanction those actions that we did take, and to make sure people understood that this was a legitimate exercise of the legal authority of the president, the attorney general, and those charged with carrying out their directives. In 1982 I recommended, and William Webster, who had been appointed director of the FBI in 1978, agreed, that we designate terrorism a national priority of the FBI, as were counterintelligence, organized crime, and white-collar crime.

In the late 1970s and early 1980s, in addition to domestic groups, numerous groups whose cause was overseas had been committing violent acts in the United States. We had Sikh terrorism, Armenian terrorism, Croatian terrorism, terrorism from virtually every continent. There were groups carrying out attacks against the Soviet Union, Turkey, and India, all operating in the United States. It was a precursor to what we have today.

In 1982, there were fifty-one terrorist incidents in the United States, in which seven people were killed and twenty-six were injured. Between 1982 and 1988, because of the renewed vigor of the counterterrorism program, we were able to reduce that level to only five to ten incidents a year. We were able to prevent fifty-six terrorist incidents that would have resulted in massive loss of life in the United States and the assassination of some visiting foreign leaders. Some incidents similar to the blowing up of PanAm flight 103 in 1988 were prevented because of our ability to collect and utilize information under the Attorney General's Guidelines.

The CISPES Affair

By 1988 only three or four terrorist groups were still functioning; we had been able, through the use of legal procedures, to preempt and neutralize most of the organizations, both domestic and foreign, that were committing acts of terrorism in the United States. But this was the time when President Reagan's policy in Central America had become very controversial, and another situation developed that again set back the counterterrorism program. This was a series of cases concerning CISPES, the Committee in Solidarity with the People of El Salvador. In 1982 or 1983 the FBI learned from the CIA that this group in the United States was a front organization for Communist guerrillas in El Salvador and was largely funded by Cuba and by the Sandinista regime in Nicaragua. The FBI developed a Salvadoran informant, and we found out that CISPES had been formed to support the revolutionary element in El Salvador, which directly supported the terrorist organizations there, particularly the Farabundo Marti National Liberation Front (FMLN). Information also indicated that CISPES was using the United States for raising money, gathering arms, and even recruiting people to go to El Salvador—all in violation of U.S. law.

An investigation began within the FBI's terrorism section, using field offices in several locations. The case, one of several hundred pending in the terrorism section, never reached the level of the assistant director in charge of criminal investigations, which was my post when the case began, or, later, that of the associate deputy director, the post I held when the difficulties developed. The reason it didn't reach my desk is that no extraordinary investigative techniques were used. There were no wiretaps, no undercover operations; the information was gathered from public meetings, from physical surveillance, and from the use of informants, all of which were authorized under the Attorney General's Guidelines. But because of the heightened political dichotomy and the disagreement between the Republican president and the Democratic Congress, the case was drawn into the spotlight.

Unfortunately, at about this time an FBI agent who happened to be the case agent for the CISPES investigation in Dallas became involved in misconduct, and his handling of this case came under scrutiny. We found that he had abused his authority in dealing with the informant, had fabricated information, and had not done his job in controlling and directing the informant. He was fired. The Justice Department chose not to prosecute, but there was certainly was a basis to prosecute. The Salvadoran informant became disenchanted and went to some of the political opponents of the Administration to allege that this was a politically motivated investigation. Then, because the Bureau had closed the case, CISPES was able to get access to information through the Freedom of Information Act. It became a *cause célèbre,* with congressional hearings and the like.

As it happened, the FBI had a new director, William Sessions, a federal judge from Texas. In October 1987, when Sessions came in, he knew almost nothing about the FBI's responsibilities in counterintelligence and terrorism—in fact, he said he hadn't even known that the FBI *had* counterintelligence responsibilities before he became director. Obviously the Bureau was at a considerable disadvantage in the representation of its position.

The charges against the FBI were that it (1) was involved in a political investigation, (2) was using illegal tactics, and (3) was violating the constitutional rights of those involved in this movement. Well, the investigation by the FBI, the Justice Department, and the Senate Intelligence Committee found that none of those allegations was true (though it *was* true that mistakes had been made in the investigation and some of our own regulations had been violated). There was no political involvement whatsoever on the part of the Reagan administration. The investigation had been reviewed by the Justice Department's Office of Intelligence Policy and Oversight early on and had been sanctioned as a legitimate investigation. No one's constitutional rights had been violated. No one had been obstructed or intimidated with regard to attending meetings, expressing his views, or engaging in any other protected activities. Nor had any FBI agent—other than the Dallas case agent, who was involved in a financial fraud in dealing with informant payments—committed any violation of law.

Unfortunately, after the CISPES inquiry Sessions went to Congress and engaged in a *mea culpa,* not only for the things the FBI had done wrong but for anything else that anybody wanted to throw at him. This, of course, just fed the fire. Then the *New York Times* and the

Washington Post said, "So, the FBI admits that it engaged in illegal activities just as it did during COINTELPRO," which was nonsense. As I said, I had not been involved in the CISPES investigation, because it had never risen to my level for approval. But in looking at the case, I felt there was substantial justification for at least part of the investigation, and I was extremely worried that the Bureau would again suffer what we had gone through in the late seventies and early eighties: congressional inquiry would jeopardize careers of people who were honestly trying to do their best to prevent acts of terrorism in the United States, and who had no motive except to defend their country. Unfortunately, that is exactly what happened. In 1988 we again went down almost to ground zero in carrying out our counterterrorism responsibilities.

The Kahane Assassination

All this set the stage, in my view, for what happened at the World Trade Center in February 1993. A few years earlier, in November 1990, there had been an assassination in New York of Rabbi Meir Kahane, an extremist who had created an organization—the Jewish Defense League—that engaged in acts of terrorism in the United States. Kahane also engendered a group in Israel that ultimately, I think, committed or at least facilitated terrorist acts. Some of his more active followers fled from the United States while under investigation for assassinating a Palestinian-American in Los Angeles and were essentially given sanctuary in Israel—one of the difficulties we had at the time. The investigation of the assassination of Meir Kahane was carried out largely by the police, with the FBI looking over their shoulders to see if there was anything of interest for the Bureau. Although I was in charge of the Bureau's intelligence and counterterrorism operations at the time, I was never informed that the assassin of Kahane was connected with any sort of organization that might have a terrorist agenda.

As it turned out, information had been available that, had it been properly processed and analyzed, would have led to a direct association between the assassin of Meir Kahane and the group that later bombed the World Trade Center and was conspiring to carry out a number of other heinous acts of terrorism. But the Kahane assassination was not properly analyzed, because of the political climate. FBI agents were loath to undertake anything that had any appearance of being involved in the political process. That includes anything that can be said to be protected by the Constitution, such as religious activity and free speech.

When I left Washington in May 1991, we were feeling pretty good. The Cold War had ended, and our side had won. Communism in the United States and the affiliated organizations were largely defunct, and Communism as a global movement was essentially discredited. Terrorism was being held in check in the United States. International acts of terrorism were decreasing, although terrorism was still very evident in certain countries, such as Algeria, Israel, India, and Northern Ireland. We had defeated Saddam Hussein in an unprecedented alliance and in doing so had countered his threat of global terrorism without any serious losses. All in all we had done a good job in dealing with the threat of terrorism, despite a lot of problems along the way. By 1991 I felt confident about leaving Washington, finishing my FBI career in Texas, and moving on into another life after government.

Then came the bombing of the World Trade Center. I was in Texas at the time, and we started seeing a link between certain people in Texas, particularly in the Dallas area, and those directly involved in the World Trade Center. This heightened my interest. Was this the act of a very small, independent group, or did it indicate a much larger operation?

A Global Conspiracy Revealed

Unfortunately, perhaps the most informative trials the United States had ever had concerning the whole matter of terrorism were virtually ignored. During the New York trials, important revelations were made about an international movement that had targeted the United States for vicious acts of terrorism. But the terrorism trial of the century was totally overshadowed by a tragic soap opera from Los Angeles. It would have been very instructive for academia, the media, and the public to pay attention to what was going on in New York, because it revealed, indeed, a global conspiracy, not necessarily of a great magnitude but of a very sophisticated capability. One of the persons who had escaped the initial arrests, Ramzi Yousef, had gone on to plan a whole series of further acts. These were to include the simultaneous bombings of between eleven and thirteen U.S. airliners flying from Asia to the United States in January 1995. The terrorists had already developed the technology and had tested it. It had in fact worked—it had killed a Japanese citizen aboard a Philippine airliner. They had developed the techniques to put explosive devices on board aircraft, and were fully engaged in the plot to carry out these simultaneous bombings of about a dozen U.S. aircraft.

We also detected a continuing conspiracy—it had not even slowed down because of the arrests—to bomb other major New York sites: the Lincoln Tunnel and the Holland Tunnel, the George Washington Bridge, the U.N. building, and the federal building housing the FBI. This group also planned to assassinate a number of political leaders, including the president of Egypt and a senator from New York. The people who were to do these things were already present in the United States and were using the protections of our Constitution to facilitate their planning of these heinous acts. We also saw certain potentially connected activities: the bombing of the Israeli embassy in Buenos Aires, followed by a terrible bombing of the main Jewish community center in Buenos Aires, an attempted bombing in Bangkok, a bombing in London. All these things were being planned and carried out by an apparatus that neither the U.S. government nor allied governments knew much about.

We finally started to get a handle on this group. Through the help of some counterterrorism experts like Yigal Carmon and Steve Emerson, the Bureau began to realize that it was dealing with a much wider conspiracy than just the group involved in the World Trade Center bombing. These investigations fall under the Foreign Counterintelligence Guidelines, which give somewhat more latitude than the domestic guidelines do.

The Militia Movement

Certain developments in the domestic arena are just as frightening for the long term. The standoffs in Waco, Texas, with the Branch Davidians, and in Ruby Ridge, Idaho, involved anti-government elements that are opposed to gun control, to the federal tax system, to federal ownership of land—indeed, to the federal government *in toto*. This movement, known as the militia movement, is growing, particularly in the western and southwestern parts of the country. The militia movement has many different components, not all of which call themselves militias. Examples are the Freemen and the Republic of Texas, both of which have been involved in standoffs with authorities. What they have in common is an absolute distrust of the federal government, a belief that the government does not have the authority to exercise any sort of control over their lives, including taxation, and that the only way to deal with the government is through armed force, or the threat of armed force.

The Waco incident was a terrible tragedy for all involved, including the FBI agents. It was their intention that everyone would come out of that situation alive, and particularly that the women and children would not be harmed. Forty agents from my office were at Waco—it was not in my territory, thank God, but I had to deal with the consequences of it. Waco generated a tremendous emotional outpouring and demand for revenge from a segment of society that has become more and more alienated not just from our government but even from our *system* of government.

After Waco a resentment began building that was almost palpable. I went on a number of television talk shows and entered into discussions on issues such as the Brady Bill and the assault-weapons ban. The government-haters were there. It was almost eerie to get the feel of them—they were so adamant in their beliefs, so disconnected from reality. There started to be a lot of traffic on the Internet about Waco and Ruby Ridge and the FBI and ATF (the Alcohol, Tobacco, and Firearms bureau). It seemed almost inevitable that sooner or later some group would act on the paranoia that was spreading across the country. So when Oklahoma City occurred, I was not surprised that finally we had seen a major manifestation of this hatred.

The FBI was ill prepared to deal with this phenomenon because it was not investigating the militias at the time. In fact, had it not been for the Anti-Defamation League and the Southern Poverty Law Center, I don't think many people in the United States, including the FBI, would have known much about the militia movement at all. Why? Because under the Attorney General's Guidelines as they were interpreted at the time—and still are—the FBI and the Justice Department did not think the FBI had the authority to collect information on groups that openly espouse the use of force and violence unless and until there is a criminal predicate, that is, an action taken that would indicate that a criminal offense either was in progress or had already occurred. The espousal of violence, the collection of arms as long as the arms were not illegal, organizing to commit violence—these things would not necessarily have caused an investigation, and in fact with the militias they had not.

And so, not only did we have evidence of a growing militant, extremist element from overseas based on a misinterpretation of Islam, but we also had within our own country a growing network of groups and individuals who misperceived the entire rationale for our constitutional form of government and blamed the government for all the ills that they and our society are subject to. These twin developments, one totally domestic, one primarily international, had a great bearing upon the safety and the security of the people of the United States.

Since the Oklahoma City bombing in April 1995 there have been other developments on the terrorism front. One was the phenomenon of the Unabomber: an alienated individual carried out a number of attacks that, while the FBI could investigate them as *criminal* acts, were not classified as terrorist acts until his manifesto surfaced. Then we were able to determine that his actions met the criteria for terrorist acts, because they were committed for a political purpose. A second occurrence was the bombing that occurred during the Olympics in Atlanta, even though years of planning had gone into the prevention of terrorism there. Was it carried out by a terrorist group? Probably not. But it had the same impact, because it was global theater, an act that gained immediate notoriety throughout the world. It certainly focused attention on the fact that no government can totally protect all its people all the time. No matter how high the level of security, there cannot be full protection against a person or group that is prepared to carry out a terrorist act no matter what risks are involved and what the consequences might be.

The U.S. Dilemma

The dilemma we face is this: We as a people do not entirely *trust* our government to use its power to protect us from acts of terrorism, particularly if those acts are motivated by political or religious beliefs; but at the same time we *expect* our government to give us that protection. We cannot decide how much authority we should grant to the counterterrorism agencies to do their job; but at the same time we expect them to be effective in doing that job, in combating terrorism. A very strange coalition has developed over the past few years in Congress, where the most extreme elements of the left and the most extreme elements of the right have come together to oppose the attempt by a Democratic president and a Republican congressional leadership to put together anti-terrorism legislation that has been supported through three administrations. This legislation would withstand constitutional scrutiny; most elements of it have already been ruled on by the Supreme Court in other forms, such as the roving wiretap issue, adjudicated in organized-crime and drug cases as being constitutional. Still, there is no consensus in our society as to how far we will allow the counterterrorism forces to proceed.

Under the guidelines as they are today, FBI agents are in the very unusual position of being perhaps the only people in our society who cannot take official cognizance of what other people say they are going to do until they actually do it. A professor, a private researcher, a writer, a reporter, can collect such information, analyze it, collate it, pronounce on it, issue statements of concern, say the government should be doing something or should not be doing something; but the FBI cannot. Under the current guidelines and a provision of the Privacy Act, the FBI is prohibited from collecting public information even from groups that directly espouse the use of violence to accomplish their objectives.

In March 1995 we saw a Japanese terrorist organization—which was really both a political movement and a religious cult—called the Aum Shinrikyo release a very dangerous gas in the Tokyo subway. A dozen Japanese citizens were killed and thousands were sickened, but that was fortunate: the group's intention was to *kill* thousands. Fortunately, they hadn't perfected their delivery system. The Aum specifically targeted the Japanese national police and tried to assassinate the commissioner general of the police. Their ultimate goal was to bring down the government of Japan.

We've seen chemical weapons used by outlaw regimes; we've seen terrorist organizations gain the capability to use chemical weapons. In the United States, people who are involved in the militia movement collect biologicals, including anthrax, one of the most lethal substances that could ever be released, yet easily obtainable. Botulism can be cultured and proliferated from a small amount of the toxin. We've already seen terrorist organizations and state sponsors of terrorism use these types of weapons of mass destruction. We also know there is a continuing outflow of nuclear materials from the former Soviet Union; even without the development of a nuclear device, deadly contamination could be spread by the use of a conventional explosive device.

So the threat escalates while we as a society cannot even decide how we're going to use our counterterrorist forces to prevent acts of terrorism. In a debate with Senator Arlen Specter during the CISPES inquiry, I asked, "Senator, do you want us to wait until there's blood on the streets to act? Or are you going to authorize us to act on information that any reasonable person would assume to be true?" His reply was, "In a democratic society, you may have to wait until there's blood on the streets." If it's the blood of a small number of people, maybe society can accept it. But if 50,000 people had been killed in the World Trade Center bombing, which was the intent of the terrorists, would we as a society accept that? The death of 168 people in Oklahoma City traumatized the American people. What would the death of 50,000 have done? What would the blowing up of a dozen PanAm 103s do to our society? How would Congress act? No doubt it would give the FBI full power to collect public information. But would we also see internments, mass expulsions, suspension of the writ of habeas corpus?

I fear that our society would overreact. And as someone who has dealt with enforcing the law for thirty years, I find that very troubling. In the United Kingdom, from whose legal system ours was developed, they have suspended the right of trial by jury and the writ of habeas corpus, they've allowed investigative detention without charge, they've engaged in wiretaps and electronic surveillance without court order—this in a society that is civil and democratic, one of the founding nations of democracy. It is also, of course, a society that is the target of terrorists. The British, the French, and the Germans all use extra-legal means to combat terrorists. We do not, we should not, and we need not. But we have to reach a reasonable balance that allows those parts of our society charged with preventing terrorism to do their jobs. Right now the balance is not there.

I wish I could say that I don't think we will have additional World Trade Centers, PanAm 103s, and Oklahoma Citys—but I have no such expectation. Although there have been some improvements in our counterterrorist capacities, they are not sufficient to give us a reasonable chance to prevent these kinds of terrible incidents. And as the potential use of even more devastating weapons increases, we are not increasing our capabilities. The Congress of the United States in its infinite wisdom has said, "You cannot use the technological resources of the Defense Department in biological and chemical areas to aid law enforcement in the prevention of these types of acts." If ever there was a nonsensical decision on the part of our elected representatives, it is that one. And what is it based on? The gun lobby's concern that in some way this would pose a threat to their political agenda. And the objections of organizations such as the ACLU, which have always been opposed to any sort of government intervention before the fact. That's where Congress is today in the battle to deal with the potential of terrorism.

Do I think we ought to impose draconian measures on our society to prevent terrorism? Absolutely not. That would allow the terrorists to win. But we must find a reasonable balance, and we *can* find a reasonable balance under the Constitution. We need the political will, and we need public attention for more than twenty-four hours. In our society, that is very difficult to achieve. But this is a battle we must win to protect our nation from the scourge of terrorism.

13

Counterterrorism and Democratic Values

An Israeli Practitioner's Experience

Yigal Carmon

Israel's experience with terrorism goes back almost a hundred years to the very beginning of the twentieth century, when the Jewish people—led by the Zionist movement—began their slow and arduous return to their homeland after two thousand years of exile.

The movements that have espoused terrorism against the Jews, though ideologically diverse (i.e., Marxist, nationalistic, Islamist), are all characterized by a lack of moral restraint regarding targets. Both in Israel and in its outposts abroad, hardly a category of citizen or field of human endeavor has been spared attack throughout the past century. Among the targets have been men, women, children, and the elderly; homes, offices, schools, universities, hotels, hospitals, and synagogues; beaches, market places, and entertainment centers; agriculture, industry, water, electricity, transportation (air, land, and sea), and sports.

Yigal Carmon holds the rank of colonel in Israeli intelligence and served prime ministers Shamir and Rabin as advisor on countering terrorism. He now heads the Palestinian Media Review (TV), which monitors change in the ideology and conduct of the PLO.

Another characteristic of the terrorism Israel has faced is that it has been integral to "conventional" military confrontations, some of which were even precipitated by a strategically premeditated escalation of terror. The Six Day War of 1967, for example, began with a wave of terror along the Syrian border. Successful in their military strategy, the terrorist organizations actually brought about a full-scale war between the Arab states and Israel.

Furthermore, the terrorism against Israel has always been sponsored by at least one major Arab state (usually by all) and—of no less importance—by the Soviet superpower until its collapse. And, since 1974, terrorism has also been indirectly sponsored by the United Nations, which adopted a series of resolutions in support of the Third World's struggle against "colonialist and imperialist powers." One of these resolutions, adopted by the General Assembly, sanctioned "all means" that "anti-imperialist" movements and organizations might use to pursue their goals. As a U.S. ally, Israel fell prey to gradual delegitimization by the Soviet and Third World blocs in the U.N., as well as to Soviet-sponsored struggle. Tragically, this only enhanced the ideological motivation of the various terrorist organizations to pursue their unrestrained war against the Jewish state.

Given Israel's small size and resources, the factors I have mentioned add up to a situation that is extremely difficult, one in which the victim is fighting against almost all possible odds.

A Strategy of Defense

Whenever a notorious terrorist is killed anywhere in the world, Israel is automatically blamed. Herein lies a myth created and perpetuated by false assumptions. Contrary to popular belief, Israel's approach to terrorism has always been primarily defensive. Those who see us as taking the strategic offensive lack knowledge of the enormous effort we have invested in prevention and self-defense. Having coordinated Israel's national counterterrorism deployment for five years (under premiers Shamir and Rabin), I would like to describe this defensive approach about which so little is known.

The fact that we chose a strategy of defense as our primary response to terrorism is, in itself, an expression of our democratic system and values. Democracies think not how to attack evil but how to protect themselves from it. It takes deep conviction and self-restraint on the part of decision-makers in democratic societies to resist the temptation to attack, the temptation to preempt rather than to stand by and wait for another blow.

The four main components of Israel's defensive strategy against terrorism are these: (1) national reinforced deployment, (2) intelligence diffusion and dissemination, (3) technology, and (4) special elite units. Before elaborating on each, let me describe their role in general.

Given the morally unrestrained range of potential terrorism targets, countering terrorism by defensive and protective means is a labor-intensive operation. But democracies—Israel included—do not have available anywhere near the number of workers required for such a gargantuan task. The total number of people employed by the FBI, for example, is incredibly small. Totalitarian regimes, on the other hand, have as much manpower at their disposal, for whatever task, as they want. The four components mentioned above, then, are used in an effort to overcome this fundamental problem of democracies: the labor-intensive nature of the defensive approach to countering terrorism.

1. National Reinforced Deployment

This reinforcement developed in three stages. First, we did what other democracies facing the terrorist threat do: we recruited to the counterterrorist effort all government branches and organs, not only those dealing with security, thereby adding a significant number of people, capabilities, and budgetary resources. Under the new system, for example, no longer did the police or General Security Services perform the technological inspection of incoming and outgoing mail, in the attempt to prevent a form of terrorist attack from which Israelis have suffered both at home and abroad. Instead, it has become the responsibility of the Ministry of Communications to deal with recruiting and training professional personnel, purchasing the equipment required, and executing the task effectively. Other similar examples can be seen in all government ministries.

The second step in increasing deployment was to open the doors for volunteers to join the regular security forces. This was done by the creation in 1974 of a new organ, the Civil Guard, as an auxiliary force under the Israeli police. In its first years the Civil Guard consisted of about 100,000 volunteers performing part-time missions to assist the police in counterterrorist activities. It was five times the size of the police force! In later years, the Civil Guard shrank to about half that size—still a significant number, however—and the forces became more professional, better trained, and more experienced. They were sometimes successful in foiling terrorist acts; the Civil Guard is a success story.

Nevertheless, these first two steps were not sufficient. The third step—or rather, series of steps—involved legislation and was the most effective, with immense impact. In a gradual process that has intensified significantly since 1973, the government of Israel, through legislation enacted by the Knesset (Israel's parliament), has imposed security responsibilities on its private sector, i.e., on the whole people. These duties are performed under government supervision and authority, but are done mainly at private expense—though sometimes with a limited government subsidy.

Almost every sector of public and private life falls under this legislation, being required by law to build security systems and to hire security guards. For example: as a result of the 1974 terrorist attack on a school in the Israeli town of Ma'alot—and given the obvious fact that there is no way to have sufficient security forces to guard all schools that might become a terrorist target—the government brought to the Knesset a law that obligates all parents to guard their children's schools. That simple legislation added about a million new "soldiers" to the national deployment. In similar ways, all other sectors of public life were required to do similar things. The task of supervising this vast undertaking was divided among Israel's three main security organs: the Israel Defense Forces (IDF), the Israeli police, and the General Security Services (GSS), each of which was responsible for training, instructing, and otherwise sponsoring a cluster of public and private institutions placed under its administrative jurisdiction.

If this massive imposition on public and private life causes some to wonder (a) how a government enforcing such legislation got re-elected, and (b) how such a huge endeavor did not turn into total chaos, the answers are at once simple and complicated.

In Israel, given its history of the last century (or shall we say the past two millennia), people understand the need to take such responsibilities upon themselves in order to survive. The cohesiveness of Israeli society—born out of suffering and tribulation—is what makes such a widespread effort viable, even today. This is the simple explanation for the public's lack of resentment toward its elected officials for enacting such laws.

More complicated is the explanation of how the whole system did not become a chaotic mess. Coordinating such a vast operation is no easy task. We set up committees, at all levels, for this purpose. My own position as advisor to the prime minister was the highest of these levels; I was a kind of "chief coordinator." Nevertheless, the system is so complex that if I were to try to explain it here, I would only manage to create confusion. (The good news is that it probably confused our enemies as well.) But the fact is that it has worked. When people feel they must cooperate to survive, nothing will prevent them from doing it.

2. Intelligence Diffusion and Dissemination

Israel's decision-makers have always deemed intelligence crucial to the country's security and therefore have always invested heavily in it. This accumulation of intelligence over a fifty-year period has given Israel an unmeasurable advantage over its enemies.

One of the most important aspects of Israel's use of intelligence as part of its counterterrorism strategy is the open or overt approach. Though seemingly a contradiction in terms, this open approach to intelligence has been integral to Israel's strategy since 1967.

After the Six Day War, a national center for the diffusion and dissemination of intelligence was established within the framework of the Israel Defense Forces. Some years later, another such center was created within the Israeli police, and the two are interconnected. All raw material relating to potential terrorist activities is funneled directly through these centers, where the personnel in charge—officers by rank—are responsible for maximizing the dissemination of relevant information. This information is passed on to the security officers of the appropriate security systems of the institutions, public or private, that are in danger of terrorist attack. (It might be noted here that all these "security officers" belong to a kind of "good old boy" network in which everybody knows everybody else—a phenomenon that, though common enough elsewhere, reaches unprecedented proportions in Israel.)

Of course, Israeli intelligence is guarded enough not to reveal sources or to release reports in full. But when all is said and done, top priority is given to dissemination—for the sake of early warning.

3. Technology

Israel has invested in technological innovations far beyond its means, and the investment has paid off. Though unable to elaborate freely on Israel's efforts in this area, I can point to a few projects that, though not particularly advanced or sophisticated, are innovative.

First, never having enough explosive disposal teams to meet the threats, decades ago we invented what are known in Israel as "security holes." These are literally holes in the ground into which suspicious parcels can be thrown, preventing casualties in the vicinity should an explosion occur. Some years later, the idea to "lift" these holes above ground arose, as did the invention of decorative "security trash cans." These cans—which today can be seen in many shopping malls in Israel—can contain an explosion of up to half a kilo of advanced explosives without harming anyone standing even within half a meter radius.

A second Israeli invention is the "security fence." So renowned have these fences become that even the British royal family uses them to protect its palaces. (The fact that someone succeeded in penetrating one a few years ago and making his way into the Queen's bedroom is evidence less of the failure of the fence than of the inexorable fascination with the royal bedroom.)

A third innovation is the "profile" system used in civil aviation, according to which passengers are questioned by airport security personnel before being allowed to proceed to boarding gates. Now, it may seem unlikely that questioning passengers can provide an effective substitute for manual automatic overall searches. But this "sniffing" method has proved successful. For instance, in April 1986 the lives of 400 El Al passengers were saved when the profile system uncovered a pregnant young Irish woman about to aboard the flight with an explosive device given to her by the terrorist father of her unborn baby.

Like other technological superpowers, Israel has tried its best to invent other methods of "sniffing." For example, it has succeeded in creating an explosives sniffer, one that competes with equipment developed by bigger countries with more resources.

4. Special Elite Units

The mission of these special units is to contain any massive terrorist act, to stop it as soon as possible and at minimum cost in human life. Such units are used in many other countries. But for a tiny country like Israel to have many such units is as unusual as it is necessary—owing to the need to be prepared to deal with several emergencies simultaneously.

These units require special equipment, and much has been done to enhance their technical capabilities. But solutions to critical situations cannot always be achieved by means of technological innovations. Take the case of a hijacked bus in the Negev Desert—filled primarily with women passengers—en route to the town of Dimona in March 1988. The bus was stopped in an open area. The hijackers threatened to kill the hostages if their demands were not met—and actually began to do so. What can be done in such a case to shock or distract the terrorists, so as to prevent them from murdering hostages, and at the same time break into the bus? The answer, in this case, did not lie in technology. Rather than storming the bus from one direction, the fighters of the elite unit attacked the bus from *all* directions—running the risk of shooting at one another. This maneuver was just what was needed to shock the terrorists for four or five seconds, giving the unit enough time to rescue the hostages without no additional casualties.

The Need for Emergency Laws

Another important aspect of Israel's overall counterterrorism strategy is one that is controversial for Americans (though not for other European democracies). This is legislation banning political or religious terrorist groups and, in practical terms, allowing the indictment of individuals on the basis merely of "membership" in an unlawful organization. The legislation also prohibits "incitement," as distinct from other forms of "aiding and abetting" crimes.

Such legislation would be unheard of in America, a country founded on absolute political and religious freedom. Fortunately for the United States, it had not been challenged until fairly recently by political and religious groups that abuse these freedoms in order to incite violence and to act violently.

But every democratic society seems to reach its own moment of truth where it finds the need and justification for emergency laws. Germany reached this point in 1977—not in 1976, when its attorney general was killed by terrorists, but a year later, when the head of an industrial association, Martin Von Schleier, was kidnapped and murdered. At this point Germany adopted rather draconian legislation, of the sort Israel has had since British rule under the mandate. The British, of course, have long had such emergency laws—and demand parliamentary re-enactment every year. The Italians had their moment of truth in 1978, when their ex-premier, Aldo Moro, was kidnapped and murdered. This led to the adoption of strict laws in Italy. France underwent a trial-and-error process in 1985-86 until bombs began exploding in the heart of Paris, in such sites as the Champs Elysées, the Galeries Lafayette, and the Place de l'Opéra. Canada has undergone similar experiences with the terrorist liberation group FLQ. As a result, the Canadian parliament approved re-enactment of the War Measures Act of 1942 (a fifty-kilo hammer to swat a mosquito).

At the time of the Gulf War, almost all democratic countries, including the United States, appointed some kind of emergency authorities to prevent Iraqis residing within their borders from becoming a security problem. Iraqi diplomatic missions were reduced to an absolute minimum, and many Iraqis and Palestinian supporters were expelled, at least temporarily. Still, however, the Iranian government's *fatwa* calling for the death of Salman Rushdie is not considered a criminal offense in most Western democracies; nor is the Muslim *jihad*, the war against "infidels."

Today, again, the United States is approaching a moment of truth. Failure to meet the challenge now may result either in an injudicious application of constitutionally unacceptable measures in the face of future crises, or in a state of extreme weakness, which might endanger the whole democratic system.

After the Oslo Accords

Israel's hope in signing the Oslo Accords with the Palestinians in September 1993 was to try to counter terrorism through a political solution, a hope that is very typical of democracies. In the course of the past hundred years, we seem to have tried all approaches—including the idealistic one. Did it work?

Firstly, terrorism continued rising to the bloody peak of February/ March 1996, with its suicide bus bombings—tripling the number of casualties suffered prior to the accords. True, these acts were committed by Islamic extremist terrorist groups (Hamas and the Islamic Jihad). But the PLO was supposed to prevent precisely this kind of act. It proved both unwilling and unable to do so (and hence proved itself to be a *de facto* terrorism-sponsoring entity). For the Israelis, as victims, the distinction between the PLO and the extremist groups matters little. There will always be unsatisfied parties to any agreement who will continue to victimize. The PLO was supposed to be the power that would stop the terror. But it failed.

Moreover, the PLO itself has accounts to settle with Israel. Instead of cooperating with their counterparts in "peace," Palestinian soldiers and policemen have shot at Israeli soldiers, killing, for instance, sixteen in the disturbance of September 25, 1996.

The Oslo agreement was an idealistic attempt to make peace gradually, leaving the most critical points of contention to the end, meanwhile allowing our rival to return to our backyard with tens of thousands of soldiers and weapons (and an even higher unofficial number). The assumption was that, like the late President Sadat, the PLO would adopt the policy of "no more war, no more bloodshed." However, the PLO understood the whole thing quite differently. Its position is one of conditional ceasefire: if it doesn't get what it believes it deserves, it will wage war. This strategy is not a covert one. It is being stated publicly time and again by PLO spokesmen and leaders.

So now Israel is faced with a terrible dilemma. If the PLO again engages in violence as a means of pressure, what shall we do? Shall we accept the growing toll in human life? Engage our armor against hostile and armed civilians, causing devastating results? Engage our infantry, and suffer the probable casualties involved in fighting in densely populated, armed areas? Or shall we give in and accept their demands?

Israel *cannot* choose to "give in and accept their demands." This is because the PLO keeps demanding not only a Palestinian state with Jerusalem as its capital, but also the so-called right of return of at least two million refugees to *pre-'67 Israel*. Accepting this demand would entail the virtual destruction of the Jewish state.

The idea of depending upon a political solution to the terrorist threat reminds me of the saying, "The road to hell is paved with good intentions."

14

Terrorists on TV: How the Mass Media Cover Terrorism

Eric Breindel

How do the American mass media—television, large-circulation daily newspapers, and national magazines—deal with global terror? Has media treatment of terrorism changed in the last quarter century? Have things changed more recently, since terrorism began to manifest itself with serious force in this country—since, say, the 1993 World Trade Center bombing? Are demands issued by terrorists—and the concerns that ostensibly animate them—accorded inappropriately respectful treatment in the U.S. media? Are the media generally hostile to efforts by foreign governments to suppress and punish terrorism? To what extent have journalists working for American mass-media outlets applied their investigative skills in efforts to identify terror fronts based in this country?

The short answer to the big question—"Has anything changed?"—is: Yes. But though things are improving, we still have a long way to go.

Let's go back in time some twelve years. In June 1985, when a

---

The late **Eric Breindel,** formerly editorial-page editor of the *New York Post,* was senior vice president of News Corporation, moderator of the weekly TV show "Fox News Watch," and a syndicated columnist. He died in March 1998 at the age of 42.

TWA airliner was hijacked by Shiite terrorists based in Beirut, television gave the terrorists a unique propaganda platform. By interviewing the hostages, at the behest of the terrorists, television reporters placed the frightened captives in a decidedly awkward position. The hostages were compelled publicly to criticize Washington in order to save their own lives. All in all, TWA 847 was a violent, ugly episode; it involved beatings, humiliation, and—eventually—the murder of one of the hostages. Hostages who were put on the air and asked for their views by correspondents were wise to say exactly what their terrorist captors wanted them to say.

As it had done on a number of prior occasions and has done many times since, television news took upon itself a kind of middleman role. Establishing dialogue with the captives' governments is, generally, a key terrorist goal, and television has helped them achieve it on more than one occasion. Indeed, in the TWA case, TV became a conduit for negotiations between the terrorists and the U.S. government. Meanwhile, TV journalists explained—and, by extension, legitimated—the terrorists' ostensible concerns. Not surprisingly, coverage on television and in the print media was extensive. The TWA affair, recall, came only a few years after the birth of "Nightline," a program created to provide daily reportage on the Iran hostage crisis. The success of "Nightline" led network news executives to conclude that nightly television reports about ongoing terror episodes had the potential to attract viewers. Insofar as the "journalism" in the programs tended to focus on the human plight of individual hostages (the terrorists, after all, controlled the agenda), the shows inevitably assisted the terrorists by heightening pressure on Washington.

Television's role during the TWA crisis actually prompted hearings on Capitol Hill about how media institutions conducted themselves when dealing with international terrorism. This was an unprecedented and unexpected development, and the congressional hearings were viewed with a measure of dismay by the television news establishment.

Most observers, however, recognized that journalists, wittingly or otherwise, had subjected themselves to potential exploitation. To be sure, some reporters, were willing to accept the fact that in the course of doing what they perceived to be their jobs, they'd let themselves be used. And, in one case, the president of a network news division acknowledged—albeit privately, not during a hearing—that focusing on individual hostages forced substantive political issues into the background. The same executive also conceded, privately, that the push for "scoops"—an interview with a terrorist, a pilot, a crew member, or, best of all, a hostage—increased the pressure on Washington and served to limit President Reagan's options. In short, television's effort to "free the hostages" had unmistakably dubious implications.

Propaganda by Deed

The 1985 TWA affair also afforded American audiences repeated exposure to the insidious doctrine of "moral equivalence." Viewers were told, for example, that "Israel, too, holds hostages"—a reference to Shiite terrorists in Israeli prisons. (The ostensible motive of the hijacking was to force Israel to release those very Shiite terrorists.)

The method at work here was nothing new. In fact, the concept of "propaganda by deed" dates back the first century. A noteworthy public action (like a hijacking) is carried out in order to heighten public awareness of the cause to which the terrorists have dedicated themselves. Such deeds, in theory, are also meant to engender sympathy for the cause in question.

During the period before the State of Israel was established in 1948, for example, members of the Stern Group, an extremist Zionist faction, carried out a series of violent actions. Realizing that a small (400-member) organization couldn't do much militarily when faced with the might of the British Empire, the Sternists concentrated on staging high-visibility incidents, usually assassinations. If possible, they then used the ensuing legal process to explain their larger purpose; a case in point is the 1945 Cairo trial of two Sternists who had traveled from Palestine to Egypt to murder Lord Moyne, the British minister-resident in the Near East.

Today, more than ever before, this method of terrorism, "propaganda by deed," requires a measure of media acquiescence. Indeed, in the TWA 847 episode, media acquiescence served as the key factor enabling the terrorists to realize some of their goals.

Such complicity, of course, needn't be forthcoming. During wartime, after all, it is possible for honest journalists to cover the news without disregarding the national interest. Prior to Vietnam, in fact, American institutions tended, voluntarily, to take steps to ensure that their activities didn't aid the enemy. But the Vietnam experience spawned insidious changes, changes that remain evident in mass-media coverage of global terror.

In noting these changes, syndicated columnist Charles Krautham-mer points to the emergence of a "cult of objectivity." A claim issued by ABC correspondent Sam Donaldson during the 1985 TWA inci-dent—"It's our job to cover the story, not to take sides"—illustrates the phenomenon: Donaldson was not willing to choose sides between American hostages (civilians, as it happens) and Shiite terrorists hold-ing guns to their heads. More recently, during the Gulf War, CNN anchor Bernard Shaw argued that his status as a journalist rendered him a "neutral," notwithstanding the participation of U.S. troops in the conflict. (This claim prompted then Senator Alan Simpson, whose caustic wit sometimes led him into controversy, to wonder aloud "whether Bernie Shaw has confused himself with Switzerland.")

The ostensible requirements of "neutrality" served for a long period as the standard rationalization for the manner in which the mass media tended to cover terrorism. And this tendency was but-tressed by the unwillingness of most mainstream journalists to recog-nize terrorism as a genuine species of warfare.

The Berenson Coverage: Relatively Reasonable

Now, at long last, the media's quest for "neutrality" in this sphere is on the wane. The arrival of terrorism in America, the indiscrimi-nate suffering it has caused, and the seeming emergence of a peace option in the Middle East have combined to awaken many journalists. Increasingly, reporters are wary about allowing themselves to be exploited; this sense of caution was hard to find a decade ago.

The case of Lori Berenson underscores the change.

Berenson is a New Yorker who made her way to Sandinista Nicaragua after a pit stop (and brief marriage) in El Salvador. To her apparent dismay, the civil war in Salvador was drawing to a close just as she arrived. Eventually, this angry "Revolutionary Tourist" from Gramercy Park wound up in Peru where—in January 1996—she was sentenced by a military court to life in prison for aiding the Tupac Amaru Revolutionary Movement. Berenson had helped the Peruvian terror gang obtain weapons, rent safe houses, and gather information for guerrilla attacks; *her* assigned target was the Peruvian Congress.

Interestingly, the U.S. media covered the Berenson case in a relatively dispassionate fashion. True, the terrorists' cause received inordi-
nately respectful, even sympathetic, treatment in certain quarters. And
Peru's use of military courts to try terrorists was widely condemned
on editorial and op-ed pages. Many critics simply ignored the fact that
civilians—and, in particular, judges—had long been principal Tupac
Amaru targets, a circumstance that had forced the establishment of the
very military tribunals deemed objectionable by the *New York Times*
and other mainstream American media organs. (All of this, to be sure,
was before the Tupac Amaru reminded the world of what they're
about in an unmistakable way—by seizing a large group of hostages at
the Japanese embassy in Lima.) Still, even in early 1996, essays celebrating Lori Berenson and her comrades weren't easy to find outside
the precincts of the hard left.

A decade ago, on the other hand, the young American would very
likely have been lionized as a heroic idealist on the front pages of
national newspapers, in weekly news magazines, and on major television programs. In the intervening period, owing in large measure to
the abject collapse of Communism, Marxist "Revolutionary Tourists"
had become considerably less popular. Even the journals of the left
offered nuanced accounts of Berenson's history and activities and
downplayed the nature of her ideological commitments.

This new reality apparently disappointed her parents, sixties radicals
who teach in New York. The elder Berensons seem to have expected
a sort of "rally-around-the-martyr" sensibility to take hold, as might
have happened during the Vietnam War. When journalists began asking questions about their daughter's membership in CISPES (the
Committee in Solidarity with the People of El Salvador, a Communist party front) and wondered whether this affiliation meant that she
favored violence, the Berensons manifested unmistakable dismay.

Missing Links

But we still have a long way to go, as evidenced by the national
media's continuing refusal to investigate the ties between U.S.-based
groups and foreign terror organizations. A single exception was a PBS
documentary on various American front-groups for the radical Palestinian group Hamas. This 1995 film was produced, directed, and
rammed through the PBS bureaucracy by an exceedingly persistent

investigative journalist, terrorism expert Steve Emerson. The documentary, which drew a fair bit of follow-up coverage, would almost certainly not have been aired a decade ago.

But the absence of parallel attempts by major newspaper and television investigatory units to probe further in this realm is hard to ignore. True, a 1996 U.S. Senate candidate, Democratic Rep. Robert Torricelli of New Jersey (Torricelli won his race and is now a senator), ran into a fair bit of controversy over his decision to take part in a series of appearances sponsored by the American Muslim Council, a group widely considered a Hamas front. Still, even though Torricelli was forced by journalists to confront this issue, apparently no one in the media tried to learn more about the organization in question.

Similarly noteworthy was the non-coverage of President and Mrs. Clinton's June 1996 White House meeting with the leaders of a major U.S.-based Hamas front. Initially, only the *Wall Street Journal* called attention to this encounter. And while the *Journal* is an important national institution, its opinion pages are widely perceived as hostile to the Clinton administration; its report on the meeting—which appeared on its editorial page, not in the news section—was represented by many as nothing more than another manifestation of this anti-Clinton animus. The *New York Post* also discussed this decidedly unusual White House conclave on its editorial pages, but that paper, too, has acquired a (well-deserved) anti-administration reputation.

Why the lack of wider media interest? Several answers make sense.

For one thing—as noted earlier—mainstream journalists still don't recognize an equivalence between terrorists and wartime enemies. In addition, a genuine aversion to practicing "McCarthyism" permeates the media; this concern is readily exploited by those who simply don't want the entire subject explored. "Guilt by association" charges are regularly leveled at those who research links between Arab-American groups and terrorists. And there's no question that this tactic inhibits journalists engaged in such efforts.

In the end, the charge of "group slander" has helped prevent a full discussion of terrorist acts carried out by Islamic fundamentalists. The scrutiny to which journalists interested in these matters are subjected has a dual root: some of the media watchdogs whose commentary inhibits open discourse in this realm are genuinely animated by civil-liberties concerns, but others actually sympathize with the Islamist cause. Still, many reporters, anxious to avoid bias charges, take pains to refrain from linking Islamic fundamentalism with terrorism. President Clinton himself has been intimidated on this score, so much so that he found it necessary, in the aftermath of Oklahoma City, to issue an apology for seeming to suggest that such ties obtain.

Here, the story of journalist Steve Emerson's Oklahoma City "mistake" in instructive. Emerson was hounded off the air for suggesting, in the direct aftermath of the Oklahoma City bombing, that he saw in the event "earmarks" of Middle East–style terrorism. Eventually, of course, it emerged that Middle Eastern terrorists happened not to be involved. As a result, Emerson was accused of having slandered an entire ethnic group. His employer, CNN, apologized for its alleged "insensitivity," even though Emerson had offered little more than informed speculation. (The bombing, in fact, *did* have the "earmarks" of terrorism Middle East–style.) Emerson's entire television career was derailed.

Despite the violence, many in the media will not accept the fact that groups like the Committee on American-Islamic Relations or the American Muslim Council are fronts for terrorist organizations. The skeptics, of course, are the very journalists who tend to jump at opportunities to "demonstrate"—with far less "evidence"—links between, say, pro-gun groups and the Ku Klux Klan.

The reason for this disparity?

Ideology.

Groups that are said to be fronts for Palestinians in Gaza and the West Bank—violent or not—arouse residual sympathy among journalists. The fellowship of the Left still thrives, not just in the academy but also in the newsroom. In these quarters, Arab émigrés who affect to represent the interests of oppressed Palestinians engender sympathy, not suspicion.

Good Signs

Still, even in this sphere, positive change can be seen. The conviction of Sheikh Omar Abdel-Rahman and his disciples in connection with the bombing of the World Trade Center forced the very inquiries concerning terror groups operating here that many observers had long hoped would be undertaken. Moreover, press coverage of the 1996 terrorism bill encouraged the conclusion that there will be further probes of this kind. The ACLU protests about the bill's allegedly sinister implications secured less attention this time than they had just one year earlier. Even the prospect of enhanced FBI wiretap authority seems to frighten fewer Americans.

A new realism has begun to inform the treatment of terrorism in the U.S. media. While there is still a long way to go, things are moving in the right direction.

PART FOUR

Is Missile Defense Moral?

15

New Threats for Old

Margaret Thatcher

The former British prime minister gave this address at Westminster College in Fulton, Missouri, on March 9, 1996.

When my distinguished predecessor delivered his Fulton speech, exactly fifty years ago, he journeyed hither by train in the company of the president of the United States. On the way, they played poker to pass the time, and the president won $75—quite a sum in those non-inflationary times for an unemployed former prime minister to lose. But in view of the historic impact of his speech on American opinion and subsequently on U.S. foreign policy, Sir Winston Churchill later recorded that his loss was one of the best investments he had ever made.

I did not travel here by train, or in the company of the president of the United States; nor did I play poker—I don't have the right kind of face for it. But in other ways there is some similarity in the circumstances of fifty years ago and today.

Mr. Churchill spoke not long after the Second World War. Towards the end of that great conflict, the wartime allies had forged new

---

Margaret Thatcher was the prime minister of Great Britain from 1979 to 1990. She was elevated to the House of Lords in 1992. Lady Thatcher is the author of *The Downing Street Years* (1993) and *The Path to Power* (1995).

international institutions for post-war cooperation. There was in those days great optimism, not least in the United States, about a world without conflict presided over benevolently by bodies like the United Nations, the International Monetary Fund (IMF), the World Bank, and the General Agreement on Tariffs and Trade (GATT). But the high hopes reposed in them were increasingly disappointed as Stalin lowered the Iron Curtain over Eastern Europe, made no secret of his global ambitions, and became antagonist rather than ally. Churchill's speech here was the first serious warning of what was afoot, and it helped to wake up the entire West.

In due course, that speech bore rich fruit in the new institutions forged to strengthen the West against Stalin's assault. The Marshall Plan laid the foundations for Europe's post-war economic recovery. The Truman Doctrine made it plain that America would resist Communist subversion of democracy. The North Atlantic Treaty Organization mobilized America's allies for mutual defense against the Soviet steamroller. And the European Coal and Steel Community, devised to help reconcile former European enemies, over time evolved into the European Community.

Stalin had overplayed his hand. By attempting to destroy international cooperation, he succeeded in stimulating it along more realistic lines—and not just through Western "Cold War" institutions like NATO. As the West recovered and united, growing in prosperity and confidence, so it also breathed new life into some of the first set of post-war institutions, like GATT and the IMF. Without the Russians to obstruct them, these bodies helped to usher in what the Marxist historian Eric Hobsbawm has ruefully christened the "Golden Age of Capitalism." The standard of living of ordinary people rose to levels that would have astonished our grandparents; there were regional wars, but no direct clash between the superpowers; and the economic, technological, and military superiority of the West eventually reached such a peak that the Communist system was forced into, first reform, then surrender, and finally liquidation.

None of this, however, was preordained. It happened in large part because of what Churchill said here fifty years ago. He spoke at a watershed: one set of international institutions had shown themselves to be wanting; another had yet to be born. And it was his speech, not the "force" celebrated by Marx, that turned out to be the midwife of history.

Today we are at what could be a similar watershed. The long twilight struggle of the Cold War ended five years ago with complete victory for the West and for the subject peoples of the Communist empire—and I very much include the Russian people in that description. It ended amid high hopes of a New World Order. But those hopes have been grievously disappointed. Somalia, Bosnia, and the rise of Islamic militancy all point to instability and conflict rather than cooperation and harmony. The international bodies in which our hopes were reposed anew after 1989 and 1991 have given us neither prosperity nor security. There is a pervasive anxiety about the drift of events. It remains to be seen whether this generation will respond to these threats with the imagination and courage of Sir Winston, President Truman, and the other wise men of those years.

THE POST–COLD WAR WORLD

How did we get to our present straits? As always with the breakup of empires, the breakup of the Soviet empire wrought enormous changes way beyond its borders. Many of these were indisputably for the good:

- a more cooperative superpower relationship between the United States and Russia;
- the spread of democracy and civil society in Eastern Europe and the Baltics;
- better prospects for resolving regional conflicts like those in South Africa and the Middle East, once Soviet mischief-making had been removed;
- the discrediting of socialist economic planning by the exposure of its disastrous consequences in Russia and Eastern Europe; and
- the removal of Soviet obstruction from the United Nations and its agencies.

All these were—and still are—real benefits for which we should be grateful. But in the euphoria that accompanied the Cold War's end— just as in what Churchill's private secretary called "the fatal hiatus" of 1944 to 1946—we failed to notice other, less appealing consequences of the peace. Like a giant refrigerator that had finally broken down after years of poor maintenance, the Soviet empire in its collapse released all the ills of ethnic, social, and political backwardness that had been held in suspended animation for so long:

■ Suddenly, border disputes between the successor states erupted into small wars, in, for instance, Armenia and Georgia.

■ Within these new countries the ethnic divisions aggravated by Soviet policies of Russification and forced population transfer produced violence, instability, and quarrels over citizenship.

■ The absence of the legal and customary foundations of a free economy led to a distorted "robber capitalism," one dominated by the combined forces of the mafia and the old Communist *nomenklatura*, with little appeal to ordinary people.

■ The moral vacuum created by Communism in everyday life, filled for some by a revived Orthodox Church, was filled for others by crime, corruption, gambling, and drug addiction. All contributed to a spreading ethic of luck, a belief that economic life is a zero-sum game, and an irrational nostalgia for a totalitarian order but without totalitarian methods.

■ And in these Hobbesian conditions, primitive political ideologies that have been extinct in Western Europe and America for two generations surfaced and began to flourish, all peddling fantasies of imperial glory to compensate for domestic squalor.

No one can forecast with confidence where this will lead. I believe that it will take long years of civic experience and patient institution-building for Russia to become a normal society. Neo-Communists may well return to power in the immediate future, postponing normality; but whoever wins the forthcoming [June 1996] Russian elections will almost certainly institute a more assertive foreign policy, one less friendly to the United States.

New Threats for Old

A revival of Russian power will create new problems—just when the world is struggling to cope with problems that the Soviet collapse itself created outside the old borders of the USSR. When Soviet power broke down, so did the control it exercised, however fitfully and irresponsibly, over rogue states like Syria, Iraq, and Qaddafi's Libya. They have in effect been released to commit whatever mischief they wish without bothering to check with their arms supplier and bank manager. Note that Saddam Hussein's invasion of Kuwait took place after the USSR was gravely weakened and had ceased to be Iraq's protector.

The Soviet collapse has also aggravated the single most awesome threat of modern times: the proliferation of weapons of mass destruction. These weapons—and the ability to develop and deliver them—are today acquired by middle-income countries with modest populations such as Iraq, Iran, Libya, and Syria, acquired sometimes from other powers like China and North Korea, but most ominously from former Soviet arsenals, or unemployed scientists, or from organized criminal rings, all via a growing international black market.

According to Stephen J. Hadley, formerly President Bush's assistant secretary for international security policy: "By the end of the decade, we could see over 20 countries with ballistic missiles, 9 with nuclear weapons, 10 with biological weapons, and up to 30 with chemical weapons." According to official U.S. sources, all of northeast Asia, southeast Asia, much of the Pacific, and most of Russia could soon be threatened by the latest North Korean missiles. Once they are available in the Middle East and North Africa, all the capitals of Europe will be within target range; and if present trends continue, a direct threat to American shores is likely to mature early in the next century.

Add weapons of mass destruction to rogue states and you have a highly toxic compound. As the CIA has pointed out: "Of the nations that have or are acquiring weapons of mass destruction, many are led by megalomaniacs and strongmen of proven inhumanity or by weak, unstable, or illegitimate governments." In some instances, the potential capabilities at the command of these unpredictable figures is either equal to or even more destructive than the Soviet threat to the West in the 1960s. It is that serious.

Indeed, it is even more serious than that. We in the West may have to deal with a number of possible adversaries, each with different characteristics. In some cases their mentalities differ from ours even more than did those of our old Cold War enemy. So the potential for misunderstanding is great. We must therefore be very clear in our own minds about our strategic intentions, and just as clear in signaling these to potential aggressors.

And that is only the gravest threat. There are others.

Within the Islamic world, the Soviet collapse undermined the legitimacy of radical secular regimes and gave an impetus to the rise of radical Islam. Radical Islamist movements now constitute a major revolutionary threat not only to the Saddams and Assads but also to conservative Arab regimes that are allies of the West. Indeed, they challenge the very idea of a Western economic presence—hence the random acts of violence designed to drive American companies and tourists out of the Islamic world.

In short, the world remains a very dangerous place, indeed one menaced by more unstable and complex threats than a decade ago. But because the risk of total nuclear annihilation has been removed, we in the West have lapsed into an alarming complacency about the risks that remain. We have run down our defenses and relaxed our guard.

INSTITUTIONAL FAILURE

To assure ourselves that we are doing the right thing, we have increasingly placed our trust in international institutions to safeguard our future. But international bodies have generally not performed well. Indeed, we have learned that they cannot perform well unless we refrain from utopian aims, give them practical tasks, and provide them with the means and backing to carry them out.

The United Nations

Perhaps the best example of utopian aims is multilateralism, the doctrine that international actions are most justified when they are untainted by the national interests of the countries that are called upon to carry them out. Multilateralism briefly became the doctrine of several Western powers in the early nineties, when the United Nations Security Council was no longer hamstrung by the Soviet veto. It seemed to promise a new age in which the U.N. would act as world policeman to settle regional conflicts.

Of course, there was always a fair amount of hypocrisy embedded in multilateralist doctrine. The Haiti intervention by U.S. forces acting under a U.N. mandate, for instance, was defended as an exercise in restoring a Haitian democracy, though that democracy had never existed; the intervention might be better described in the language of Clausewitz as the continuation of American immigration control by other means. But honest multilateralism without the spur of national interest has led to intervention without clear aims.

No one could criticize the humane impulse to step in and relieve the suffering created by the civil war in Somalia. But it soon became clear that the humanitarian effort could not enjoy long-term success without a return to civil order. And no internal force was available to supply this. Hence the intervention created a painful choice: either the U.N. would make Somalia into a colony and spend decades engaged in "nation-building," or the U.N. forces would eventually withdraw and Somalia would revert to its prior anarchy. Since the United States and the U.N. were unwilling to govern Somalia for thirty years, it followed that the job of feeding the hungry and helping the sick must be left to civilian aid agencies and private charities.

Conclusion: Military intervention without an attainable purpose creates as many problems as it solves.

This was further demonstrated in the former Yugoslavia, where early action to arm the victims of aggression so that they could defend themselves would have been far more effective than the U.N.'s half-hearted multilateral intervention. A neutral peacekeeping operation, lightly armed, in an area where there was no peace to keep, served mainly to consolidate the gains from aggression. Eventually the U.N. peacekeepers became hostages, used by the aggressor to deter more effective action against him. All in all it was a sorry episode, ended by the Croatian army, NATO air power, and American diplomacy.

The combined effect of interventions in Bosnia, Somalia and, indeed, Rwanda has been to shake the self-confidence of key Western powers and to tarnish the reputation of the U.N. And now a dangerous trend is evident: as the Haiti case shows, the Security Council seems increasingly prepared to widen the legal basis for intervention. We are seeing, in fact, that classically dangerous condition—a growing disproportion between theoretical claims and practical means.

Ballistic-Missile Defense

Compare this hubris with the failure to act effectively against the proliferation of nuclear, chemical, and biological weapons, and the means to deliver them. As I have already argued, these are falling into dangerous hands.

Given the intellectual climate in the West today, it is probably unrealistic to expect military intervention to remove the source of the threat—against North Korea, for example—except perhaps when the offender invites us to do so by invading a small neighboring country. Even then, in the case of Iraq, as we now know, our success in destroying the aggressor's nuclear- and chemical-weapons capability was limited. And we cannot be sure that the efforts by inspectors of the International Atomic Energy Authority to prevent Saddam from putting civil nuclear power to military uses have been any more successful; indeed, we may reasonably suspect that they have not.

What then can we do? There is no mysterious diplomatic means to disarm a state that is not willing to be disarmed. As Frederick the Great mordantly observed, "diplomacy without arms is like music without instruments." Arms-control and non-proliferation measures have a role in restraining rogue states, but only when combined with other measures.

If America and its allies cannot deal with the problem directly by pre-emptive military means, they must at least diminish the incentive for the Saddams, the Qaddafis, and others to acquire new weapons in the first place. That means the West must install effective ballistic-missile defense that would protect us and our armed forces, reduce or even nullify the rogue state's arsenal, and enable us to retaliate.

The potential contribution of ballistic-missile defense to peace and stability seems to me to be very great:

- First and most obviously, it promises the possibility of protection if deterrence fails, or if there is a limited and unauthorized use of nuclear missiles.

- Second, it would preserve the capability of the West to project its power overseas.

- Third, it would diminish the dangers of one country's overturning the regional balance of power by acquiring these weapons.

- Fourth, it would strengthen our existing deterrent against a hostile nuclear superpower by preserving the West's powers of retaliation.

- And fifth, it would enhance diplomacy's power to restrain proliferation by diminishing the utility of offensive systems.

Acquiring an effective global defense against ballistic missiles is therefore a matter of the greatest importance and urgency. The risk is that thousands of people may be killed by an attack that forethought and wise preparation might have prevented.

The European Union and Central Europe

It is often the case in foreign affairs, of course, that statesmen are dealing with problems for which there is no ready solution. They must manage them as best they can. But while that might be true of nuclear proliferation, no such excuses can be made for the European Union's activities at the end of the Cold War. It faced a task so obvious and achievable as to count as an almost explicit duty laid down by history: namely, the speedy incorporation of the new Central European democracies—Poland, Hungary, and what was then Czechoslovakia—within the EU's economic and political structures.

Early entry into Europe was the wish of the new democracies. It would help to stabilize them politically and smooth their transition to market economies, and it would ratify the post–Cold War settlement in Europe. Given the stormy past of that region—the inhabitants are said to produce more history than they can consume locally—everyone should have wished to see it settled economically and politically inside a stable European structure.

Why was this not done? Why was every obstacle put in the way of the new market democracies? Why were their exports subject to the kind of absurd quotas that have until now been reserved for Japan? And why is there still no room at the inn?

The answer is that the European Union was too busy contemplating its own navel. Both the Commission and a majority of member governments were committed to an early "deepening" of the EU (that is, centralizing more power in the EU's supranational institutions), and they felt that a "widening" of it (that is, admitting new members) would complicate, obstruct, or even prevent this process. So, while the "deepening" went ahead, they arranged to keep the Central Europeans out by the diplomats' favorite tactic: negotiations to admit them. In making this decision, the European Union put extravagant and abstract schemes ahead of practical necessities in the manner of doctrinaire "projectors" from Jonathan Swift down to the present.

And with the usual disastrous results. The "visionary" schemes of "deepening" either have failed or are failing. The "fixed" exchange rates of the European Exchange Rate Mechanism have made the yo-yo seem like a symbol of rigidity; they crashed in and out of it in September 1992 and have shown no signs of obeying the *diktats* of

Brussels since then. The next stage of monetary union agreed upon at Maastricht—the single currency—is due in 1999, when member states will have to achieve strict budgetary criteria. With three years to go, only Luxembourg fully meets these tests. The attempts by other countries to meet them on time have pushed up unemployment and interest rates, depressed economic activity, and created civil unrest.

And for what? Across the continent, businessmen and bankers increasingly question the economic need for a single currency at all. It is essentially a political symbol—the currency of a European state and people that don't actually exist, except perhaps in the mind of a Brussels bureaucrat.

Yet these symbols were pursued at a real political cost in Central Europe. The early enthusiasm for the West and Western institutions began to wane. Facing tariff barriers and quotas in Western Europe, the Central Europeans began to erect their own. And those politicians who had bravely pursued tough-minded policies of economic reform, believing that they were following the advice of European leaders, found themselves left in the lurch when the going got rough. Only the Czech Republic under the leadership of Vaclav Klaus has remained on course to a normal society.

In the last few years, the democratic reformers have fallen one by one in the former Communist satellites, to be replaced by neo-Communist governments promising the impossible: transition to a market economy without tears. This is a tragedy in itself, and an avoidable one. But with Russia lurching politically into a more authoritarian nationalist course, and the question of Central Europe's membership in NATO still unsettled, it has more than merely economic implications.

NATO

This brings me to my last example of institutional failure, mercifully a partial one, counterbalanced by some successes. NATO is a very fine military instrument; it won the Cold War when it had a clear military doctrine. But an instrument cannot define its own purposes, and since the dissolution of the Warsaw Pact, Western statesmen have found it difficult to give NATO a clear purpose. Indeed, they have shilly-shallied on the four major questions facing the Alliance:

■ Should Russia be regarded as a potential threat or a partner? (Russia may be about to answer that in a clearer fashion than we would like.)

■ Should NATO turn its attention to "out of area," where most of the post–Cold War threats, such as nuclear proliferation, now lie?

■ Should NATO admit the new democracies of Central Europe as full members with full responsibilities as quickly as prudently possible?

■ Should Europe develop its own "defense identity" in NATO, even though this concept is driven entirely by politics and has damaging military implications?

Such questions tend to be decided not in the abstract, not at inter-governmental conferences convened to look into the crystal ball, but on the anvil of necessity in the heat of crisis. And that is exactly what happened in the long-running crisis over Bosnia. At first, the supporters of a European foreign policy and a European defense identity declared the former Yugoslavia "Europe's crisis" and asked the United States to keep out. The United States was glad to do so. But the European Union's farcical involvement only made matters worse and, after a while, was effectively abandoned.

Then the United Nations became involved, and asked NATO to be its military agent in its peacekeeping operations.

Finally, when the U.N.-NATO personnel were taken hostages, the United States intervened. It employed NATO airpower with real effect, forced the combatants to the conference table, for better or worse imposed an agreement on them, and now heads a large NATO contingent that is enforcing the agreement.

In the course of stamping its authority on events, the United States also stamped its authority on the European members of NATO. And since the logistical supply chain goes through Hungary, it drew the Central Europeans into NATO operations in a small way. Whether NATO will apply the logic of this crisis in future strategic planning remains to be seen; but for the armchair theorists of a closed, passive, and divided NATO, Bosnia has been no end of a lesson.

The West and the Rest

These various institutional failures are worrying enough in their own terms and in our own times. If we look ahead still further to the end of the twenty-first century, however, an alarming and unstable future is on the cards.

Consider the number of medium-to-large states in the world that have now embarked on a free-market revolution: India, China, Brazil, possibly Russia. Add to these the present economic great powers: the United States and Japan, and, if the federalists get their way, a European superstate with its own independent foreign and defense policy separate from, and perhaps inimical to, the United States. What we see here in 2096 is an unstable world in which there are more than half a dozen "great powers," all with their own clients, all vulnerable if they stand alone, all capable of increasing their power and influence if they form the right kind of alliance, and all engaged willy-nilly in perpetual diplomatic maneuvers to ensure that their relative positions improve rather than deteriorate.

In other words, 2096 might look like 1914 played on a somewhat larger stage.

That need not come to pass if the Atlantic Alliance remains as it is today: in essence, America as the dominant power surrounded by allies that generally follow its lead. Such are the realities of population, resources, technology, and capital that if America remains the dominant partner in a united West, and militarily engaged in Europe, then the West can continue to be the dominant power in the world as a whole.

WHAT IS TO BE DONE?

I believe that what is now required is a new and imaginative Atlantic initiative. Its purpose must be to redefine Atlanticism in the light of the challenges I have been describing. There are rare moments when history is open and its course changed by means such as these. We may be at just such a moment now.

Reviving the Alliance

First, security. As my discussion of the Bosnian crisis demonstrated, the key lies in two reforms: opening NATO membership to Poland, Hungary, and the Czech Republic, and extending NATO's role so that it is able to operate out of area.

Both reforms will require a change in NATO's existing procedures. An attack on the territory of one member must, of course, continue to be regarded unambiguously as an attack on that of all; but that principle of universality need not apply to out-of-area activities. Indeed, it needs to be recognized that a wider role for NATO cannot be achieved if the participation of every member state is required before an out-of-area operation can go ahead. What is required is flexible arrangements that, to use a fashionable phrase, permit the creation of "coalitions of the willing."

Would NATO expansion mark a new division of Europe and give Russia the right to intervene in states outside the fold? Not in the least. Among other reasons, we could hold out the possibility of admitting those countries that (a) demonstrate a commitment to democratic values and (b) have trained military forces up to an acceptable standard. That would be a powerful incentive for such states to pursue the path of democratic reform and defense preparedness.

NATO also provides the best available mechanism for coordinating the contribution of America's allies to a global system of ballistic-missile defense: that is, a system providing protection against missile attack from whatever source it comes. If, however, the United States is to build this global ballistic-defense system with its allies, it needs the assurance that the Alliance is a permanent one resting on the solid foundations of American leadership. That raises, in my view, very serious doubts about the currently fashionable idea of a separate European "defense identity" within the Alliance.

Essentially, this is another piece of political symbolism, associated among European federalists with long-term aspirations for a European state with its own foreign and defense policy. It would create the armed forces of a country that does not exist. But, like the single currency, it would have damaging practical consequences in the here and now. In the first place, it contains the germs of a major trans-Atlantic rift. And in the second, it has no military rationale or benefits. Indeed, it has potentially severe military drawbacks. Even a French general admitted that during the Gulf War the U.S. forces were "the eyes and ears" of the French troops. Without America, NATO is a political talking shop, not a military force.

Nor is that likely to be changed in any reasonably foreseeable circumstances. Defense expenditure has been falling sharply in almost all

European states in recent years. Even if this process were now halted and reversed, it would take many years before Europe could hope to replace what America presently makes available to the Alliance by way of command-and-control facilities, airlift capacity, surveillance, and sheer firepower. Defense policy cannot be built upon political symbolism and utopian projects of nation-building that ignore or even defy military logic and fiscal prudence.

Trans-Atlantic Free Trade

But even a vigorous and successful NATO would not survive indefinitely in a West divided along the lines of trade and economics. One of the great threats to Atlantic unity in recent years has been the succession of trade wars—ranging from steel to pasta—that have strained relations across the Atlantic. So the second element of a New Atlantic Initiative must take the form of a concerted program to liberalize trade, thereby stimulating growth and creating badly needed new jobs. More specifically, we need to move towards a Trans-Atlantic Free Trade Area, uniting the North American Free Trade Area with a European Union enlarged to incorporate the Central European countries.

I realize that this may not seem the most propitious moment in American politics to advocate a new trade agreement. But the arguments against free trade between advanced industrial countries and poor Third World ones—even if I accepted them, which I do not—certainly do not apply to a Trans-Atlantic Free Trade deal. Such a trade bloc would unite countries with similar incomes and similar levels of regulation. It would therefore involve much less disruption and temporary job loss—while still bringing significant gains in efficiency and prosperity. This has been recognized by American labor unions, notably by [AFL-CIO president] Lane Kirkland in a series of important speeches. And it would create a trade bloc of unparalleled wealth (and therefore influence) in world trade negotiations.

Of course, economic gains are only half of the argument for a TAFTA. It would also provide a solid economic underpinning for America's continued military commitment to Europe, while strengthening the still fragile economies and political structures of Central Europe. It would be, in effect, the economic equivalent of NATO and, as such, the second pillar of Atlantic unity under American leadership.

Political Foundations

Yet let us never forget that there is a third pillar—the political one.

The West is not just some Cold War construct, devoid of significance in today's freer, more fluid world. It rests upon distinctive values and virtues, ideas and ideals, and above all upon a common experience of liberty.

True, the Asia-Pacific region may be fast becoming the new center of global economic power. Quite rightly, both the United States and Britain take an ever closer interest in developments there. But it is the West—above all, perhaps, the English-speaking peoples of the West—that has formed that system of liberal democracy that is politically dominant and, as we all know, offers the best hope of global peace and prosperity. In order to uphold these things, the Atlantic political relationship must be constantly nurtured and renewed.

So we must breathe new life into the consultative political institutions of the West such as the Atlantic Council and the North Atlantic Assembly. All too often they lack influence and presence in public debate. Above all, however—loath as I am to suggest another gathering of international leaders—I would propose an annual summit of the heads of government of all the North Atlantic countries, under the chairmanship of the president of the United States.

What all this adds up to is *not* another supra-national entity. That would be unwieldy and unworkable. It is something more subtle, but I hope more durable: a form of Atlantic partnership that attempts to solve common problems while respecting the sovereignty of the member states. In the course of identifying those problems and cooperating to solve them, governments would gradually discover that they were shaping an Atlantic public opinion and political consciousness.

The Highroads of the Future

The reaction, fifty years ago, to that earlier Fulton speech was swift, dramatic, and, at first, highly critical. Indeed, to judge from the critics you would have imagined that it was not Stalin but Churchill who had drawn down the Iron Curtain.

But for all the immediate disharmony, it soon became evident that Fulton had struck a deeper chord. It resulted in a decisive shift in opinion: less than two months later, the opinion polls recorded that 83 per cent of Americans now favored the idea of a permanent alliance between the United States and Britain, which was subsequently broadened into NATO. By speaking as and when he did, Churchill guarded against a repetition of the withdrawal of America from Europe that, after 1919, allowed the instability to emerge that plunged the whole world—including America—into a second war.

Like my uniquely distinguished predecessor, I too may be accused of alarmism in pointing to new dangers to which present institutions—and attitudes—are proving unequal. But, also like him, I have every confidence in the resources and the values of the Western civilization we are defending. In particular, I believe (to use Churchill's words) that: "If all British moral and material forces and convictions are joined with your own in fraternal association, the highroads of the future will be clear, not only for us but for all, not only for our time, but for a century to come."

That at least has not changed in fifty years.

16

A Just War Argument for Ballistic-Missile Defense

James Turner Johnson

An important feature in American debate over military issues since the early 1960s has been the recovery of just war thinking as a basis for moral analysis of policy options. This is significant for two main and interrelated reasons. First, the ideas about politics and the use of force that developed in just war tradition are deeply embedded in Western thought; collectively they reflect how people in the West think when they think about morality and war. Second, the just war approach to questions of war, peace, and military preparedness bridges the gulf between realism and idealism, incorporating elements of both and bringing them into engagement while avoiding their extremes.

The idea of just war, as Paul Ramsey argues, defines a *theory of state-craft* that recognizes the integral relation of ethics to politics. "These two distinguishable elements," Ramsey says, "are together in the first place, internally related," not separate and unconnected. The problem

---

James Turner Johnson is professor of religion at Rutgers University, where he also teaches in the graduate department of political science. Among the books he has written are *Can Modern War Be Just?* and *The Quest for Peace: Three Moral Traditions in Western Cultural History*.

addressed by the idea of just war is to develop the specific ethical wisdom related to political uses of force "as human activities properly related and subordinated to the purposes of political communities in the international system."[1] Similarly, Michael Walzer connects just war thinking to the "sense that war is a human action, purposive and premeditated, for whose effects someone is responsible."[2] The purposiveness of the resort to force in the context of statecraft is, for both these theorists, a key to recognizing the inherent presence of moral concerns. Purposiveness implies ethical meaning and responsibility, both before and after the fact of a particular decision.

In the classical just war terminology, the link between ethics and politics is incorporated into the core requirements of the *ius ad bellum*, that part of the tradition that determines when resort to force is justified: the requirements of competent authority, just cause, and right intention. The first of these restricts the right and responsibility to employ military force to only the highest political authority, while the second and third requirements lay on that authority the responsibility of resorting to force only when it is genuinely justified as a response to some form of evildoing and when it is intended to promote justice and peace. The structures and purposes of the life of the political community are thus understood in moral terms, and the use of force is placed squarely within this frame of understanding.

The just war idea, with its central insight about the integral relation of ethics and politics and the role of force in statecraft, is carried in various ways within different sectors of Western culture. This reflects the diversity of its roots. When the just war tradition first coalesced as a cultural consensus in the late Middle Ages, it incorporated insights from theology and philosophy, canon law and civil law, chivalric self-understanding, the practice and experience of war, and the developing patterns of relations among sovereign rulers. At the dawn of the modern period, as a result of the work of theorists like Francisco de Vitoria and Hugo Grotius, the just war idea was developed as an expression of natural law; these and subsequent theorists extended just war tradition into a theory of the law of nations, which in turn provided the basis for the development of modern international law. Not only international law on armed conflicts but national codes of military discipline reflect, draw upon, and further develop the just war *ius in bello*, that portion of the tradition dealing with what it is right to do in carrying out the use of force. Similarly, modern political theory, with its definition of war as justified only in terms of the rights and responsibilities of states, reflects and incorporates ideas fundamental to the *ius ad bellum* of the inherited just war consensus. Among these are the conceptions that only sovereign political entities have the necessary authority and responsibility to employ force for political purposes, and that these purposes are defined by the state's obligation to ensure justice, to establish a peaceful order and put down threats to it, and to defend the rights and property of its citizens.

These examples underscore the solid presence of just war ideas within the mainstream of Western thought, not only the religious and philosophical spheres but also law, politics, and military theory and practice. The examples also show how just war tradition has developed and been carried through history by the engagement of moral reflection on politics and war with practical questions of statecraft and the use of military force.

Because this tradition has developed through an ongoing interaction between theoretical principles and practical experience, it bridges the divide between realism and idealism in American policy circles. Evidence of this can be seen clearly in the policy debates on military matters since the early 1960s in which theological versions of just war thought—for example, the contributions of Paul Ramsey and of the American Catholic bishops—have figured prominently. The character of such religiously based analysis has throughout been shaped, not only by reflection on religious principles, but also by an ongoing engagement with the world of policy and strategic thought. That certainly can be said as well of the work of Michael Walzer, the foremost example of a political philosopher in recent debate seeking to "recapture the just war for political and moral theory."[3] From another perspective, William V. O'Brien has explicitly linked just war theory to the contemporary idea of limited war[4] and to the present shape of the international law of war.[5] Regarding the policy sphere, I have argued that just war ideas can be read through the debate over the "Weinberger Doctrine" of 1986,[6] and a great deal of engagement with just war thinking has taken place in military contexts, particularly in the service academies and the war colleges.

Just war thinking thus is not an imposition of disengaged ideal principles upon the harsh realities of international politics. Rather, it is a tradition of reflection that draws realist concerns and ideal ethical principles into engagement as equally necessary elements in considering the proper nature and role of force in statecraft.

THE MORAL OBLIGATION OF DEFENSE

The idea of defense against violated rights is at the core of just war reasoning about the use of force. "He who does not keep harm off a friend," wrote the fourth-century Christian theologian Ambrose of Milan, echoing established classical thought, "is as much in fault as he who causes it."[7] Ambrose, like his Stoic and other predecessors, associated this maxim with the virtue of justice: warding off an unjust assault on a friend is the just thing to do. Yet he also recognized that for a Christian the command to love one's neighbor brought a different virtue into play, that of *caritas*, the love that proceeds from divine grace and motivates the Christian to love others. Thus for him the moral obligation to defend the other when the other is attacked followed from both natural justice and Christian love.

Ambrose's pupil Augustine justified Christian participation in military service by expanding the duty to prevent harm: he took it beyond friends to include all innocent "neighbors," whatever their status in life or their relation or non-relation to the potential protector. For Augustine, a key concern was that the soldier serves under public authority and thus can provide this defense without being guilty of "wrong desire," as he might be if he were to act simply out of his own motivation.[8]

In Christian moral reflection, the understanding that love for the neighbor requires the defense of another person or persons who are being unjustly threatened or subjected to harm was an especially important and powerful moral insight, since it countered a form of Christian pacifism. For the pacifists, Christ's injunction to "turn the other cheek" when confronted with violence meant a total rejection of the use of force by Christians. For Ambrose and Augustine, though, it did not follow that Christ's words meant the Christian should allow evil to happen to the innocent neighbor without acting in his or her defense. Rather, their moral insight was that where another person is under attack, another kind of moral obligation held sway: that of the Christian's willingness to give of himself for the need of the other.

Defense of the neighbor thus follows as an implication of the obligation to love the neighbor.

For the modern theorist Paul Ramsey, this line of argument provides the genesis of a specifically Christian idea of just war: a realization that while the words and example of Jesus prevented a Christian from defending himself or herself by force, the obligations of divinely given love for the neighbor in need actively require a Christian to defend that neighbor against unjust attack. Those obligations justify the use of force against the evildoer.[9]

Ramsey, in developing this argument, attached it to the New Testament parable of the Good Samaritan. Reasoning from the care given by the Good Samaritan to the man who had been assaulted and robbed by thieves on a lonely road, Ramsey arrived at a rationale for defense preparedness to prevent such harm from befalling other travelers:

> . . . [I]t would have been a work of charity, and not of justice alone, to maintain and serve in a police patrol on the Jericho road to prevent such things from happening. By yet another step, it might well be a work of charity to resist, by force of arms, any external aggression against the social order that maintains the police patrol. . . . [W]hat do you think Jesus would have made the Samaritan do if he had come upon the scene while the robbers were still at their fell work?[10]

The theological argument from love of neighbor to the moral obligation of defense is not intended to *replace* the duty that flows from justice but to enhance it. As the language cited from Ambrose and from Ramsey in the above passage shows, the responsibility to defend the other against unjust harm comes in the first place from natural justice and applies to all humankind.

The natural origin of the right of defense provides the basis of Michael Walzer's argument. His approach to the justification of resort to force focuses directly on what he believes to be a trait common to all humanity: the ability to recognize wrong when confronted with it. As Walzer develops his understanding of this justification, he moves from the nature of the evildoing to the moral response it evokes: the wrong done is aggression, and defense is the moral answer to it. Put broadly, what justified war is about is the response of defense to the evil of aggression:

Aggression is the name we give to the crime of war. We know the crime because of the peace it interrupts—not the mere absence of fighting, but peace-with-rights, a condition of liberty and security that can exist only in the absence of aggression itself. The wrong the aggressor commits is to force men and women to risk their lives for the sake of their rights. . . . [T]hey are always justified in fighting; and in most cases, given that harsh choice, fighting is the morally preferred response.[11]

All these theorists, from Ambrose and Augustine to Ramsey and Walzer, point to the fundamentally defensive nature of just war, whether their reasoning is based on religious norms, like love of neighbor, or on norms rooted in nature, like the need to protect justice or individual and social rights. The core justification of the resort to force in just war tradition is the obligation to defend against harm values threatened or assaulted by another, to restore these values if necessary, and to prevent a recurrence of the threat or harm if possible. Thus the classic statement of just cause for use of force in just war tradition is that force is justified for defending against harm either in progress or threatened, for restoring that which has been wrongly taken away, or for punishing the wrongdoer from whom the evil threat or actions have come. Resort to war, in this view, is a mournful necessity, but no less a moral necessity because mournful. Augustine well conveys this tension in the following passage:

But, say they, the wise man will wage just wars. As if he would not rather lament the necessity of just wars, if he remembers that he is a man; for if they were not just he would not wage them, and would therefore be delivered from all wars. For it is the wrongdoing of the opposing party which compels the wise man to wage just wars; and this wrongdoing, even though it give rise to no war, would still be a matter of grief to man because it is man's wrongdoing.[12]

Augustine here captures the fundamental problem with which the tradition of just war wrestles: that even though resort to the use of military force is to be lamented, it is both justified and necessitated by the wrongdoing of others, over whose actions one ultimately has no control. The moral justification of resort to force follows from the need to defend against and combat such wrongdoing.

The moral obligation of defense and the primacy of defense in justifying military force are central to both American politico-military
doctrine and the structure of the international order. United States
military forces are organized under a Department of Defense, not (as
earlier in our history) a Department of War (or even a "Department
of Just War"), and it is fundamental American military doctrine that
these forces exist for the purpose of defending American lives and
property and the values on which this society is built. In the international order, the primacy of defense, long a stable feature of customary relations among nations, is written into international law in the
form of the Charter of the United Nations. In Article 2 the Charter
prohibits member states from employing "the threat or use of force
against the territorial integrity or political independence of any state."
The Charter thus identifies such threats or uses of force as attacking
the justice of the international order itself, and not only that of the
states subjected to aggression and the people whose rights are assaulted
and endangered. When this article goes on to empower the Security
Council to preserve international peace, it provides a basis in the
international order for defensive action, including uses of force,
against the prohibited unjust threats or uses of force. Laying out the
right of defense further, Article 51 of the Charter explicitly grants the
power of self-defense against "armed attack" to all nations, whether
acting individually or collectively.

Thus the fundamental moral priority of defense against evil established in just war reasoning is translated into concrete forms both in
international law and in national policy.

Defining Defense

But what counts as defense? The concept is not easy to define,
though it may seem straightforward. Within the broad moral tradition
of just war, defense and its justification are interlinked; a use of force
must be justified for defensive purposes in order to be considered an
act of defense.

As I have argued above, two main lines of justification can be identified in just war reasoning. One, exemplified in modern debate
by Paul Ramsey, proceeds from the Christian idea of love of neighbor. On this line of reasoning, as we have seen, the Christian has an

obligation in love to defend the neighbor who is unjustly attacked, and this obligation provides the justification for resort to force. Just war is thus by definition defensive war: war waged to protect against unjust attack one's neighbors in the political community—and by extension the structures of that community which they have forged and on which they depend.

A second and considerably broader segment of just war tradition justifies defense in terms of natural justice, or the natural rights of those attacked. In recent just war thought, Michael Walzer's argument on defense well exemplifies this approach, which traces back through such earlier theorists as Grotius and Thomas Aquinas. What justifies the defensive use of force, as Walzer puts it, is aggression against "peace-with-rights, a condition of liberty and security."[13] As Walzer casts his argument, the right of defense is collective—he speaks of defense against aggression in terms of the reaction of "groups of citizens"—and so the action of defense serves both the self and the neighbor in the community that is the object of aggression.

In practical terms, where the issue is defense of the political community against unjust attack, these two approaches to the justification of defense merge within just war tradition: the same justified defense that protects the community and the neighbor in that community also protects the self. The commonality between these lines of moral argument is thus what is important: both contribute to defining the just war idea of defense as the morally justified resort to force to combat wrongdoing.

Just War and Active Defense

The fundamental just war paradigm of the use of force to defend someone under unjust attack exemplifies a concept of *active* defense: the evildoer's weapon is upraised, ready to strike, and the defender interposes his own weapon and his own strength to ward off the blow. While the most minimal concept of the right of active defense would limit the defender's action to that alone, just war tradition goes further. First, use of force in defense against unjust attack is not only a right but an obligation. Although this obligation is not exceptionless or absolute, it is nonetheless powerful; as Walzer puts it, "in most cases, . . . fighting is the morally preferred response."[14] Second, the defender is justified not simply in warding off the attacker's blows but also in directing force against the attacker to end the unjust attack.

Both religious and secular versions of the tradition define the force that may be used in this way as limited by considerations of proportionality and discrimination. As to proportionality, the defender should not do to the attacker more than what is necessary to prevent the attack from succeeding. For specifically Christian versions of the tradition, the harm that may be done to the assailant is limited by the realization that he, too, however unjust, is someone the Christian is commanded to love; yet he may receive the same degree of harm as he was prepared to give his victim. At the extreme this would justify the assailant's death, though lesser measures, if effective to disarm or incapacitate him, are morally preferable. Ramsey's rhetorical question, what should the Good Samaritan have done if he had come upon the attack in progress, is intended to elicit this answer. Thus active defense is defined as a right and as a moral obligation, and it includes the use of force not only to ward off the attack but, using proportionate means, to punish the attacker and stop the attack.

Considerations of discrimination place a further limit on what counts as defense: the defensive use of force may never extend to a retaliatory attack on the innocent among the attacker's own people. As Ramsey puts it, "This is the distinction between *legitimate* and *illegitimate* military objectives. The same considerations which justify killing the bearer of hostile force by the same stroke prohibit noncombatants from being directly attacked with deliberate intent."[15] In the nuclear debate, this stance led Ramsey to reject counterpopulation or countervalue targeting but to approve counterforce or counterforces targeting—that is, strikes aimed at the enemy's nuclear forces or his military forces in general. What rules out some uses of force—the requirement that they must not be disproportionate or aimed at noncombatants—permits others. According to just war reasoning, a justified use of force in defense is not restricted to only those forces used in the unjust attack; it extends in principle to all the attacker's military forces (but not his noncombatants), where the limit of specific action is determined by considerations of proportionality.

Just War and Passive Defense

Just war reasoning also includes the concept of *passive* defense. Defense in this sense focuses on advance provisions that render means of attack impotent. To extend Ramsey's extrapolation of the Good Samaritan story, passive defense would include building a fort on the Jericho Road to provide travelers with refuge from attackers. Such passive means of defense have the advantage of not endangering potential Good Samaritans or members of police patrols who otherwise might have to engage in combat (active defense) against evildoers.

When one reads of the ascendancy of defensive warfare over offensive in certain periods of history, it is *passive* means of defense that are usually meant: means that impede attack, provide shelter from harm, or both. Examples include the castles of the Middle Ages, constructed to protect not only soldiers but also people from the countryside, along with their farm animals and movable goods, from marauding armies; the mathematically designed fortifications of the seventeenth-century military engineer Vauban and his imitators; and the log forts built along the American frontier during the westward expansion. Passive defense also includes such means as the late eighteenth-century practice of stretching chains across rivers to block the passage of a potential invasion force of sailing ships and the barbed wire protecting the trenches of the western front in World War I.

A completely passive means is the only form of defense that persons opposed to military action in any form can accept. In just war terms, however, such defense has no clear moral advantage over active means; each case depends on the circumstances. In practice, a completely passive means of defense is an abstraction in any case, and historically preparations for defense have joined passive means with provision for active means. Neither the medieval castles nor Vauban's star-shaped earthen forts could have indefinitely outlasted the siege weapons of their times, and so they were constructed to allow an active defense from soldiers inside. Chains across rivers could be cut by invaders, and so they had to be protected by well-positioned forts armed with long-range cannon. Similarly, barbed wire had to be defended against cutting by machine-gun emplacements. Even when provision is made for passive defense against attack, an active defense still remains necessary.

Further, a strategic defense may require a tactical offense. This is the connection, in just war terms, between the idea of defense against specific attack and the other two recognized just causes, that is, retaking things unjustly taken and punishing the attacker. It is also the underlying reason why, according to international law, defense against aggression includes the possibility of retaliation. Yet retaliation, as I have noted, may raise moral problems.

THE NUCLEAR-WEAPONS DEBATE

Good defenses, whether active or passive, not only promise protection against attack but offer the added benefit of deterring attacks that might otherwise be launched. Deterrence created in this way does not raise the moral concerns attaching to deterrence by threat of nuclear retaliation, and indeed, in just war terms, defense, as described above, if efficacious, avoids the moral problems raised by critics of strategic nuclear deterrence. A critic of nuclear deterrence on moral terms should thus be positively disposed toward development and deployment of an efficacious defense system that would lessen the risk that the nuclear retaliatory force would be called into use.

The particular circumstances of the nuclear debate, however, have contributed to a certain confusion in moral reasoning about defense. As a result, the clarity of the idea of defense has been muddied, and the central place of this idea in just war reasoning has been challenged by arguments that have perverted the moral logic of *ius ad bellum*. These arguments in their cumulative effect virtually deny the possibility of a right to use force of any kind, even in the face of grave injustice. They raise several prudential concerns to a higher priority than the moral duty of defense. Collectively, they depict contemporary war as inherently disproportionate, define the moral concept of last resort in a way that almost always rules out the use of force, and offer the deeply pessimistic calculation that the use of military force holds out little or no hope of combating injustice and producing peace. When such argumentation is joined to a concept of defense defined in terms of strategic deterrence by threat of nuclear retaliation, the effect is that even the strictly defensive resort to force is all but ruled out as a moral possibility. This is the exactly opposite conclusion from that which moral reasoning based on just war tradition, rightly understood, should reach.

The Policy Argument

Because the often intense moral debate over nuclear weapons continues to shape the way many people think about issues of defense, it is important to look more closely at the conditions that shaped that debate. Specifically, the development of moral reasoning on nuclear weapons was deeply influenced by a policy argument focused on a strategy of deterrence to the exclusion of active and passive means of defense.

The logic of strategic deterrence came into being as a result of a radical change in the balance of offensive means—the hydrogen bomb, with destructive capacity measured in megatons of TNT, and the development of intercontinental ballistic missiles—against which existing passive and active means offered only an ineffective defense. Earlier in the nuclear age, when the offensive means were atomic weapons with destructive power measured in kilotons and the means of delivery were relatively slow bombers, there was still an argument in policy circles that defensive means might effectively counter these weapons. By 1981, though, when Lawrence Freedman's *The Evolution of Nuclear Strategy* was published, strategic deterrence had become orthodoxy. In his conclusion Freedman catalogued "three basic responses" to nuclear weapons in strategic thought: first, "to exploit the destructive power to make total war appear a greater folly than ever before," the response that led equally to the logic of deterrence and the logic of disarmament; second, to develop "either an effective defense or a form of first strike that could eliminate the enemy's capacity to retaliate," a position Freedman characterized as "futile" and to be "considered exhausted for the moment"; and third, the effort "to deny the essence of nuclear weapons and to contrive to develop types of weapons and tactics for their use which minimize their destructive power."[16] While Freedman admitted that "new technological developments" may make defense or first strikes viable, his treatment of these three types of response leaves no doubt that he, like the main line of strategic nuclear theory and policy at the time he was writing, favored the first and had a very low opinion of the second and third.

The Moral Argument

Moral debate on nuclear weapons generally followed the lines traced out by the developing strategic thought and responded in similar ways. Clearly the dominant positions in the moral debate were of the type Freedman included in his "first response": efforts "to make total war appear a greater folly than ever before." Viewing the prospect of war led to the denial that nuclear war, or even any form of war in the nuclear age, could be moral. This was the position known as "just war pacifism" or "modern war pacifism."

Many American Catholics took this to be the position expressed in a much cited passage from Pope John XXIII's 1963 encyclical *Pacem in Terris*: "In this age which boasts of its atomic power, it no longer makes sense to maintain that war is a fit instrument with which to repair the violation of justice" (par. 127).[17] Taken in one direction, this line of thought led to a moral argument in which nuclear deterrence can be justified, but not any actual use of nuclear weapons—or perhaps of any other weapons either, because of the threat of escalation. By 1984 this reasoning had taken a morally authoritative form in the position of the American Catholic bishops that tolerated possession of nuclear weapons for the purpose of deterrence but denied that any use of nuclear weapons could ever be morally contemplated. The tolerance of nuclear deterrence, moreover, was limited: "Nuclear deterrence should be used as a step on the way toward progressive disarmament."[18] An even more extreme conclusion was reached by the bishops of the United Methodist Church in their 1986 statement *In Defense of Creation*: contemporary war threatens creation itself.[19]

It was easy to forget, as the policy and moral debates developed, that the foundations on which the dominant conclusions rested included various contingent elements. Freedman had granted that "new technological developments" might change the strategic scene. But the image of mutual destruction associated with the idea of using nuclear weapons—powerfully exemplified for many in the debate by Jonathan Schell's "republic of insects and grasses"—took on a more absolute character: this is what modern war is like, and it will not change. In this context, any attempts to bring about a shift in the strategic balance, even efforts to shield against the threatened destruction or limit its effect, became immoral, because they were viewed as violating a fundamental taboo: they accepted the possibility of the use of nuclear weapons in war.

With regard to measures of active defense, this approach effectively freezes the moral debate in the posture reached strategically in May 1972, the date of the first ABM Treaty between the United States and the Soviet Union. This posture carries within it an unfortunate paradox: that the massive destruction feared from the use of nuclear weapons becomes a self-fulfilling prophecy if one or more such weapons is ever used on a population center, since means of defense against such destruction are viewed as making the use of nuclear weapons more likely.

MISSILE DEFENSE AS A MORAL PRIORITY

Notwithstanding the long shadow cast by the debates over nuclear deterrence, the contemporary policy argument for missile defense reflects a changed security environment. Two features stand out: the threat is different from that which strategic deterrence sought to counter, and the possibilities of responding to the current threat are different from those available a decade or more ago. Moral analysis and argument must take account of these changes.

The threat that the policy of strategic deterrence aimed to counter had three major characteristics. First, this threat was posed by a single enemy, the Soviet Union, the other nuclear superpower. Second, given the resources of the USSR, a first-strike attack was expected to be massive enough to overwhelm defenses, so that the response was defined as avoiding such a strike by deterrence. Third, the threat was of massive nuclear devastation on a scale never before achieved in war if a strike were carried through, so that the aim was to prevent war from beginning.

The current security environment is one in which this threat has receded, principally because of a changed political climate but also because the breakup of the Soviet Union has left the United States in a position of clear military superiority. In place of the former threat, though, are multiple new threats that are not addressed by the old strategy of deterrence.

The New Security Environment

In this new environment, the potential sources of danger are many, not one. The strategy of deterrence always depended on more than simply possession of a retaliatory force and perceived willingness to use it; that strategy relied on the structural relationship that had been established between the two superpowers and the predictability that grew out of a history of interaction between them. The enmities to be guarded against today lack these features and are hence more dangerous. In place of structured mutual expectation is unpredictability; in place of tension over interests is often a deep ideological hatred; in place of an expressed mutual desire not to make war against the adversary's people is often a history of acts aimed directly at noncombatants.

Fashioning a strategy of deterrence against threats posed by such enemies is extremely hard. What may deter one may not deter another. Deterrence as such may not be effective in the face of a willingness to experience martyrdom and an ideology that reinforces this willingness. In some cases a deterrent may not be credible because an adversary can plausibly judge that a retaliatory threat either will never be carried out or will not cause unacceptable damage. Indeed, domestic and/or international opinion may be such that, paradoxically, it is the United States that is deterred from retaliation for an attack by such an adversary.

Besides the multiplicity of threats, a second important issue is the character of acts that may need to be countered. Security analysis identifies four possibilities in particular that need to be taken into account: (1) an accidental launch of a nuclear-armed ballistic missile from the old Soviet arsenal, a launch occasioned by deterioration in training, maintenance, and oversight; (2) a terrorist attack using one of these missiles or a shorter-range nuclear weapon acquired clandestinely; (3) a missile attack by a new nuclear power unremittingly hostile to the United States; and (4) a missile attack involving not a nuclear but a biological or chemical warhead. In the latter three cases there need not be an actual attack; rather, the threat of such an attack could be used to gain concessions, and the actual weapon could be reserved for another day.

Following the logic of just war tradition, the degree to which noncombatants are affected by these threats is a central concern. What I find particularly troubling, from the standpoint of moral reflection, is that the principal effect of all four of the above possibilities is directly to threaten noncombatant life. In the case of an accidental launch, its programmed target, whether military or civilian, is by definition in peacetime a noncombatant target. In the case of the three other possibilities, all of which involve purposeful action rather than accident, a directly intended noncombatant target is far more plausible than a military one. The proven *modus operandi* of terrorism is to target noncombatants; furthermore, whether the agent of threat is a terrorist group or a rogue state, a threat to cause devastation and the deaths of multitudes in a major city is likely to appear a more effective way to use one of a limited number of weapons and/or delivery vehicles than a threat against a military installation. In addition, a population center is an easy target: large and undefended.

The Moral Obligation of Defense

The logic of just war reasoning imposes a moral obligation of defense. In the most basic terms, what this tradition is about is defense of justice against injustice, innocence against evil, right against wrongdoing. The fundamental purpose of military force in a just society is to provide this defense for the members of that society and to defend itself so that it can carry out this task. These considerations argue for the provision of active defense measures against the forms of contemporary threat identified above, forms that all involve attacks or threats of attacks by missile-borne warheads of mass destructive capability. In simple language, the obligation to defend implies developing an effective means of defense. In the present security environment, then, putting in place an effective missile-defense system follows from the moral logic of defense that is at the core of just war tradition.

The moral obligation of defense is supported by four other considerations. First, as already argued, existing means of providing national security—including in particular the deterrent strategy developed to counter the Soviet threat—do not address the kinds of threat identified above. Second, the arguments against an active missile defense developed in the former strategic environment are irrelevant in the present one. In particular, it is not credible to argue today that deploying such a system would be a destabilizing force. Indeed, just the opposite is likely: that adding such a system to the national defense capacity of the United States would increase international stability by deterring potential adversaries from developing the above kinds of threat.

A third consideration follows from this: putting in place a credible missile-defense system would enhance overall deterrence by subtracting from the likelihood that a threat would achieve its end. A good defense, and not only the threat of retaliation, deters attack. Together their deterrent effect is multiplied. Thus a missile-defense system would support the cause of peace by magnifying the likelihood that aggression would not succeed.

A fourth consideration is that an effective missile-defense system seems technically feasible today, whereas at the time of the original ABM Treaty in 1972 the likely effectiveness of existing anti-missile technology was very limited. There can be no moral obligation to do the impossible, and thus the moral context in 1972 was not the same as that of today. The obligation to defend can now be acted upon to provide an active defense.

Each of these considerations can be restated in terms of classic just war language. The obligation of defense is simply a statement of the idea of *just cause* for use of force. Increasing international stability and deterring aggression speak to the just war requirements of use of force only *in last resort* and of directing the use of force to *the goal of peace*. The technical ability to put in place an effective missile-defense system fulfills the just war requirement of *reasonable hope of success* in the decision to employ forceful means. Finally, the fact that a missile-defense system would aim only at the weapons used in an attack well satisfies the just war criteria of *right intention* and *proportionality of ends*, and it also satisfies the *ius in bello* criteria of *proportionality of means* and *discrimination*.

To my mind, the moral logic is overwhelmingly in favor of the policy choice of putting a missile-defense system in place.

17

Ballistic-Missile Defense in the New Strategic Era

Robert Kagan

I n America, there is no such thing as strategic thought divorced from politics—the endless competition for political advantage suffuses even the most earnest debates over foreign and defense policies. Notwithstanding this truism, historians are unlikely to record that the transfer of the presidency from Republican to Democratic hands for the first time in a dozen years was a critical factor in shaping U.S. strategy in the post–Cold War era. For the result of these simultaneous revolutions—in the global strategic environment and in domestic politics—was a wholesale jumbling of the inherited strategic wisdom in both parties. Once out of the White House and with no Communist enemy to struggle against, many erstwhile Republican anti-Communist internationalists in the Reagan mold reverted to something approximating an earlier style of Republican isolationism. Meanwhile, many Democrats who had spent the seventies and eighties reviling the evils of American power now found themselves trying to use that power for what they considered good ends in the

---

Robert Kagan is Alexander Hamilton Fellow at the American University, Washington, D.C., and a contributing editor of *The Weekly Standard*. He held State Department posts from 1984 to 1988.

world, thus making an equally rapid transformation from McGovernism to an earlier Democratic tradition of Wilsonianism.

Yet both parties brought with them considerable baggage from the Cold War era. The not surprising result is that in foreign policy and defense strategy, inconsistencies abound. The most glaring of these have been in attitudes toward defense spending and the use of military force. Post–Cold War Republicans now regularly decry the use of U.S. military force for any purpose other than the protection of a narrowly defined set of "vital strategic interests." Yet most of them stand for increases in the defense budget, at least relative to the Clinton administration's preferences, continuing a party habit from the Reagan years. Democrats, on the other hand, including the Clinton administration, have declared the United States the world's "indispensable nation." They have urged U.S. military interventions in Bosnia, Haiti, Rwanda, and Zaire; they have recognized the need to deter Iraq and Iran in the Middle East, China in the Taiwan Straits, and North Korea along the demilitarized zone; and they have proposed extending U.S. military guarantees in Central and Eastern Europe. Yet in an inconsistency even more striking than that of Republicans, most of these Democrats nevertheless continue to see the increasingly strapped defense budget as bloated and an inviting target for cuts, as they did throughout the post-Vietnam era.

Such cognitive dissonance is strikingly present in the debate over one particular weapons program: ballistic-missile defense. In the post–Cold War era, Republicans have made anti-ballistic-missile systems their defense program of choice. They have championed this marquee item of the Reagan era partly out of habit; indeed, it is not the only Reagan-era weapons system to have maintained support among Republicans in Congress even as Congress has actively turned away from the global mission of the Reagan era. But many conservatives have also seen ballistic-missile defense as particularly well suited to their preferred strategy in the new era: a strategy of minimal foreign involvement, if not outright isolationism. It is no accident that the resurrection of an "America First" attitude in conservative ranks has been accompanied by an increasing clamor for ballistic-missile defense. National missile defense is to modern isolationists what the concept of a naval strategy of "coastal defense" was to the isolationists of the nineteenth century, a weapon that presumably insulates

America from an ugly and dangerous world but does not provide over-eager presidents with means to entangle the nation in foreign squabbles. Ballistic-missile defense holds special attraction for many conservatives because it offers the promise of a new, space-age "fortress America." It seems to provide the basis, for the first time in a hundred years, of a minimalist foreign policy freed from the dangers posed by a tumultuous world.

Liberal Democrats, meanwhile, have been opposing missile-defense systems almost entirely out of old habits developed during the Cold War. If conservative isolationists see ballistic-missile defense as well suited to their policies in the current age, liberal and Democratic opponents are simply refighting old battles that are no longer relevant. In the 1980s, they opposed the building of ballistic-missile-defense systems chiefly because they placed their faith in the doctrine of Mutual Assured Destruction and considered any missile-defense program destabilizing and likely to engender a nuclear confrontation with the Soviet Union. Today, with the demise of the Soviet Union, and the corresponding decline in importance of bilateral arms-control agreements to reduce nuclear arsenals, the ABM Treaty has risen to a top position in the liberal arms-control pantheon. But opposition to ballistic-missile defense has become more a shrine to be worshipped at than a considered strategic judgment.

THE NEW DANGERS

These attitudes toward ballistic-missile defense held by conservative isolationists and liberal internationalists contain abundant ironies. For conservative isolationists hoping that a national missile-defense system can draw the United States backward to a less globally involved era, the irony is that ballistic-missile defense is, on the contrary, the one thing that can preserve and extend America's global engagement in the present evolving strategic environment. If conservatives succeed in their goal of building advanced ballistic-missile defenses, they will be laying the essential foundation for the next phase of American global activism.

As for liberal internationalists, the consequences of their opposition to missile defense would be more than just ironic. Were they to succeed in stopping or significantly slowing the development of missile-defense technologies, they would undermine the very internationalist posture they seek for the United States in the post–Cold War world. Liberal internationalists both inside and outside the Clinton administration today do not realize how indispensable missile defense is if the United States is to remain the "indispensable" nation of the future.

An Ever-Widening Circle

Neither conservative isolationists nor liberal internationalists have fully come to grips with the fundamental shift in the international strategic environment that has occurred in recent years and is bound to continue into the next century. American intelligence agencies estimate that at least twenty countries "already have or may be developing weapons of mass destruction and ballistic missile delivery systems."[1] Not all of these countries are today adversaries of the United States, although domestic instability in the Middle East or South Asia, where nearly half of them are located, could change that assessment rapidly. But some of the states that are engaged in particularly aggressive campaigns to develop weapons of mass destruction and delivery systems are among the most dangerous and unpredictable on earth. The Central Intelligence Agency has identified five nations—North Korea, Iran, Iraq, Libya, and Syria—that "already have or are developing ballistic missiles that could threaten U.S. interests."[2] Much ink has been spilled in the debate over whether the United States will or will not face the prospect of a missile attack against its own territory within the next decade or so.[3] What should be obvious is that our ability to make such determinations with any precision is limited. Intelligence estimates of weapons development in hostile states have proved inaccurate in the past—one need only recall the severe underestimation of the extent of Saddam Hussein's weapons program before the Gulf War revealed how much more advanced the Iraqi program really was.

What is certain is that the new strategic environment has increased the likelihood that more states will try to acquire weapons of mass destruction and the means to deliver them, and that the threat or use of such weapons is going to become an increasingly standard feature of international life.

The reasons are twofold. First, the collapse of the Soviet empire, and with it the bipolar world of the Cold War era, loosened constraints on states whose behavior was once fairly tightly regulated by Moscow. The Iraqi invasion of Kuwait could probably not have occurred during the Cold War; the danger that a regional crisis could escalate to a nuclear confrontation between the two superpowers was so great that the Soviet Union, as Iraq's major patron and weapons supplier, would almost certainly have prevented the invasion. In the post–Cold War world, the smaller rogue states and would-be aggressors have greater freedom to pursue their goals in regions of strategic importance to the United States and its allies. Indeed, the only constraint they now face is the prospect that the United States will respond with its overwhelming military power, as it did in the Gulf War against Iraq.

That constraint is, of course, considerable. The Gulf War resoundingly demonstrated that U.S. conventional military superiority over any of these small or middle-sized states is and will continue to be an obstacle to ordinary modes of aggression. As one expert on proliferation has put it, "a key lesson potential challengers . . . will presumably have drawn from the [Gulf] war is that, for the foreseeable future, the United States is simply too strong to be challenged by conventional means."[4]

Circumventing Conventional Firepower

This enormous disparity in conventional power is precisely why such states are turning to unconventional weapons. For the Gulf War also yielded another lesson to potential challengers: The United States and its allies have no effective answer to a hostile force equipped with mobile ballistic missiles. Iraqi Scud missiles proved a dangerous wild card in the Gulf War, raising a number of difficult problems both for U.S. military forces and for U.S. diplomacy. About a quarter of all American casualties came from the launch of a single Scud missile against U.S. military facilities at Dhahran. American pilots flew more than two thousand sorties to find and destroy Scud missiles hidden in the Iraqi desert, a tremendous diversion of valuable resources that proved only minimally successful.[5] Meanwhile, Iraqi Scud missile attacks on Israel, designed to provoke Israel's entry into the war, threatened to break apart the fragile coalition of Arab states that the United States had laboriously constructed and maintained. In the face of overwhelming U.S. conventional military superiority, in other words, Saddam Hussein nevertheless retained the capacity to inflict a possibly catastrophic strategic blow.

That lesson is not lost on present and future challengers to regional peace. Now and in the years to come, ballistic missiles are likely to become the "'weapon of choice' for Third World governments who understand that attempting to match the United States plane for plane, tank for tank, is a costly and, ultimately, a losing proposition."[6] As the Indian army's chief of staff commented after the U.S. victory in Desert Storm, "the Gulf War emphasized once again that nuclear weapons are the ultimate coin of power. In the final analysis, they [the Americans] could go in because the United States had nuclear weapons and Iraq didn't."[7]

American military planners are aware of the new threat to U.S. strategy. In the Pentagon's Quadrennial Defense Review (QDR) issued in 1997, officials noted that U.S. conventional military superiority could well encourage the development of weapons of mass destruction as an "asymmetric means to attack our forces and interests overseas and Americans at home. That is, they are likely to seek advantage over the United States by using unconventional approaches to *circumvent* or *undermine* our strengths while *exploiting* our vulnerabilities."[8]

UNDERMINING AMERICA'S GRAND STRATEGY

The impact of this changing strategic environment on America's ability to defend its global interests will be significant. The United States has assumed the role in the post–Cold War world of principal guarantor of both international and regional peace and stability. But the United States remains, in classic geopolitical terms, an "island nation." To pursue its grand strategy, it must have both the ability and the will to project force into unstable regions far from home.

Until the recent shift in the strategic environment, America's ability to project power was limited only by constraints imposed on its capacity to bring sufficient forces to bear at the appropriate point in a timely manner. But in the new age, with weapons of mass destruction and ballistic-missile capabilities proliferating, the United States and its armed forces face an entirely new set of "asymmetrical" challenges. These challenges, if not addressed by the development and deployment of ballistic-missile defense technologies, threaten to undermine American grand strategy.

The Deterrent Effect

Without ballistic-missile defenses, both in the United States and in the appropriate theaters, American leaders may find themselves deterred in a number of ways from launching missions to protect U.S. and allied interests.

If foreign powers possess missiles capable of reaching U.S. territory, an American president would have to weigh this risk in deciding whether to challenge the behavior of such a regime with the threat or use of military force. During the crisis in the Taiwan Straits in 1996, the Chinese government sent a not-so-subtle warning about the capacity of Chinese missiles to strike at Los Angeles. American strategists may take this threat more or less seriously, but such a warning is almost certain to be part of a U.S. president's calculations the next time there is a crisis over Taiwan.

Even if a foreign aggressor does not have missiles capable of reaching the United States, it may be able to hold American allies hostage in any crisis. If Iraq had managed to produce even one nuclear-tipped ballistic missile capable of striking Munich or Rome before the outbreak of the Gulf War, one wonders what effect the existence of such a threat might have had on America's ability to pull together a NATO-led coalition to drive Saddam's army out of Kuwait. Perhaps it would have been sufficient to tip the scales in favor of containing Saddam in Kuwait rather than evicting him.

We can already see this deterrent effect at work in the international diplomacy of Northeast Asia. The fact that North Korea has developed ballistic missiles capable of striking Japan, Alaska, and Hawaii has given that desperately poor, famine-ridden dictatorship vastly disproportionate influence on the international scene. As a 1996 Heritage Foundation report pointed out, "the mere possession of ballistic missiles and a program to develop nuclear weapons have given North Korea . . . substantial political power, leading the United States and its allies to make previously unthinkable concessions."[9] North Korea's ability to threaten Japan puts strains on the U.S.-Japanese alliance and limits U.S. options in dealing with potential crises on the Korean peninsula. As more states like North Korea acquire such capabilities, in the absence of effective national and theater missile defenses the diplomacy of the United States and its relations with its allies will increasingly be influenced by this new kind of threat.

Finally, the deterrent effect created by proliferation of nuclear weapons and delivery systems can have a direct and potentially disastrous impact upon America's ability to project force into regions of vital importance. Bases, troop concentrations, port facilities, airfields, and logistics centers are all vulnerable to ballistic-missile strikes. As defense planners pointed out in the QDR, potential adversaries can exploit this vulnerability to deter or even defeat a conventional attack by an otherwise vastly superior American military force. If "an adversary ultimately faces a conventional war with the United States, it could employ asymmetric means to delay or deny U.S. access to critical facilities; disrupt our command, control, communications, and intelligence networks; deter allies and potential coalition partners from supporting U.S. intervention; or inflict higher than expected U.S. casualties in an attempt to weaken our national resolve."[10] Obviously, even the threat of such actions might make an American president hesitate before sending U.S. forces to the scene of a crisis.

If not countered by effective national and theater missile-defense programs, the cumulative effect of these various threats—against the U.S. population, against U.S. allies, and against U.S. forces abroad—is likely over time to weaken the sinews of American global leadership. It has been difficult enough these past few years to sustain a commitment to play the dominant role in enforcing peace and international rules in key regions around the world. Even if the increasing risks posed by the proliferation of weapons of mass destruction and delivery systems were to have only a marginal effect on the decisions of U.S. politicians and policy-makers, that margin might just prove the difference between effective global leadership and a more uncertain and unreliable America.

Such uncertainty and unreliability on the part of the world's most powerful nation would have profound effects on the international system it has constructed and upheld. It would loosen the bonds of alliances that depend, above all, on the reliability of the U.S. military commitment. It would encourage the rise of regional powers that, with little actual military strength, can nevertheless limit America's capacity to resist their drive for regional hegemony. It would elevate the status of so-called rogue states, which will increasingly be capable of molding the international environment to suit their needs. Even a hint of increased timidity on the part of the United States can encourage potential adversaries and discourage friends and allies, who may feel compelled either to make concessions or to seek other means of pursuing their interests. If the United States and its allies feel vulnerable to the potentially catastrophic consequences of a missile attack, even if the probability of such an attack is low they may be inclined to make compromises to avert it. The accumulation of such compromises can gradually have the effect of wearing out the fabric of the present international order.

Unpromising Alternatives

In theory, there are alternatives to developing and deploying effective national and theater missile-defense systems. The United States and its allies could, for instance, rely on the international nonproliferation regime to prevent this spread of weapons and delivery systems. Or the United States could act unilaterally, whenever it deemed it necessary, to destroy plants and facilities where the development of such weaponry is suspected—as the Israeli government did in Iraq in 1981.

Unfortunately, neither of these alternatives is very promising. International efforts to prevent proliferation may slow the trend toward ever-wider dispersion of weapons technologies, but significant players in the international system—for instance, Russia and China—have both strategic and financial reasons to be lax in their enforcement of international safeguards. China's supply of weapons, equipment, and technology to Iran and Pakistan has been difficult to stop over the past ten years, and there is little reason to suspect the task will be any easier over the next ten.

It is even less likely that the United States will act preemptively to destroy suspected weapons sites or weapons-production facilities in the absence of some other, unrelated justification for the use of military force.[11] Presidents Bush and Clinton both balked at such an action when confronted with North Korea's nuclear-weapons development program, thus leaving as the only option the far less reliable diplomatic process now under way. Nor can U.S. intelligence be relied upon to discover with a high degree of accuracy the extent of any hostile nation's weapons development program—as our pre–Gulf War intelligence failure in Iraq demonstrated.

That leaves missile defense as the only practical response to the new strategic environment. For the United States to maintain and extend its support of the present international system will require rapid development of both national and theater missile defenses. In order to carry out our grand strategy of preserving peace in vital regions and deterring aggression against our allies and our interests, we will have to acquire the capability to defend American cities from single-missile launches by rogue states—if not from more massive barrages by states possessing much larger arsenals. Equally important, we will have to establish theater missile-defense systems to protect our friends and allies from blackmail, and to shield our own troops and overseas bases from attack.

Such defenses, whether conservative isolationists like it or not, will be the underpinning of an America actively engaged in the world. For liberal internationalists, the challenge is even greater. In the coming years they will have to decide between two opposing principles. Their rigid commitment to the ABM Treaty and their equally rigid opposition to more spending for missile defense have now become the enemy of their commitment to internationalism. As weapons of mass destruction proliferate, the time is fast approaching when they will have to make a choice.

18

The Opposition to Missile Defense: Why Some Things Never Change

Jeffrey Salmon

In July 1996 *Slate*, the webzine (if that is still the correct jargon) from Microsoft, carried a debate among a group of prominent national-security experts and commentators over the need for the United States to deploy a defense against ballistic missiles. Returning to a controversy that has been carried on for at least thirty years—one that virtually drew the line between hawks and doves during the Cold War—the five contestants (Morton Halperin, Walter Slocombe, John Rhinelander, Richard Perle, and Charles Krauthammer, with Herb Stein as moderator) refought the old battles over the nature of the threat, the feasibility of missile-defense technology, the costs, the merits of arms control and the ABM (Anti-Ballistic Missile) Treaty, the effectiveness of deterrence, and the impact ballistic-missile defense might have on stability. It would be hard to imagine how anyone could add something original to the sea of words already poured out

---

Jeffrey Salmon is executive director of the George C. Marshall Institute in Washington, D.C. He was Senior Speechwriter to both Secretary of Defense Caspar Weinberger and Secretary of Defense Richard Cheney and has been a senior fellow at the Institute for National Strategic Studies at the National Defense University.

over this issue. And except for the fact that this was probably the first ballistic-missile defense (BMD) debate to take place entirely online, it broke no new ground. The forum, however, did highlight some curious things about the debate, both how it has changed since the Cold War ended and, perhaps more striking, how it has not.

For example, there was a general agreement, one that would have been hard to come by in the 1980s, that a *theater missile defense* (TMD) to protect our troops in the field and our allies—such as the Patriot used during the Gulf War—is feasible. Designing a defense against the entire Russian ICBM (intercontinental ballistic missile) force, which would involve thousands of warheads with accompanying decoys coming at us virtually all at once, presents a qualitatively different technological challenge than building a defense against the handful of Scud-like missiles now possessed by rogue states such as Iraq and North Korea, or even the more sophisticated threat from China. At least within this diverse group, there was a consensus that our experts are smart enough to engineer an effective TMD.

But Morton Halperin, for one, rejected the need for such a defense no matter what its feasibility. He called the threat against which it was to be deployed "hypothetical" and suggested that the better course was deterrence through the threat of preemption. According to Halperin, it would be much easier and cheaper simply to destroy the missile forces of the rogue states if they ever appeared menacing, a view that was shared by none of the other participants and was ridiculed by Richard Perle.

Even with respect to the more expensive, controversial, and technologically difficult defense of the United States—the so-called *national missile defense* (NMD)—there were some notable agreements. NMD immediately suggests the need for highly sophisticated space-based defenses, which in turn suggests President Reagan's Strategic Defense Initiative (SDI) and "Star Wars." But with the end of the Cold War, the technological requirements for NMD have decreased along with the feelings of urgency about deploying a global protection against ballistic missiles. The greatest concern is no longer a massive, coordinated Soviet first strike but rather the accidental or unauthorized launch of one or two missiles from Russia or an intentional but relatively limited strike from North Korea or China. In either case the ABM system faces a significantly easier job. Nor is there as great a sense of immediacy about deploying a national missile defense as there was when the Soviets were a hostile superpower. Even among traditional proponents of SDI, notably Perle, there was no call for NMD to be put on an emergency footing. He agreed with Clinton administration official Walter Slocombe that NMD could wait at least seven years, if only because that was the earliest that one could realistically be assumed ready to go.

The entire missile debate (which has been going on at least since the early sixties, when Robert McNamara was Secretary of Defense), rather than revolving around the need for highly complex, space-based defenses against a robust Soviet strategic missile force, now seems to turn on questions surrounding deployment of TMD: Is TMD confined by the ABM Treaty in the same way as strategic missile defense? Do the intentions and capabilities of the rogue states suggest the need for TMD? What can we afford? Which systems are best?

Plus Ça Change . . .

The *Slate* forum also revealed some amusing role reversals. For example, Perle, perhaps the most fearsome hard-liner of the 1980s, lectured Halperin, a well-known dove and pillar of the arms-control community, on why we should no longer fear, or even pay much attention to, Russian ICBM forces, while Halperin sounded dark warnings of a Russian missile threat. According to Halperin, virtually any deployment of missile defenses, especially a defense of the United States, would violate the ABM Treaty, leading to a Russian refusal to reduce its arsenal as agreed to under START II. To this the hard-liners responded, in effect, "Who cares about the Russian missile force?" "Whether the Russians are aiming 2,000 or 4,000 ballistic missiles at us makes no difference to our security," Charles Krauthammer noted. Perle went further: "Mort Halperin's analysis of the Russian attitude toward a U.S. ABM system could have been written in the 1970s. Hey Mort, the world has changed. The Cold War is over." The idea that an impoverished, post-Communist Russia would respond to a U.S. deployment of missile defenses with a modernization of its ICBM forces was, Perle contended, "ludicrous."

For his part, Halperin insisted that "our most urgent goal should be to seek to reduce the size of the Russian ICBM force," since it is the only force with the "capacity to destroy the United States." "The Cold War is over," he wrote, "but the arguments against constructing weapons to shoot down long-range ICBMs remain essentially unchanged: too expensive to build, too risky to rely upon, and ultimately, counterproductive."

In effect, Halperin was saying that missile defense is wrong no matter what the distribution of power in the international system or what types of political regimes wield that power. This is a remarkable admission. BMD grew up in the context of a superpower contest that has evaporated, and the Russian successor to the Soviet regime appears to be both uninterested in and incapable of continuing the traditional East-West conflict. But taking its place as a reason for concern in the national-security arena is the rapid spread of weapons of mass destruction to rogue states.

Now, it is not remarkable that Halperin simply dismisses the rogue-state threat. But it is puzzling to find him fretting so about the Russian threat, a threat he spent an earlier part of his life explaining away. Even more curious is the fact that he and indeed the arms-control community in general appear not to give proper attention to the fundamental regime change that has taken place in Russia.

Apparently, opposition to ballistic-missile defense transcends the heterogeneous nature of international politics. In other words, the reasons why the United States should not deploy defenses are unconnected to the character of the threats and the kinds of regimes that make up the international system. The opposition also goes beyond mere partisanship. The traditional arms-control community, at least as represented in the pages of *Arms Control Today*, the house organ of the Arms Control Association, has consistently campaigned against missile defense no matter who occupies the White House. The journal even sounded a warning against President Clinton's modest BMD program with the headline "A New Threat to the ABM Treaty: The Administration's TMD Proposal."

Why is it that so fundamental a change in the character of international politics—the collapse of the Soviet empire—has had so little impact on the arguments against missile defense? How can one sustain a military strategy that is indifferent to changes in threat? These questions go to the core, not only of the opposition to BMD, but of the theory underlying U.S. strategy in the nuclear age.

THE ABM TREATY

Before exploring these questions directly, let us look more closely at some issues brought up in the *Slate* forum and what they reveal about the character of the post–Cold War debate on ballistic-missile defense.

Central among these issues is the ABM Treaty. The primary argument today concerning missile defense turns on whether or not TMD falls under the tight restrictions of the ABM Treaty. The arms-control community would have virtually all TMD systems, save for the most limited Patriot-type interceptors, bound by ABM Treaty restraints. Their argument is that a theater defense can easily be upgraded to a strategic defense and so must be limited. Arms Control Association president Spurgeon Keeny wrote in *Arms Control Today* that the Army's THAAD (Theater High Altitude Area Defense) system, currently the leading U.S. TMD program, could with only slight modifications be used to defend U.S. cities and if "coupled with satellite tracking" "could in theory" defend "a large portion of the eastern U.S."[1] Consequently, such advanced theater defenses must come under the ABM Treaty. Moreover, Keeny argues, a U.S. deployment of THAAD even overseas would "threaten" the United States because it would require "substantial ABM Treaty amendments, thereby reducing U.S. security." In Keeny's mind, our security requires our continued vulnerability to missile attack, even if the aggressor turns out to be North Korea.

Keeny and others still consider the ABM Treaty between the United States and the Soviet Union to be the backbone of our security although there no longer is a Soviet Union. Why? Because it is the foundation for arms control. Take, for example, Gerard C. Smith, who headed the U.S. negotiating team when the treaty was signed in 1972. On the treaty's twentieth anniversary, Smith attempted to draw some distinctions between the Cold War and post–Cold War justifications for banning missile defense. But his distinctions merely served to highlight his tenacious embrace of the past.

"The key ABM problem today," Smith argued, "is no longer that defenses might provoke a buildup of offensive weapons, but that they could block an unprecedented opportunity to reduce strategic forces."[2] BMDs still complicate arms reductions because "the more defenses one side has the more offensive forces the other side will retain, to ensure that some would penetrate the defenses," Smith noted. The action-reaction scenario would stall U.S. and Russian efforts to reduce their nuclear arsenals. However, as Smith was aware, the ABM Treaty was first justified on the grounds that it would help *prevent* an offensive arms race. With a superpower arms race an unlikely possibility, Smith finds a new justification: by taking away the incentive for more missiles that would naturally arise if missile defenses were widely deployed, the treaty provides the framework for the great powers to *reduce* their arsenals.

This continuing focus on Russian strategic systems suggests a refusal to believe that the Soviet menace has disappeared or at least has changed significantly. Other problems may have arisen to complicate relations between the former rivals, but arms races and arms reductions are no longer a serious concern because the Russians are in no position to compete in this arena, nor do they seem willing to do so. Smith rests his argument on the difference between increasing and reducing strategic arms—a largely meaningless distinction in the context of current relations between the United States and the former Soviet Union. Smith's mind is running on autopilot.

What the Treaty Accomplished

Aside from this outdated thinking, an additional problem for Smith is his assumption that the ABM Treaty actually achieved its primary goal of controlling the superpower arms race. There is considerable historical evidence to call this assumption into question. By the mid-1980s, after well over a decade under the powerful arms-control influence of the ABM Treaty, the superpowers had together deployed some 9,000 strategic offensive weapons. Under the circumstances, it is difficult to see how the United States and the Soviet Union could have spent *more* on nuclear weapons over this period. Indeed, if there had been no restraints on developing ABM systems, a significant portion of the money spent on strategic offensive forces would surely have been spent on defensive deployments, thus starving offensive weapons of at least some resources. As it was, the competition was confined to the most dangerous set of weapons imaginable. It seems reasonable to conclude that, far from impeding the arms race, the ABM Treaty actually contributed mightily to acceleration of that race, especially in land- and sea-based ballistic missiles.

Moreover, the treaty had the perverse strategic impact of locking the arms race into an area where the Soviet Union's raw productive capability could be put to its best advantage. A competition in technologically sophisticated ABM systems was one in which the West would have excelled and the Soviets would have found it hard to keep up. This is surely one reason why Moscow was so insistent on killing SDI: Soviet officials knew they could not successfully compete in the high-tech, computer-driven contest of deploying a space-based missile defense.

In short, in terms of both arms control and broader strategic objectives, the ABM Treaty was counterproductive. Still, the arms-control community holds to the treaty as its holy writ. Of course, the personal stake that individuals have in ideas they helped to formulate— Halperin wrote some of McNamara's most influential speeches— should not be overlooked, nor should the natural unwillingness to admit that things did not go as one had planned. But there is a deeper reason why the ABM Treaty and the prohibition against missile defense that it enshrines are so critical to Halperin and his fellow arms controllers. The reason stems from theories that have guided U.S. defense policy in the age of nuclear weapons.

DETERRENCE THEORY IN THE NUCLEAR AGE

The current opposition to missile defense is the child of a peculiar concept of strategy in the nuclear age. Its roots lie in a theory of international relations that is divorced from politics and a hubristic belief that modern science has given leaders a way to overcome the chance circumstances that lead to war and prevail during it.

Near the beginning of *The Absolute Weapon*, one of the first serious studies of nuclear strategy after Hiroshima, Bernard Brodie argues that the incredible power of nuclear weapons does not in itself offer a guide to making strategic policy.[3] For Brodie, the mere existence of power tells nothing about how that power should be used. This might be called the traditional view of power. In contrast, the post–nuclear view holds that the destructive potential of the atom bomb gives those who possess the bomb a moral duty to see that it is never used. To employ nuclear weapons for a political goal is not only immoral but irrational, given that victory in the traditional sense is no longer possible.

A striking thing about the writings of Brodie and those of other civilian strategists at the dawn of the nuclear era is that they give both of the above views of power more or less equal weight. From the first, strategic analysts were in agreement that nuclear weapons could have only one purpose: deterrence. Colin Gray, for example, argued that "from the very beginning of the nuclear age, American so-called defense intellectuals have proclaimed that 'the name of the game is (pre-war) deterrence.'"[4] Brodie's *Absolute Weapon* certainly seemed to support this view, in arguing that "thus far the chief purpose of our military establishment has been to win wars. From now on its chief purpose must be to avert them. It can have almost no other purpose." Yet Brodie also wrote that "regardless of technological changes, war remains as Clausewitz put it, an 'instrument of policy,' a means to realizing a political end." Indeed, he continued: "Nations can still save themselves by their own armed strength from subjugation, but not from a destruction so colossal as to involve complete ruin." Therefore, we must "reorganize ourselves to survive a massively more destructive 'Pearl Harbor' than occurred in 1941."[5]

There is clearly a tension here between what Gray called "pre-war deterrence and operational strategy," or what might be called political and apolitical views of power. But a discussion of post-nuclear-exchange survival, such as Brodie's, suggests that these absolute weapons may actually have some traditional function in war fighting. Still, tension or no, at least Brodie was grappling with the two critical questions inherent in strategy in the nuclear age: What do we do if deterrence fails? What would our political goals be in such a war? Eventually it became unfashionable to raise these questions.

Some ten years after the publication of *The Absolute Weapon*, Brodie wrote a more complete study entitled *Strategy in the Missile Age*. There he looked to theories of air power developed in the early 1900s to discover the origins of the revolution in military strategy that saw victory coming through the intimidation and destruction of an enemy's society rather than the traditional tactic of defeating the opponent's armed forces. From this perspective, Brodie looked into the abyss. Deterrence, he argued, was "relative, not absolute; its effectiveness must be measured not only according to the amount of power that it holds in check, but also according to the incentives to aggression which form the pressure behind that power." Minimum deterrence, therefore, was unacceptable. Not only must the structure of force change relative to threat, but "if deterrence fails we shall want enough force to fight a total war effectively."[6] Additionally, while he regarded first strike as morally repugnant, Brodie believed that if deterrence was to remain credible, U.S. forces must at least be capable of delivering an effective initial blow. The outcome of nuclear war, he suggested, was fraught with uncertainty; therefore rational action could not be assumed. However, Brodie argued, "so long as there is a finite chance of war we have to be interested in outcomes, and although all outcomes would be bad, some would be very much worse than others." Consequently, a "strategy of deterrence ought always envisage the possibility of deterrence failing." This set out a requirement for damage limitation, active and passive defense, and terminating the war on the most favorable terms.

War as Process

Brodie struggled with the basic question of whether strategy in the traditional sense was really possible any longer or whether the destructive power of nuclear weapons made it unreasonable to think about much more than simply how to deter. This struggle was also apparent in Thomas Schelling's *Arms and Influence*. Schelling took deterrence further into the realm of theory and economics, making it as much as possible a question of process.

In Schelling's work, war, deterrence, and "compellence" were really processes of bargaining, negotiation, or signaling. If the process went haywire, if bargaining was poorly executed or intentions ineffectively communicated, the consequence could be conflict. As Brodie argued, the use of nuclear weapons separated victory from the infliction of pain. Schelling called this the power to "hurt," or the power to inflict suffering irrespective of the outcome. Each side's ability to hurt could be used as a diplomatic tool—to deter or compel—for "to inflict suffering gains nothing and saves nothing directly; it can only make people behave to avoid it."[7]

War is not the exercise of military force to accomplish a political goal but a bargaining process, subject to the same kind of analysis as any other process, e.g., cost-benefit analysis. But Schelling did not go so far as later strategists would with this concept of war as process, for he did not believe that the process could always be manipulated to avoid war. Nor did he argue, consistent with the MAD (Mutual Assured Destruction) or assured-vulnerability doctrine, that process can be so successfully mastered that the chance of war is virtually eliminated. Schelling was acutely aware of the role of "unpredictability." In fact, uncertainty ensures that deterrence can work, since the threat of escalation, the threat that the whole matter will get out of control, could be manipulated to make one side back down in the face of a nuclear confrontation.

According to Schelling:

> one might pretend, in order to make war as fearsome as possible, that the obvious way to fight a war if we cannot successfully destroy military forces is to destroy enemy cities, while he does the same to us with the weapons that we are powerless to stop. But once the war started, that would be a witless way to behave, about as astute as a head-on collision to preserve the right of way. And general nuclear war is probably fearsome enough anyway to deter any but a most desperate enemy in an intense crisis; making it somewhat less fearsome would hardly invite efforts to test just how bad the war would be.[8]

This unflinching analysis, however, conflicts with MAD theory, which was designed to make deterrence secure by making war unthinkable.

Still, despite his hard-nosed acknowledgment that nuclear conflict remained a possibility, there was a troubling abstract quality to Schelling's work. He appeared to assume that all nations would react to the pressures of deterrence and compellence in similar and predictable ways. There was also an assumption about human nature in Schelling's thinking. He seemed to assert an economic/rational model of behavior, one that was not only optimistic but universal in application as well. In other words, for Schelling's system to work, all actors must assign equal or at least fairly similar weight to the values under threat as they calculate costs and benefits. As we shall see, this separation of strategy from political context is an essential component of assured vulnerability.

A willingness like Schelling's to think seriously about deterrence and nuclear conflict was also apparent in another influential study, Glenn Snyder's *Deterrence and Defense*, published in 1961. Snyder, a social scientist, employed game theory to understand how nuclear weapons altered the traditional calculus of defense. For Snyder, "the deterrer, in choosing his optimum military and threat posture in advance of war, must estimate not only the effectiveness of that posture for deterrence, but also the consequences for himself should deterrence fail. In short, he is interested in defense as well as in deterrence; his security is a function of both. . . ." Moreover, "a general nuclear war might not automatically be an unlimited disaster; whether it became so might depend critically on how we had planned and prepared in advance to fight it."[9]

From the Early Strategists to McNamara

Looking back, we can see several notable qualities in these three critical studies. For example, each was open to the idea that there may be more to nuclear strategy than deterrence. Brodie began with the influence of airpower on strategy to understand the place of deterrence in an age of potential massive population destruction. Schelling turned strategy into an economic model of negotiation and calculation of cost and benefits without ignoring the possibility that war was still possible. And Snyder's game theory, while it might prefer deterrence, remained open to its failure.

There was also a clear tendency in their work (less pronounced in Brodie's, perhaps) to build deterrence theory outside a political context, workable no matter what nations happen to dominate the international system. From the beginning, it seems, deterrence theory was presumed to transcend politics.

By the time Robert McNamara was finished with this issue, however, the complexity of the early thinkers with respect to how deterrence might operate had given way to "pure deterrence," and to the rejection of the suggestion that damage-limitation through active and passive defense could play anything but a destabilizing role in U.S. strategy or that missile defense could actually contribute to deterrence. This turn by McNamara made possible the arguments against all forms of missile defense that remain the dominant paradigm of the arms-control community.

Early in the Kennedy administration, McNamara briefly entertained the more comprehensive view of deterrence and defense outlined by Brodie and others. In fact, McNamara argued in 1962 that "the United States has come to the conclusion that, to the extent feasible, basic military strategy in a possible general nuclear war should be approached in much the same way that more conventional military operations have been regarded in the past."[10] This left open the requirement for missile-defense as well as civil-defense measures.

It was not long, however, before McNamara repudiated this view in favor of a posture of assured vulnerability in which anti-missile defense played no role. In fact, ABM was seen to undermine the very credibility of assured destruction and to contribute to the arms race. (The idea here was the Soviets would simply increase their offensive forces to overcome our ABM system, leading the United States to respond by building up its own offensive forces, and so on.) The Soviet arsenal was growing, and McNamara became convinced that our ABM deployments could never keep up with Soviet offensive forces. (It was cheaper, he calculated, to add offensive muscle—particularly by MIRVing [i.e., using Multiple Independently targeted Re-entry Vehicles] to overcome defenses—than to build new ABM sites.) It therefore seemed necessary to abandon any thought of war-fighting and active defenses in favor of a policy that would simply make war so horrendous as to become unthinkable.

A Doomsday Machine

After years of thought on this topic, Brodie too changed his mind about deterrence. In his last published article, Brodie went so far as to argue that response initiative should be taken away from the President so as to make a destructive retaliation certain; i.e., he wished to remove the chance that a president might be either unwilling or incapable of executing the retaliatory threat. It is sheer fantasy, he suggested, to permit retaliatory options, because the notion of options assumes that the discrete use of nuclear weapons, or indeed damage-limitation, is feasible. "Any rigidity which keeps us from entering the new horrors or from nibbling at it in hopes that a nibble will clearly be seen as such by the other side, is a salutary rigidity," Brodie wrote.[11] Rigidity was in the service of solidifying the deterrence process and of overcoming the chance of war. In practice, Brodie's concept equaled a doomsday machine.

In this view, war between the superpowers has become irrational. Leaders, however, need not even act irrationally to be caught in a chain of events that draws them, against their will, into the abyss of war. Rather, as Schelling taught, war is a process of negotiation by threat of violence where each side manages the risk as best it can to secure what success it can.

If this is so, the problem has moved from one of positioning the nation to achieve its political goals in case war breaks out, to one of understanding the mechanism of negotiation and the process that sometimes drives nations to war. Because war is no longer a reasonable choice, the *process* must be mastered, not to secure political goals but to secure peace, which was widely recognized as the precondition for achieving any end.

Conquering Chance

Now, if leaders would never choose war, how could it happen? As Schelling noted, deterrence and the process of bargaining were highly uncertain and unpredictable. An understanding of the process required conquest of the factor that kept total manipulation beyond our grasp: chance. That was what McNamara and the latter-day Brodie aimed toward in constructing a doctrine that made deterrence absolute by assuring that in the event of war all would die. Anything that got in the way of this conquest of chance, such as anti-missile defenses, was a supreme threat to the process that sought to assure everyone that war was not an option. Once war was considered an option, once one entered into a debate about the role of missile defense in damage-limitation or even in strengthening deterrence, the delicate mechanism that keeps the chance of war at bay was called into question.

Physics gave us the opportunity to conquer the chance of war by taking away the very possibility that war could have a meaningful outcome or that it could contribute to achieving some political end. Missile defense, on the other hand, suggested that human beings cannot successfully manipulate chance, that our ability to understand the processes that might lead to war is forever limited, and that, consequently, a defense against nuclear missiles is necessary, for all the reasons so cogently set out by the early Brodie, Schelling, and Snyder.

Ballistic-missile defense was so nettlesome to the modern deterrence theory that it was opposed even when it could actually contribute to an assured-destruction capability. It certainly would have been possible, for example, to deploy an ABM system around our retaliatory-missile and command-and-control sites (a so-called point defense) and yet still follow the bizarre logic of MAD, which dictates that cities should remain vulnerable to attack. The ABM Treaty even allows for a limited deployment of this kind.

This use of missile-defense technology, however, has always been vigorously opposed by the arms-control community. "It would be very difficult to amend the ABM Treaty to permit extensive deployment of point defenses without severely eroding the effectiveness of the treaty's ban on nationwide defense," writes Peter Clausen in a 1986 book opposing SDI published by the Union of Concerned Scientists. "If the treaty were so amended," Clausen suggests, "each superpower would be able to deploy a significant part of the technical base for a territorial defense, and neither could be confident that the other would not attempt to quickly expand and upgrade its system."[12] In other words, if the firewall against missile defense were ever breached, the next step would inevitably be the provocative step of protecting cities.

Thus, even a defense that helps to preserve our ability to retaliate (and so lends confidence to our assured-destruction capability) is unacceptable for what it might somehow, someday contribute to a more robust defense of cities. But how can a defense of a nation's population possibly be destabilizing?

Again, one must understand the logic of MAD. Population defense is objectionable because it provides an incentive for a preemptive attack. Especially in McNamara's time, it was assumed that missile defenses would not be particularly effective against a robust, full-scale first strike. However, defenses *could* provide protection for the initial aggressor against a limited or "ragged" retaliation from a nation that had already had a large percentage of its missile force devastated in a preemptive strike. Defenses then could best be used by the aggressor because they could help protect his population centers from the necessarily limited retaliation of the poor soul that took the first hit. In this logic, defense of cities provides an incentive to first-strike and so adds weight to the argument that defenses should be abandoned altogether.

Assuming Strategic Symmetry

Now the major argument against the MAD doctrine was always its apolitical nature. At one level it assumed that the Soviets would be as convinced as we were of the impossibility of prosecuting a successful nuclear war. Next, it assumed they would share our attitude about the unwisdom of ABM systems and would forgo any attempts at damage-limitation in the event of war. What is more, MAD assumed that the economic/rational behavior model spelled out by Schelling applied to the Kremlin as well as to the White House. Individuals, it asserted, would behave in a fairly predictable manner no matter what the political or psychological pressures. In short, MAD assumed that a strategic symmetry would develop between the superpowers and that the Soviets would ultimately adopt our view that the goal of the relationship was to ensure strategic stability and peace.

Despite ample evidence to the contrary—for example, that the Soviets spent as much on the entire range of missile-defense preparedness as they did on strategic systems—the United States persisted throughout the Cold War in believing that Moscow had adopted its peculiar view of deterrence.

This was, of course, consistent with the apolitical nature of deterrence theory itself, from which the MAD doctrine was derived. For all their insights into the nature of conflict in the nuclear age, Brodie's, Schelling's, and Snyder's writings were oddly divorced from the kinds of day-to-day political calculations and considerations of risks and uncertainties that drive the behavior of responsible leaders. This failure to take into account the context and indeed the way human beings actually behave under pressure, or under the sway of a powerful political idea, infected assured-destruction thinking from the beginning, and led to an unjustified confidence in America's ability to predict how deterrence would actually work. Nothing could simplify deterrence more than removing politics and human behavior from the calculation.

Still, we did not go to war with the Soviets. Can we give deterrence the credit? Keith Payne argues in *Deterrence in the Second Nuclear Age* that we have the right to conclude only that deterrence did not fail, not that it was effective. "We simply do not know with . . . certainty why Soviet leaders did not do what they did not do," Payne notes.[13] We do not know how close we came to the abyss during the Cold War, nor do we know what role assured destruction played in keeping us from falling in. What is more, we can never know what would have happened had we taken a different road in the early years of the nuclear era and engaged in a robust arms race with the Kremlin on *defensive* systems. What is clear is that assured destruction was disconnected from the heterogeneous character of the international system and rested on the assumption that technology had given us the tools to overcome the chance of war.

From Bipolarity to Multiplicity

Whatever one concludes about the wisdom of forgoing missile defense during the Cold War on the grounds of an abstract theory, there is certainly reason to question the application of this theory today, in the second nuclear age, as Payne calls it. If the first nuclear age was defined by a bipolar competition, the second is defined by a multiplicity of nations vying for regional dominance. In this context, one in which very diverse political systems must be understood, it makes even less sense to rest security on a strategy that is so explicitly indifferent to the political and psychological forces that drive nations and human action. As Payne suggests,

> confident statements about [deterrence in the post–Cold War era] are expressed without knowing who the opponent is, whether the opponent is risk-tolerant or risk-adverse, what the context of the assumed conflict or crisis is, how the opponent calculates the potential cost of inaction on its part, what the stakes involved are, what the domestic political condition of the opponent is, what credibility the opponent attaches to our deterrence threat, or anything other than the type of forces available to the U.S. leader.[14]

We appear confident that deterrence works because the theory of deterrence tells us it should work, not because we have attempted to understand the character of the nations we wish to deter. During the bipolar superpower conflict, this meant ignoring the political system of just one nation; in a multipolar world it means assuming that a half dozen or so regimes as diverse as Syria, North Korea, and India will calculate risks just as we predict.

Our confidence in deterrence is indeed hubris, as Payne points out. It is hubris to think we have the ability to deter all nations with a single threat of annihilation; and it is hubris to think that nuclear physics provides us with a way to remove the very chance of war.

There is something characteristically Western about this idea of overcoming chance. Ever since Francis Bacon, science has aimed to understand nature so that it can be predicted and controlled. Science has now discovered a weapon so devastating that it is capable of destroying life on earth. The Western reaction is to use that discovery to control human behavior to the point that human beings will, for the first time in history, never engage in war.

It is rather easy to see why the arguments against missile defense have not changed even though the international political system has changed. Halperin and the rest of the arms-control community were never really interested in how or why the Soviets acted the way they did, how or why they calculated risks in a certain way. The arguments against missile defense were always abstracted from politics so that there would be no reason for them to change when the context of international politics itself changed. Deterrence theory stands no matter what look international politics assumes. Missile defense is dangerous within the context of assured-destruction theory no matter if the aim is to deter the Soviet Union, Russia, India, North Korea, Great Britain, or the Holy Roman Empire. In the end they are all the same.

There is something almost comical about a view of national security that insists with Halperin that it is better to engage in a preemptive war against, say, North Korea than to deploy a missile defense, and with Brodie that it is better to build, in effect, a doomsday machine that removes a president's prerogative power in the face of war. In the abstract both ideas make sense. In practice they are nonsense.

As both Walter Slocombe and Richard Perle point out to Halperin in the *Slate* forum, an actual American president faced with real-life risks would be unlikely (to say the least) to engage in preemptive war against North Korea (or anyone else, for that matter) because it appeared to be threatening some kind of aggression. Could the president trust CIA intelligence? Would his action cause an invasion of South Korea? How many people might be killed as a result of this action, which was based on a CIA estimate? And is it any more likely that a president would actually allow his hands to be tied by an automatic-response mechanism in the time of great crisis and possible war?

Comical or not, this abstraction from the actual way nations and leaders act, which forms the core of the consistent opposition to missile defense, can easily lead to tragedy. The tragic characters in literature seem to fall because of hubris. We should learn from their example.

19

Ballistic-Missile Threats and U.S. Policy

R. James Woolsey

The following is adapted from testimony given by the former Director of Central Intelligence to the U.S. Senate Committee on Foreign Relations on September 24, 1996.

In March 1996 I was visiting Taipei when the Chinese government announced its intention to begin ballistic-missile launches three days later into two twenty-mile-square impact areas, one a mere twenty miles off Taiwan's northeast coast and the other thirty miles off the southwest coast. These launches interfered with access to Taiwan's principal port, Kaohsiung, to Taipei's international airport, and to rich fishing grounds. At first the Clinton administration stated that the firings did not constitute a blockade and were only political theater—albeit "a little too close to the edge of the stage"—but that "there will be consequences should these tests go wrong." Subsequently, I was glad to see, the Administration called the firings reckless and provocative.

But the main point here should never have been what the conse-

---

R. James Woolsey was the Director of Central Intelligence from 1993 to 1995. He currently is a partner with the Washington law firm Shea & Gardner.

quences would be in the event that China proved unable to hit even a square in the ocean twenty miles on a side. The main point is what the consequences are when such tests go *right*. Off Taiwan in early 1996, as well as in the streets of Tel Aviv and Riyadh in early 1991, we were given an important insight into the future of international relations. It is not an attractive vision. Ballistic missiles can, and in the future increasingly will, be used by hostile states for blackmail, for terror, and to drive wedges between us and our friends and allies. It is my judgment that the Administration is not giving this grave problem the attention it deserves.

The Ballistic-Missile Threat

Let me say a few words in general about the threat that ballistic missiles are coming to pose to American interests in the world. First, although ballistic missiles are normally discussed in the same breath with weapons of mass destruction, it is important to realize that it is not always necessary to deploy nuclear, chemical, or bacteriological warheads in order to use ballistic missiles—even with current accuracies—as weapons of terror and blackmail. The Chinese have admitted that they were using those missile launches near Taiwan to attempt to influence Taiwan's presidential elections and to affect Taiwan's relations with other countries. Saddam's Scud missile attacks on Israel, using conventional high-explosive warheads, were clearly an attempt to provoke an Israeli response and to split the coalition against Iraq, which included a number of Arab states that would have had great difficulty fighting alongside Israel against another Arab nation.

Second, we are in the midst of an era of revolutionary improvements in missile guidance. These improvements will soon make ballistic missiles much more effective for blackmail purposes—again, even without warheads containing weapons of mass destruction. The press has reported, for example, that the U.S. government is adopting a policy to permit non-government users of the Global Positioning System (GPS) satellite network to have much greater confidence that the government will not interrupt or degrade the satellites' signals. The press also reports that the Administration believes regional agreements will ensure that the signals cannot be used by hostile forces. But the efficacy of such arrangements remains to be seen. The current type of GPS access is adequate for many commercial purposes. But if the policy of "selective availability" of GPS is abandoned, there will be a definite risk not only that other nations will be able to use guidance signals provided by the United States for their ballistic-missile systems (that is true today) but also that they will thereby be able to achieve truly excellent accuracy for their missiles.

With such guidance improvements, it is quite reasonable to believe that within a few years Saddam or the Chinese rulers will be able to threaten something far more troubling than firings of relatively inaccurate ballistic missiles. They may quite plausibly be able to threaten to destroy, say, the Knesset, or to create a Chernobyl incident at a Taiwanese nuclear-power plant.

Third, even relatively inaccurate ballistic missiles may have awesome power if equipped with weapons of mass destruction. Although attention is usually focused on the possibility of various countries' obtaining nuclear warheads, nuclear capability is at least somewhat constrained by the difficulty of acquiring fissionable material. Loose controls over fissionable material, particularly in the former Soviet Union, are nevertheless quite troubling, because unauthorized sales and smuggling of fissionable material to rogue states are becoming increasingly likely.

But it is even easier to acquire the wherewithal to produce chemical or, much worse, bacteriological warheads. Chemical and bacteriological weapons will be available far sooner and to a much larger number of countries than will nuclear warheads. Bacteriological warheads in particular will serve about as well as nuclear ones to turn a country's ballistic missiles into extremely effective tools of terror and blackmail, even if they are never launched. A large number of countries are working on ballistic missiles, and there is considerable international traffic in technology and equipment—much of it out of Russia, China, and North Korea—that helps other nations develop and improve both weapons of mass destruction and the ballistic missiles to carry them.

Fourth, to use ballistic missiles for terror and blackmail directly against the United States, it is not necessary to be able to conduct an effective counterforce strike with ballistic missiles against ICBM silos, bomber bases, and other nuclear facilities in our continental heartland. This concern with a counterforce strike against nuclear facilities in the interior of the lower forty-eight states was, of course, a principal issue for us during the long Cold War standoff against the Soviet Union. Much of our strategic analysis during those years centered on the ability of our ICBMs and strategic bombers to withstand such a strike and retaliate effectively. (For example, the Scowcroft Commission Report in 1983, of which I was the principal drafter, was heavily devoted to this question.) But in current circumstances, nuclear blackmail threats against the United States may be effectively posed by, e.g., North Korean intermediate-range missiles targeted on Alaska or Hawaii, or by relatively inaccurate Chinese ICBMs targeted on Los Angeles.

Fifth, we should not automatically assume a benign post–Cold War world order in which Russia is a friendly democracy—with a few inconsequential anomalies—that is steadily developing a free-enterprise economy, and China is a free-enterprise economy—with a few inconsequential anomalies—that is steadily becoming a friendly democracy. It is at least as likely, in my judgment, that the Russia that will face us will come to be autocratic and imperialistic; we may hope, but we should not be confident, that it will retain some measure of civil liberties and some free sectors in its economy. As for the new China, in addition to our serious differences with its leaders over civil liberties, nuclear proliferation, and trade, we may well have seen its international face in the Taiwan Straits in March 1996. In short, we cannot discount the possibility that serious international crises will develop in the future with either or both of these countries.

A Deficient "Intelligence Estimate"

I will turn now to the presentation given to the U.S. Congress in February 1996 by Richard Cooper, chairman of the National Intelligence Council, covering the new National Intelligence Estimate (NIE 95-19), "Emerging Missile Threats to North America During the Next Fifteen Years." (I must stress that this unclassified presentation by Dr. Cooper and other unclassified sources are my only sources of information about this estimate.) The answers provided to the questions that were asked—based on the public record—during the process of writing this NIE may well be the best consensus that the intelligence community could produce, and may be consistent in many ways with earlier work. However, one major reason, it seems to me, why this estimate seems to differ from the major assessments made during my tenure as Director of Central Intelligence (1993-95) lies in the questions that were asked. To focus an NIE on the threat to the contiguous forty-eight states is, in my judgment, to focus on a subset, and not a particularly useful subset, of the strategic problems posed for us by other countries' possession of ballistic missiles.

If broad conclusions are drawn from an NIE of such limited scope, as they apparently were—for example, that "intelligence indicates" that ballistic missiles do not pose a serious threat to U.S. interests—the conclusions could be quite wrong, even if the drafters of the NIE answered as best they could the questions they were asked. If decision-makers conclude, and I believe this would be a serious error, that this NIE—at least as it has publicly been described—covers the most important questions about ballistic-missile threats to U.S. interests, what would they say about, e.g., nuclear blackmail threats against Alaska and Hawaii? These sorts of threats will in great likelihood be present from North Korean intermediate-range missiles in well under fifteen years. Such questions as these seem to be an afterthought, at least in the public description of the NIE. But Alaska and Hawaii were not admitted to the Union on terms that exclude them in some way from the common defense called for in the preamble to the Constitution. As objects of blackmail they are of no less concern to us than Oklahoma and Kansas.

I believe that the "contiguous forty-eight" frame of reference for this NIE, if the document is used as a basis for drawing general policy conclusions, can lead to a badly distorted and minimized perception of the serious threats we face from ballistic missiles now and in the very near future—threats to our friends, our allies, our overseas bases and military forces, our overseas territories, and some of the fifty states. Using an estimate that focuses on the ICBM threat to the contiguous forty-eight states to make *general* judgments about our need for ballistic-missile defenses is akin to saying that because we believe that for the next few years local criminals will not be able to blow up police headquarters in the District of Columbia, there is no serious threat to the safety and security of police in the District.

There are other troubling aspects of the scope of this NIE. The unclassified version of the report on it by the General Accounting Office (GAO) makes several important points. First, and most significantly, the GAO stressed that the NIE does not "identify explicitly its key assumptions" and does not "account for alternative economic and political futures." The GAO also pointed out that the NIE fails to "quantify the certainty level of nearly all of its key judgments." Although quantification can be overused, I believe, in intelligence estimates, some use of rough "gambler's odds," such as "a one-in-three chance," can assist understanding. The GAO added that the evidence presented in the NIE "is considerably less than that presented in the earlier NIEs, in both quantitative and qualitative terms."

Other Undue Restrictions

I would add several other points about this NIE, as it is set out in the unclassified February statement to the Congress. Again, the NIE's answers may be reasonable in view of the questions it seeks to answer. If you are assessing *indigenous* capabilities within *currently hostile* countries to develop *ICBMs* of *standard design* that can hit the *lower forty-eight states*, the NIE's answer that we have fifteen years of comfort may well be plausible. But each of these qualifications is an important caveat; each severely restricts the ability to generalize legitimately, or to make national policy, based on such a limited scope.

The concentration on *indigenous* ICBM development seems to me to limit sharply any general conclusions that might legitimately be drawn. Dr. Cooper testified that "the potential for foreign assistance introduces some uncertainty into our predictions of timelines." That is putting it mildly. Indigenous development of ICBMs was of interest during the Cold War because the Soviets sought to maintain a monopoly on their most precious military capabilities, and so export of fully developed ICBMs was not in the cards. But in the aftermath of the Cold War, Russia, China, and North Korea are in the export business for missile technology and components, and for some technologies related to weapons of mass destruction as well. Moreover, with respect to some such exports, the degree of control exercised by Moscow, and perhaps by Beijing, may not be at all complete. Consequently, transfers deserve more attention than they did during the Cold War.

A further problem is created by transfers of ballistic-missile technology or components to a country that, though now friendly to the United States, might later turn hostile through a revolution or radical change in government. Even with the best intelligence in the world it is impossible to forecast fifteen years in advance such events as the Iranian revolution of the late 1970s, which turned a friendly state into a hostile one.

Moreover, indigenous capabilities may be enhanced by unconventional means. A country without traditional ICBM technology that has been able to produce warheads carrying weapons of mass destruction—such as biological—may be able to produce a functioning ICBM by strapping several smaller boosters together, a technique sometimes used for space launches. Even if accuracy and performance were not up to our standards, such a missile, equipped with such a warhead, might serve quite adequately for purposes of blackmail and terror.

Because of these uncertainties we should study carefully the possibility of *technically feasible* threats, not only threats for which we actually see countries assembling components and conducting tests. One reasonable course of action, for example, would be for the government to assemble a small technical "red team" of bright young American scientists and engineers and let them see what could be assembled from internationally available technology and components. I would bet that we would be shocked at what they could show us about available capabilities in ballistic missiles. We should remember that by assessing only what we could actually see, we badly underestimated Iraq's efforts in the years before the Gulf War, especially with regard to weapons of mass destruction.

It may be that the President was relying on something other than this recent National Intelligence Estimate when he said, in vetoing the 1996 Defense Authorization Bill, that U.S. intelligence "does not foresee" the existence of a ballistic-missile threat to the United States "in the coming decade." But to the degree that the President was extrapolating a general conclusion from the very limited part of the overall ballistic-missile threat that appears to be assessed by this NIE, I believe that this was a serious error.

Arms Control and Missile Defense

Finally, let me turn briefly to the current state of arms-control negotiations as they might affect our ballistic-missile-defense (BMD) programs and to those programs themselves as set forth in the defense budget for 1997 as originally proposed by the Administration. Here too my information comes from public reports.

In 1995, my law partner and friend Steve Hadley, who was Assistant Secretary of Defense for International Security Policy in the Bush administration, set out in testimony before the Congress the history of the negotiations in 1992 that followed President Yeltsin's January speeches of that year. President Yeltsin called for "a global system for protection of the world community [that could be] based on a reorientation of the U.S. SDI to make use of high technologies developed in Russia's defense complex."

Earlier this year [1996], according to press reports, the new Russian foreign minister, Mr. Yevgeny Primakov, threatened to withhold Russian ratification of the START II Treaty unless the United States agreed to restrictions that could substantially limit even our *theater* ballistic-missile defenses, in the context of distinguishing such theater systems from those limited by the treaty.

Among the many things that have changed since 1992 are that President Yeltsin is now surrounded by advisors, such as Mr. Primakov, who are generally less inclined to promote cooperation with the United States than their predecessors and who have very close ties to the rulers of rogue states that are at the heart of our proliferation concerns. But whatever the reasons, the shift during these four years from Russian willingness to propose overall cooperation with the United States on ballistic-missile defenses to Mr. Primakov's effort to undermine the effectiveness of our theater missile-defense programs is quite striking.

During these same four years, the Russians have expressed substantial disagreement with one particular aspect of the treaty that I negotiated in 1990 covering conventional armed forces in Europe (CFE)—the special limitations that apply to the share of their total conventional armed forces that the Russians can deploy to their northern and southern flanks. The United States has worked with its NATO allies during the last year or so to accommodate some of the Russian concerns by making certain adjustments in the map defining the CFE flank zones. Assuming that the Administration seeks appropriate congressional approval for any map changes, I have no quarrel with these efforts, since they have been coordinated with our NATO allies, especially Turkey and Norway, who are principally interested in these particular limitations.

The point is that while we are being quite reasonable regarding CFE Treaty adjustments, Russia is headed the opposite direction with respect to adjustments to the ABM Treaty. The Russian government is now trying to make the ABM Treaty *more* restrictive on the United States—for example, by trying to get us to agree to limitations on the speed of our theater ballistic-missile interceptors. It is my understanding that the Administration has resisted these Russian efforts, but it is unfortunate that—again according to press reports—we have apparently agreed to language that establishes interceptor speeds (below three kilometers per second) that would *not* violate the treaty. I hope we will continue to insist that faster interceptors (such as those that would be used for the Navy's Upper Tier theater defense system) are also treaty-compliant, but I am concerned that we have agreed to discuss interceptor speed at all. Limitations on the range and speed of *targets* for theater systems should be sufficient to establish that our theater systems are not being "tested in an ABM mode" in violation of the treaty.

I also have difficulty in understanding the reasons for adding other nations, such as other former Soviet republics, to the ABM Treaty. Multilateralizing the treaty will make it harder to amend and adjust it in order to accomplish the purposes President Yeltsin set out in 1992. The original purpose of the ABM Treaty was to prevent a Soviet ABM deployment that would endanger our ability to retaliate following a Soviet counterforce strike against the United States. We fear no such strike from, e.g., Belarus. I see no reason why we are moving to make it harder rather than easier to adjust the treaty to the realities of the post–Cold War era.

Finally, I was quite disappointed that the Administration's original defense budget for 1997 delayed and cut the funding for the theater and national BMD programs that Congress has called for. I am sympathetic with the dilemma faced by the senior leaders of the Defense Department as they were forced to set priorities among BMD programs, given the fact that the funds available for defense procurement overall were less than two-thirds of the sustaining level of approximately $60 billion that was needed. The problem is not so much, in my view, the choices that the Defense Department leadership made in the face of these fiscal constraints. It is the constraints themselves.

Some Recommendations

Any overall assessment of the risks and needs facing the United States should, in my judgment, indicate the primary importance of a vigorous program for *theater defenses* (Navy Upper Tier and THAAD, the Army's Theater High Altitude Area Defense program) and also the importance of a sound program to move toward some type of *national defense*, coupled with a diplomatic effort to increase, not decrease, the flexibility in the ABM Treaty. I would personally put the top priority at the present time on the theater defense programs, in addition to the shorter-range systems that are already being pursued. The reasons are set forth very well in the 1996 report by the Heritage Foundation, *Defending America*. In general, much of the work on theater systems, particularly in connection with space-based sensors, is also relevant to national defenses.

I would defer for the time being the question whether we should consider withdrawing from the ABM Treaty. I believe that, with an appropriately firm negotiating approach to the Russians and with adequate funding for our own BMD programs, we should be able to accommodate our needs within the treaty for some time if it is appropriately interpreted and, possibly, modified.

In 1992 we explored seriously with the Russians how we might cooperatively move toward limited national defenses so that both countries could be defended from a wide range of ballistic-missile threats. With any reasonable Russian government, this approach should eventually bear fruit. As only one example, if we could reach agreement on returning to something very similar to the ABM Treaty's original 1972 form (permitting two sites, not one, in each country), a thin national defense against most threats other than a large attack by Russia would be made substantially easier. As part of a combined approach, we might be willing to supply the Russians, as well as other nations, with data from our space-based sensors such as Brilliant Eyes. This would substantially enhance the performance of their theater defense systems. Such a combined approach of treaty modification and cooperative programs would give us a few more years to assess the direction in which we want to move over the long run.

One final point. The Russians should be made aware that we expect them to be reasonable and that we will weigh their international conduct and military programs as we make long-term decisions

about our approach toward the ABM Treaty and cooperative programs. We have no reason to hesitate to make clear what American
needs and desires are. We are dealing from a position of strength. It
was our Cold War adversary's political and economic system that was
cast onto the ash-heap of history, not ours.

20

Global Missile Defense: Effective, Affordable, and Available

Henry F. Cooper

The question is no longer *whether* to defend the American people against ballistic-missile attack but *when* and *with what kind of defense*. In their 1996 platforms, both Republicans and Democrats espoused programs that could deploy *ground-based* defenses by 2003.[1] But both positions are deficient because of ideological concerns, primarily associated with the ABM Treaty.

The answer to "when and with what kind?" should be "as soon as possible, with the most effective global defenses technically feasible": *as soon as possible* (beginning as early as three years from now), because the threat to the American people warrants a prudent response and, given the uncertainties of today's threat projections, prudence demands a sense of urgency; *global* defenses, because increasingly

---

Henry F. Cooper is the chairman of High Frontier, a non-governmental authority on missile-defense issues. From 1990 to 1993 he was director of the Strategic Defense Initiative (SDI). Among his previous government posts were Chief U.S. Negotiator at the Geneva Defense and Space Talks with the Soviet Union (1985-89), Assistant Director of the Arms Control and Disarmament Agency (1983-85), and Deputy Assistant Secretary of the Air Force (1979-82).

longer-range missiles being developed in states around the world can threaten American interests at unpredictable times and places world-wide; and *with the most effective defenses technically feasible*, because high effectiveness is required to protect cities against even limited attacks.

Surprisingly, the most effective defenses can be built fastest and for the least money. *Sea-based* and *space-based* defenses are the most effective and also the least expensive, and can be deployed soonest. Whether they *will* be deployed is an issue of policy, not technology or affordability. If current policies—particularly those related to the ABM Treaty—are not changed, much more money will be spent on much less effective ground-based defenses.

My main purpose here is to describe how to build quickly the least expensive, most effective defenses and to discuss how current policy is limiting our ability to do so. But first, a brief comment on the threat.

Russia and China are modernizing their ballistic missiles, which today could be used to attack U.S. cities. Neither state is a model of stability in the new world disorder. The uncertain control of Russian missiles is particularly troubling, despite Russia's commitment not to target missiles at American territory.[2] That commitment is unverifiable and can be rescinded in minutes, as the commander-in-chief of the Russian Strategic Rocket Forces, General Igor Sergeyev, acknowledged in a January 22, 1995, interview on "60 Minutes." Early in 1996, Chinese officials made a not-so-subtle threat to attack Los Angeles if the United States interfered with their attempt to influence Taiwan's election, an effort that included "test" launching of ballistic missiles toward Taiwan.[3]

Additional nations could threaten the United States with attack by missiles now under development faster than we could deploy defenses against them.[4] Rogue states could threaten to attack a totally vulnerable United States—and, as former Defense Secretary Les Aspin frequently argued, the United States could find itself the "deterree" rather than the "deterrer." Such states as North Korea, Iran, Iraq, Libya, and Syria are among the more than twenty already possessing ballistic missiles and associated weapons of mass destruction. As they obtain longer-and longer-range missiles, it becomes increasingly difficult to predict where and when an actual threat might develop and who might be threatened. With sufficiently long-range missiles, an unpredictable rogue leader could hold the entire world hostage to his whims.

Imagine how the Gulf War might have gone if Saddam Hussein had fielded longer-range missiles that could threaten European—or possibly American—cities. It is doubtful that, under such circumstances, President Bush could have formed the coalition that performed so brilliantly during the 1991 Gulf War—or that Congress would have approved the U.S. involvement. The vote was extremely close as it was.

Having on-the-scene effective defenses before such a threat develops is strategically important. Without such global defenses, the United States cannot protect its allies and friends, and its security interests around the world will be severely limited, with potentially long-term negative strategic consequences. If such defenses are not on the scene already, they will be very difficult to deploy—as illustrated by the difficulty the United States had in moving Patriot defenses to South Korea in 1994 to counter North Korea's threatened aggression.

The distinction between long-range "strategic" and shorter-range "theater" ballistic missiles—and defenses against such missiles—is a misleading vestige of Cold War arms-control language, which used a definition based on a weapon system's range instead of a more appropriate definition based on its function. In fact, "theater" missiles are "strategic" weapons in the truest sense of the word. As observed by the co-chairmen of a recent joint Defense Science Board/Defense Policy Board Task Force, theater ballistic missiles are not just another battlefield weapon:

> The motives of potential adversaries to possess these weapons [theater ballistic missiles] are decidedly strategic. They offer a relatively low cost way to threaten population centers and crucial military targets like ports and other points of entry in order to coerce neighbors, break up coalitions and deter U.S. military involvement in their region. They can raise the stakes even higher when they carry chemical, biological, or nuclear payloads. The gravity of this threat requires that continued special attention be given to efforts to counter it.[5]

THREE PHASES OF MISSILE DEFENSE

Acquiring a 90 per cent effective defense is a demanding but achievable goal. This degree of effectiveness would be expected to permit one in ten attacking missiles to break through to its intended target—

and of course, a single nuclear warhead could destroy a major city, while a single chemical or biological warhead could kill a major portion of a single city's population. A single-layer 90 per cent effective defense would not be able to defend one city against even a dozen missiles armed with weapons of mass destruction. A defense with two 90 per cent effective layers would permit one in a hundred attacking missiles through, but would be effective enough to defeat several dozen warheads—a plausible threat, as the Clinton administration has acknowledged.[6]

Boost-Phase Defenses

The diagram below shows the three stages at which a missile can be intercepted: the *boost phase*, when it is being powered into space by rockets; the *mid-course phase*, during which it travels outside the earth's atmosphere, ascending to its highest point and then beginning to descend; and the *terminal phase*, when it reenters earth's atmosphere and descends toward its target. Assuring two independent shots at an

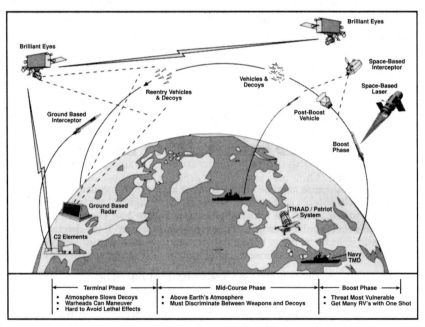

THREE STAGES OF MISSILE DEFENSE

attacking missile would be very difficult for the ground-based defenses being developed by the Clinton administration.

Furthermore, such ground-based defenses would be totally ineffective against ballistic missiles that release multiple warheads—or submunitions—while they are rising from their launchers in their boost and ascent phases of flight. Boost-phase defenses will be needed to defeat this predictable threat development.[7] In fact, unless effective defenses of this kind receive priority, rogue states are likely to develop a multiple-warhead capability in the near future—perhaps before currently planned U.S. ground-based defenses are even deployed.

To defeat submunitions released early in the attacking missile's flight, defenses must be located near the missile's launch point, close enough to intercept it within a period of tens of seconds to minutes after it is launched. (The longer the range of the attacking missile, the more time the defense has to respond.) Generally, ground-based defenses cannot be placed close enough to achieve boost-phase intercepts. In some instances—e.g., for some launch sites in Libya, Syria, and North Korea—sea-based defenses can be stationed near enough to permit boost-phase intercepts; often they can be stationed close enough to intercept missiles in their ascent phase. Manned and unmanned aircraft also can, in some scenarios, operate close enough, but the cost and logistic-support requirements for maintaining such operations are daunting.

In most cases, space-based defenses are the best means of achieving boost-phase intercepts.[8] Space-based lasers and interceptors can be placed in low earth orbit over threatening missile launchers, and they can intercept attacking missiles early in their flight—in the boost phase, if they have enough time. Because laser beams travel at the speed of light, space-based lasers (SBLs) can intercept even short-range (as short as seventy miles) missiles in their boost phase. Space-based interceptors (SBIs), employing today's technology, can intercept intercontinental-range ballistic missiles in their boost phase; using plausible future technology, they could intercept much shorter-range missiles—down to a few hundred miles—in their boost phase.

Mid-Course-Phase/Exo-Atmospheric Defenses

After its boost phase, when its rockets have completed burning, the attacking missile begins to "coast" through space in a ballistic trajectory until it re-enters the earth's atmosphere and begins to decelerate because of atmospheric drag. Early in this mid-course phase, it can begin dispersing warheads and decoys, providing numerous targets to confuse or overwhelm the defense. This "discrimination" problem continues throughout the mid-course phase of flight above the earth's atmosphere, where there is no air resistance to slow down lightweight decoys that can be carried in large numbers. "Exo-atmospheric" defenses must discriminate between warheads and decoys—a daunting task requiring high-fidelity sensors—and then attack the warheads. Space-based sensors such as the Brilliant Eyes system (now called the Space-based Surveillance and Tracking System, SSTS) are very important in providing this high-fidelity information to defeat probable offensive countermeasures.

Together, SBIs and SBLs compose a robust space-based defense architecture. SBIs can be very effective in destroying warheads during the mid-course phase, provided the discrimination problem is solved. SBLs, though ineffective as interceptors during the mid-course phase, are quite effective in perturbing a cloud of warheads and chaff, enabling sensors to discriminate warheads from lighter decoys.

Once the discrimination problem is solved, exo-atmospheric defenses can defend large areas, particularly if they are located close enough to the launch point to intercept the attacking missile in its ascent phase. All basing modes offer the potential for intercepting a missile during this longest phase of its flight, which lasts many minutes—up to twenty in the case of intercontinental ballistic missiles. However, because of timing constraints, ground-based interceptors located near the intended target cannot attack the missile before it begins its descent after traveling halfway to that target. Consequently, the area that such ground-based interceptors can defend is much smaller than the area defended by ascent- or boost-phase interceptors.

Terminal-Phase/Endo-Atmospheric Defenses

As the warheads and decoys reenter the earth's atmosphere for the final minute or so of their flight, the air resistance causes light elements, e.g., decoys, to decelerate more rapidly than heavier elements, such as a nuclear-armed re-entry vehicle. This simplifies the discrimination problem, enabling "endo-atmospheric" defenses to attack the warhead inside the earth's atmosphere—preferably high up, before the warhead can maneuver to avoid defensive interceptors.

Terminal-phase defenses, which make up most of the development programs of the Clinton administration, are usually ground- or sea-based. However, spaced-based interceptors can be designed to penetrate the atmosphere and intercept reentry vehicles, at least down to about thirty miles altitude.[9] All endo-atmospheric defenses are limited to defending relatively small areas because they cannot engage until late in the attacking missile's flight, as it nears its target.

Achieving a maneuvering capability to defeat terminal defenses is not particularly challenging, as the illusive Gulf War Scud missile demonstrated. There, the crudely modified Scud design simply broke up on reentry, became aerodynamically unstable, and followed a very hard-to-hit corkscrew path to its intended target. Such a crude design is not very accurate, but great accuracy is not required to hit a city with a weapon of mass destruction. To counter even such a crude design, a defensive interceptor must also be highly maneuverable— much more maneuverable than Patriot, and probably more maneuverable than any of the endo-atmospheric interceptors currently being developed for deployment.

THE FASTEST ACHIEVABLE DEFENSES

As we have seen, it is most useful to intercept missiles in their boost and ascent phases—and the earlier the better for defending large areas and defeating offensive countermeasures. Furthermore, an early intercept would cause the debris to fall on the territory of the country launching the attack, a factor that could deter such an attack in the first place.

If a missile can be destroyed in its boost phase, the location of its target is immaterial. Thus a boost- or ascent-phase defense can protect very wide areas—possibly even the entire world. A striking fact is that boost- and ascent-phase defenses not only are more effective wide-area defenses but also can be built before ground-based defenses—and for less money.[10]

Sea-Based Interceptors

The earliest deployable, highly effective defense—called the Navy Upper Tier or Navy Theater Wide Defense—would exploit the U.S. Navy's fleet of Aegis cruisers stationed worldwide, a system in which the United States has already invested about $50 billion. For an additional $2-3 billion, 650 long-range defensive interceptors could be put on twenty-two cruisers over the next three to five years. This investment would also provide for improvements to the associated battle-management, command, control, and communications (BMC3) systems to enable a worldwide, or global, capability.

Such sea-based defenses would exploit the geographical fact that about two-thirds of the earth's surface is covered by water. Ships can be stationed in international waters between many threatening and threatened states. For example, Sixth Fleet cruisers in the Mediterranean Sea could protect all of Europe from ballistic missiles launched from North Africa and the Middle East. And Seventh Fleet cruisers in the Sea of Japan could protect East Asia from missiles launched from North Korea. These same cruisers could also protect the United States from launches from rogue states, provided that U.S. policy permits the full exploitation of readily available technology. Other cruisers in the North Atlantic or North Pacific could provide additional intercept opportunities against long-range missiles launched from numerous states over the North Pole toward the United States. An appropriate deployment of Aegis cruisers worldwide could provide multiple shots at long-range missiles aimed at the United States from many rogue states.

Space-Based Interceptors

After sea-based wide-area defenses, the next fastest way to provide an effective defense is to build space-based interceptors. These "hit-to-kill" interceptors would be placed in orbit and would maneuver into the path of attacking missiles, destroying them on impact. If the SBI acquisition programs canceled by the Clinton administration were reestablished, fully funded, and managed by a streamlined, competent team, deployment of a first-generation global space-based defense could begin in three or four years. When fully deployed another two years later, after a total investment of $6-7 billion, this system would provide multiple intercept opportunities worldwide against ballistic missiles with ranges greater than about 300 miles. These intercepts could begin as early as the boost phase of sufficiently long-range missiles, before the missiles could release multiple warheads and/or decoys.[11]

This system would use hardware and software space-qualified on the 1994 Clementine program, which demonstrated Brilliant Pebbles technology in returning to the moon for the first time in twenty-five years. Clementine provided much, much more multi-spectral data of the entire surface of the moon than was obtained by the much larger and much more expensive Apollo program.[12] So, building a first-generation space-based defense is not just a hypothetical possibility. Existing technology, pioneered by the Strategic Defense Initiative (SDI), makes it a manageable engineering problem.

This fact is not lost on the private sector. Bill Gates of Microsoft fame and Craig McCaw of McCaw Cellular fame have joined forces to invest millions of their own dollars in a new company, Teledesic, that will build a telecommunications system employing several hundred satellites in low earth orbits, similar to the Brilliant Pebbles constellation. Teledesic's president, Russell Daggatt, gave credit to SDI—and Brilliant Pebbles in particular—for the enabling technology that makes the Gates and McCaw investment a good one. More recently, Boeing agreed to invest up to $100 million for up to 10 per cent ownership of Teledesic and the prime contract to build a $9 billion constellation early in the next decade.

And Teledesic is not alone in exploiting SDI-pioneered space technologies for profit. Motorola is developing Iridium (with several satellites already in orbit), TRW is developing Odyssey, and Loral is developing Globestar. These major aerospace companies are not seeking money from the federal government for such development, because the strings attached would slow their race to make money in a growing, competitive global marketplace; all they want from the government is licenses. Interestingly enough, the first license to exploit Brilliant Pebbles technology was obtained in 1993 by a new remote-sensing company, WorldView (now called EarthWatch), supported entirely by venture capital.[13]

Hard-nosed leaders in industry are not investing in a "Star Wars" fantasy—as politicians often refer to efforts to build effective ballistic-missile defenses. Urged on by the profit motive, they will probably exploit SDI technology to build effective space systems by the end of this decade. The civil and national-security sector will probably take longer because of the bureaucratic and political pressures that always resist innovation. And unless there is a change in attitude, it will take even longer for missile-defense applications because, as we shall see, of the added "political correctness" burden associated with the ABM Treaty.

In the far term—after about ten years and an investment of about $15 billion—space-based lasers, or SBLs, could be built to intercept, in their boost phase, ballistic missiles with ranges greater than about seventy miles.[14] Contrary to the images conjured up by "Star Wars" rhetoric, the technology is sufficiently mature to justify building such a system—as acknowledged by William Broad, science reporter for the *New York Times* and no friend of SDI or ballistic-missile defenses in general, in a December 1994 article headed "From Fantasy to Fact: Space-Based Laser Nearly Ready to Fly."[15] At the initiative of Senate Majority Leader Trent Lott, Congress began in 1997 to appropriate substantial funding in order to accelerate SBL development.

The combination of SBLs and SBIs would provide an impressive defense that would be difficult to defeat, short of a massive attack. SBLs would provide boost-phase intercept capability against all but very short-range (less than about seventy miles) missiles and would help discriminate between warheads and lightweight decoys during the mid-course phase in outer space. SBIs would provide multiple intercept opportunities: starting as early as the boost phase for sufficiently long-range missiles, extending through the mid-course phase in outer space, and continuing into the terminal phase (down to about thirty miles altitude) as the attacking missiles reenter the earth's atmosphere.

The annual cost of a program to build these very effective global defenses to defend both the United States and its friends and allies around the world would be less than what the Clinton administration is currently spending (about $3 billion a year) to protect only a limited area overseas from a few short- and intermediate-range ballistic missiles. These theater defenses will provide no protection for the American people. And a modestly effective multi-site ground-based defense to protect the American people against a few dozen missiles (a realistic threat, as acknowledged by then Defense Secretary William Perry) would cost about $35 billion—three to four times the cost to field *both* the Navy's wide-area sea-based defense and the Air Force's space-based interceptors. Deployment of such a ground-based system could not begin before the end of the decade,[16] would not be completed until at least the middle of the next decade, could be severely stressed by a few dozen warheads,[17] and would be totally ineffective against ballistic missiles that released their warheads and decoys in the boost phase.[18]

Thus, if ground-based defenses are developed and deployed, additional defenses will be needed to provide intercept opportunities earlier in the flight of attacking missiles. This is precisely what sea- and space-based defenses can provide—and if they are deployed first, a major investment in ground-based defenses can be avoided.

THE POLITICAL OBSTACLES

If the threat is urgent and the most effective defenses are the most immediately available and the least expensive, why then is the U.S. government primarily investing in less effective, less immediately available, and more costly defenses?

This bizarre state of affairs is the consequence of an ideological debate, too long characterized by bumper-sticker arguments. The debate began right after Ronald Reagan's March 23, 1983, speech announcing his intention to establish what became known as the Strategic Defense Initiative, or SDI. Almost immediately, the Soviets charged that Reagan's initiative would lead to all sorts of instability, a new arms race in space, and the end of arms control, particularly as focused on the ABM Treaty, and U.S. arms-control advocates mirror-imaged these arguments.[19] "Star Wars" imagery was introduced, by those ideologically opposed to ballistic-missile defense in general and to space-based defenses in particular, to suggest that SDI was the dream of a misguided actor who confused fantasy with reality.

Setbacks continued. Even though the technology for space-based defenses was more mature, Congress in the Missile Defense Act of 1991 directed that building ground-based defenses—beginning with a treaty-compliant site—be given priority; the validation phase of the then fully approved Brilliant Pebbles program was reduced to a "robust" research and development activity. Two years later, to take the "stars out of Star Wars," as he said, Les Aspin, President Clinton's first Secretary of Defense, changed the name of the Strategic Defense Initiative Organization to the Ballistic Missile Defense Organization. Aspin curtailed the "theater defense" programs (particularly boost-phase interceptor programs and the Navy Upper Tier) he had inherited even while claiming to give them first priority, severely cut all programs to defend the U.S. homeland, and scuttled all space-defense development programs. In the congressional debate on missile defenses in recent years, some proponents of building effective defenses have focused their advocacy on a multi-site ground-based defense, which they have repeatedly argued "is not Star Wars." At the other end of the spectrum, some who oppose all missile defense, however based, have argued that even ground-based defenses are "Star Wars."

SDI was never about the stars or wars. It was about non-threatening, non-nuclear defenses of Americans and America's overseas troops, friends, and allies from attack by missiles armed with weapons of mass destruction. The Reagan/Bush administrations invested more in ground-based defenses than in space-based defenses, so the suggestion of an undue emphasis on space systems was also wrong.

Some missile-defense advocates in the current debate no doubt fall prey to the misperception that ground-based defense costs less and can be built faster than other types. Others know better but nonetheless support ground-based defense even though it is more expensive and must be built at a slower pace. They believe that this defense is all that the political/ideological traffic will bear, that any program that might be perceived as threatening the ABM Treaty, which is idolized by the Cold War arms-control community, will fail.

But as we have seen, ground-based defenses simply will never be able to defeat likely countermeasures such as submunitions released in the ascent phase of an attacking missile's flight—and they may have difficulty with high-fidelity mid-course decoys. Better defenses will be needed if the American people are to be protected from the rogue states that are obtaining longer- and longer-range ballistic missiles, plus associated chemical, biological, and nuclear weapons.

Fix the ABM Treaty

If ever the American people are to be defended by technically feasible and less expensive sea- and space-based defenses, something must be done about the ABM Treaty. Nowhere is the difficulty made more plain than in the plight of sea-based wide-area defenses. In 1995-96, Congress directed that the Navy Upper Tier be developed and deployed as soon as possible. However, the Clinton administration has been reluctantly pursuing a scaled-down program that does not fully exploit available technology to make Upper Tier all it can be—because of assumed ABM Treaty restrictions. For over nine months the Clinton administration withheld funds appropriated in 1995 while conducting no fewer than six internal reviews of Upper Tier—all of which substantiated the technical, programmatic, and cost estimates that had been well known for at least four years.[20] And funds appropriated in 1996 were held up also, slowing development of a much needed defense, as the Administration continued to delay the program. During 1997, the Administration finally included the Navy Upper Tier—now called Navy Theater Wide—defense in its core theater defense acquisition programs, but without the needed funds to proceed at a technology-limited pace. Consequently, Congress more than doubled the Administration's 1998 funding request of $149 million by appropriating $410 million. If this is spent wisely and willingly—and if the program is fully funded in the future—the first Aegis-based interceptors could be deployed in three years.

The program the Administration is pursuing is deliberately *not* using readily available technology to provide the most effective defense. Why? Because the Administration seeks to make sure that the system intended to protect our overseas troops, friends, and allies has no ability to protect the American people. For example, the system is being designed to employ sensors that can "see" only warm "theater" warheads against a cold space background, to assure that the defense will be ineffective against cold "strategic" warheads that might threaten the United States—even though sensors to "see" cold warheads would cost little more and could be available at the same time. Also, to assure ABM Treaty compliance, the system is being designed not to take advantage of sensors other than ship-based radar, a restriction that markedly reduces the defense coverage characteristics.[21] The use of forward-based sensors—in the same architecture already being used to defend against cruise missiles—would increase the area that a given Aegis cruiser could defend by ten to one hundred times. But this capability is being excluded because it might also give that cruiser the ability to defend the United States against missile attack.

This is a particularly ironic double standard because the Soviet Union/Russia has long exploited large phased-array radar on the periphery of the former Soviet Union in exactly the same way as "external" sensors, in order to improve the capability of the Moscow ABM system. The United States has declared this to be consistent with the ABM Treaty. Yet the Clinton administration is denying U.S. theater defenses the same benefits—and theater defenses were not supposed to be restrained by the treaty. If this constraint is not removed to permit the use of readily available technology, some future captain of a "dumbed-down" Aegis cruiser in the Sea of Japan may confront the absurd situation of being able to intercept a missile launched from North Korea if it is directed toward Tokyo but not, as a matter of policy, if it is directed toward Seattle.

As for space systems, building SBIs and SBLs would seem to be entirely consistent with the National Space Policy, released by the White House in September 1996.[22] However, the ABM Treaty again blocks the path to building such defenses.

Clearly, no effective defense of the U.S. homeland can be built within the terms of the ABM Treaty. Furthermore, the treaty is corrupting the so-called theater defense programs to defend overseas U.S. troops, friends, and allies. It costs us dearly in treasure; we can only hope that it will not cost us dearly in lives.[23] Actually, it probably has already cost us lives—the twenty-eight military personnel killed when an Iraqi Scud missile hit their barracks during the 1991 Gulf War might have been spared had Patriot not been dumbed-down and delayed because of treaty concerns.[24] America's continuing vulnerability is making the ballistic missile the surest way to threaten the United States and therefore the weapon of choice of state terrorists.

Cooperation on Missile Defenses?

From 1985 through 1992, the United States tried to persuade the Soviets/Russians to move beyond confrontation and threats of mutual annihilation to cooperation—including cooperation on missile defenses. In 1992, in the same U.N. speech in which he proposed the deeper reductions that became START II, Russian president Boris Yeltsin proposed that SDI be redirected to take advantage of Russian technology and build a global defense for the world community.

Yeltsin's proposal reversed the long-standing Soviet/Russian argument that defenses were incompatible with arms-control reductions.

The Bush administration made progress toward agreement on that agenda, but in the final analysis it failed to capitalize on Yeltsin's initiative. And the Clinton administration did not continue on that negotiating path. Rather, it called the ABM Treaty the "cornerstone of strategic stability" and has sought from the outset to "strengthen" it by making it a theater ballistic-missile defense treaty as well. This regrettable action ignored the advances made in response to Yeltsin's 1992 initiative and reintroduced the linkage arguments, reinforcing the Mutual Assured Destruction (MAD) ideas that are the foundation of the ABM Treaty and suggesting that all defenses are incompatible with arms reductions. On August 21, 1997, the Administration announced an agreement with Russia, Belarus, Kazakhstan, and Ukraine that would, in effect, turn the ABM Treaty into a multilateral Theater Missile Defense Treaty, making the "dumbing-down" trends discussed above a matter of international law. A Senate debate over these unlawful amendments is certain—and thirty-four or more "no" votes could stop the ratification process.

This trend is contrary to U.S. national interests. Indeed, it is even contrary to Russia's interests in the long run, if cooperation is truly Russia's objective. In any case, the United States. should clearly state its intention to build the most effective, affordable defenses that current technology permits, with or without Russia's cooperation. If Russia chooses to cooperate, a global defense could serve our mutual interests. Otherwise, the United States should withdraw from the ABM Treaty as permitted in Article XV.

Cooperation in building a global defense for the world community, as Yeltsin proposed, could also serve as a new unifying mission for NATO. This was the essence of Lady Margaret Thatcher's proposal on the fiftieth anniversary of Sir Winston Churchill's "Iron Curtain" speech, which focused the West's strategic thinking for the duration of the Cold War. (See chapter 15 of this volume.) In her survey of post–Cold War dangers, Mrs. Thatcher urges that NATO coordinate the contributions of America's allies in acquiring an effective global defense as "a matter of the greatest importance and urgency." She aptly argues that such a global defense would contribute to peace and stability by: providing the possibility of protection should deterrence fail—or if there were a limited and unauthorized use of nuclear missiles; preserving the capability of the West to project its power overseas; diminishing the danger that one country will overturn the regional balance of power by obtaining nuclear missiles; strengthening our existing deterrent against a hostile superpower by preserving the West's power of retaliation; and enhancing diplomacy's power to restrain proliferation by diminishing the utility of such systems.

Indeed, it is important that America's allies contribute—and not only to help develop complete systems. Radar and other sensors in strategic locations around the world could greatly enhance the effectiveness of a global defense. And all would benefit.

With or without the cooperation of others, the United States should put behind us the era of dumbing down systems according to our perceptions of the constraints imposed by ambiguous Cold War treaty terms. We should end America's total vulnerability to missile attack as soon as possible with the best defenses we can afford.

Notes

CHAPTER 1

"Just Cause Revisited"

JAMES TURNER JOHNSON

1. Thomas Aquinas, *Summa Theologica,* 2/2, q. 40, a. 1.

2. Gratian, *Decretum*, pars secunda, causa 13, q. 2, canons 1, 2.

3. Aquinas, *Summa Theologica*, 2/2, q. 40, a. 1.

4. Alfred Vanderpol, *La Doctrine scolastique du droit de guerre* (Paris: A. Pedone, 1919), 250.

5. St. Ambrose, *On the Duties of the Clergy*, 1.41.211.

6. Ibid., 3.4.27.

7. Ibid., 1.36.179.

8. Paul Ramsey, *War and the Christian Conscience* (Durham, N.C.: Duke University Press, 1961), 15-39.

9. St. Augustine, *Contra Faustum*, 22.70.

10. Aquinas, *Summa Theologica*, 2/2, q. 40, a. 1, reply obj. 1; emphasis in text.

11. James Turner Johnson, *Just War Tradition and the Restraint of War* (Princeton: Princeton University Press, 1981), 15065.

12. Vitoria, *De Jure Belli*, sec. 10.

13. Ibid., sec. 13.

14. Ibid., secs. 14-16; Vitoria, *De Bello*, sec. 3.

15. Vitoria, *De Jure Belli*, sec. 15.

16. Vitoria, *De Bello*, sec. 4.

17. Vitoria, *De Jure Belli*, secs. 18-19.

18. Vitoria, *De Indis*, sec. 3, 7.

19. Grotius, *The Law of War and Peace*, bk. 3, chap. 3; cf. bk. 1, chap. 3.

20. Ibid., bk. 2, chap. 1, sec. 2; emphasis added.

21. Ibid., bk. 2, chap. 1, sec. 4.

22. James Brown Scott, *The Spanish Origin of International Law*, (Oxford: Clarendon Press, 1934), 200ff.

23. Grotius, *The Law of War and Peace*, bk. 2, chap. 1, sec. 4.

24. Ibid., bk. 2, chap. 1, sec. 17.

25. Ibid., bk. 2, chap. 25, sec. 9.

26. Ibid., bk. 2, chap. 26, sec. 4.

27. Cf. Geoffrey Best, *Humanity in Warfare* (New York: Columbia University Press, 1980), chap. 3.

28. Ibid., chap. 2.

29. All these are included in Dietrich Schindler and Jiri Toman, eds., *The Laws of Armed Conflicts* (Leiden: A. W. Sijthoff; Geneva: Henry Dunant Institute).

30. For discussion in the context of European balance-of-power politics see Henry Kissinger, *Diplomacy* (New York: Simon and Schuster, 1994), chaps. 6, 7.

31. Morton A. Kaplan and Nicholas deB. Katzenbach, "Resort to Force: War and Neutrality," in Richard A. Falk and Saul H. Medlovitz, eds., *The Strategy of World Order*, vol. 2: *International Law* (New York: World Law Fund, 1966), 290, n. 3.

32. Henri Meyrowitz, *Le Principe de l'égalité les belligérents devant le droit de la guerre* (Paris: A. Pedone, 1970), 144-47.

33. Kaplan and Katzenbach, "Resort to Force," 290, n. 3.

34. John Eppstein, *The Catholic Tradition of the Law of Nations* (Washington, D.C.: Catholic Association for International Peace, 1935), 132.

35. Ibid., 140.

36. John Courtney Murray, *Morality and Modern War* (New York: Council on Religion and International Affairs, 1959), 9.

37. Cited ibid., 11; emphasis added.

38. Ronald G. Musto, *The Catholic Peace Tradition* (Maryknoll, N.Y.: Orbis Books, 1986), 190.

39. Paul Ramsey, *The Just War* (New York: Scribner's, 1968), 190-210.

40. Pope Paul VI, *Never Again War!* (New York: United Nations Office of Public Information, 1965), 37-39.

41. National Conference of Catholic Bishops, *The Challenge of Peace* (Washington, D.C.: United States Catholic Conference, 1983), para. 70.

42. Bryan J. Hehir, "Just War Theory in a Post–Cold War World," *Journal of Religious Ethics* 20, no. 2 (Fall 1992): 250; emphasis in text.

43. Ibid., 251.

44. Augustine, *Contra Faustum*, 22.74; as cited by Thomas Aquinas, *Summa Theologica* 2/2, q. 40, a. 1.

45. Paul Fussell, *The Great War and Modern Memory* (New York: Oxford University Press), 314.

CHAPTER 2

"Competent Authority Revisited"

EUGENE V. ROSTOW

1. Pungently recalled in the title of Isaiah Berlin's book *The Crooked Timber of Humanity* (1991).

2. William V. O'Brien, *The Conduct of Just and Limited War* (New York: Praeger, 1981 and 1983), 10.

3. Myres S. McDougal and Florentino P. Feliciano, *Law and Minimum World Public Order* (New Haven: Yale University Press, 1961).

4. *Filartiga v. Pena-Irala,* 630 F(20) 876 (C.C.A.2d. 1980); *Tel-Oren v. The Arab Republic of Libya* (470 U.S. 1003 [1985]). Scoble, "Enforcing the Customary International Law of Human Rights in Federal Courts," *California Law Review* 74 (1986): 127.

5. Julius Stone, *Conflict Through Consensus* (Baltimore: Johns Hopkins University Press, 1977).

6. The opinions are magisterially reviewed in Lori F. Damrosch, ed., *The International Court of Justice at a Crossroads* (Dobbs Ferry, N.Y.: Transnational Publishers, for the American Society of International Law, 1987).

7. Elihu Root, "The Real Monroe Doctrine," *American Journal of International Law* 35 (1914): 427.

8. See Yoram Dinstein,*War, Aggression and Self-Defense,* 2d ed. (Cambridge: Cambridge University Press, 1994), 231-48.

9. *Corfu Channel* case, Merits (1949) I.C.J. Report 4.

10. I discuss this issue briefly in remarks in *Proceedings,* Seventy-Seventh Annual Meeting, American Society of International Law (Washington D.C., April 14-16 1983), 33-36, 50-51, 217-23.

11. *Namibia* case (1971) I.C.J. 16.

12. Security Council Resolution 54 (July 15, 1948); 61 (Nov. 4, 1948); 62 (Nov. 16, 1948); 73 (Aug. 11, 1949); 89 (Nov. 17, 1950); 93 (May 18, 1951); 242 (Nov. 22, 1967); 338 (Oct. 22, 1973).

13. International Court of Justice, "Certain Expenses of the United Nations" (1962), 151.

14. Martin Wight, "The Balance of Power," in Herbert Butterfield and Martin Wight, eds., *Diplomatic Investigations: Essays in the Theory of International Politics* (Cambridge: Harvard University Press, 1966), 149, 174-79.

15. Dinstein, *War, Aggression and Self-Defense,* 143.

16. International Court of Justice, "Certain Expenses."

17. Ibid.

18. Immanuel Kant, "Thoughts on Eternal Peace," reprinted as appendix in D. J. Friedrich, *Inevitable Peace* (1948; reprint, Greenwich, Conn.: Greenwood Press, 1969), 257.

19. Julius Stone, *Visions of World Order: Between State Power and Human Justice* (Baltimore: Johns Hopkins University Press, 1980), xii-xiv.

CHAPTER 3

"Just War in a New Era of Military Affairs"

A. J. BACEVICH

1. "Transcript of President Bush's Address on End of the Gulf War," *New York Times,* March 7, 1991, A8.

2. B. H. Liddell Hart, *The Real War, 1914-1918* (Boston: Little, Brown, 1930), 273.

3. Michael S. Sherry, *The Rise of American Airpower: The Creation of Armageddon* (New Haven: Yale University Press, 1987). Although Sherry focuses chiefly on the development of the long-range bomber, his argument is equally applicable to the evolution of naval air power.

4. Although the U.S. Navy had developed earlier vessels for attacking shore targets—for example, the shallow-draft, rocket-launching craft designed to support World War II amphibious landings—these were categorized as auxiliaries rather than major combatants.

5. Enhanced technological capability may well generate its own headaches. As precision increases, so do expectations, constantly "raising the bar" of acceptable performance. As a result, tolerance for inaccuracy or even human error diminishes. Soldiers in the field may find themselves hard pressed to satisfy demands for virtually no-fault performance—especially in a media-saturated theater of operations. In such circumstances, the act that in former days was dismissed as part of the "fortunes of war" becomes "immoral." Consider, for example, the brouhaha following U.S. destruction of the al-Firdos bunker in Baghdad during the Gulf War. Consider in particular the sensitivity of the U.S. military to the criticism it received as a result of the incident: embarrassed by this ugly exception to what they had portrayed as a virtuoso performance, U.S. commanders of their own volition restricted further attacks on downtown Baghdad.

6. This analysis does not consider adversaries who either are very stupid or have a penchant for astonishing miscalculation—those willing to challenge the United States to fight a high-tech, conventional war. As Saddam Hussein reminds us, such adversaries exist. But a bumbling opponent is not an advantage that the United States can count on having in all cases.

7. The large number of Somali civilian casualties that were a by-product of U.S. efforts to capture Aidid—an aspect of the story that has gone largely unremarked—suggests that the advent of the latest military technology has not yet reversed the phenomenon whereby forces designed for conventional war become compromised when obliged to fight unconventionally. Unconventional forces carry high potential to thrust conventional forces into morally compromising circumstances.

8. Although overstated, Samuel P. Huntington's comment that "global political and security issues are effectively settled by a directorate of the United States, Britain, and France" contains a core of truth. But that arrangement is supported less by any substantive claims to power by the latter two nations than by (fading) memories of the days of empire. Such an arrangement is not sustainable. Samuel P. Huntington, "Clash of Civilizations?" *Foreign Affairs* 72 (Summer 1993): 39.

CHAPTER 4

"NBC-Armed Rogues"

BRAD ROBERTS

1. Philip Shenon, "Perry, in Egypt, Warns Libya to Halt Chemical Weapons Plant," *New York Times,* April 4, 1996, 4.

2. W. Anthony Lake, "Confronting Backlash States," *Foreign Affairs* 73, no. 2 (1994). The author recognizes that Lake's views are not broadly accepted and that many question

the right of the United States to deem others "rogues." But for lack of a better short-hand, the term is used here to refer to the category of states as defined.

3. For a summary discussion of the just war tradition, see chapter 1, "The Catholic Tradition of Moderate Realism," in George Weigel, *Tranquillitas Ordinis: The Present Failure and Future Promise of American Catholic Thought on War and Peace* (Oxford: Oxford University Press, 1987), 25-45. See also Michael Walzer, *Just and Unjust Wars*, 2d ed. (New York: Basic Books, 1992).

4. For a review of these themes, see Brad Roberts, "1995 and the End of the Post–Cold War Era," *Washington Quarterly* 18, no. 1 (Winter 1995).

5. Walzer, *Just and Unjust Wars*, xiv.

6. See Jane M. O. Sharp, "Appeasement, Intervention and the Future of Europe," and Ken Booth, "Military Intervention: Duty and Prudence," in Lawrence Freedman, ed., *Military Intervention in European Conflicts* (Oxford: Blackwell Publishers, 1994).

7. James Turner Johnson, "Just Cause Revisited," this volume, 26.

8. Francisco de Vitoria, *On the Law of War*, sec. 13.

9. Walzer, *Just and Unjust Wars*, 62.

10. Johnson, "Just Cause Revisited," 26.

11. Hugo Grotius, *The Law of War and Peace*, bk. 2, chap. 1, sec. 2.

12. Elihu Root, "The Real Monroe Doctrine," *American Journal of International Law* 35 (1914): 427.

13. Walzer, *Just and Unjust Wars*, 74, 80.

14. Morton A. Kaplan and Nicholas deB. Katzenbach, "Resort to Force: War and Neutrality," in Richard A. Falk and Saul H. Mendlovitz, eds., *The Strategy of World Order*, vol. 2, *International Law* (New York: World Law Fund, 1966).

15. Johnson, "Just Cause Revisited," 25.

16. Clausewitz, *On War*, trans. Michael Howard and Peter Paret (Princeton, N.J.: Princeton University Press, 1976), 370.

17. Walzer, *Just and Unjust Wars*, 81.

18. George Weigel, "Just War After the Cold War," in *Idealism Without Illusions: U.S. Foreign Policy in the 1990s* (Washington, D.C.: Ethics and Public Policy Center, 1994), 155.

19. Ibid., 153.

20. Johnson, "Just Cause Revisited," 9.

21. Ibid., 19-24.

22. See Weigel, *Tranquillitas Ordinis*, 257-85.

23. A. J. Bacevich, "Just War in a New Era of Military Affairs," this volume, 74.

24. Eugene Rostow, "Competent Authority Revisited," this volume, 55.

25. Johnson, "Just Cause Revisited," 31.

26. Walzer, *Just and Unjust Wars*, xxi.

27. Lake, "Confronting Backlash States."

28. Michael Klare, *Rogue States and Nuclear Outlaws: America's Search for a New Foreign Policy* (New York: Hill and Wang, 1995).

29. See Rosemary Righter, *Utopia Lost: The United Nations and World Order* (New York: Twentieth Century Fund Press, 1995).

30. The term is Charles Krauthammer's, used to describe the United States as the dominant power in a world no longer bipolar, because of the collapse of the Soviet Union, but not yet multipolar. See Krauthammer, "The Unipolar Moment," *Foreign Affairs* 70, no. 1 (1991): 23-33.

31. Weigel, *Tranquillitas Ordinis,* 37.

32. John Kelsay, *Islam and War: A Study in Comparative Ethics* (Louisville, Ky.: Westminster/John Knox Press, 1993).

CHAPTER 6

"Complex Humanitarian Emergencies and Moral Choice"

ANDREW NATSIOS

1. Study conducted by Faye Henderson of the LAI/OFDA (Office of Foreign Disaster Assistance) staff (August 3, 1992) for the author, then assistant administrator of FHA/USAID, Bureau of Food and Humanitarian Assistance.

2. See "Global Humanitarian Emergencies, 1996," study by U.S. Mission to the United Nations, ECOSOC section, February 1996.

3. This includes aggregated budget data from the offices of Food for Peace and Foreign Disaster Assistance in the U.S. Agency for International Development and the State Department's Office of Population, Migration and Refugees for fiscal year 1995.

4. See Michael Mandelbaum, "Foreign Policy as Social Work," *Foreign Affairs,* January/February 1996.

5. See Henry Kissinger, *Diplomacy* (New York: Simon and Schuster, 1994), 79.

6. See, e.g., "Dictatorships and Double Standards," *Commentary,* November 1979.

7. See Telford Taylor, *Munich: The Price of Peace* (New York: Random House, 1979), 165, 228-32.

8. Larry Minear and Thomas Weiss, *Mercy Under Fire* (Boulder, Colo.: Westview Press, 1995), 63.

9. See Gilbert A. Lewthwaite and Gregory Kane, "Witness to Slavery" (special three-part series), *Baltimore Sun,* June 16-18, 1996.

CHAPTER 8

"Somalia and the Problems of Doing Good"

ALBERTO R. COLL

1. *Lives Lost, Lives Saved: Excess Mortality and the Impact of Health Interventions in the Somalia Emergency* (Refugee Policy Group, Center for Policy Analysis and Research on Refugee Issues, November 1994), 16-17, 21, 24.

2. Andrew Natsios, "Food Through Force: Humanitarian Intervention and U.S. Policy," *Washington Quarterly,* Winter 1994, 135.

3. George F. Kennan, "Somalia, Through a Glass Darkly," *New York Times,* September 30, 1993, A25.

4. *The United Nations and Somalia, 1992-1996* (New York: United Nations Department of Public Information, 1996), 261-63.

5. John L. Hirsch and Robert B. Oakley, *Somalia and Operation Restore Hope: Reflections on Peacemaking and Peacekeeping* (Washington, D.C.: U.S. Institute of Peace Press, 1995), 121-22.

6. Keith B. Richburg, "In War on Aideed, UN Battled Itself," *Washington Post,* December 6, 1993, cited by Hirsch and Oakley, *Somalia and Operation Restore Hope,* 121-22. Hirsch and Oakley add, "There is no doubt that the militia leaders had studied not only Operation Desert Storm but Vietnam and Lebanon to understand the domestic political impact of American casualties."

7. Chester Crocker, "The Lessons of Somalia," *Foreign Affairs,* May/June 1995, 7.

8. *Lives Lost, Lives Saved,* 32.

CHAPTER 9

"The Duty to Intervene"

DREW CHRISTIANSEN and GERARD F. POWERS

1. John Paul II, "Address to the International Conference on Nutrition," *Origins* 22, no. 28 (Dec. 24, 1992): 475.

2. For moral assessments of humanitarian intervention, see J. Bryan Hehir, "Intervention: From Theories to Cases," *Ethics and International Affairs* 9 (1995): 1; Kenneth Himes, "The Morality of Humanitarian Intervention," *Theological Studies* 55 (1994): 82; James Turner Johnson, "The Just War Idea and the Ethics of Intervention," Reich Lecture, U.S. Air Force Academy, November 17, 1993; Pierre Laberge, "Humanitarian Intervention: Three Ethical Positions," *Ethics and International Affairs* 9 (1995): 15; John Langan, "The Ethics of Intervention in the Nineties," Sr. Virginia Geiger Lecture, College of Notre Dame of Maryland, May 6, 1993.

3. This breakdown is adapted from a helpful taxonomy of "peace operations" outlined by Denis McLean in *Peace Operations and Common Sense: Replacing Rhetoric with Realism* (Washington, D.C.: U.S. Institute of Peace, 1996), 3-4.

4. See Michael Walzer's moral analysis of this case in *Just and Unjust Wars,* 2d ed. (New York: Basic Books, 1992), 105-6.

5. Citing five years during which they have "unwittingly provided resources to factions/warlords and contributed to their war effort," the major international non-governmental organizations operating in Liberia announced in May 1996: "We feel a great obligation to the innocent victims of recent violence in Liberia, but will not return there if our presence could lead to more suffering for the Liberian people." "Announcement to the Liberian People from the Major International NGOs Operating in Liberia," May 28, 1996; available in the Office of International Justice and Peace, U.S. Catholic Conference, Washington, D.C.

6. John Pomfret, "Aid Dilemma: Keeping It From the Oppressors," *Washington Post,* September 23, 1997, A1, 12-13.

7. John XXIII, *Peace on Earth (Pacem in Terris),* papal encyclical (Washington, D.C.: USCC Office of Publishing and Promotion Services, 1963).

8. Ibid., par. 53-66.

9. Ibid., 61, 132-37.

10. John Paul II, "Address to the Diplomatic Corps," January 16, 1993, *Origins* 22, no. 34 (Feb. 4, 1993): 587.

11. For example, the Pope's outspoken opposition to the Gulf War raised serious questions about whether major modern wars could meet just war norms. The Pope's statements are collected in *John Paul II for Peace in the Middle East* (New York: Paths to Peace Foundation, 1992). According to Cardinal Angelo Sodano, Vatican secretary of state, the same principles undergird the Vatican's opposition to use of force in the Gulf and support for limited forms of humanitarian intervention in Bosnia-Herzegovina. In the Gulf War, the possibilities of negotiation did not seem to be exhausted, and the devastating effects of a full-scale military intervention appeared greater than the evil to be combatted. In Bosnia, numerous formal and informal negotiations led nowhere; the type of limited intervention the Vatican supported (e.g., enforcement of economic sanctions, the "no-fly zone," and safe havens) fell far short of full-scale military intervention, and thus involved much lower risks of being disproportionate. See Cardinal Sodano's interview with the Turin daily *La Stampa,* cited in Catholic News Service, December 28, 1992, 20-21.

12. See Frederick Russell, *The Just War in the Middle Ages* (Cambridge: Cambridge University Press, 1975).

13. National Conference of Catholic Bishops (NCCB), "The Harvest of Justice Is Sown in Peace," November 1993, reprinted in G. Powers, D. Christiansen, R. Hennemeyer, eds., *Peacemaking: Moral and Policy Challenges for a New World* (Washington, D.C.: U.S. Catholic Conference, 1994), 338.

14. NCCB, "Harvest of Justice," 337. Bryan Hehir balances international law's reluctance to legitimize humanitarian intervention with morality's appeal to a duty to intervene by arguing for maintaining the presumption for non-intervention while expanding the causes that justify intervention beyond genocide. J. Bryan Hehir, "Intervention: From Theories to Cases," *Ethics and International Affairs* 9 (1995): 7-9. For an overview of Catholic teaching on sovereignty and humanitarian intervention and the problems associated with enlarging the justifications for humanitarian intervention, see Kenneth Himes, "Catholic Social Thought and Humanitarian Intervention," in Powers, Christiansen, Hennemeyer, *Peacemaking,* 215.

15. NCCB, "Harvest of Justice," 338.

16. Tom Farer argues that the U.N. has improperly defined impartiality as applying no external standards rather than as applying standards equally. See "Intervention in Unnatural Humanitarian Emergencies," *Human Rights Quarterly* 18, no. 1 (February 1996): 1-22. Farer argues against a strict separation of mediation and coercion, peacekeeping and peace enforcement, criticizing Boutros Boutros-Ghali's contention that these should be seen as alternative techniques, not adjacent points on a continuum. For Boutros-Ghali's position, see his *An Agenda for Peace: 1995* (New York: United Nations Publications, 1995), 15.

17. See, e.g., NCCB, "Harvest of Justice," 338; "Interview with Cardinal Joseph Ratzinger," head of the Vatican Congregation for the Doctrine of the Faith, Catholic News Service, June 25, 1993; Bryan Hehir, "Intervention: From Theories to Cases," *Ethics and International Affairs* 9 (1995): 10-11.

18. Cf. Walzer, *Just and Unjust Wars,* 108.

19. Pope John Paul II has said that humanitarian intervention is "not primarily a military intervention but forms of action aimed at 'disarming' the aggressor," especially prayer. "Remarks at General Audience," January 12, 1994, reprinted in Catholic News Service, January 17, 1994, 18. The breadth of the Pope's understanding of intervention is evident in that he considers the "principle of humanitarian intervention" as simply the positive form of the "principle of non-indifference." John Paul II, "Address to the Third International Convention of Military Ordinaries," March 11, 1994, *L'Osservatore Romano,* English weekly edition, March 23, 1994, 6. In urging humanitarian intervention in Bosnia-Herzegovina, beginning in mid-1992, the Vatican has emphasized the need for the international community to provide humanitarian aid, to establish "safe havens" and a "no-fly zone," to impose an arms embargo and economic sanctions, and to provide political support to democratic forces. Msgr. Alain Lebeaupin, "Remarks before the Committee of Senior Officials, Conference on Security and Cooperation in Europe," September 16, 1992, in *L'Osservatore Romano,* English weekly edition, September 23, 1992, 2. In calling for international intervention, the Vatican's emphasis has been on diplomatic initiatives. It has acknowledged the need to back these initiatives by force, if necessary, but has frequently cautioned against more aggressive uses of force, given the risks of aggravating conflicts, causing disproportionate harm, and putting civilians at risk.

20. In their 1993 statement "The Harvest of Justice Is Sown in Peace," the U.S. Catholic bishops gave new emphasis to non-violence as not only an option for individuals but also a duty for states. NCCB, "Harvest of Justice," 319.

21. See, e.g., Timothy Garton Ash, *The Uses of Adversity: Essays on the Fate of Central Europe* (New York: Vintage Books, 1990); Tad Szulc, *Pope John Paul II: The Biography* (New York: Scribner's, 1995); George Weigel, *The Final Revolution: The Resistance Church and the Collapse of Communism* (Oxford: Oxford University Press, 1992).

22. NCCB, "Harvest of Justice," 318.

23. See, e.g., D. Christiansen and G. Powers, "Economic Sanctions and the Just-War Doctrine," in D. Cortright and G. Lopez, eds., *Economic Sanctions: Panacea or Peacebuilding in a Post–Cold War World?* (Boulder, Colo.: Westview Press, 1995): 97.

24. Ibid., 104-12. On the need for humanitarian provision, see also Walzer, *Just and Unjust Wars,* 172-75.

25. Cf. James Turner Johnson, "The Just War Idea," 21-24.

26. Cf. ibid, 22.

27. For two views on the possibilities and limits of U.N. intervention in internal conflicts, see Paul F. Diehl, "The United Nations and Peacekeeping," in E. Kolodziej and R. Kanet, *Coping with Conflict After the Cold War* (Baltimore: Johns Hopkins University Press, 1996), 147-67; Jack Donnelly, "The Past, the Present, and the Future Prospects," in M. Esman and S. Tehami, *International Organizations and Ethnic Conflict* (Ithaca: Cornell University Press, 1995), 48-71.

28. Walzer, *Just and Unjust Wars,* 87.

29. See Donnelly, "The Past, the Present, " 69-71.

30. Alvaro de Soto, a senior advisor to U.N. Secretary General Boutros-Ghali, believes the U.N. has been effective in intervening in internal conflicts in Namibia, El Salvador, Cambodia, Mozambique, and elsewhere. Where it has been less effective, that

is due to uncertainty among member states about the role they want the U.N. to assume in these conflicts and an unwillingness to provide the U.N. with the political backing and resources necessary to be effective. Alvaro de Soto, "Strengthening Global Institutions," in Powers, Christiansen, Hennemeyer, *Peacemaking,* 149-64.

31. According to a statement of a commission of the Council on Foreign Relations, "Bosnia shows both the limits and the value of the United Nations. When member states, including the United States, sought to hide their own indecision about what to do in the former Yugoslavia—as well as their unwillingness to act—by giving assignments to the U.N. peacekeeping force that it was not capable of carrying out, the results were unacceptable. On the other hand, the U.N. agencies active in Bosnia, including the High Commissioner for Refugees, have helped to alleviate human suffering." Statement of an Independent Task Force on the United Nations, "American National Interest and the United Nations," August 1996, 5. The fact that the United Nations has been used in this way indicates the need to give considerable weight to probability-of-success concerns in evaluating legitimate authority for humanitarian intervention. Given the risks of misusing intervention for narrow interests of the powerful, the presumption should be for multilateral over unilateral interventions. But the lack of institutional capacity and the tendency for the U.N. and other multilateral bodies to be used as an excuse for inaction suggest that unilateral action by one or several states may sometimes be justified, in part on grounds of probability of success. On the limits of collective action, see, e.g., David C. Hendrickson, "The Ethics of Collective Security," *Ethics and International Affairs* 7 (1993): 10-15.

32. "Statement by the Administrative Board," U.S. Catholic Conference, March 25, 1993, in *Origins* 22, no. 43 (April 8, 1993): 733; See also Archbishop John Roach, "Letter to the Secretary of State," May 11, 1993, *Origins* 23, no. 2 (May 27, 1993): 22.

33. It remains unclear whether massive force was necessary, as Western military commanders tended to believe, or whether, as the locals contended, active military defense would have been enough to deter an undisciplined army used to bullying unarmed civilians and to shelling cities from a safe distance.

34. The failure of the international forces (IFOR/SFOR) in Bosnia to use the means necessary to implement the civilian aspects of the Dayton Accords is another example of what might be considered self-fulfilling predictions of impotence. See, e.g., Diane Paul, "Don't Whitewash Phony Elections," *Washington Post,* August 20, 1996.

35. NCCB, "Harvest of Justice," 337.

CHAPTER 10

"Weinberger Triumphant"

ROBERT KAGAN

1. "Defining Missions, Setting Deadlines: Meeting New Security Challenges in the Post–Cold War World," speech delivered by Anthony Lake at George Washington University, Washington, D.C., March 6, 1996.

2. John Hillen, "American Military Intervention: A User's Guide," *Heritage Foundation Report* No. 1079, 2 May 1996.

3. The National Security Strategy is a presidential document required by Section 603 of the Goldwater-Nichols Defense Department Reorganization Act of 1986. See Hillen, "American Military Intervention," 18.

4. John Lewis Gaddis, *The United States and the End of the Cold War: Implications, Reconsiderations, Provocations* (New York: Oxford University Press, 1992), 190-91.

5. John Shy, "Jomini," in Peter Paret, ed., *Makers of Modern Strategy: From Machiavelli to the Nuclear Age* (Princeton: Princeton University Press, 1986), 143-49.

6. Peter Paret, "Clausewitz," in Paret, *Makers of Modern Strategy*, 212.

7. Hillen, "American Military Intervention," 3.

8. Ibid., 1.

9. George P. Shultz, *Turmoil and Triumph: My Years as Secretary of State* (New York: Scribner's, 1993), 650.

10. Michael Mandelbaum, "Foreign Policy as Social Work," *Foreign Affairs* 75, no. 1 (January/February 1996).

11. Paul Kennedy, "Grand Strategy in War and Peace: Toward a Broader Definition," in Paul Kennedy, ed., *Grand Strategies in War and Peace* (New Haven: Yale University Press, 1991), 5-6.

12. A. J. Bacevich, "Military Culture and Institutional Change," in George T. Raach, ed., *Peace Operations: Developing an American Strategy* (Washington: National Defense University Press, 1995); cited in Hillen, "American Military Intervention," 6.

13. Charles J. Dunlap, Jr., "The Origins of the Military Coup of 2012," *Parameters* 22 (Winter 1992-93), 2-20.

14. Karl von Clausewitz, *On War,* trans. and ed. Michael Howard and Peter Paret, rev. ed. (Princeton: Princeton University Press, 1984), book 1, chap. 1, 81.

15. See Paret, "Clausewitz," 200-201.

16. James A. Baker III with Thomas M. DeFrank, *The Politics of Diplomacy: Revolution, War and Peace, 1989-1992* (New York: Putnam Publishing Group, 1995), 649.

17. John Keegan, editorial, *Daily Telegraph,* London, December 2, 1994, 27.

18. Mandelbaum, "Foreign Policy as Social Work," 21; cited approvingly by Hillen, "American Military Intervention," 1.

CHAPTER 11

"Terrorism and Just War Doctrine"

ANTHONY CLARK AREND

1. Among the most important works on the just war tradition are: Paul Ramsey, *The Just War: Force and Political Responsibility* (1968); James Turner Johnson, *Ideology, Reason, and the Limitation of War* (1975) and *Just War Tradition and the Restraint of War: A Moral and Historical Inquiry* (1981); Michael Walzer, *Just and Unjust Wars* (1977); William V. O'Brien, *The Conduct of Just and Limited War* (1981) and, earlier, *War and/or Survival* (1969).

2. See Robert J. Beck and Anthony Clark Arend, "Don't Tread on Us: International Law and Forcible State Responses to Terrorism," *Wisconsin International Law Journal* 12 (1994): 153-219, for an examination of recent forcible responses to terrorism.

3. This is a point made by William V. O'Brien in *Law and Morality in Israel's War with the PLO* (1991), 275.

4. St. Thomas Aquinas, *Summa Theologiae, secunda secundae*, 15, Q. 40 (Art. 1); cited in O'Brien, *The Conduct of Just and Limited War*, 17.

5. Ibid.

6. See National Conference of Catholic Bishops (NCCB), *The Challenge of Peace: God's Promise and Our Response* (1983), 28-29.

7. O'Brien, *The Conduct of Just and Limited War,* 18-19.

8. U.N. Charter, Arts. 39-51.

9. War Powers Resolution, sec. 2(c).

10. Beck and Arend, "Don't Tread on Us," 175-76.

11. NCCB, *The Challenge of Peace*, 27.

12. Ibid.

13. Ibid.

14. St. Augustine, Book LXLLIII, *Super Josue*, qu. X; cited in O'Brien, *The Conduct of Just and Limited War*, 20.

15. James A. Childress, "Just-War Criteria," in Thomas A. Shannon, ed., *War or Peace: The Search for New Answers*, 46; cited in O'Brien, *The Conduct of Just and Limited War*, 20.

16. U.N. Charter, Art. 51.

17. See, for example, Richard B. Lillich, ed., *Humanitarian Intervention and the United Nations* (1973); Natalino Ronzitti, *Rescuing Nationals Abroad Through Military Coercion and Intervention on the Grounds of Humanity* (1985); Fernando Teson, *Humanitarian Intervention* (1988).

18. NCCB, *The Challenge of Peace*, 28.

19. Ibid., 29.

20. Ibid.

21. As Professor O'Brien observes, "right intention insists that charity and love exist even among enemies." O'Brien, *The Conduct of Just and Limited War*, 34.

22. Augustine, *Contra Faustum* (LXXIV); cited in O'Brien, *The Conduct of Just and Limited War,* 33-34.

23. See John Foster Dulles, *War, Peace and Change* (1939), for a fascinating discussion of this dilemma.

24. See O'Brien, *The Conduct of Just and Limited War*, 34-35.

25. NCCB, *The Challenge of Peace*, 30.

26. O'Brien, *Law and Morality in Israel's War with the PLO*, 280.

27. NCCB, *The Challenge of Peace*, 30.

28. Ibid.

29. Ibid., 31.

30. See Anthony Clark Arend and Robert J. Beck, *International Law and the Use of Force* (London: Routledge, 1993).

31. NCCB, *The Challenge of Peace*, 31.

32. O'Brien, *Law and Morality in Israel's War with the PLO*, 281.

33. Ibid.

34. See Beck and Arend, "Don't Tread on Us," 206-9, for a discussion of different *legal* interpretations of proportionality.

35. Oscar Schachter, "The Extra-Territorial Use of Force Against Terrorist Bases," *Houston Journal of International Law* 11: 215, 315 (emphasis added).

36. Beck and Arend, "Don't Tread on Us," 207.

37. Ibid.

38. William V. O'Brien, "Reprisal, Deterrence and Self-Defense in Counterterror Operations," *Virginia Journal of International Law* 30: 462, 477.

39. Ibid., 472.

40. O'Brien, *The Conduct of Just and Limited War*, 42.

41. Ibid.

42. See NCCB, *The Challenge of Peace*, 31-34.

43. This draws upon recommendations that Robert Beck and I presented in "Don't Tread on Us," 216-19.

44. See Beck and Arend, *International Law and the Use of Force*, 71-79, for a discussion of anticipatory self-defense under international law.

45. These recommendations also draw upon Beck and Arend, "Don't Tread on Us," 218-19.

CHAPTER 16

"A Just War Argument for Ballistic-Missile Defense"

JAMES TURNER JOHNSON

1. Paul Ramsey, "A Political Ethics Context for Strategic Thinking," in Morton A. Kaplan, ed., *Strategic Thinking and Its Moral Implications* (Chicago: University of Chicago Center for Policy Study, 1973), 125.

2. Michael Walzer, *Just and Unjust Wars* (New York: Basic Books, 1977), 15.

3. Walzer's characterization of his purpose, ibid., xiv.

4. William V. O'Brien, *The Conduct of Just and Limited War* (New York: Praeger, 1981), 1-10 and passim.

5. William V. O'Brien, "Just War Doctrine's Complementary Role in the International Law of War," chap. 7 in Alberto R. Coll, James S. Ord, and Stephen A. Rose, eds., *Legal and Moral Constraints on Low-Intensity Conflict,* International Law Studies, vol. 67 (Newport, R.I.: Naval War College, 1995).

6. James Turner Johnson, "Just War Thinking and Its Contemporary Application: The Moral Significance of the Weinberger Doctrine," chap. 5 in Alan Ned Sabrosky and Robert L. Sloane, eds., *The Recourse to War: An Appraisal of the "Weinberger Doctrine"* (Carlisle Barracks, Pa.: Strategic Studies Institute, U.S. Army War College, 1988).

7. St. Ambrose of Milan, *On the Duties of the Clergy* 1.36.179, in Philip Schaff and Henry Wace, eds., *Nicene and Post-Nicene Fathers,* 2d series, vol. 10 (New York: Christian Literature Publishing Co., 1896; Peabody, Mass.: Hendrickson Publishers, 1994).

8. St. Augustine, *On the Free Choice of the Will* (Philadelphia: Peter Reilly, 1937), 1.5; see Augustine, *Contra Faustum* 22.75, in John Eppstein, *The Catholic Tradition of the Law of Nations*

(London: Burns, Oates, and Washbourne, 1935), 69-70; see further Frederick H. Russell, *The Just War in the Middle Ages* (Cambridge: Cambridge University Press, 1975), 16-20.

9. Paul Ramsey, *War and the Christian Conscience* (Durham, N.C.: Duke University Press, 1961), 33-39.

10. Paul Ramsey, *The Just War* (New York: Scribner's, 1968), 142-43.

11. Walzer, *Just and Unjust Wars*, 51.

12. St. Augustine, *The City of God* 19.7, in Whitney J. Oates, ed., *The Basic Writings of St. Augustine*, vol. 2 (New York: Random House, 1948).

13. Walzer, *Just and Unjust Wars,* 51.

14. Ibid.

15. Ramsey, *The Just War,* 144.

16. Lawrence Freedman, *The Evolution of Nuclear Strategy* (New York: St. Martin's Press, 1981), 396.

17. Ronald G. Musto, *The Catholic Peace Tradition* (Maryknoll, N.Y.: Orbis Books, 1986), 190.

18. National Conference of Catholic Bishops, *The Challenge of Peace: God's Promise and Our Response* (Washington, D.C.: United States Catholic Conference, 1983), pars. 175, 188.

19. United Methodist Bishops, *In Defense of Creation* (Nashville, Tenn.: Graded Press, 1986), 6, 11, 92; see Paul Ramsey, *Speak Up for Just War or Pacifism* (University Park, Pa.: Pennsylvania State University Press, 1988), 20.

CHAPTER 17

"Ballistic-Missile Defense in the New Strategic Era"

ROBERT KAGAN

1. Central Intelligence Agency, *The Weapons Proliferation Threat*, March 1995.

2. Ibid.

3. The debate arose over the November 1995 National Intelligence Estimate (NIE) prepared by the intelligence community. That NIE declared that no significant shift in the threat to the continental U.S. was likely before 2010.

4. Gary Schmitt, "Missile Defenses in an Uncertain World," draft of report prepared for the Marshall Institute, January 1997.

5. See *Gulf War Air Power*, vol. 2, part 2, a study commissioned by the U.S. Air Force and released in 1993.

6. Schmitt, "Missile Defenses."

7. Selig S. Harrison and Geoffrey Kemp, "India and America After the Cold War" (Carnegie Endowment for International Peace, 1993), 20.

8. The Defense Department's Quadrennial Defense Review was released in May 1997. Emphasis in original.

9. Heritage Foundation, *Defending America: Ending America's Vulnerability to Ballistic Missiles*, 1996, 17.

10. Defense Department, Quadrennial Defense Review.

11. Were the United States to make retaliatory strikes against Iran in response to suspected terrorist attacks, for instance, military planners might target such facilities.

CHAPTER 18

"The Opposition to Missile Defense"

JEFFREY SALMON

1. Spurgeon Keeny, "The Theater Missile Defense Threat to U.S. Security," *Arms Control Today*, September 1994, 5.

2. Gerard C. Smith, "Two Decades Later: The ABM Treaty in a Changed World," *Arms Control Today*, May 1992, 3.

3. Bernard Brodie, *The Absolute Weapon: Atomic Power and World Order* (New Haven: Yale Institute of International Studies, 1946), 14.

4. Colin Gray, *Strategy and the M-X* (Washington, D.C.: Heritage Foundation, 1980), 4.

5. Brodie, *Absolute Weapon*, 76, 89, 72.

6. Bernard Brodie, *Strategy in the Missile Age* (Princeton, N.J.: Princeton University Press, 1961), 275, 277.

7. Thomas Schelling, *Arms and Influence* (New Haven: Yale University Press, 1966), 93.

8. Ibid., 197-98.

9. Glenn Snyder, *Deterrence and Defense: Toward a Theory of National Security* (Princeton, N.J.: Princeton University Press, 1961), 30, 38.

10. Robert N. McNamara, Address at Ann Arbor, Michigan, June 16, 1962, *New York Times*, June 17, 26:1.

11. Bernard Brodie, "The Development of Nuclear Strategy," *International Security*, vol. 2, no. 4 (1978), 65.

12. Peter Clausen, "Limited Defense: The Unspoken Goal," in *Empty Promise* (Boston: Beacon Press, 1986), 156.

13. Keith Payne, *Deterrence in the Second Nuclear Age* (Lexington: University Press of Kentucky, 1996), 50.

14. Ibid., 46.

CHAPTER 20

"Global Missile Defense"

HENRY F. COOPER

1. The Republican Platform, following the pattern of the Republican-led Congress, called for building the first site by 2003. The Democratic Platform, following the lead of the Clinton administration, called for research and development for three years, after which the initial site could be deployed in another three years—by 2003—if warranted by the threat.

2. Shortly after James Woolsey resigned as Director of Central Intelligence in 1995, he gave a Washington audience his personal assessment that, within the next ten years, there was a two-in-three chance that Russia would be engaged in violent conflicts with one or more of its neighbors—and a one-in-three chance that Russia would again threaten the United States. In August 1995 hearings before the Senate Foreign Relations Committee, David Osias—a close advisor on Russian activities to the current Director of Central Intelligence—observed that Russia has "insufficient accountability" over its weapons-grade

nuclear materials, and that Russia's control over its nuclear arsenal is endangered by political forces it was "not designed to withstand." At the same hearing, Bruce Blair, a Brook-
ings Institution expert on the Soviet/Russian command-and-control system, commented
that thousands of nuclear weapons are in the hands of a Russian command system "totter-
ing on the edge of collapse." Bill Gertz (in "Russian Renegades Pose Nuke Danger," *Washington Times,* October 22, 1996, A1) disclosed similar conclusions from a top-secret CIA
report. He reported that the CIA cited evidence that "despite official assurances, high level
Moscow officials are concerned about the security of their nuclear inventory."

3. See Patrick E. Tyler, "As China Threatens Taiwan, It Makes Sure U.S. Listens,"
New York Times, January 24, 1996, A3. The prospects of growing adventurism by China,
as discussed in several reviews, were summarized by Stewart M. Powell in "The China
Problem Ahead," *Air Force Magazine,* October 1995, 60-63. A sobering analysis of the
prospective threat from China is also given by Samuel P. Huntington, "The Clash of
Civilizations," *Foreign Affairs,* Summer 1993, 47.

4. Contrary press accounts notwithstanding, the U.S. intelligence community
acknowledged in 1995 that North Korea could begin fielding Taepo Dong II intercontinental-range ballistic missiles (ICBMs) within the next three to five years if it chose to do
so—and North Korea's propensity to sell missiles to rogue states in the Middle East and
North Africa is well known. (See "Senate Intelligence Committee Releases Unclassified
Intelligence Assessments," Senate Select Committee on Intelligence News Release,
May 1, 1995.) Furthermore, Russia might sell SS-25 ICBMs as space launchers, which
could be rapidly reconverted into ICBMs—without violating treaty constraints.

5. Theodore Gold and David E. Jeremiah, in their transmittal letter to the chairmen
of the Defense Science Board and the Defense Policy Board for their *Report of the Defense
Science Board/Defense Policy Board Task Force on Theater Missile Defense,* Office of the Secretary of Defense, Washington, D.C., January 1996.

6. Then Defense Secretary William Perry acknowledged that realistic scenarios
could include several dozen missiles. (See Federal News Service Transcript, "Remarks by
Secretary of Defense William Perry at the Regional Commerce and Growth Association
of St. Louis, Missouri," September 28, 1995.) At the same time, he reiterated that the
Clinton administration proposed to meet this threat with a defense that involved ground-
based interceptors and space-based sensors—an inadequate response.

7. This was emphasized in Gold and Jeremiah, *Report of the Defense Science Board.*

8. For further discussion of this important aspect of the threat and the consequent
requirements for space-based boost-phase defenses, see Lawrence Goldmuntz, "Poor
Man's MRVs and Space Defense," *Strategic Review* 24, no. 4 (Fall 1996): 41-48.

9. Lawrence Livermore National Laboratories demonstrated this ability to maneuver down to about thirty miles altitude, using first-generation Brilliant Pebbles hardware.
Deeper penetration might be possible if such an endo-atmospheric intercept capability
were sought as a serious design objective. However, the added cost may not be justified,
because SBIs may have as much difficulty keeping up with maneuvering reentry vehicles
as do other endo-atmospheric terminal defenses.

10. Programmatic possibilities discussed in this section are based on the recommendations of the Heritage Foundation's Missile Defense Study Team (which I was privileged to
lead) in *Defending America: A Near-and Long-Term Plan to Deploy Missile Defenses* (Washington, D.C.: The Heritage Foundation, 1995), updated in *Defending America: Ending America's Vulnerability to Ballistic Missiles* (Washington, D.C.: The Heritage Foundation, 1996).

11. It is generally incorrectly assumed that the technology to support ground-based defenses is more mature than that for space-based defenses. In fact, the Pentagon's acquisition bureaucracy approved a major defense acquisition program for the Brilliant Pebbles space-based interceptor fully two years before one was approved for the first ground-based interceptor. Technology innovation in the SDI program flowed from space to the ground, not the other way around. Congress slowed Brilliant Pebbles development in 1991, and the Clinton administration killed it in 1993 for political, not technical, reasons. In April 1994, the Pentagon's Inspector General found the Brilliant Pebbles program had been managed "efficiently and cost-effectively within the funding constraints imposed by Congress" and observed that termination of key contracts "was not a reflection on the quality of program management."

12. This joint DoD-NASA mission won well-deserved awards from NASA and the National Academy of Science for the small team of scientists and engineers that "made it happen." The entire December 16, 1994, issue of the academy's journal, *Science,* recounted preliminary results of this impressive mission, which was accomplished in less than two years from conception in my office to lift-off. At a cost of only about $80 million, Clementine demonstrated the feasibility of NASA administrator Dan Goldin's call for a "faster, cheaper, better" approach to the nation's space programs—as well as the space-worthiness of first-generation Brilliant Pebbles sensors, computers, and software.

13. In an article entitled, "Brilliant Pebbles Inspired First Commercial Sensing Venture," the Space Marketplace Supplement to the June 25, 1993, edition of *Aerospace Daily* reported that WorldView Imaging Corporation, financed with venture capital, had obtained the first-ever Commerce Department license to launch and operate remote sensor satellites with three-meter or better resolution.

14. See March 14, 1995, letter to Senator Strom Thurmond from the industrial team conducting research and development on space-based lasers. The letter was signed by Vance Coffman, president of the Space and Missiles Sector of Lockheed-Martin Corporation; Timothy W. Hannemann, executive vice president, Space and Electronics Group, TRW; and Edward T. Gerry, president, W. J. Shafer Associates. While Senator Thurmond solicited the analysis provided in the letter to him, its content does not necessarily reflect his views on deploying space-based lasers.

15. William J. Broad, "From Fantasy to Fact: Space-Based Laser Nearly Ready to Fly," *New York Times,* December 4, 1994.

16. The Clinton administration is conducting a "technology readiness" program for defending the United States and has suggested that a ground-based defense could be deployed at one site within four to five years for under $5 billion. However, such a defense could not defend the entire United States and could be overwhelmed by more than a few attacking missiles. An acquisition program to develop and deploy a multi-site ground-based defense for about $35 billion was fully approved by the Defense Department's acquisition bureaucracy in 1992.

17. Forward-based sea-based defenses—and space-based defenses—would provide much greater confidence since they could provide multiple shot opportunities, beginning as early as in the attacking missile's boost phase.

18. Intelligence officials believe the capability to release submunitions from ascending ballistic missiles could be on the world market within five years, according to David M. North, "Washington Outlook—Danger Ahead," *Aviation Week,* July 24, 1995, 19.

19. Three days after Reagan's March 23, 1983, speech, Soviet General Secretary Andropov asserted, "Should this [SDI] conception be converted into reality, this would actually open the floodgates to a runaway race of all types of strategic arms, both offensive and defensive." The harmonious response of the U.S. arms-control elite was summarized by McGeorge Bundy, George Keenan, Robert McNamara, and Gerard Smith in "The President's Choice: Star Wars or Arms Control," *Foreign Affairs,* Winter 1984/85. (Reprinted in the anthology published by the Ethics and Public Policy Center in 1986, *Promise or Peril: The Strategic Defense Initiative.*)

20. For example, they were included in my January 20, 1993, "End-of-Tour Report" when I stepped down as SDI director. That report also laid out the Bush-administration costs and schedules that had been approved and included in Pentagon plans—subsequently dropped by the Clinton administration.

21. As then Deputy Secretary of Defense John Deutch explained to the Navy League on April 13, 1995, the Clinton administration's version of the Navy Upper Tier limits this potential benefit by constraining the system to use only data from the Aegis SPY-1 radar—a constraint that assures compliance with the ABM Treaty but also severely restrains the effectiveness of the Navy Upper Tier as a theater missile defense. See Bill Gertz, "Navy Missile Defense Shouldn't Be Issue in Talks, Deutch Asserts: Upper Tier Legal Under ABM Treaty," *Washington Times,* April 14, 1995, A3.

22. See "President Clinton Issues New National Space Policy," press release, The White House, Office of the Press Secretary, September 19, 1996, and the associated National Space Policy Fact Sheet, The White House, National Science and Technology Council, September 19, 1996.

23. See Henry F. Cooper, "ABM Treaty Costs," testimony before the Senate Foreign Relations Committee, September 26, 1996 (mimeograph; published in the committee hearing report).

24. Patriot was not initially given an ability to defend against ballistic missiles—probably because of ABM Treaty concerns. During the mid-1980s, arms-control experts testified that providing Patriot with a ballistic-missile-defense capability would violate the treaty—even though the treaty was not supposed to limit theater defenses. With considerable debate each year, the upgrade proceeded, and Patriot barely made it to the Gulf War. The production lines were turned on before the system had completed its tests, and every Patriot fired in the war was built after Iraq invaded Kuwait in 1990.

Index of Names